IMPOUNDED PEOPLE

IMPOUNDED
PEOPLE

Japanese-Americans
in the Relocation Centers

EDWARD H. SPICER   ·   ASAEL T. HANSEN
KATHERINE LUOMALA   ·   MARVIN K. OPLER

THE UNIVERSITY OF ARIZONA PRESS
Tucson   Arizona

About the Authors

From community analysis of relocated Japanese-Americans in World War II
to full-time diverse participation in anthropological teaching, writing, and research
has been the recent history of the four authors of IMPOUNDED PEOPLE. As
professors of anthropology their interest has remained intense in the problems
of administrated communities. Edward H. Spicer was community analyst at the
Poston, Arizona, Relocation Center and later headed the Community Analysis
Section of WRA in Washington, D.C., at the time the original report was
printed (Washington, D.C., WRA, GPO, 1946). A member of the anthropology
faculty at the University of Arizona, Professor Spicer wrote the introduction to
this book. Katherine Luomala, professor of anthropology at the University of
Hawaii, was assistant to the head of Community Analysis and detailed to the
West Coast for field work. Asael T. Hansen, professor of anthropology and
sociology at the University of Alabama, was community analyst at Heart
Mountain Center, Wyoming, and Marvin K. Opler, professor of anthropology
at the State University of New York at Buffalo, was community analyst at
Tule Lake Center, California. During the last six months of the existence of
the War Relocation Authority, the four analysts gathered at Washington, D.C.,
to write the original report on relocation as it was experienced by Japanese-
Americans and the Government of the United States.

THE UNIVERSITY OF ARIZONA PRESS

Copyright © 1969
The Arizona Board of Regents
Library of Congress Catalog
Card No. 68-9340
Manufactured in the U.S.A.

CONTENTS

LIST OF ILLUSTRATIONS

PHOTOGRAPHS

viii

FIGURES

INTRODUCTION: THE RELOCATION CENTERS IN RETROSPECT

The story of the evacuation and relocation of the West Coast Japanese-Americans during World War II has been told many times and in many different ways. The issue of the constitutionality of the evacuation order has been repeatedly reviewed, but, despite a majority decision by the United States Supreme Court, not settled to the satisfaction of all Americans. The forced uprooting of 110,000 peaceable people—more than the whole population of the Five Civilized Indian Tribes who were similarly dealt with a century ago—has become, like the Indian "Trail of Tears" before it, a theme of our literature. The singling out of the West Coast Japanese from those in Hawaii (and from the descendants of Germans and Italians) for suspension of civil rights has emphasized the danger ever present in the United States, no less than in Germany, of race prejudice in high places. The wide range of reactions of the people of the United States to evacuation and its aftermath of impounded people has revealed with peculiar clarity the opposing sentiments and principles out of which the American value system is constantly reforged.

Judging from the amount of published discussion, Americans have been more interested in the civil rights aspect of the Japanese-American experience than in any other. Dozens of articles in a wide variety of periodicals through the years since 1942 demonstrate this persistent preoccupation. Major studies thus far indicate even in their titles the prevailing sense of outrage which accompanies this interest: *Americans Betrayed, Politics and the Japanese Evacuation* (by a distinguished political scientist)[1]; *Prejudice, War and the Constitution* (by a trinity of lawyers)[2]; *The Spoilage* (by a team of sociologists).[3] These show, among other things, how the evacuation decision was powerfully influenced by anti-Oriental groups on the West Coast who also had special economic interests to be served by the evacuation. Thus far no refutation of these careful studies has been made. They also open up for

1

reconsideration the basis of the Supreme Court's decision that military necessity justified the evacuation. It is clear that this fundamental issue remains a vital one in American life one that was by no means settled by the Supreme Court. In the study called *The Spoilage* some of the most extreme consequences of evacuation in the lives of American citizens of Japanese descent have been documented in great detail. Here the pressures, confusions, and despairs following evacuation are recounted as they impelled some 6,000 young people to renounce their American citizenship. Perhaps the theme of the destruction of loyalty and hope, even though it involved only a small part of all the Japanese-Americans, will stand out in history as the point of greatest interest. For here there is an unforgettable parable in which the abstraction of constitutional rights is placed in the context of distraught and suffering human families.

Nevertheless, these extreme reactions of a relatively few constitute only one part of the whole experience of the 30,000 evacuated families. Americans have shown great interest also in the human drama of uprooted people, old and young, Japanese and American, farmer and businessman, trying to pull back together the pieces of their lives in the midst of the pressures generated by nations at war. Such accounts as *Citizen 13660*,[4] in which black-and-white sketches by an inhabitant of a relocation center portray the emotional shock of suddenly being outcast in one's own society, or *The Moved Outers*,[5] which tells for children what being an evacuee was like, or *Born Free and Equal*,[6] in which fine photographs give vignettes of feeling and activity in a relocation center, or the remarkable picture record of the flourishing of the arts as presented in *Beauty Behind Barbed Wire*[7]—these tell us many things about the nature of the life in the relocation centers.

There is a great difference between these and the books which focus on civil rights. While moral indignation is by no means absent, there is an emphasis on human universals, suffering and courage, loyalty and disillusion, family values and cultural tradition, and how these were expressed in the bleak barracks cities. The writers are interested in how people feel and think and what they do in a crisis, conceived more in general human terms than in terms of the Japanese-Americans of 1942–46. It is only incidental that the people are of Japanese background. The violation of civil rights is merely a particular expression of the universal and recurrent theme of humanity in conflict with itself.

These two approaches, civil rights and human drama, have provided us with a basis for an understanding of an event of some importance in the history of the United States. They have not, however, exhausted the significance of that event. It has further meanings which cry for fuller exploration. One such theme is that of the courage of the men and women who undertook to manage the War Relocation Authority which was established by the President to solve the problems created by the evacuation. This staff found themselves suddenly confronted with a completely unprecedented task in the midst of national forces let loose by war. Ignorant of the Japanese-Americans to begin with, they were nevertheless charged with their welfare in a nation in which hostility towards Japanese increased parallel with intensification of war efforts—and defeats—in the Pacific. They were pushed into the limelight of conflicting forces bitterly expressed in the national Congress, in excited state legislatures, and among powerful national associations. What they did under these circumstances resulted in a new chapter in the growth of American culture. Thus far only the protagonists—the WRA staff—have tried to interpret for us the significance of this episode in the national life. In the final report of the agency, called *WRA—A Story of Human Conservation,*[8] they give us glimpses of the frequently dramatic conflicts as they saw them from the inside. What they sketch should be explored further by persons other than the protagonists themselves, for the process in which they participated is of great importance for understanding the foundations of American freedom.

Another theme of this human experience was opened up in a study called *The Governing of Men.*[9] This vivid account of one of the "disturbances" during the early months in the relocation centers portrays the confrontation of the mass of evacuees and the agency staff as they began, in ignorance of one another, to try to make some order out of the chaos created by the evacuation in 110,000 individual lives. In contrast with civil rights-focused studies, this account describes the conflicts and problems which arose as thousands of people of many different backgrounds suddenly confronted one another in a new and unfathomable situation. It tells us dramatically about the cross-currents of emotion and purpose which threw evacuees and War Relocation Authority administrators alike into turmoil. It deals, however, with only the very beginning of the experience in one of the relocation centers. There have been no studies which tell the story of the whole four years of mutual adaptation by administrator and evacuee.

Written in 1946 as one of the final reports of the government agency— the War Relocation Authority—the account presented in the following pages is a narrative of what happened in the relocation centers during the four years of their existence. Except for a few simple corrections, nothing has been changed. It is offered again because the authors believe that the situation it describes is timeless in its bearing on the problems of the relations between bureaucracy and local initiative. The destructive consequences of the government actions leading through evacuation to renunciation of citizenship by some of the young people are presented only as a part of the total experience of the Japanese-Americans. The drama and heartbreak of people under relentless pressures interweave the whole account. The emphasis, however, is on that other theme of how, given chaos and betrayal as the starting point, people strive to bring meaning back into their lives. This is the story primarily of the people who were uprooted—the evacuees—revealing at point after point what also was happening to the administrators charged with the management of the relocation centers.

In this report, more descriptive than analytical, the writers were striving to record, while they were still close to the events, what seemed to be the major developments in the growth of community life under the peculiar circumstances of the relocation centers. It seems necessary, therefore, to provide here some statement of the significance of what happened in the centers as viewed from the standpoint of the impact of government administration on human communities.

WRA POLICY AND THE RELOCATION CENTERS

The men who had to hammer out policy for the War Relocation Authority were inventors working under extreme pressure. The evacuation order did not indicate, except in a most general way, what the procedure of the new agency should be. The agency was at first independent of any established department of government, and was enjoined to insure "the welfare" of the persons evacuated. What the best interests of these people might be could have been construed in any of a half-dozen different ways. Even the basic physical circumstances under which they were to continue their existence were still in process of determination during the first three months after evacuation. What their status as a part of American society should be remained undefined.

Although the War Relocation Authority was empowered to decide these questions, the responsibility of decision could not be undertaken in isolation from the rest of the people of the United States. Not only were the agency's tasks unprecedented, but it was also under immediate and powerful pressures by a variety of interests and opinions in the welter of American democracy. Under such pressures the policy makers not only had to formulate guidelines, but they also had to work extremely fast. In the midst of mounting emotions and intense mobilization for war, they had to "care for" 110,000 people whom thousands of Americans identified with the nation's enemy. This identification, focused by the evacuation itself, was spreading widely as Japanese victories in the Pacific took in the Philippines and seemed to proceed unchecked.

Perhaps the easiest course would have been to assume that the decision to move the people from their homes had defined them as dangerous;

hence, until the war's end, they should be held securely in the barracks camps which the Army was already building in inland "wilderness" areas. Governors of states, Congressmen, and leaders of influential national organizations were strongly advocating such detention. To have accepted these demands as the determinants of policy would undoubtedly have quieted excited spokesmen for segments of the American population. The first tendency of the policy makers was to think somewhat along these lines. The idea of productive, largely self-sufficient communities maintained in isolation from the rest of the nation was alluring at first as the simplest solution. Indeed, what other course could be pursued in the face of the accomplished fact of the uprooting and in the midst of spreading hostility over the nation? That the policy of the War Relocation Authority did not crystallize in this direction is of great significance for American history.

The first phase in the forging of policy extended over some eight months, from April to December, 1942. During these months the men directing the WRA operations faced not only the immense physical problems of setting up living quarters, hospitals, schools, and productive enterprises in the centers, but also the vastly more complex problem of trying to see into the future of the evacuees in the United States. They considered, but did not finally accept, the idea of isolated settlements where people might suspend their readjustment in the nation until after the war should end. They chose rather to go to work immediately on the problems of readjustment, in spite of the war and public hostility to the evacuees. They decided that the "group stigma" ought not to be encouraged by the creation of a limbo where people should sit it out in the centers; they believed that continued residence as a people singled out from the whole would in the long run work against a satisfactory reintegration. This decision called for a complex job of planning the movement of the evacuees back into a nation at war. It also called at every point for cooperation with the Army which had assumed the responsibility for the operation of the evacuation; for close work with the Department of Justice and other branches of government; and above all for the agency itself to do all within its power to mobilize the sentiments and the organizations among the American people which were favorable towards the evacuees. In the view of the WRA staff, the decision defined the relocation centers as temporary stopping places, as way stations back into American society; it defined the field of operation of the agency not as the little enclosures of the relocation centers, but as the United States as a whole, with all of its counterforces and contradictions.

The policy objectives which the WRA worked out during the summer and fall of 1942 rested on the foundation of certain basic assumptions which the policy-making staff wrestled with beginning in May. These did not involve practicalities, but rather principles of human rights and constitutional government. The actual starting point for the policy makers developed from neither the conference of state governors in April—amid the consternation, anger, and prejudice flaring up over the "dumping" of the evacuees in the mountain states—nor from the American Legion convention in August where it was concluded that every man, woman, and child among Japanese-Americans was a menace to the United States. The starting point was an interpretation of the law of the land, and the first basic assumption was that the law should not be set aside with respect to the evacuees. The WRA faced the fact that American citizens were being detained in the relocation centers without due process of law and that this situation could not be defended—a position later confirmed by a Supreme Court decision. This led the agency to immediately make it possible for the evacuees to do seasonal work in agriculture outside the centers and later to institute a determined and hard-driving program to resettle all willing evacuees in all parts of the United States outside the West Coast exclusion zone. Ultimately this principle at the base of WRA policy led logically to the expulsion of all the evacuees from the relocation centers as soon as the Western defense zone, the scene of their original homes, was again declared open to them by the Army.

The administrative consequences of the basic position of the WRA in its policy formulation will not be discussed here; the progression of programs unfolding from preceding ones has been eloquently presented in the final official report of the agency. The target of attention here will be a conception of the *nature* of the relocation centers which, equally with the constitutional principle, lay at the heart of the over-all WRA policy. In explanation of its policy the agency in its final report presented considerations which it held were consistent with the decision to keep the centers open and get the evacuees released as soon as possible. It is clear that the policy-makers decided as early as the summer of 1942, while evacuees were still being poured into the centers, that these places created by government fiat were undesirable and that evacuees should not be permitted to stay in them. In the final report of the agency they were spoken of as "bad," as an "unnatural environment," and as a "fundamental negation of American democracy and incapable of ever becoming anything else." Writers of the report also emphasized the "abnormal, highly charged atmosphere of the centers" and "the deadening effects of institutionalized life at the centers," leading to a general recommendation for the future, that "the camp approach" should be avoided because, "Inevitably, this makes for an institutionalized environment which in turn, produces frustration, demoralization, and a feeling of dependency among the residents."

Although the WRA policy makers may have been more articulate as a result of hindsight when they wrote the final report, there is no doubt that a decision was made before the end of 1942 about the nature of the relocation centers and what they could and could not become. This became a twin point in the program, along with the principle of prompt integration back into the mainstream of American society. The centers were incapable of being anything except undesirable places in which to live, therefore people should not remain in them. It was the obligation of the government, since the government had uprooted them, to find more "normal and natural" places to live wherever that should be possible in the United States. This was the foundation position of the WRA, and this position rested solidly on the conception that no citizens of the country should be involuntarily detained anywhere without specific charges. The WRA rejected flatly the principle that the war made any difference whatever. The principles in terms of which it worked being quite independent of any temporary condition such as a government being at war, it moved consistently and with firm determination toward the goals which its analysis of the principles involved had led it to define.

Two circumstances gave the agency a good deal of trouble in carrying out its program. The first of these—that the relocation centers must be maintained as "as decent as possible places to live in" as long as evacuees should be in them—was thoroughly understood by staff members who foresaw inherent contradictions between accepting this principle, which WRA did fully, and the major policy-guiding principles that the centers were undesirable places in which to allow people to live. As young people did resettle and leave the centers, there were "manpower shortages," and center operation sometimes became difficult. Many problems arose, but the WRA decided them in favor of the dominating idea of getting people to resettle and found no insurmountable obstacles in maintaining basic necessities and even certain comforts in the relocation centers.

The other circumstance was a puzzle to the administration: American well-wishers who gave valuable aid to the evacuees—ranging from placing Nisei* students in colleges immediately after evacuation to providing help of all kinds in the big cities where some evacuees resettled—could not understand the WRA's concept that the people should "not be permitted" to remain in the centers. This became especially a point of difference when the West Coast was reopened to the return of the evacuees even before the war had ended. The WRA took the stand that the lifting of the exclusion orders removed the last excuse for maintaining the

---

*Nisei: American-born children of immigrant Japanese.
Issei: Japanese immigrants forbidden to become U.S. citizens by the Oriental Exclusion Proclamation of 1907—a ban not lifted until 1952.
See Review laid in.

relocation centers. It declared a firm policy of forcing evacuees out, if necessary, by certain assigned closing dates. This was logical in conformity with the principles which the WRA had adopted earlier. But to evacuees and to many of their friends it appeared as a final brutal twist in the WRA program. The WRA staff complained of the apparent impossibility of getting such friends of the evacuees, let alone evacuees themselves, to understand the necessity for the forcible closing of the centers. Apparently this resistance to closure remained something of a mystery to the WRA policy makers to the very end.

EVACUEE PURPOSE AND THE RELOCATION CENTERS

It can be said that for the top staff of the War Relocation Authority the centers came early to be seen in wholly negative terms. Within a few months they came to be conceived as places to be eliminated, a viewpoint rooted in fundamental American values, and formulated in the belief that the WRA staff could see, by taking thought, what was best for the evacuees. It was considered unnecessary to consult the evacuees with regard to what was best for them. The weighing of their future was taken as a matter for administrative decision.

Meanwhile, during the very months when the WRA administration was thinking out its course, the heads of the evacuee families were arriving at a very different and almost opposite conception of the relocation centers. The main features of their view crystallized during the summer and fall of 1942. There were later changes in response to changing conditions, but the general, basic meaning of the centers to the evacuees persisted, a meaning which was at odds with the view dominating the WRA staff. The evacuee viewpoint was founded on their experience as a people in the United States. Evacuation was the climax of a series of events. They saw it, and the subsequent moves of the United States government, in relation to some forty years of living as persons of Japanese descent in this country.

The WRA staff had not had that experience. It is evident by hindsight that the reading of reports and books about the Japanese-Americans, no matter how full and accurate could not substitute for that experience. To some staff members the attitudes of the evacuees actually appeared to be those of people suffering from a "persecution complex" or, that is to say, abnormal behavior. It was a full year before the simple fact that the United States had forced the first-generation immigrants to retain their Japanese citizenship had any impact on policy. The administrators were aware that the United States had denied Issei the right be become American citizens; but the implications of that solid fact for the Japanese-

Americans in time of war between Japan and the United States did not sink in. Not until the Issei were forced to take a stand during the Army registration program did the Issei point of view finally come across to the administrators, and this was in February, 1943. In short, the realities of life for persons of Oriental background on the West Coast of the United States were not real for the WRA policy makers, and it was these realities as felt by the evacuees which gave rise to formulation by them of the meaning of the relocation centers.

One of the most striking developments in the growth of community life in the centers was the very early appearance of viewpoints about the significance of evacuation and its aftermath in relation to the total international scene. Evacuee leadership had been promptly crippled by shipping the most prominent older men from all West Coast communities to enemy alien internment camps. The Federal Bureau of Investigation, in handling this operation, immediately instituted a screening program which led to the release of the great majority of such persons, as it was found that their records indicated no subversive or potentially dangerous inclinations. These mature persons who had borne most leadership responsibility in the Japanese-American communities were coming into the relocation centers in increasing numbers during 1942. They were thinking soberly of what the future of Japanese-Americans might be, and their conclusions for the most part were that the future depended heavily on the course of the war and its ultimate outcome with respect to the relations of the United States and Japan. In short, they were very far removed from thinking of the relocation centers as a meaningless interlude in the life of their people, believing instead that the approach of the evacuees to life in the centers had to be conceived in the broadest political terms. As they came into contact with one another in the relocation centers, they steadily formulated a conception of the significance of their new enforced situation in relation to their past and to their future.

The concept of the centers, developed among these older men now scattered throughout the new communities, can best be summed up in the phrase "neutral haven." They took the view that they had been forced by the United States into a neutral position. If they had been allowed to remain on their farms and in their businesses on the West Coast they would have necessarily taken part in the mobilization of the United States for the war effort. This was now denied them, and neutrality had been forced on them. Moreover, it was felt by many that this situation had its advantages. Regardless of the decision of the great majority to remain in the United States, the bitter fact that they had all along been denied citizenship, put emphasis on the obverse fact that they were citizens of Japan. If Japan were to win the war, (and this seemed a possibility during 1942) a strong Japan might have an important influence for the better on their life in the United States. Particularly if they emerged from a position of neutrality without having engaged in the U.S. war effort, Japan might take their part and remove such discriminations as denial of naturalization privileges and the right to hold land. If, on the other hand, the United States should win the war, their enforced neutrality could not be held against them. Obviously, then, with respect to the politics of international relations, the relocation centers offered an advantageous position, so long as their neutral character remained clear. Looking at the centers from this point of view there were some who advocated a formal prisoner-of-war status, in which case the Geneva Convention might be invoked to prevent the WRA from turning the centers into war-production communities. For most, however, this carried the neutrality concept too far, and they were content to accept the havens as offered without further formalization.

In fact, even though the evacuees held the concept of "neutral haven," most regarded as somewhat dangerous any discussion of the idea with the WRA staff. It was thought, and probably rightly, that it would be misconstrued as had been in the past many other features of Japanese-American status. Since it could be misinterpreted in terms of anti-American sentiments, it was regarded as a delicate subject. The returned internees discussed it in their blocks with the people there who could be trusted to be discreet, but it was not until a year later when army registration threatened them with being forced into the situation of "men without a country" that they let down the barriers. From then on the international aspects of Japanese-American status were more freely discussed.

Consistent with the "neutral haven" concept, but oriented toward and stimulated by the practicalities of getting along with each other and with the WRA staff, was another view of what the relocation centers should mean in evacuee lives. It was sometimes voiced during the summer of 1942 in the terms "ideal cities," "harmonious communities," or some similar phrase. This concept is not to be interpreted as an ideal of simple cooperative living together. It had important political aspects. In fact, it involved recognition of the existing political differences among Japanese-Americans and a prescription for achieving unity. Somewhat apart from aspects of the international position of the Japanese-Americans, there were opposing viewpoints in the West Coast communities which had developed long before evacuation. These were usually inter-generational differences, common between almost all parents and all children. But the age gap between Issei and Nisei was unusual as a result of delay in starting families by the first generation of immigrants. Thus there was a discontinuity in age in any community, making for a sharper division between generations of Japanese than among most immigrant groups, particularly in attitudes towards life in the United States. As described in the following report, evacuation itself intensified these issues. The relocation centers suffered from immediate and intense conflict which wrenched families apart and produced tension during early months in the close contacts in mess halls and all the phases of life in the blocks.

Out of this tension grew the concept of the relocation centers as "ideal cities," embodying an aim which at the very least would hold in check and, hopefully, smooth over permanently the internal political schisms in the Japanese-American communities. The guiding principle could be stated simply as, "We are all in the same boat, young and old, Japanese citizens and American citizens. Regardless of birth, our fate in the United States has turned out to be the same. Therefore, we must stick together and seek with determination to harmonize whatever differences we may have felt or even continue to feel. This means working together on everything to make life as satisfactory as possible here in the relocation centers." Each relocation center of approximately 10,000 persons, was to be a community in which harmony should reign and life should be peaceful and secure. The ideal called for close cooperation of the generations and for the unity of all in confronting the representatives of the government which had created the centers.

This concept of the centers became the dominant one and, in its main features, persisted until the centers were closed. It was subject to a variety of interpretations by the evacuees themselves. In the first place it was a solution to the almost unbearable tensions of the first months because it placed highest value on the harmonizing of the internal differences. It was political in this sense, but it was based on political sentiments of narrower scope than those supporting the "neutral haven" view. Yet at the same time it was logically consistent with the latter. It was also in harmony with the WRA objective of keeping the centers as places decent as possible to live in, so long as they remained in existence, and thus provided a foundation for the development of what the WRA called "community government." It contained within its implications a maximum of what the great majority of people in the centers wanted. Its dominance as a guiding principle is therefore easy to explain.

It was also less subject than the "neutral haven" concept to strain and reinterpretation as the course of war veered and changed during the next four years. This concept, obvious and simple as it may appear, did not grow merely out of the necessities for cooperation of individual with individual in the satisfying of elemental needs in the new setting. On the contrary, it emerged from the discussions of the meaning of the Japanese-American experience carried on among the older influential men. Meetings were formal in some cases, informal in innumerable others. From these interchanges in which the significance of what had happened was discussed and rediscussed the phrases took form and began to be accepted. By the end of 1942 they became, or were in process of becoming, something like sacred symbols, embodying major values in the Japanese-American world view as developed in the crisis. Their acceptance meant a new dominance of the older family heads such as had become impossible in the ordinary context of American life. The multiform influences present in the pre-evacuation communities had been pushed a little distance away. And the hostile action of the United States government against the younger men and women stimulated wide acceptance of this view in a way that could not have taken place in the old communities.

These growths of community at the political and symbolic level changed as the WRA program unfolded. The neutral haven concept slowly disintegrated as Japan's military power disintegrated, its ultimate political meaning having depended on uncertainty in the outcome of the war. The ideal community concept also declined in relevance as the resettlement program drained the communities of much of their most vigorous manpower. Yet through all but the last three or four months, when the WRA's determination to close the centers by certain definite dates was undebatable, the concept was still strong and constituted an ideological bulwark for the majority of people. But at the bitter end a metamorphosis took place. The concept eroded to the point that most people began to interpret it only in terms of its security aspect and as a necessity for others, not for themselves. The "others" began to be thought of as "the residue," "the unrelocatables."

The concept of ideal community as a source of security in a world that had become insecure is indicated in this review of its widest political meaning and its final narrowest scope as home for "the residue." Certainly the provision of security was an important and in many ways fundamental function of the concept, but this was by no means its only, or perhaps even its major, function. In a peculiar way it was also an outlet for the aggressions built up against the government in its position as arbitrary dictator of the Japanese-American destiny. Indications of this function were apparent during the earliest months of life in the centers. Jokes were told and conversations spiced with phrases which characterized the relocation centers as examples of the stupidity of the government. The cost of the centers to the government, the idling of important productive manpower, the failure of the original work corps idea of the WRA were stigmatized and bitterly joked about. The rows of barracks filled with unnecessarily immobilized people began to be seen as a forlorn testimony to the ignorance and foolish judgment of the government. The "play-toy" community councils, the unenforceable work standards, the duplication of hospital service and school systems which the evacuation had brought on and which were observable all around them became for the evacuees symbols of the ignorance and prejudice which had beset their life in the United States from the beginning. At least a little of the aggression which they felt was relieved in the pervasive reference to the centers in these terms. The ideal communities which they themselves were building underneath the meaningless bureaucratic framework gave a vantage point from which to jibe at and ridicule the imposed structure.

There was in addition a more positive symbolic meaning of the relocation centers. Communities organized by evacuees in accordance with their own political orientations and cultural values—that is, the ideal communities in process of realization—became symbols of the worth of the Japanese as a people. They were asserting themselves in the face of innumerable pressures to conform to someone else's view of what they should be. As they formulated programs for bringing Issei and Nisei together in regulating the community, regardless of the regulations of the WRA, and as they found means for influencing the selection of evacuees for the various jobs, they were exploring the limits of autonomy. A process of accommodation took place as they sought to expand to the maximum their sphere of self-determination within the government framework. The process was accommodation, not acceptance. It was the accommodation of the evacuee concept of inner harmony in human relations to the administrators' concept of efficient management. Insofar as there was any possibility of self-assertion, the evacuees tried to realize it. Insofar as they succeeded, self-respect was built and reinforced. Thus the ideal communities, as they took some evacuee direction, became symbols of the human dignity of the people. To some, this had strong connotations of the superiority of the Japanese over anyone else. For most, the self-assertion involved in each evacuee-initiated feature of relocation center relations was symbolic of refusal to submit any longer to being "pushed around," and the ethnocentric meaning was of little or no significance. Whatever the individual meanings, those working relationships which the evacuees regarded as bearing their stamp came to stand for human dignity and importance. In this sense they were not only the mechanisms of the ideal communities, they were also symbols of the basic pride and spirit of the people.

The ferment of the relocation centers during the first year or more was the turmoil of people getting their values straight again after a crisis. The most important of these values were expressed in the conceptions of the centers that we have just considered. Simple as they may seem when reduced to a few phrases, they were nevertheless embodiments of complex experience. They represented the adaptation of longheld belief and deeply felt value to the new set of conditions, as the evacuees saw those. They were important less as phrases in themselves than as end products of the process of reorientation in which thousands of men and women participated. The phrases, once formulated, had different connotations for different individuals, but whatever the connotations the phrases themselves served finally as symbols of the unity of the people. Leaders who emerged had to learn how to use the phraseology in formal meetings and in casual conversations or they could not remain in positions of respect.

Another process took place simultaneously. This was the adjustment of individual personalities to one another in the give-and-take of daily life. New people surrounded everyone, even though families and to some extent old friends had stayed close enough together to form neighborhood groups within blocks as the centers were filled. Everyone was faced with more new than familiar persons in the unaccustomed intimacy of the imposed block basis of social life.* Moreover these strangers faced one another in wholly new roles, as chefs and workers in the mess halls as well as table companions, as block managers entirely outside the Japanese-American experience, and in a host of other roles required in the organization of center life. Personal differences were ironed out steadily, and people adjusted to getting along with one another as new roles were defined in the action of getting the necessary things done. Expectations of everyone became clearer during the first six months, and people learned to conform to these expectations. The specifics of the process are described at some length in the following report. It seemed to some observers that the first of the new social units to take form was the block. This was expectable since there the intensity of interaction rapidly reached a maximum in response to the need for getting the mess halls and other basic institutions into operation. However, it was not actually true that the blocks formed first and that the community of a relocation center was built on a foundation of block organizations.

The block organizations took form indeed in the first few months, and they rapidly became the effective social units through which evacuees met the immediate issues of practical living. But the process of formation of these face-to-face groups did not take place before, but rather concurrently with the defining of the larger community of a whole center. That larger community, as we have seen, depended on the definition of values derived from the whole experience of the evacuees and the application of these to the new situation. Face-to-face groups of family heads intent on furthering this process crosscut the blocks, and the interaction in these groups profoundly affected the development of organization in the block life. It would be more correct to say that the foundation of social life in the relocation centers consisted in the common understandings epitomized

---

*A diagram of the block plan and more detailed explanation of its operation are given on page 70.

in the phrases "neutral havens" and "ideal cities." The social unit of the block as it finally took form was not an organization of people concerned merely with taking care of the physical necessities. It was a unit which managed such things satisfactorily only as its members integrated the new roles with a meaningful scheme regarding the significance of relocation center life in the total life of the evacuees.

It is doubtful that there would have been serious disturbances during the first months of the centers if community growth had consisted simply in the mechanical stabilization of people's relations as they settled into the new physical mold. Disturbances would have been highly localized, if personal disputes had become serious enough to merit being called disturbances. The process of community growth was much more complex. It did not involve, first, the taking care of physical necessities and then, when such matters were settled, some attention to values. On the contrary, the practicalities of block life could not be organized and relations in the blocks stabilized until the broader orientations and purposes were defined and people had got their bearings with reference to these ultimate values. The organization of block affairs was indeed dependent on and in a sense a function of the broader organization which took place. Sensing if not actually making contact with the process as it took place especially among the older men, administrators tended to interpret what was going on as a subversive rather than a constructive development. This tendency was aggravated by the fact that evacuee leadership generally regarded important aspects of what they were discussing and feeling as too delicate to be mentioned to persons who were not Japanese-American in experience. They felt that the ignorance and inexperience of the WRA staff in such matters made any mutual discussion of the issues impossible. It required a popular movement over immediate center issues, such as the general strike which developed in the Poston relocation center in November 1942, to effect a first step in bringing evacuees and administrators together on any sort of common ground with respect to goals for the community life.

The question has been raised as to whether communities did in fact develop under the relocation center conditions or whether the people remained an "aggregate of frustrated and confused individuals."[10] Throughout the preceding discussion I have used the term "community" and thereby implied an answer to this important question. I have used the term "community" to apply to a condition in which families of men, women, and children accept organizational forms and symbols rooted in traditional custom and belief for the purpose of realizing common purposes. It seems apparent that a process of community building did take place in the relocation centers in this sense. The organizational forms remained tentative, chiefly as a result of the fact that during their four years of development important conditions affecting them changed repeatedly. Nevertheless it is obvious from the report that a structure did grow up through which interaction among evacuees and administrators was guided, and evacuees played an important part in the development of the remarkable variety of forms which appeared in the various centers. The symbolic phrases and ideas were also subject to change in the course of the four years, but they nevertheless developed into very definite forms readily apparent to any reasonably sensitive observer.

It has also been suggested that there was no real economic base and hence that no community in any ordinary sense could develop. However, there was an economy in the relocation centers, highly managed in most respects. Very limited in the production of goods but productive of services, it was characterized by a market system organized in terms of the cooperative enterprises of the stores. In addition there were social organization, politics, religion, symbol systems, and the arts. The manner in which these essentials of community life were oriented and given meaning by the evacuees under these special and peculiar circumstances is what the following report attempts to show. It falls short of being an adequate ethnography, but it makes clear that such a description could be made. The kind of stability which the community achieved and the kind of vulnerability to which it was subject emerge from the report.

It seems doubtful that thousands of people can remain together for any number of days without developing community in the sense in which it is used here. Only concentration camps of the most brutal kind, such as those in which Bruno Bettelheim[11] lived and which he has described for us, approach conditions in which human communities become impossible because of the disintegration of the personalities and their transformation into something which we would hesitate to call human. The relocation centers had a sufficient margin of autonomy to make it very clear that we should not speak of them as the concentration camp kind of social unit.

The outstanding fact about the relocation centers was the the Japanese-Americans did not remain aggregates of frustrated and confused individuals. They did not become people without hope and they did not become apathetic. They did not, in short, respond as the WRA administrators predicted, even though a few individuals did seem to fit that prescription and could be pointed to as examples of what WRA policy wished to avoid. The important fact to understand is that a certain kind of community life did develop which made sense for the evacuees out of a devastating experience. This growth, this human response, was either ignored or deplored by the administrators because it did not quite fit with their view of the situation.

THE SIGNIFICANCE OF THE OPPOSING VIEWS

The opposing positions which the following report describes and of which the authors have attempted to give some interpretation may be taken for granted as inevitable in all encounters between administrators and the administered. On the other hand one may raise questions concerning it. Is, indeed, this kind of opposition inevitable and necessary? Is the behavior of the evacuees to be judged as perverse because the administrators so regarded it? Was the energy which the evacuees put into the ordering of their world anew purely wasted effort? Could this energy have been turned to account within a different administrative framework? Was the behavior of the evacuees what should be expected usually to take place in similar situations? If it gives any clues to how people may be expected to behave in such situations, may there not be some virtue in considering other types of administrative context in which the evacuee initiative could have contributed constructively to the situation?

One raises such questions not in the conviction that the WRA administration was unsuccessful, but only in the interest of developing that useful instrument which is called "public administration" to its full potential in solving human problems. The head of the agency was honored by our government after he had liquidated the War Relocation Authority, and it was the opinion of many fellow administrators that this had been a job unusually well done. Nor does one raise questions in the belief that the WRA was purely oppressive. Quite the contrary—its policy makers and staff generally seem to have been unusually imaginative, adaptable to emergent needs of the evacuees, considerate of individual hardship, and courageous in fighting for the carefully thought-out program against the opposition of other agencies and various hostile groups and individuals. The record of success in achieving the goal set and the maintenance of humane conditions in the centers are perfectly clear. Nevertheless the questions keep nagging.

Was the atmosphere of opposition and forced compliance which unquestionably pervaded the relocation centers a necessary condition? Is this kind of condition, which if one looks about one recognizes as characteristic not only of relocation centers but also of Indian reservations in the United States, the colonial countries before independence, and a host of modern national government programs for the improvement of life at the local level in various parts of the world—is this condition inevitable? If it is not inevitable, what are the alternatives?

One matter must be clear before considering possible alternatives. This is the fact that the condition of opposition to which special attention has been called is not what the WRA policy makers predicted would develop under the circumstances of the relocation centers. They predicted apathetic response to institutionalized living conditions, individual frustrations, and an inevitable growth of dependency. There were indeed such symptoms among the evacuees and it seems probable that there would have been further development of these if the relocation centers had continued in existence. It should be understood, however, emphasis is put upon the point that the pervasive opposition of purpose was the circumstance which caused such responses, and given a longer period in which to operate would have made them general in the centers. The overwhelmingly dominant response was the immediate and continuing effort to build conceptions of the centers meaningful in relation to the Japanese-American experience. It was this behavior which the administrators either attempted to ignore or else regarded as perverse. Having made up their own minds as to goals, they continued firmly to behave in a manner calculated to promote apathy, frustration, and dependency. They, in short, seemed to regard their kind of administration as something inevitable. In this sense, then, *their behavior embodied a self-fulfilling prophecy and was little related to what was actually taking place in the relocation centers.*

It would seem that the administrators accepted a particular tradition of administration which has been developed in the Western world, a tradition designed to "get things done." It is adapted for accomplishing certain specialized work through the means of an office force consisting of paid employees who are responsible upward to the top administrative official in a hierarchy. It is built on impersonality, specialized competences, and the separation of policy-making functions from program execution functions. Policy making is reserved to the top level of administrators or to some type of board to whom the top administrators are ultimately responsible. This device, this set of administrative techniques, has become a most useful tool in our industrial world. It is in fact an integral part of the organizations and goals which make up the industrial aspect of our civilization. Like all good things, however, it becomes dangerous if its uses and their limitations are not well understood.

This administrative instrument is often regarded as capable of doing jobs for which it is not designed, resulting not only in failure in the completion of such jobs, but often in the destruction of the materials which the instrument mishandles. An example is the attempts to use the instrument in situations where the ends of administrative lines are not paid office forces and technicians, but communities of ordinary people where the basic difficulty is in connection with policy determination. When applied to problems of such groups the traditional administrative arrangement becomes destructive. A community of human beings seeks constantly to take part in planning its own future or, at the very least, in maintaining the feeling that it is participating in the working out of its own destiny. It is true that many human communities have existed for long periods under various oppressive regimes without any control over their future, but in these circumstances they often embrace religious beliefs which give people some sense of control of their individual destinies.

However, in terms of such a value system as has become dominant in the United States, participation in the working out of the collective future has become fundamental. Administrative technicians such as those who are interested in careers in government are not regarded as having the competence to choose among future courses for ordinary communities of people—persons whom "the people" choose have these ultimate policy-making functions. Technically trained people may advise, but they should not choose courses of action and paths of development. Our system depends on maintaining in the hands of our communities the fundamental choices which mold our destiny. Cynicism about the actual working out of the election system or other aspects of democratic procedure does not change the fact that there is acceptance of the fundamental principle of participation. There is a growing tendency to transfer to administrative agencies of the traditional sort many functions of policy making for various communities under the guise of "special circumstances." This has been done in the case of the Indians of the United States. Something of this sort has developed in many countries in connection with one or another kind of economic or community development program for betterment of living conditions. The tendency is strong everywhere in the United States as the federal government assumes functions which local governments cannot, or will not, undertake. We may see in the WRA experience, in rather exceptional circumstances it is true, the mechanism of maladaptation of the traditional administrative arrangements to the fundamental solution of local community problems.

To summarize briefly the sequence of events as seen from the standpoint which is presented here: A government agency was set up to deal with newly created problems of human beings uprooted from their home communities. The agency was manned by administrators brought up in the traditional pattern of administration adapted to employee staffs. They proceeded quickly and efficiently to "think through" aspects of the problems as they gathered information. They made decisions promptly about the nature of the "camps" and about the best course for the welfare of the evacuees. They went through this process in the best traditional administrative manner, gathering information about the Japanese-Americans, but not bringing Japanese into responsible policy-making positions. The WRA staff did not have the experience of facing life as Japanese-Americans, and thus the viewpoint growing out of such experience was not included in the cauldron of policy discussion.

The result was a paternalistic set of decisions, despite the WRA's disclaimer in this regard. Men without Japanese-American experience made decisions about the future course of action and then asked for cooperation in accomplishing what they had decided on. The Japanese-American families composed largely of United States citizens had not asked these administrators to represent them. They had not given a mandate to the WRA to decide policy for their group. The process of policy making was split into two courses: On the one hand policy decisions were made by the technicians of the administrative agency who lacked the experience which could make them competent; on the other hand the people whose future was at stake moved in isolation to the making of their own policy decisions. The policies thus formulated were at odds on fundamental points and could have been reconciled only through exchange of ideas at the policy level. The basic decision to operate as an administrative agency of the traditional sort created a situation in which administration and people moved farther apart rather than closer together. The requested participation was denied and each later effort on the part of evacuees in connection with, for example, proposed general conferences on resettlement[12] found the agency adhering to its policy of making its own decisions in isolation from the evacuees.

It is very clear that the administrative tradition within which War Relocation Authority worked is increasingly being applied in situations for which it is unsuitable. The WRA experience, if carefully considered, suggests certain guides for the development of an administrative tradition adapted to the situation of the linkage of government, or other large organizations, and communities of people. A fundamental of the approach is recognition of the fact that administrative technicians as such are not equipped to be designers of public policy. If they do undertake the role of policy makers, it demonstrates a failure to understand the limits of their own specialized competences. Public policy involving the future of human communities *must be made by those communities,* or the destruction of some of the most important human qualities is certain to take place, resulting in frustration, apathy, and dependency.

It would be impossible to trace out the full extent of the indebtedness of the authors of the report presented below. There is, however, a primary debt which I mention with deep gratitude. It was John Collier, then Commissioner of Indian Affairs, who first realized the importance of a running analytical account of what was happening to the evacuees and to the administrators charged with their welfare. He conceived the idea of an action research unit at the Poston center (for which the Bureau of Indian Affairs had initial responsibility). Alexander H. Leighton undertook the direction of the unit which was called the Bureau of Sociological Research. During the summer of 1942 Leighton initiated research which insofar as possible was to be utilized to help solve the immediate administrative and other human problems. His work was an important influence on the research later developed by the War Relocation Authority. By the end of 1942 John H. Provinse, Chief of Community Services for WRA, was able to put into operation a plan with which he had been concerned for action research as an integral part of the new agency. John F. Embree became the first head of a Community Analysis Section and employed analysts for each of the centers. The subsequent work of the section owed much to the foundation ideas of both Leighton and Embree. The whole of the original report was typed by Miss Joan Ishiyama, secretary of the Community Analysis Section, who contributed far more than secretarial services.

The authors hope that this report will not only help correct the widespread misunderstanding of the nature of the relocation centers, but also contribute to better understanding of administrative structures and processes as they relate to human needs.

Edward H. Spicer
January, 1969

Notes

1. **Grodzins, Morton,** 1949, *Americans Betrayed. Politics and the Japanese Evacuation.* The University of Chicago Press, Chicago.

2. **Ten Broek, Jacobus, Edward N. Barnhart, and Floyd W. Matson,** 1954, *Prejudice, War and the Consitution. Japanese-American Evacuation and Resettlement.* University of California Press, Berkeley and Los Angeles.

3. **Thomas, Dorothy Swaine and Richard S. Nishimoto,** 1946, *The Spoilage.* Japanese-American Evacuation and Resettlement Series. University of California Press, Berkeley and Los Angeles.

4. **Okubo, Miné,** 1946, *Citizen 13660.* Columbia University Press, New York.

5. **Means, Florence Crannell,** 1945, *The Moved-Outers.* Houghton Mifflin Co. Boston.

6. **Adams, Ansel,** 1944, "Born Free and Equal." *U.S. Camera.*

7. **Eaton, Allen H.,** 1952, *Beauty Behind Barbed Wire. The Arts of the Japanese in Our War Relocation Camps.* Harper and Brothers, New York.

8. **United States Department of the Interior,** (n.d.), *WRA—A Story of Human Conservation.* U.S. Government Printing Office, Washington, D.C.

9. **Leighton, Alexander H.,** 1945, *The Governing of Men. General Priniciples and Recommendations Based on Experience at a Japanese Relocation Camp.* Princeton University Press, Princeton, N.J.

10. **Provinse, John H. and Solon T. Kimball,** 1946, "Building New Communities During Wartime." *American Sociological Review,* Vol. XI, No. 4:396–410 (Aug.).

11. **Bettelheim, Bruno,** 1943, "Individual and Mass Behavior in Extreme Situations," *The Journal of Abnormal and Social Psychology,* Vol. 38, No. 4: 417–52 (Oct.).

12. **United States Department of the Interior,** (n.d.) *Community Government in War Relocation Centers.* U.S. Government Printing Office, Washington D.C.

FOREWORD TO THE ORIGINAL

This is a report concerning a group of people during a crucial period in their experience; it is not a report on the policy or operation of the Government agency which played a considerable role in the crucial experience. The group consists of one of America's minority peoples, and the crisis was the loss of self-determination. Implicit in the account is the assumption that any sort of people would have behaved in much the same way if they had been dealt with similarly. The fact that a minority of the people were brought up in Japan is important for interpreting minor aspects of their behavior during the crisis, but chiefly for understanding the behavior of Americans towards them.

The report deals specifically with four years in the life of Japanese-Americans—from 1942 to 1946. The Prologue attempts to show what in their relations with other West Coast people led to their being singled out for evacuation and placement in the relocation centers. The body of the report takes up in outline the experiences of the people in the relocation centers: first, the period of Moving In, from May 1942 through January 1943, which was a time of conflict and tension as people made the adjustment to living in artifical communities under Government supervision; second, the period of Being Sorted, from February 1943 to November 1943, during which new tensions arose in response to the Government program of separating the loyal and the disloyal; third, the period of Settling Down, from about November 1943 to December 1944, during which the majority of people completed their adjustment to life in the artificial communities; and fourth, the period of Getting Out, from December 1944 to December 1945, when the communities broke up. In the Epilogue an attempt is made to sketch the process, as it appeared in early 1946, of transition from Government supervision to life in free communities.

The writing of the report, as well as the gathering of data, has been a cooperative enterprise. All those who ever worked in the Community Analysis Section of the War Relocation Authority have contributed; in addition many evacuees and other WRA staff members have participated. The report is designed not as an exhaustive analysis of the attitudes and organization of the evacuees in the relocation centers, but rather as an outline of major developments. It seeks to report what, at the time of the liquidation of the agency, seem to have been the most important psychological and social effects of the crisis which Japanese-Americans have undergone—most important, that is, for an understanding of what happens to people when democratic processes go wrong and a Government seeks to set them right.

PROLOGUE

The two months after the attack on Pearl Harbor were black for all America, but California and its two neighbors to the north knew literal blackness when the air-raid sirens cut the ear and lights flickered out over the cities, which then waited with traffic and radio stations quiet for whatever might happen. Planes began to roar back and forth overhead with searchlights stabbing them from the ground. Were these enemy planes? Was this at last the beginning of the expected attack from the Pacific? The panic-stricken reaction to a careless neighbor's light during a blackout was that saboteurs and fifth columnists were signalling the enemy.

The shock of Pearl Harbor did not fade, and the rumor-ridden mystery of what had really happened in Hawaii grew deeper. It was all the more acute for Californians because they identified their defense problems with Hawaii, which had been so close for the past century through business and friendly ties. The open sesame of conversation was the whisper, "A friend of mine heard a sailor in a bar (or an officer's wife) was back from the islands say that . . . ."

During those two months after December 7, HMS *Resolute,* Guam, Wake, Colin Kelly, Hong Kong, and Manila were in the headlines. Below the headlines was the familiar box with instructions for what to do in an emergency attack. Rumors of what had happened at Pearl Harbor grew more horrifying; more and more ships were being listed. The Pacific Coast was more vulnerable than it dared imagine.

People flocked to sign up for civilian defense, but no one knew what to tell them to do—except wait to be called. Runs were started on flashlights, batteries, buckets, and shovels. Dirty bags of sand for incendiaries littered city sidewalks and buildings. Signs on stairways, "This Way to Air Raid Shelter," made one look with new eyes at familiar buildings to judge their relative safety under bombing. People coming from the movies talked of where to go and what roads to take if there should be an attack. Women rushed to stores to buy nylons and rubber

25

girdles; grocers began to limit sales on sugar, coffee, and canned goods. A few people complained about "Made in Japan" goods in dime stores. Others excitedly called their friends about the sacrifice sales on Oriental art in Japanese-owned stores. There would be no more such art until after the war, perhaps never, and they were now a bargain—better than a bargain if you quibbled about the price with the owners who seemed inclined to accept any price offered.

Quisling had become an international noun two years before, but it and the concept of fifth columnism had for Americans the garbled slickness and fascinating unreality of a Sunday feature story. That was before the Sunday of Pearl Harbor and the rumors (later proved false) of fifth columnism in Hawaii. Americans then began to reproach themselves, "We're such trusting suckers." But yet to believe that a fifth column actually existed was to deny faith in the nation at a time when the urge was for unity and to avoid, even in thought, taking the first step in helping the enemy to divide and conquer. It became a painful dilemma, but the American people had (and continued to have), by and large, a phenomenal willingness not to solve the dilemma between faith and distrust for themselves. They let the FBI investigate their reported suspicions about neighbors and fellow workers. They tried to put suspicion on an individual basis rather than to direct it against any particular group as a whole. In contrast to the behavior at the time of World War I, they hesitated to suspect people just because of their descent and to assume that people born in a nation now at war with the United States must therefore be disloyal.

World War I was not so distant that people had overcome their shame about the witch hunting of Americans of German descent twenty-five years earlier and the hysterical excesses of renaming sauerkraut, changing Schmidt to Smith, and banning German music. Lack of complete confidence in war news, especially atrocity stories, lingered on from the last war together with a determined skepticism and sophistication about any kind of propaganda. Only the oldsters of World War I called for parades, flying flags, military bands, and a rah-rah war. For most people, the depression, unemployment, years of isolationism and pacifism, debunking of war and the exposure of war-making munitions industries, and the speed of the Axis military machine topped by Pearl Harbor made this a different kind of war.

These attitudes, and confidence in the FBI to investigate suspected individuals, helped, during the two months after Pearl Harbor, to break whatever runaway emotions a frustrated nation, not yet geared for war, might have turned upon its own people. Later it was to be some of the leaders, not the people as a whole, who decided to judge a part of the population as a group, irrespective of citizenship and loyalty, rather than as individuals.

THE PROCESS OF SCAPEGOATING

Nonetheless, persons of German and Italian ancestry on the West Coast were uneasy during the first two months of the war. Those of Japanese descent were even more uneasy. Their Oriental faces identified them in a region whose greatest physical danger was from that part of the World War being fought in the Far East. Also, it was the surprise attack by Japan that had made America take sides and had catapulted it into war with the Axis nations. Before America had made her decision, some of the less well-assimilated residents with ties through birth or descent with countries later to become our enemies, had taken one side or another about the war in the Old Country. Most, however, were indifferent. A few Italians praised Mussolini; others denounced him. A small proportion of Germans (largely post-World War I immigrants or disaffected citizens) believed Hitler to be the savior of Germany; others called him a menace to the world. Some Japanese collected funds and tinfoil to help Japan fight China; others picketed American steamships loading scrap iron for Japan.

The lines of these differences also cut across the general public regardless of nationality or descent. Americans whose ancestry was as complicated as a patchwork quilt formed societies with first-, second-, and third-generation Americans to help the United States by helping England fight the Axis. People whose former homeland or parental homeland had been ravaged by the Axis were prominent among those taking sides. For example, after the Manchurian incident, some Chinese boycotted Japanese-owned stores in California, wore signs saying, "I am a Chinese-American," and sent money to help China fight Japan. Other Chinese said, "This is America and no place to fight with other Americans over Old Country politics." People of many nationalities agreed with that point of view. Either they desired to emphasize their identification with America over former ties, or they believed that anything happening outside America was none of America's business.

As insults by Japan to Americans in the Far East grew in the two years before Pearl Harbor, the tide of public opinion on the West Coast began to rise against Japan. Nearly fifty years of McClatchy and Hearst propaganda against the California Japanese began to fester like an old sore and lead some Americans to identify people of Japanese ancestry in California with those in Japan. American school girls and boys of Oriental appearance sometimes had the experience of being spit on and cursed because of their ancestry. People of German and Italian descent, being less racially visible, had fewer such experiences. However, the antagonism rising as Hitler swept over Europe made them feel self-conscious, although like most of the German aliens in California in 1941, many of them, too, had been refugees from economic and political oppression.

By the time of the attack on Pearl Harbor, these hostile undercurrents with their paradoxes and dilemmas were part of the mental climate of the West Coast. To be normal—that is, to maintain the values and thoughts of the half hour before one heard about Pearl Harbor—was now the height of abnormality, because it violated the instinct for self-preservation. The abrogation, or at least the restriction, of some civil rights was expected, tolerated, and by a few even desired as proof that the higher authorities, after the failure at Pearl Harbor, once again had their hands firmly on the wheel. However rough and mysterious a course they pursued, survival required that the secret knowledge which they could not share with us for security reasons dictated that course which was best for our preservation as a people and as a nation. They knew also, as part of the secret knowledge, what our losses, which now placed the West Coast in such extreme jeopardy, had been. We took for granted that their shame, eagerness to get into action, and instinct for survival was as strong, if not stronger, than our own.

Within a few days after Pearl Harbor, the assignment of Lieutenant General J. L. DeWitt as Commanding General of the Western Defense Command was announced. The very name, Western Defense Command, was both terrifying and reassuring; the West Coast was a theatre of war but would be defended; there would be organization, plans, and leadership. West Coast residents breathed a little more evenly as they read that the General was firm, determined, a stickler on the job, even a martinet. Curiously, the word then seemed to lack a derogatory connotation. It suggested instead that he would leave nothing undone to prevent a second Pearl Harbor.

The West Coast was frightened. An ordinary person could do nothing to stop the nightmare progress of the Japanese in the Pacific. Rushing down to enlist was and could be an outlet for only a small part of the population. The story of the blocked roads of France seemed about to become our story too. In case of attack, should we stay home like rats in a trap so that the roads would be free for the Army, or should we flee to the Sierras? The only authoritative general order given for a long time (if more were given, they never reached the ordinary person) was to keep lights out during a blackout. Even so, instructions were always so complicated or so changing that no one ever was sure which siren meant "all clear." To settle the family quarrel by following what the people across the street did might be, for all we knew, following a fifth columnist. The very rarity of orders made those which were given all the more acceptable, respected, and reasonable to an unmobilized, frustrated people who still complained, chiseled, and scurried about for the easier way but also wanted to do something constructive and heroic.

Differences about foreign politics faded as everyone rallied to the United States. It is one thing to defend and aid the Old Country when the United States is at peace, but when the adopted land and the homeland are at war, discretion and common sense make conformity and unity with the adopted land a necessity. He who had argued Italian or Japanese politics like a lion with the rest of the fishing fleet suddenly became, within the hour on December 7, a confused, weary, frightened old man with stumbling English and the frightful label of "enemy alien." Was the freedom of speech so vociferously enjoyed earlier a sugar-baited trap of the democracies? Or would people understand that an old man liked to argue with his cronies about Old Country politics when that country and America were still friends and not enemies?

Before sunset of December 7, the intelligence authorities had started to pick up individuals on their lists who were suspected of disloyalty. Most were enemy aliens. Enemy aliens and their families were anxious. Who would be next? The senile, German-speaking mother-in-law who hysterically demanded that they leave this dangerous coast and return to Germany was kept out of sight as much as possible. The Italians played up their fun-loving, innocuous qualities and illiteracy. Some Japanese, hearing that books and mementoes of the Old Country were suspect, undertook a frightened burning of valuable books, irreplaceable family portraits, and prized collections of dolls. What little the general public knew about the pickups had the dual effect of giving them confidence in the alertness of the authorities and of shocking them that a trusted neighbor or business acquaintance of German, Italian, or Japanese descent was a traitor, as suggested simply by the FBI picking him up and holding him until they could get around to questioning him. Many were released, but their neighbors rarely came to know exactly what happened. Doubt about them lingered on.

Indirectly the public felt more strongly the effect of another restriction on enemy aliens, particularly on the Japanese. On December 8, funds of enemy aliens were frozen. When the public learned that the sudden scarcity of fresh vegetables and fruits and their sky-rocketing price was due to frozen funds of enemy aliens among the Japanese, there were murmurs of protest. Mrs. Franklin D. Roosevelt, who visited the Coast immediately after Pearl Harbor, was popularly credited with getting the order relaxed so that enemy aliens could get enough cash to meet necessary business and living expenses.

During those first two months after Pearl Harbor, the people of the West Coast, despite their genuine fear of attack from outside and the possibility of fifth columnism at home, were remarkably calm. They shared the feeling of unity which had swept the nation. That unity precluded unreasonable suspicion of fellow American residents. State and local officials as well as the general public acceded to the request of the FBI that it handle investigations of reported subversive activities in order that witch hunts might be prevented, counter-espionage not hindered, and possible patterns of fifth columnism not obscured.

People who before the war had not hated fellow townsmen because of their descent did not do so when war was declared. Those who had denounced them before the war as "Dagos," "Germs," and "Japs" continued their former pattern of belief and speech with more fervor and noise, and sported windshield stickers, "Open Season on Japs," directed against the California Japanese. When civilian defense units were organized, Nisei (American citizens of Japanese descent) were prominent in many of them. A Modesto unit spontaneously elected a Nisei as their chairman. As they tell it in Modesto, it began to dawn on them that their Chairman was of the same ancestry as the most feared enemy. They suffered a little bemused and amused embarrassment because, "Well, he was a darn swell guy, better American than some of the rest of us," but still, "It sure made us feel funny when it struck us that he was a Jap and here we had picked him as the best one for the job; we didn't know what other people would think." The matter was left to limp along.

But events beyond the control of the community were to make the decision and give needle sharpness to the dilemmas and paradoxes.

Conflicting Responsibility for Enemy Aliens

Under the Presidential Proclamations of December 7 and 8, the Department of Justice was responsible for controlling enemy aliens in the continental United States and Alaska. It had the authority to apprehend and intern dangerous enemy aliens; to seize short-wave radios, guns, ammunition, and other articles declared contraband to enemy aliens; and to exclude enemy aliens from certain zones. However, enemy aliens who brought contraband to local law enforcement officers were often turned away as full handed as they had come because the officers were not prepared to receive, receipt, or store such articles. Instructions to them and to aliens were slow to percolate. Aliens were handicapped by the almost entire suspension of their language newspapers and the absence of those leaders who had been picked up. Nevertheless, the collection of contraband was progressing toward the deadline of January 5, and the FBI was busy apprehending aliens and citizens suspected of subversive activities. No areas from which enemy aliens were to be excluded had been announced; apparently the Department of Justice felt its vigilance and knowledge of conditions in crucial areas made this extreme measure unnecessary.

Californians debated among themselves about how to protect effectively the thousands of miles of western coastline. Campers thought of "dandy invasion coves," difficult to guard. It seemed reasonable to them, as armchair strategists, that the enemy would bypass obvious ports of entry in favor of infiltration. Heavily populated ports knew they would receive the first attack. Each city and hamlet on the coast or in the mountains felt, with local pride fiercely turned inside out, that if the enemy got control of a certain nearby road or installation, it would have the key to California. To succeed in these armchair strategies, the enemy would need fifth columnists. Had each community which regarded itself as the key to California asked to be declared a restricted zone, most of California would have been included. But there was no storm of demand for such action. Discussion continued, in most regions, to have an academic or cracker-barrel quality. Feelings about enemy aliens remained diffuse and uncrystallized.

Because the authorities frequently changed and inadequately communicated their instructions about alien travel, funds, and related matters, enemy aliens and their families fell prey to anxieties, insecurity, rumors, and nervous speculations about the future. For their own sake and that of their children most of the aliens wished to observe the regulations and behave in the way satisfactory to officials and the general public, but conflicting advice and information handicapped them.

Aliens had, in general, three possible courses of action: to withdraw into a shell, to stress loyalty to the United States, or to continue about usual affairs as normally as possible. Citizen counselors themselves did not agree on the best course. Consequently, aliens and their families were caught in a cross fire. Whatever they did was sure to displease some valued adviser. If they kept to themselves, as some police officers advised them, in order not to attract curious kibitzers and perhaps "trouble," they were criticized by those people who felt that if they had nothing to conceal they should participate more fully in the community life to prove their Americanism. When they attempted to do that, their alien origin or obvious race led occasionally to their being turned away by civilian war-relief groups. These rejections were so multiplied in the telling that even the thickest-skinned individual was discouraged. Just to act normal was impossible since official restrictions and nervousness affected home life and business.

As to the general public, the aliens felt relieved that the pattern of World War I hysteria was not being repeated. While some of the public might be curious and watchful in the way that some people are about the misery and anxiety of others, very few were openly hostile. Most had the attitude of reserving judgment, and in the meantime of continuing whatever courtesy or kindness they had shown before the war. Many were indifferent to everyone but themselves because of the sudden changes in job, residence, and family readjustments which the war was making in their own microcosms. It was easy to note casually but not to inquire about the glumness and sorrow on the Italian barber's face or the disappearance from the flower kiosk on the avenue of the old Japanese woman and her high school son. People who ordinarily would have concerned themselves with the welfare of those who were on the peripheries of their microcosms of personal life now felt too oppressed by their own problems. When an employee of alien birth or parentage quit his job after customers had made unpleasant remarks about enemy aliens, or when such a person dropped out of the choir, the employer or fellow choir members often felt relieved, much as they might like the individual personally, that this embarrassment and uncertainty was over. However, if they had aggressively befriended the individual they felt hurt at being rejected and would vindictively condemn his entire national group.

The Attorney General of the United States, Francis G. Biddle, was determined that enemy aliens should not become scapegoats any more than any other group. As long as they obeyed the regulations pertaining to their status, they need not be afraid, he assured them. They would be judged individually, not categorically. A month or two before Pearl Harbor, he had said:

In tense times such as these, a strange psychology grips us. We are oppressed and fearful and apprehensive. If we can't get at the immediate cause of our difficulties, we are likely to vent our dammed-up energy on a scapegoat. That scapegoat may be someone whose views are contrary to our own. It may be someone who speaks with a foreign accent, or it may be a labor union which stands up for what it believes to be its rights. That sort of psychology is the very essence of totalitarianism. On the other hand, civil liberties are the essence of the democracy we are pledged to protect. Insofar as I can by the use of the authority and influence of my office, I intend to see that civil liberties in this country are protected; that we do not again fall into the disgraceful hysteria of witch hunts, strike-breakings, and minority persecutions which were such a dark chapter in our record of the last World War.

After Pearl Harbor, he pressed forward in his battle, this time against those who were discharging aliens and citizens from jobs only because of their ancestry. He said:

War threatens all civil rights; and although we have fought wars before, and our personal freedoms have survived, there have been periods of gross abuse, when hysteria and hate and fear ran high, and when minorities were unlawfully and cruelly abused. Every man who cares about freedom, about a government by law—and all freedom is based on fair administration of the law—must fight for it for the other man with whom he disagrees for the right of the minority, for the chance for the underprivileged with the same passion of insistence as he claims for his own rights. If we care about democracy, we must care about it as a reality for others as well as for ourselves; yes, for aliens, for Germans, for Italians, for Japanese, for those who are with us as those who are against us. For the Bill of Rights protects not only American citizens but all human beings who live on our American soil, under our American flag. The rights of the Anglo-Saxons, of Jews, of Catholics, of Negroes, of Slavs, Indians—all are alike before the law. And this we must remember and sustain—that is, if we really love justice, and really hate the bayonet and the whip and the gun, and the whole Gestapo method as a way of handling human beings.

Instead of using his authority to restrict enemy aliens to the hilt, the Attorney General tried to see that every enemy alien (as well as every friendly alien and every American citizen), if there was no cause to doubt his loyalty, received every right permissible to him in wartime. The Attorney General declared that inevitably there were some disloyal aliens— and citizens—but the Government was aware of them and had control of their activities. It would not, however, condemn any alien group wholesale. People would be judged as individuals and not as members of a race or nationality.

President Roosevelt followed up Mr. Biddle's plea with the statement:

It is one thing to safeguard American industry, and particularly defense industry, against sabotage; but it is very much another to throw out of work honest and loyal people who, except for the accident of birth, are sincerely patriotic . . . . Remember the Nazi technique: "Pit race against race, religion against religion, prejudice against prejudice. Divide and conquer." We must not let that happen here. We must not forget what we are defending: Liberty, decency, justice.

Most Californians agreed, or at least fell into line. As 1941 drew to a close, certain distinguished Californians, who, under the chairmanship of Governor C. L. Olson, had formed the Northern California Committee on Fair Play for Citizens and Aliens of Japanese Ancestry, reported:

Californians have kept their heads . . . . There have been few if any serious denials of civil rights to either aliens or citizens of Japanese race, on account of the war. The American tradition of fair play has been observed . . . all the organs of public influence and information—

press, pulpit, school welfare agencies, radio, and cinema—have discouraged mob violence and have pleaded for tolerance and justice for all law-abiding residents of whatever race.

Federal and local agencies that maintained order and suppressed sub versive activities were praised for their vigor and sympathetic consideration. Private civic agencies had promptly assisted enemy aliens suffering from wartime restrictions. To most Californians at the end of 1941, enemy aliens were not a threat to state and national security. Not many were clamoring for any more restraint of aliens than existed. They were satisfied that the intelligence agencies and the Department of Justice were not overlooking dangerous enemies. The FBI was easy to reach by telephone. The public had confidence in its respect for clues reported by citizens and its thorough investigations. The swiftness with which it had moved after December 7, indicating previous preparation, had much to do with both the public calm and the absence of sabotage.

The tense two months after Pearl Harbor marked a high point in American respect for the civil rights of enemy aliens and their citizen children. This respect existed without endangering national safety or lapsing into complacency. The excitement of later events has clouded the fact that the confidence of the people, shown during the early period, in the power of democratic ideals to win the loyalty of residents in America had been justified. The aliens had not betrayed the trust of citizens in their loyalty or neutrality. Attorney General Biddle and Secretary of War Stimson announced in February that there were no substantial evidences of sabotage anywhere in the United States. About the same time, the attorney general of California stated, "We have had no sabotage and no fifth column activity since the beginning of the war."

Through most of January the "organs of public influence and information" continued the policy which had won the praise of the Committee on Fair Play. But counterforces, opposed to the confidence shown in the loyalty of enemy aliens and the scrupulous observance of their civil rights, were beginning to operate beneath the surface of the public awareness. Once these forces gained momentum, they ground on as imperviously, relentlessly, and powerfully as a glacier gathering size and speed once it was on the move.

The first major engagement in the war between two different points of view regarding enemy aliens and their children began to take shape late in December with the Attorney General of the United States on the one side and the Commanding General of the Western Defense Command on the other side.

To the Commanding General, military security required that enemy aliens be prohibited from strategic areas and that every piece of contraband be collected. Late in December he asked the War Department "to acquaint the Department of Justice with the need for vigorous action along the Pacific Coast." Because he believed that there had been "almost complete absence of action on the part of the Department of Justice over a period of nearly four weeks," he asked it to "act with expedition and effectiveness in the discharge of its responsibilities." The Army did not wish, he explained, "impressions to the contrary notwithstanding," to take from Justice the conduct and control of alien enemies. If this became necessary, the Army would accept the transfer with the greatest reluctance.

In the first week in January representatives of the Department whose head had declared that the Bill of Rights protected even enemy aliens met in San Francisco with the head of the Western Defense Command. James Rowe, Assistant Attorney General, presented a memorandum to answer the Commanding General's criticisms and requests. It described the progress of contraband collecting, a new registration of enemy aliens, and requests to Army and Navy to recommend prohibited areas. The Department was giving in, under arguments of military safety, on the issue of enemy aliens, for it agreed to permit a warrant to be issued with the cause to be met only by the statement that an enemy alien exclusively occupied the premises to be searched. However, it continued to hold strictly to the line of the civil rights of American citizens by refusing to raid and search every house in a specific locality without first finding out if enemy aliens or American citizens lived in the houses entered. It had not abandoned the enemy aliens entirely, for it was still determined to judge each as an individual and not to apprehend or search any alien unless there was cause to suspect him. There would be no mass raids on enemy aliens, taking the term "mass raid" to mean that eventually every enemy alien in the Western Defense Command would be raided with or without cause. If the President overruled Justice on this, it would ask the Army to take over the control of enemy aliens in the Western Defense Command.

The Commanding General was responsible for national safety in his defense zone. Normal processes of law about warrants hampered and delayed him. To require a warrant, he said, before searching a home occupied jointly by citizens and aliens might permit suspected individuals to escape. His eagerness to permit no dangerous person to be loose, no matter how many innocent people suffered or were inconvenienced, led him to prejudge any alien or citizen as disloyal if any suspicious person reported him as such. He also suspected even those who had not aroused suspicions. He asked Justice what control it had over those disloyal, subversive citizens who had not been detected in any overt act and over dual citizens.

The meeting ended. Justice still refused to make mass raids. It still required a warrant before permitting houses occupied jointly by citizens and aliens to be raided. However, it gave in some more on the aliens by permitting officers to search and apprehend enemy aliens without a warrant if they would get a warrant later. This was not enough for the the Commanding General. Most of the dwellings he wanted searched were occupied by both citizens and aliens and not by aliens exclusively. Until Justice permitted any home shared by citizens and aliens to be searched without a warrant, he felt unable to protect the West Coast adequately. Most of the premises he was thinking about, he said, were Japanese.

Three weeks later the Attorney General announced the first two areas from which the Commanding General had recommended that enemy aliens be excluded. They were the San Francisco waterfront and a Los Angeles rectangle which included the municipal airport and shore line.

The waterfronts were considered particularly vulnerable to outside attack. They also had the "actual or potential menace" (a popular phrase of the time) of large numbers of alien enemies. Significant of the change in official thinking, more and more the enemy aliens were being called alien enemies. One might assume that all aliens would be cleared off the waterfronts before being moved from less vulnerable inland areas. However, the waterfront aliens could stay until February 24; the inland aliens had to move by February 15. The reason given was that the waterfronts had "large numbers of alien enemies, Japanese particularly, either living or working in them." The obvious inference was that their welfare required more time for moving. This contradiction between the urgent needs of military safety and solicitude for the welfare of alien enemies believed dangerous to that safety reappears in the announcement. It adds that exclusion "not only will aid national defense but also will protect the aliens themselves."

An obvious question left unanswered is why enemy aliens now needed such an unusual measure as mass evacuation to protect them when Californians had, according to the Committee on Fair Play, kept their heads. However, the Commanding General contradicts the Committee in his final report:

. . . press and periodical reports of public attitudes along the West Coast from December 7, 1941, to the initiation of controlled evacuation clearly reflected the intensity of feeling. Numerous incidents of violence involving Japanese and others occurred; many more were reported but were subsequently either unverified or were to be cumulative.

Though the Commanding General was reporting on a much longer period, he still contradicted the Committee in regard to December, 1941.

Unfortunately, he does not document his remark about "numerous incidents." Writers differ sharply about how much violence was actually suffered by enemy aliens between December 7 and the Japanese evacuation. Those favoring evacuation declare that incidents were many, especially toward persons of Japanese ancestry. Those opposing evacuation declare incidents were few and due largely to long-standing bad relations between California Filipinos and Japanese, aggravated by Christmas liquor and the fall of Manila. No objective account has been published as yet of the number and nature of verifiable incidents reported to local, state, or national law enforcement officials as distinguished from wild, barroom threats of violence which came to official ears.

February climaxed the war of nerves against the three enemy alien groups. Intense anxiety and disorganization afflicted the approximately 120,000 German, Japanese, and Italian enemy aliens on the West Coast. From one day to another they did not know what new regulation or area would be announced, or whether the new area would include their homes, or if they had already had to leave, their new residences. The Commanding General states, " . . . public excitement in certain areas reached a high pitch, and much confusion, the result of conflicting reports and rumors characterized the picture." Rumors flew that this piecemeal dislodging of aliens was the forerunner of a mass evacuation of all German, Italian, and Japanese aliens from the Pacific Coast. Most of the aliens were adults with children who were American citizens and not subject to the regulations, but since they were still dependent on their parents they also had to move. Other aliens were aged and dependent on adult citizen children who felt morally obligated to move with their parents to care for them. People such as these lived in the homes occupied jointly by aliens and citizens, which the Department of Justice would not raid without a search warrant.

Separating the Japanese from Other Enemy Aliens

As early as mid-January, efforts to sort Germans and Italians out from among enemy aliens and to concentrate on rounding up Japanese aliens and their citizen children became evident. The glacier was gaining momentum to sweep all persons of Japanese ancestry off the West Coast and into camps guarded by barbed wire and armed soldiers. The overt dynamic reasons were that they needed "protective custody" from other West Coast people and that since the authorities could not distinguish the loyal from the disloyal it was necessary in the interest of military security to remove all. Although serious consideration continued to be given until March to the mass evacuation of the Germans and Italians, they were not, to the authorities and general public, quite such an undistinguishable mass as the Japanese or in as much danger from hoodlums. The earlier promise of Attorney General Biddle that no alien group would be condemned wholesale was to be kept in mind for the Germans and Italians but completely forgotten, except by a relatively few people, in regard to the Japanese.

The general public began to feel actively sorry for the German and Italian aliens described in the newspaper human-interest stories and whom they knew personally. The most publicized of the alien enemies evacuated from the San Francisco waterfront were the Italian parents of San Francisco's popular favorite, baseball player Joe DiMaggio. The numerous politically important leaders of German and Italian descent pleaded for the aliens of their nationality. The Japanese aliens, who under American laws have never been permitted to become naturalized citizens of the United States, had no mature leaders of their ancestry in high political, social, and financial circles to apply pressure; their children, who were citizens, were too immature and disorganized to be effective. The five-decade-old hostility cultivated by certain sections of the West Coast population toward the Japanese and other Asiatics inhibited stories about them as human beings with names, personalities, and roots in America. Though westerners had known many Japanese personally for some thirty or forty years, they had a mental block which made them think of Japanese as mysterious, inscrutable, and latently dangerous and not as a group made up of persons as individual and different as the ones they did know.

February was the month of decision about mass evacuation. It was to end with the general public watching the boys and girls, young men and women, and older people of Japanese descent stand by piles of baggage waiting for Greyhound buses to take them to camps on former fair grounds and race tracks. The public was not as passive as it appeared. It merely felt worn but relieved. A scapegoat was carrying off the baggage of their fears, anxieties, doubts, and frustrations. Attorney General Biddle's forgotten words echo:

In tense times such as these, a strange psychology grips us. We are oppressed and fearful and apprehensive. If we can't get at the immediate cause of our difficulties we are likely to vent our dammed-up energy on a scapegoat. . . .

What happened in February to make people forget their intention not to "again fall into the disgraceful hysteria of witch hunts, strike-breakings, and minority persecutions which were such a dark chapter in our record of the last World War," and which the Attorney General had warned about?

The Philippines were going. The enemy Japanese were rapidly pouring through the Malay jungles the British had called natural fortresses. Who can forget the February evening when the newspapers reported that residents of Singapore were dancing at the Raffles Hotel while waiting for their Japanese conquerors to enter the lobby? Up in Placerville, California, people in the lobby of the hotel named after the one in Singapore gathered around the radio to listen to President Roosevelt's speech. Even as he talked, a Japanese enemy submarine fired at the oil tanks near Santa Barbara. People gossiped that local Japanese had signalled the submarine. The Commanding General received "hundreds of reports nightly of signal lights visible from the coast, and of intercepts of unidentified radio transmissions." The Battle of Java Seas came and went, an Allied defeat. "Too little and too late" became too familiar. America in her haste to convert to war was mixed up in her own hands and feet and short tempered. There was reconversion unemployment, shortages, crowding cities, emptying villages. On a farm near Auburn, California, a tall boy in his best clothes met the bus, a ten-year-old handed up his suitcase, told him to come back a sergeant, whistled for his dog, and as the bus pulled away ran into the field crying. People told each other, "What we need is a bomb to wake us up. Some people don't know there's a war on."

The chairman of the Tolan Committee* told San Francisco late in February when it came to investigate the evacuation of enemy aliens and citizens of Japanese descent:

It is possible that the entire Pacific Coast may be evacuated. They tell me back in Washington that it is not only possible but probable that the Pacific Coast will be bombed. That has come to me from men who are supposed to know.

Over and over, the Committee told its witnesses, "We can lose this war. They tell me in Washington we can lose this war."

More people were talking like the district attorney of Madera County who wanted martial law by the Army with its first act to be the removal of all persons of Japanese descent. He said:

Our State and Federal laws, supported by a Bill of Rights are entirely inadequate to meet the situation. If we are not to run the risk of disaster we must forget such things as the writ of habeas corpus, and the prohibition against unreasonable searches and seizures. The right of self-defense, self-preservation, on behalf of the people, is higher than the Bill of Rights.

It was getting so that anyone who thought of protecting the constitutional rights of anyone, let alone of persons of Japanese ancestry, was accused of being unpatriotic. The Attorney General of the United States with Edward Ennis and James Rowe, who were on his staff, and

---

*A congressional committee under the chairmanship of Congressman John Tolan of California to investigate problems of "national defense migration." It held hearings on the West Coast in February and March, 1942.

others who fought with them to hold back the tide of hysteria were called "cookie pushers" and enemies of national security. People were reluctant to protest about any regulation connected in any way with national defense for fear of being labeled communist, fascist, or fifth columnist, or of being asked, "Don't you know there's a war on?" A spokesman for a small coastal city with a grievance about a prohibited zone boundary which excluded enemy aliens, most of them Italians, from a shopping district where all doctors' offices, hospitals, the principal stores, the prison, and the jail were located, started his remarks to the Tolan Committee with the statements, "Local authorities appreciate that we are at war, but . . . . " and, "While we are all out for the Army, and appreciate that many people hesitate asking a question about any ruling for fear of being accused as a fifth columnist . . . .

There were dissenting voices, however, which spoke out loudly for the Japanese. The Secretary of the Committee on Fair Play declared:

Our citizens of Japanese parentage are just as trustworthy now as they were a few weeks ago when Governor Olson and other publicists paid tribute to their loyalty and civic devotion. Has the setback given to the Allied arms by the military machine of Japan made our political leaders in state, county, and municipality play the bully and turn against our Japanese citizens as scapegoats for the remote culprits, in Japan, whom our Japanese-American citizens have repeatedly denounced?

These dissenting voices frequently said that economic self-interest and not fear of danger to military security prompted some of the talk about disloyalty of persons of Japanese descent and the necessity for evacuating them. An Oakland attorney stated to the Tolan Committee:

I find no popular demand for the efforts to drive the so-called alien enemies from California. (Chester Rowell, [a prominent San Francisco columnist] has also stated this as his impression). The clamor seems to come from Chamber of Commerce, Associated Farmers, and the newspapers notorious as spokesmen for reactionary interests. In view of this fact, effort should be made to determine whether there is any connection between the clamor for the dispossession of the Japanese farmers and the desire of these clamoring interests to get possession of the Japanese farms and the elimination of the Japanese competition . . . . So far the Attorney General has resisted the mad pressure; but the mad pressure mounts. Even now we hear the rumble of the threats of martial law for all of California—a state of "nonlaw" which would abolish the rights of all of us and make many wonder whether totalitarianism is to be fought with the same and so reduce the struggle to an abstraction.

Leading the demand for the removal of the Japanese was the California Joint Immigration Committee which named as its sustaining bodies the American Legion, the California State Federation of Labor, California Grange, and the Native Sons of the Golden West. Originating in 1905 as the Japanese and Korean Exclusion League, the Committee had the assistance of both the Hearst and the McClatchy papers to keep alive fears of the "Yellow Peril." It declared:

We were largely instrumental in the passage of the 1913 Alien Land Act . . . and . . . instrumental, in 1924, in securing the adoption of the present immigration law which now excludes any Asiatics from a quota as such, as distinguished from the quota of 100 that is accorded to all nations if there are people therein eligible for citizenship.

It considered the granting of citizenship to Negroes after the Civil War a "grave mistake." Unlike Adolf Hitler, who had similar doctrines about citizenship for the white race only, the Committee stated that it did not claim that the white race was superior to another. Its strongest foe, in getting the Exclusion Act passed, it said, was the Federal Council of the Churches of Christ in America.

On February 13, 1942, the Committee which through December and most of January had not been able to turn West Coast residents against the persons of Japanese ancestry in their midst stated, "Neither fear, timidity, nor cost should delay action. Japanese should be removed now!" It demanded that the entire Pacific Coast as far inland as necessary and such other interior regions as necessary be called a combat zone from which all Japanese aliens and American citizens of Japanese ancestry should be removed. All civil authorities of the states should be required to help federal authorities in this program.

At this time the Commanding General was still wrestling with the problem of how to protect the Western Defense Zone while handicapped by Department of Justice regulations about having a search warrant before entering and searching a home occupied jointly by citizens and aliens. The problem, he said, required immediate solution and called for measures not then in being.

He had recommended to Attorney General Biddle that virtually all the territory lying west of the Cascades be declared a prohibited zone. The Attorney General replied that since Portland, Seattle, and Tacoma were included, it would involve a mass evacuation of many thousands; no reasons were given for such a mass evacuation; and if it were contemplated, the War Department would have to do it itself because the Department of Justice did not have the equipment and personnel. The Attorney General took the occasion to add a reminder of the disputed issue. He wrote:

The proclamations directing the Department of Justice to apprehend, and where necessary, to evacuate alien enemies, do not, of course, include American citizens of the Japanese race. If they have to be evacuated, I believe that this would have to be done as a military necessity in these particular areas. Such action, therefore, should in my opinion be taken by the War Department and not by the Department of Justice.

In his final report, the Commanding General pointed out that the western theatre would not have been made secure as long as more than two-thirds of the total Japanese population on the West Coast was not subject to alien enemy regulations. These two-thirds were American citizens. American law at that time had no provision for treating its citizens as alien enemies.

A way was to be found. On February 14, 1942, the Commanding General wrote to the Secretary of War about the "Evacuation of Japanese and other Subversive Persons from the West Coast." He requested authority to name military areas from which he could exclude all alien enemies, American citizens of Japanese ancestry, and all other suspected

Signs such as these soon ringed vital areas of the West Coast.

persons. He asked for authority to requisition the services of any and all other federal agencies, and for a law to provide penalties. On the previous day, the West Coast congressional delegation in Washington had recommended to the President that all persons of Japanese lineage and all others, aliens and citizens alike, who might be deemed dangerous should be evacuated. It will be recalled that a third petition using almost identical language had been prepared and issued on the same day by the California Joint Immigration Committee.

By mid-February, those forces which had long been determined to move all persons of Japanese ancestry off the West Coast had converged. They got results. On February 19, 1942, the President of the United States as Commander in Chief issued Executive Order 9066, which closely follows the wording and ideas in the three petitions. The Secretary of War and the military commanders he designated were to prescribe military areas in such places and of such extent as he or the commanders might determine. Any and all persons could be excluded from such areas. All agencies were to assist in implementing the program. Within a month Congress passed Public Law 503, to provide the penalties for disobedience. Lieutenant General J. L. DeWitt of the Western Defense Command was appointed by the Secretary of War as one of the military commanders.

On March 2, the Commanding General announced the two military areas in his Command from which all persons of Japanese ancestry, citizens and aliens, were to leave voluntarily. Nine thousand left voluntarily to go inland, but the dislocation of the evacuees and the new communities to which they went caused so much trouble and confusion that on March 27, all Japanese were ordered to remain within Military Area No. 1 until plans had been completed for their controlled evacuation by military and civil agencies to assembly centers from which they would be transferred to relocation centers. The Western Defense Command established a civil agency within itself, the Wartime Civil Control Administration, to take charge of evacuation. A few days later the War Relocation Authority was established to take charge of the relocation center phases of evacuee life.

The greatest mass migration of American residents in history was to follow, far greater than any movement of American Indians from tribal lands to reservations. America had learned something about human engineering since the Indians were moved. The engineering exhibited in the evacuation of the Japanese from the West Coast was a magnificent tour de force, as different and superior in technique and administrative management from the transfer of Indians as the oxcart differs from the latest bomber.

A WEST COAST DILEMMA

The two principal arguments for the wholesale evacuation of the Japanese involved (1) doubt of the ability of anyone to distinguish between the loyal and the disloyal among persons of Japanese ancestry, whether born in Japan or in the United States; and (2) doubt of the ability of non-Japanese residents of the West Coast to safeguard the Japanese residents from vigilantism (the traditional California term of Spanish origin for mob lawlessness).

The first Japanese immigrants arrived on the Pacific Coast nearly fifty years before World War II. People born in Japan pioneered the wilderness of California, Washington, and Oregon with people of many other nationalities. As on all American frontiers, the pioneers were young and of diverse origins—old Americans, European immigrants, Mexicans, Chinese, Japanese, and a few Negroes. They built the railroads together, cut the lumber, broke the soil for farms, and gave three Pacific states to the Union. They established homes and businesses. They hired each other and worked for each other. They met in stores, schools, churches, theatres, and homes. Their children went to the same schools.

The West is a new and young country. Many pioneers were still alive in 1942. During fifty years of pioneering, of home and state building, and of raising a generation or two of children, West Coast people, though of different races and nationalities, had shared many experiences through which they should have come to know each other well. Yet when the crisis of World War II came, some looked with the narrowed and suspicious eyes of strangers at the elderly Japanese among them and even at young Americans whom they had known from birth. The doubters asked, "Who is who among the Japanese? Who is loyal to the rest of us? Who is a traitor? We must be sure. Remember Pearl Harbor. How can we tell which is which?"

Why should anyone have such doubts after so many years of shared experiences? Why should people suddenly begin to look at Japanese neighbors and acquaintances as if they were sinister strangers whose bowing, gifts, and many friendly services had cloaked espionage? Many residents, of course, simply ignored the climate of doubt and suspicion about their Japanese friends. They were sure of them, but what of the other Japanese they did not know? They perhaps were the ones about whom rumors and disturbing anecdotes were going around, like the one about the old gardener in the next block who, when jokingly addressed as "Captain" by his employer, a Navy officer, straightened up, looked him in the eye, and said, "Admiral to you," and then disappeared forever, presumably to carry on nefarious activities elsewhere.

Suddenly it seemed that the Japanese had always lived to themselves with a one-way screen between them and the Caucasians. The screen permitted the Japanese to see and understand the Caucasians and to calculate carefully what action to take toward them, but made it impossible for the Caucasians to see any farther into Japanese life than they permitted them. A Washington banker spoke to the Tolan Committee about his many and he hoped (but he was not sure) loyal, old friends of Japanese descent. He said that he found it "exceedingly difficult to divine the oriental . . . their mental processes may not be identical with our own." The word "alien" and particularly "enemy alien" became synonymous with the word "Japanese" in 1942.

Doubts of loyalty had been stimulated and multiplied by decades of anti-Oriental propaganda of the Hearst and McClatchy newspapers and the California Joint Immigration Committee. Even people who had dismissed the Sunday feature stories about the "Yellow Peril" who were "infiltrating" into California to raise potatoes around Stockton and strawberries on the wasteland of Florin began to wonder if there might not have been a grain or two of truth in the inflammatory articles.

The mayor of Tacoma, Washington, said he thought he could tell which Japanese were loyal and which were disloyal because,

. . . a man's background, regardless of who he is, very generally has much to do with what he is going to do. If born in this country; if a Christian; if employed side by side with others who fill that same classification . . .; if educated in our schools; if a producer now and in the past; if maintained in a position of production—I should think that person could be construed to be a loyal American citizen.

He did not think eye slant or skin color had anything to do with loyalty.

The chief of police of Los Angeles County where one-third of all American Japanese lived did not agree. He said,

. . . I feel that they (American citizens of Japanese descent) present as difficult, if not a more difficult, problem than the enemy alien. They are cognizant of the American custom of living; they are capable of understanding the American language and inference; and subject to small limitations, are allowed to associate and mingle with the general American public. . . . In addition to the family traits and the patriotism for the native country of Japan, you have racial characteristics, that of being a Mongolian, which cannot be obliterated from these persons, regardless of how many generations are born in the United States.

The attorney general of California also thought the American-born Japanese, the Nisei, were more dangerous than the Issei, their Japan-born alien parents, because there were twice as many Nisei as Issei and most Issei were over fifty-five years of age. Singled out for special suspicion were the Kibei, those Nisei who had lived in Japan and had attended school there for a few years before returning to the United States.

Historic Problems of Minority Groups on the West Coast

The pioneers of the West Coast had not always got along together amicably during their decades of shared experiences. At different times, the Armenians, Italians, Portuguese, and Dust Bowl in-migrants as well as the Chinese, Japanese, Negroes, and Mexicans were called undesirable foreigners and treated as outcasts. Some still are. Many share traits and attitudes resulting from discrimination. Though intense at times, prejudice and discrimination never became codified or rigid on the West Coast for any of the nationalities. One community differed from another; one individual differed from another; one decade differed from another. Minority groups learned from experience which communities and individuals were friendly and avoided the others.

To non-Caucasians, prejudice and discrimination were as real and concrete a factor in their lives and fortunes as weather and taxes. They learned to let the Caucasians make the first move, for the Caucasians had two standards, one for themselves, one for non-Caucasians. Only the unusual had a single standard. This waiting led to reserve, caution, mysteriousness, inscrutability, deviousness, or sinisterness, or whatever word one chooses to call the one-way screen which came to separate, as the result of prejudice, Caucasians and Orientals. Experience taught the Japanese and Chinese, as it taught other minority group members, that the burdens of adjustment were on their backs. If they could not get them off they would have to learn to carry them as easily as possible.

What West Coast residents, including some Japanese, called "Japanese psychology" did not have a "Made-in-Japan" label but a "Made-in-California" stamp. This Japanese psychology would have been unrecognizable as native Japanese in Tokyo or in Hiroshima. It had its roots in American attitudes toward non-Caucasians and had been fed with Old Country values reinterpreted in the light of decades of West Coast living.

Japanese immigrants inherited the pattern of fears, suspicions, and jealousies which some white pioneers had whipped up earlier on the West Coast toward the Chinese because of desire to eliminate as much economic competition as possible in the rich new land and because of the primitive fear of strangers who are bizarre and externally different, as the Chinese were from Westerners in facial characteristics, pigtails, clothing, language, food, and manners. Other Caucasians protested the mistreatment of the Chinese and the passage of the Chinese Exclusion Act because of desire to get them, like European immigrants, as cheap labor, because of humanitarian reasons as well as fear of international complications with the Far East over discrimination against Asiatics.

When the Chinese were excluded, the Japanese were brought into a ready-made climate of hatred and tension toward Orientals. Organizations were waiting to get the Japanese excluded as they had the Chinese. The Chinese Exclusion League changed its name to the Japanese and Korean Exclusion League and went to work. Later it took the name of the California Joint Immigration Committee. It substituted the slogan "The Japs must go" for the slogan "The Chinese must go." At times the excesses of the anti-Orientalists were so notorious that Presidents of the United States had to request the West Coast, led by California, to moderate its behavior because of the threat to American relations with Japan and the Far East in general. Protests of church and educational leaders as well as Presidents, did not prevent restrictive and discriminatory state and national legislation from being passed. The alien land laws prohibited the Chinese and Japanese from purchasing farm land. The Exclusion Act of 1924 denied Japan the token number of 100 immigrants a year, a courtesy extended to all other nations with limited immigration. Some of the same people and same organizations, still active in 1942, led the demand for wholesale evacuation, and saw their slogan, "The Japs must go," temporarily realized.

Had it not been for their race, or rather had it not been for those who made an issue of race, Americans generally would have welcomed the Japanese immigrants, the Issei or first generation, as desirable newcomers. Their high standards of literacy, education, industry, thrift, family ideals, community cooperation, respect for law, and desire for self-improvement were qualities admired by an American with Puritan and pioneer traditions. Although many immigrants came from the Japanese peasantry, a goodly proportion were younger sons from middle-class families. Of the men still alive and in America in 1940, 80 percent had received, before leaving Japan, the equivalent of American high school education; 10 percent had been to college either in Japan or the United States; most of the others had been to primary schools.

The Issei put their roots down in America. Like most immigrants they saved their low wages from heavy labor on ranches, railroads, mines, and lumber camps to start their own farms, small businesses, and professions. The cultural background and character traits of the stable and adaptable Issei insured that they did not remain in the lower economic and social stratum, but soon climbed the various rungs of the middle-class ladder. Their pioneer period from 1870 to 1908 ended with many of them financially able to send back to their native prefectures for wives and to go into business for themselves. Relatively few remained bachelors and lived as transients following the crops.

During the second period from 1908 to 1921 they built families and businesses and nurtured sentimental and economic bonds with the adopted country. Many who failed, or had made the money they had come for, went back to the old country. The hardy and successful remained to build up a stable community life, to adopt American modes of living and business practices, and to give their children American educations. The peak of the birth rate occurred in 1921. From 1921 to 1941 the Issei were busy raising and providing for their American-born children, the Nisei, most of whom were barely on the verge of maturity when Pearl Harbor came. After 1924 when the Exclusion Act was passed, agitation and persecution of Issei by anti-Oriental groups quieted down. Few Nisei, therefore, had much first-hand experience with discrimination except in getting white-collar and professional positions until Pearl Harbor. Stories of burned homes, smashed windows, and personal attacks were familiar to them only from reminiscences of their parents about the old rough-and-tumble days of the California frontier.

Like other immigrants, Issei sought out people from their own country and particularly from their own prefecture. In their pioneer days they worked in gangs under a boss who served them as business manager and negotiator with employers. Later when they married they drew together into communities either in scattered rural districts or in congested city areas. During the years just before Pearl Harbor, some were moving into better residential districts, away from the Japanese community.

San Francisco, the original nucleus because it was the major port of entry, was replaced as their population center by Los Angeles. When Southern California began to boom, the Japanese, like millions of other American residents, were attracted to the region. Japanese settlements sprang up also in Washington and Oregon. Because northern discrimination never was as virulent as California, the Japanese to the north were better assimilated and tended to belong to a higher income and educational level than those to the south. Around Hood River, Oregon, a few acquired land, before the alien land law was passed, in partial payment for clearing off the forest. This land they developed so well that their less energetic neighbors have tried to get it away from them ever since.

Like other immigrants, the Japanese clung to their native language and depended on their American-born children to aid them in affairs outside the colony which required a knowledge of English. They also tried to pass on their language and cultural values as a heritage to their children. Their emphasis on respect for age and family ties created a strong and tight discipline within the family until the maturing Nisei began to rebel and reach out more successfully all the time for the independence they saw other American adolescents enjoying.

Though the Issei had attitudes and experiences similar to those of other immigrants to America, two factors gave their pattern of life peculiar emphasis, created paradoxes, and fostered much of the Caucasian uncertainty and suspicion so noticeable at the time of Pearl Harbor. The first major factor was the discrimination and prejudice which certain West Coast groups showed the Orientals from the time they first came to America. The second major factor was the Naturalization Statute of the United States, dated 1870. Its effect denied Japanese aliens the right to become naturalized citizens of the nation where they had chosen to establish businesses, make homes, live out the major part of their lives, and raise and educate children who were legally American citizens. More than anything else this determined the essential nature of the psychology of the Japanese immigrants in America.

Because American citizenship was denied them, the Issei were involuntary subjects of the Emperor. If they did not want to become people without a country, they must maintain their citizenship in Japan, the country of their birth, since the country of their choice would not give them legal status as its citizens. The hostility of the anti-Orientalists drove home to Issei the need for a national power to protest for them to the highest American authorities whenever violence and mistreatment occurred. They must have a country to which they could return if the ever-present spectre of deportation constantly dangled before them ever became a reality.

On the foundation stone dated 1870, West Coast anti-Orientalists built a pyramid of discriminatory state legislation which permitted only citizens and persons eligible for citizenship to own and rent agricultural land and to acquire certain commercial licenses. Not only Oriental aliens but American citizens wishing to trade with them were handicapped. In an interlocking and complex society like the United States, economics ignore racial barriers when it is profitable to do so. A network of evasive techniques to carry on business within the letter of the law developed side by side with counter techniques to detect and prosecute evasions whenever political capital could be made of the "Yellow Peril." Since the Issei could not buy land in their own names, they bought it in the names of their American citizen children, thus depending more than most immigrants on their children for aid in business.

In the early years of the century, vicious attacks on Issei in San Francisco streets led President Theodore Roosevelt, at the request of Japan, to protest to California about the attacks and the attempt to segregate Oriental school children. At this same time the Issei, feeling that Japan was too distant and they must cultivate self-reliance, began to give their separate prefectural societies (*kenjinkai*) a superstructure called the Japanese Association for the purpose of protecting fellow countrymen in America from anti-Japanese factions. Almost every community had its Japanese Association which served as economic and agricultural coordinator, social service agency, chamber of commerce, town council, intermediary with the larger American community, and source of leadership.

The Association, the prefectural societies, and the producer-marketing cooperatives created a closely knit community wherever the Japanese lived in any number. This highly organized colony with its bonds tightened by the need to unite against discrimination made the Japanese known to the West Coast as a people who stuck together. They often quarreled bitterly among themselves, especially over economic matters, but when friction and dissension, whatever the cause, seemed in danger of being known to the outside, the leaders said, "Let's forget it. After all, we are all Japanese together." Community solidarity together with strong parental control over the family resulted in an almost negligible rate of crime, juvenile delinquency, and dependence on public assistance.

The concentration of the Japanese into their own colonies and their specialization in food-raising and food-distribution occupations focused attention on them as a special group, though numerically they were an insignificant percentage of the total West Coast population. Caucasians could not dismiss them with amused contempt as they did some minorities who survived only as cheap labor or tourist curiosities. They endowed Japanese success in the face of legal, social, and economic restrictions with the same aura of mysteriousness and sinisterness as their personalities. A Tulare County resident, who with others had formed the Orosi Home Guard after Pearl Harbor to protect Orosi from the men, women, and children of Japanese descent who lived in the area, told the Tolan Committee that during the depression when "good, hard-working white people went broke in the Orosi community, the Japanese did not." Nobody in the community, he said, could figure out how they did it except that they must have had help from outside—from Japan. White farmers around Hood River when hit by the depression asked, "How did the Japanese happen to find out that one could make money on pears while we were going broke on raising apples?" That "you have to get up early to get ahead of them" was literally true, much to the indignation of white farmers who would rather have started to market with their fresh produce after dawn than before like their Japanese competitors.

Because of discrimination and inability to get American citizenship, the Issei could not let themselves be swept along almost unconsciously by the tide of assimilation like European immigrants who can be naturalized and toward whom prejudice gradually dies away as the years pass. An unnaturalized European can drift along through the years, raise a family, buy land, and be buried on American soil without his legal status in America being questioned until, as in World War II, the unnaturalized among the Italians and Germans felt the sting of the label "enemy alien" despite decades of American residence.

The Issei were never permitted to forget that they were not American citizens and not eligible to become American citizens. Reminders faced them at every turn—in the law courts, at city hall license windows, in real estate offices, and at the polls.

Each new discriminatory law or wave of discrimination in the three Coastal States forced them to halt and review the paradox. They had to reconsider their involuntary dilemma between protecting their legal status in Japan and making secure their American home and the country of their children. Every time that their American roots were threatened, their legal insecurity in the United States was driven home to them afresh. Their sense of being a minority group was sharpened. They strengthened their community solidarity to survive in America. A few gave up bucking the American system and went back to Japan; others wondered how far discrimination might go some day. Would they really be sent back to where they came from, as the anti-Orientalists constantly threatened to do? They had to be prepared for either the chance of living out their lives in America with their American citizen children or the possibility of having to return to the Old Country. They must write to the half-forgotten relatives in Hiroshima, perhaps send over a child to strengthen the sentimental bond between grandparents and parents, and claim their share in the property which had until then seemed too insignificant to bother about. It was a vicious circle. When persecution drove the Issei farther behind the one-way screen, the prejudiced among the Occidentals berated them for being unassimilable as Americans and for being pro-Japan.

THE EVACUATED PEOPLE

Between 1931, the date of the Manchurian Incident, and 1941, the mounting tension between the United States and Japan was etched on the moods of the Japanese communities in America as if by a seismograph. Several splits of varying depth and importance in the community, though not caused by the Sino-Japanese war, deepened under tension. Issei were differing from other Issei; Nisei quarreled with Nisei; and Issei and Nisei were at odds with each other. It was harder to keep the differences from the larger American community and present the calm front of the past. Some of the members were acting as individuals or in groups without consulting the Japanese Association. Individualism was loosening community solidarity.

The old dilemma of the Issei ached again more poignantly. They were also concerned about the behavior and future of their children. When the United States in 1940 required all aliens to register at the post office, some of the Nisei were shaken by this reminder of the complex and insecure status of their Issei parents in America. Registration of aliens when the United States was at peace with the world was foreboding to both generations in view of the Far Eastern trouble. Throughout America, people were taking sides in the turmoil of Asia and Europe. Some of the Issei collected funds and materials for Japan relief, often working through relief societies. Once called the Military Virtue Society was renamed Cherry Blossom Society when Issei worried that American public opinion, to which decades of living with their paradox had made them keenly sensitive, would object if the warlike title came to their attention. Many such societies and collections were abandoned by 1940 for a variety of reasons. Some Issei decided that since the United States was obviously becoming more sympathetic to China in the conflict, they, as residents of America but citizens of Japan, should be neutral. Others gave up the attempt to balance themselves first on one side of the dilemma and then the other and decided to accept wholly their beclouded American status with its danger of becoming stateless. All Issei were concerned about their children who, through birth on American soil, were American citizens. They wanted to protect and enhance their children's interests. The boys were being called up in the draft to serve in the United States Army. The community gave them big parties, alternating *banzais* with "God Bless America" and congratulating the draftees on the opportunity to serve the United States and thereby satisfy both the ancient Japanese tradition of loyalty and the authority under which one lives.

What Issei worried about in regard to their Nisei children was that they sometimes seemed like strangers to them in their language, manners, and attitudes. The Japanese-language schools had been of scant value after all in teaching the children enough Japanese to talk with their parents. The broken English of some parents and the halting Japanese of the children could not bridge the gulf between generations, particularly immigrants and their children, a group with unusual problems. The Issei had expected to relinquish gradually the control of the community, the family, and the business to the Nisei after they had proven themselves mature and responsible. Most Nisei, however, were still of high school age or younger, so that this was still for the future. The children, for the most part, had distinguished themselves in public school to the pleasure of their parents for their good scholastic attainments, excellent behavior, and attractive appearance. They were kept busy with school and chores at home and a round of picnics and other social activities sponsored by the public school, language school, Buddhist and Christian Sunday Schools, prefecture societies, produce companies, Boy and Girl Scouts, and teen-age clubs called names like Aces and Acettes.

Among the older Nisei were some who were called "regular Issei type," while among the Issei were men and women with the point of view of "typical Nisei." By and large, the major lines were by generations. The older Nisei often argued among themselves and rebelled against community and Issei control. The conservative Issei leadership as represented by the Japanese Association was still unshaken, but more and more Nisei businessmen were organizing their own service clubs and chambers of commerce to do business outside the colony without consulting the Association.

One Nisei organization was the Japanese-American Citizens League (JACL) which in 1941 had some fifty chapters in the United States, most of them on the West Coast. Unsympathetic with the Issei desire to see Nisei interpret to other Americans what Issei saw as good in Japanese culture, it considered its function to be that of aiding Nisei to solve those mutual problems which could not be settled by individual effort. Because of their heritage of social and economic problems caused by American hostility toward the Issei, the JACL Nisei hoped through organization not only to protect their own civil rights as American citizens but to alleviate and improve Issei status in America. Essentially they turned their backs upon Japan and tackled the problems of life in America for persons of Japanese descent. The conservative Issei, cynical from their long-time paradox, often viewed the JACL critically and skeptically. They wondered if the Nisei should, or ever would be permitted by Caucasians, to forget that they were Japanese.

While the JACL may have seemed bold and rash to some Issei, there were a few college Nisei about the time of Pearl Harbor who dubbed the JACL as reactionary and criticized them for their frequently close relations with the American Legion, chambers of commerce, D.A.R., and similar groups. JACL leaders often regarded such Nisei (for example, some who joined Young Democrat clubs), in turn, as intellectuals, radicals, and even communists.

The Kibei—Nisei who had received some education in Japan—had their own groups. Those who did join the JACL often organized their own chapters. They felt "different" and were regarded somewhat as outcasts by Nisei whose education had been entirely in the United States. The Kibei were no more homogeneous as a group than the Issei and the American-educated Nisei. Some Kibei saw eye to eye with elderly Issei. Others bitterly condemned their parents for having sent them to Japan which did not want them and because when they returned to America they were handicapped by their poor English, greater emotional maturity, and un-California-like manners. Diverse reasons had led the Issei to send one or more children to Japan—to please the child's grandparents, to take off some of the parents' economic burden until they had established themselves, to be cared for if one parent had died, to learn Japanese language and culture to prepare for exporting and other positions. Whatever the parents' reasons, the returning Kibei often exhibited the psychology of a rejected child who finds it difficult to adjust himself to the parents and siblings who had rejected him earlier. Some Nisei claimed that the Kibei were like bats in the old folk tale of the war between mammals and birds: whichever side was winning would be joined by the bats.

Not all, even of the mature Nisei, Kibei, and Issei, had taken well-defined stands on the issues that faced them regarding the future of both aliens and citizens of Japanese origin. Most persons, and the Japanese in America were no exception, drifted along, vaguely arguing at times over the international and national problems affecting them, but usually living from day to day and settling questions as they arose. By the time of Pearl Harbor, the groups described were fairly well outlined. They were bickering with each other, and when the crisis of the declaration of war came, the splits were to tear the disintegrating community asunder.

Despite the long-strained relations between the United States and Japan, Pearl Harbor was as much of a shock to the West Coast Japanese as to the rest of the United States. They too heard the news with incredulity. They had the additional anxiety, however, of what it would mean to them as individuals with Japanese faces and as members of a group with the same racial origin as the enemy. Over and over, retrospective accounts of this period use the same stock phrases to indicate shock, confusion, and apprehension, "Then, BOOM! Pearl Harbor. We lived in darkness after that."

A high school boy wrote:

My first thought was, what will people think or feel toward us at school tomorrow. All day long, I moped around the house with a face longer than a horse, but the incident that knocked the wind out of me was when the man my father was working for was taken by the FBI because they said he was an enemy alien and very dangerous to the country . . . . The morning after, at school, I am proud to say that everyone treated us like Americans which we are.

The events of the month after Pearl Harbor were a surprise both to Issei and Nisei. Many older people had the same experience as the school children. Their Caucasian acquaintances and friends went out of their way to reassure them that they drew a distinction between them and the enemy in Japan. Most restrictions under which Issei and Nisei lived during December 1941, were self-imposed. They wished to be as inconspicuous as possible, a course of protective action for themselves recommended by some civic authorities who had not grasped the attitude of watchful tolerance most Caucasians were adopting toward the Japanese. Through the months the exceptions mounted; nonetheless, those West Coast people who spat upon the Japanese, made obscene remarks, and kept them off streetcars and buses were exceptions.

The principal restrictions on enemy aliens, which the Issei now were, included the freezing of funds, the closing down of foreign language newspapers, and prohibition on travel beyond a few miles. Many Issei who had been prominent in societies to collect funds to aid Japan in the Sino-Japanese war were picked up by the FBI. This the Japanese communities considered expectable. Nisei, though not subject to any restrictions since they were American citizens, were frequently requested, because of their Japanese appearance, to show birth certificates or other evidences of citizenship.

By February the old pack of anti-Oriental cards had been reshuffled and pressures were multiplied. The American failures in the Pacific war, the infrequent attacks by Filipinos on California Japanese, the FBI raids for contraband, the threat of mass evacuation of aliens from all countries at war, and unfounded rumors that blazed like flash fires had brought the Japanese to a state of panic. All adult men among the fishermen of Terminal Island near Los Angeles were picked up by the FBI on a blanket warrant without warning. There were more and more pick-ups everywhere. No one knew why certain men were picked and others left. Those who were left were regarded suspiciously by the communities as informers. When they in turn were apprehended they felt a sense of relief that at least the onus of being informers on innocent men had been lifted from them. A little girl wrote, "I heard that the FBIs were taking all Japanese fathers to detention camps and I was thinking that they were going to take my father too." An Issei father with a reputation in the community for his anti-fascist convictions was interned for six months. He said:

When I was first taken by the FBI I felt very much ashamed. I thought, "What have I done that this disgraceful thing should happen to me. Bad men will be interned and I will be among them." I felt very sad. But when we got to jail I saw there all the leaders of the Japanese community, men who were respected and whom I knew would not do anything wrong. I felt that I was in good company and did not feel so bad about it anymore.

The people who were left behind suffered from lack of leadership. Rumors of ill treatment by the FBI, which was equated with the dread "thought police" of Japan, spread. There were stories of pretended FBI agents who entered homes to steal money and possessions. Men reviewed their past and racked their brains to figure out what they might ever have done which to a Caucasian would be suspicious or dangerous. Anything connected with Japan and any paper with Japanese writing, even account books, were rumored to be suspected by the intelligence agencies. Families burned their collections of Japanese dolls, books, family photographs, anything and everything that would suggest Japan to a Caucasian. Men who had not yet been picked up had packed suitcases waiting since no one knew who would be next or why.

The community had lost its old and respected leaders. The offices of the Japanese Association had closed after Pearl Harbor. The office of the Japanese Consul was, of course, empty. The people left behind had no one to go to for advice and information. They turned to the JACL which the American authorities were coming to regard their liaison with the Japanese communities. In general, the JACL advocated full cooperation with the American authorities, objected to opposition to any regulations, and, told the people whatever occurred, to endure it as part of their contribution to the American war effort.

In puzzling over the reason for the apprehension of leaders whom the community was certain were not dangerous to the United States, people concluded that there must be informers among themselves who were twisting the truth and lying to get these leaders into jail. The rumor that the FBI paid an informer $25 per head created the additional rumor that informers were turning in people whom they had personal grudges against. Most suspicion centered on the JACL. It was rumored that they were advocating evacuation of the Issei in order to buy out Issei holdings and entrench themselves economically. They were accused of charging exorbitant prices for legal services which an alien could have performed for nothing at the post offices. For lack of knowing why their communities had been so disrupted by the FBI, people turned upon the JACL and used it for a scapegoat. In the meantime, despite the hostile rumors, they depended upon the JACL to represent them and keep them advised of what the authorities wanted them to do.

Community solidarity and organization crumbled. People still had an intense bond with each other since they were still "all Japanese together," but the splits had divided them. The greatest public airing of them came at a Tolan Committee hearing when one of the "Young Democrats" sent a letter to the Committee attacking the JACL and discrediting it. The unhappy Issei shook their heads. The Nisei had been demanding to be boss for a long time; they had their chance, and they were making a mess of it. Both Nisei and Issei, as well as separate factions among them, still retained enough of the old "all Japanese together" feeling to fear that hotheads among them might do something wild and rash which would plunge the entire group into danger.

As February turned into March, the communities began to fear that

even the American citizenship of the Nisei, which had been so highly regarded both by their parents and themselves, would not protect them and
that they too would be evacuated. Uprooted people from the prohibited
zones were creating a leaven of despair. No one knew which area would
be named next. Regulations changed from one day to another. Authorities denied that there would be mass evacuation; the newspapers said that
there would be. Then, early in March, the Western Defense Command
announced that all persons of Japanese descent, regardless of citizenship,
were being encouraged to leave voluntarily the western half of the Coastal
States. People got ready to move. Many households now consisted of only
a non-English-speaking Issei mother and her immature children. Upon
them fell the burden of packing and selling possessions and taking care
of property. The Issei father in jail or already in a detention camp was
unable to assist them.

As Japanese began to move into the eastern half of the Coastal States
and over the Rockies, protests began to rise from these areas against
being "dumping grounds." Even some of the Japanese communities
east of the Rockies protested. They did not want any "Japanese
Okies" from California disrupting their life and endangering their
situation. So great was the protest that voluntary evacuation was
ordered stopped until plans could be made for mass evacuation of the
remaining Japanese into reception centers and later into more permanent
camps.

March was a nightmare period for people of Japanese descent. Some
Nisei in the American Army were being discharged, and local boards
were deferring others; their American citizenship had not protected their
civil rights. They were being removed only because of suspicion, but the
very fact of their being removed at all was beginning to make the larger
American community feel that there must be cause for suspicion. Issei
saw the business and security of a lifetime vanish. However, it was the
little things, the small day-to-day incidents that hurt far more than the
mass rejection by America of a people who had helped pioneer the West.
One of the evacuees wrote:

I think some of us were a little relieved to be away from the minor
irritations, the insults, slander, and the small humiliations unthinking
people heaped upon us after Pearl Harbor. Many people may say, "Well,
that's to be expected," but to be unable to go out in the streets, or just to
the corner store, without the fear of being insulted, and being all tense
inside with that same fear, was one of the most humiliating things . . . .
What could we do? Nothing. Just endure in silence. Those are the things
that are locked in the hearts of many of us. Not big things, but many
small things. We became "sullen and morose" but can we help it? We
were not sullen and morose, just leery of any kind advance.

Another wrote later:

You can't tell me anything about military necessity in connection with evacuation . . . . One man down in Imperial Valley broadcast how much of a menace and danger the Japanese were. His brother was running up and down the Valley buying up Japanese land cheaply. In northern California they let the Japanese put in all their crops. Then about 3 days before harvest, when the Japanese had put in all the work and money, they discovered a "military necessity" and evacuated them. Others got the benefit of their investment and efforts.

A woman said:

Everybody took advantage of us. Some people took things when we were not watching. While we were packing inside the house, these people would go around the back and take everything they saw . . . . It was difficult to keep our tempers. For seventeen years, Dad and Mother had struggled to build up their business. Every profit they made was put into the store for remodeling and improving it little by little. At the same time they were raising four little kids. When they finally reached the peak of their business success and had nothing to worry about, when they finally succeeded in raising four children and sending them through high school and even had one attending college—BOOM came evacuation and our prosperity crumbled to pieces . . . . The precious 48 hours notice we had in which to pack passed like a nightmare.

Rumors spread that even the citizenship of the Nisei was to be taken from them. Some did not see what difference it made. It seemed unnecessary irony.

The buses gathered in town after town on scheduled dates—or later —and the Japanese departed. Other townspeople saw them go, some of them for the first time realizing what was happening as they saw hundreds of their friends, customers, and employees of many years with their bundles and suitcases, which was all they could take, getting on trains and buses to leave. Some evacuees remarked the kindnesses of strangers who brought them cups of water when the buses came to a temporary halt, and harked back to the day in Terminal Island when the bus driver dropped his cap and slowly picked it up to give the women and children a chance to say goodbye to the men who were being taken away to internment camps. Rumors were floating about of the bad conditions at Manzanar, one of the reception centers. Some people said the United States was gathering all Japanese into a few places; then when the Pacific war got worse they would bomb them in retaliation.

A puzzled young Nisei asked:

What had I, or, as a matter of fact, what had the rest of us done, to be thrown in camp, away from familiar surroundings, and familiar faces? What had there been in my life that made such a thing happen? The only answer is, the accident of my birth—my ancestry. There is no other logical answer.

He wondered how he ever came to be going to a camp full of Japanese, aliens and citizens alike, with nothing much in common between them and himself except the color of their skins.

Three generations of a farm family dejectedly await bus transportation on first phase of evacuation journey.

An Issei farm couple and their Nisei children equipped with identification tags reflect despair and a sense of adventure.

The federal, state, and local authorities who had evacuated them answered, and their answer was repeated to the Nisei and the Issei by the JACL:

You are not being accused of any crime. You are being removed only to protect you and because there might be one of you who might be dangerous to the United States. It is your contribution to the war effort. You should be glad to make the sacrifice to prove your loyalty.

It is notable that sworn statements from Honolulu police and FBI officials declared that all rumors of resident Japanese in the Hawaiian Islands assisting the enemy on December 7 or hindering the American forces were false. The resident Japanese, on the contrary, had cooperated with American officials in every way. The attorney general of California had said there had been no sabotage of any kind in that state since the war. There were no charges against the West Coast Japanese, therefore, of disloyalty, espionage, or sabotage. Only suspicion, fear, and uncertainty motivated their removal by the authorities.

Thus ended one chapter in the history of the Japanese in America. The next opened in the dust of Manzanar, the smell of the horse stables of Santa Anita, the quiet of the Merced Fair Grounds, and other race tracks and fairgrounds of the West Coast, where the people went to wait until the relocation centers were built.

1.

MOVING IN

By late May, 1942, all but a few thousand of the 110,000 persons of Japanese ancestry on the West Coast were confined in the Army's assembly centers. The places of confinement consisted of sixteen converted fairgrounds, race tracks and athletic stadiums, thirteen of them in California, the others in Oregon, Washington, and Arizona. In them the 30,000 families were living under crowded conditions, close surveillance, and with no knowledge of what would happen to them next. There were rumors that they would be released to seek a living somewhere to the East. There were more rumors of camps being built in remote parts of the interior, perhaps agricultural communities where they could live peacefully until the war was over. Other rumors spoke of hot and terrible places where men who protested about food or other conditions in the assembly centers were to be sent. There was despair, hope, apathy, and intense speculation, but no one knew what was in store.

Then in June, with gathering momentum, the next phase of the forced migration got under way. At the former migratory labor camp doing duty near Sacramento as an assembly center, trains were loaded with men, women, children and babies and moved northward to unload their cargo near the little town of Tulelake, California. Here the rough barracks of one of the first relocation centers which was christened Tule Lake were still under construction. Farmers from the rich Salinas Valley were transported to the Arizona desert. San Francisco businessmen were sent from the Tanforan race track to the bare, intermountain valleys of central Utah. From the fertile Central Valley of California to the sandy flat lands of eastern Colorado, from southern California to the plains of Wyoming, from the moist coastland of the Northwest to the sagebrush plains of southern Idaho, from the San Joaquin Valley to the woodlands of Arkansas the trains moved during the spring, summer, and early fall.

For the involuntary travelers, the break with the accustomed and the usual was now complete. In the assembly centers, behind fences and under guard by military police, the evacuees had suddenly found themselves, although looking out at familiar hills and highways, in a strange, new world of social relationships. They were outcast, but still in their own country. Now the new world of human relations was matched by an equally strange physical world. It was clear, as the trains moved over the wasteland of the mountain states, that they were to be exiled in desert and wilderness.

Compared with the rapidity of movement from homes to assembly centers, the second phase of the forced migration was a long-drawn-out process. Beginning in May, it was not completed until November. To those still in the assembly centers letters came back from the new places, stories of heat and dust, of fears about inadequate food and medical care, but also some mention of new freedoms and new possibilities for the

Military police keep watch from tower at Santa Anita race track near Los Angeles which was converted hastily into an assembly center in April, 1942.

Baggage being inspected for contraband before evacuees could take possession at Stockton, Calif., Assembly Center May, 1942.

future. Three of the relocation centers were filled by the end of July. The Manzanar center in California merely passed on June 1 from Army to WRA management without transfer of people. Opening in early May, Poston in Arizona received several thousand persons directly from their homes with no interval of residence in assembly centers. Tule Lake center in northern California and Gila in southern Arizona received their train-loads from the assembly centers in June and July. Another trio of centers —Minidoka in Idaho, Heart Mountain in Wyoming, and Granada in Colorado—began to be filled up in August. The last three—Topaz in central Utah and the two Arkansas centers, Jerome and Rohwer—were not occupied until September, October, and November.

The length of time that people spent in the assembly centers had important influences on their adjustment in the relocation centers. In general the longer the stay in the assembly centers, the more the relocation centers seemed at first like something of a release. There was a little more freedom of movement within the new places and a little less obvious restriction in the form of fences and guarding soldiers. Moreover those who spent two to five months in assembly centers learned much about living with one another. They had made many basic adjustments by the time they arrived in the relocation centers. Some of the friction between younger and older people and among long-standing factions in the former communities had been fought out. The adjustment in the new camps, therefore, went a little more smoothly.

What took place in the relocation centers was also related to the stage of development of WRA policy at the time people arrived. The early occupied centers—Manzanar, Poston, Tule Lake and Gila—began their efforts at community living before the framework of WRA policies had fully crystallized. Employment and resettlement plans, both of major significance for the adjustment of evacuees to their new life, as well as less vital policies were by no means defined through May, June, and July. This made for greater uncertainty, both among staff and evacuees, in the

Evacuees identifying baggage at relocation center, Poston, Ariz., May, 1942.

early centers. In the later centers, on the other hand, the people had at the start more definite understanding of the limitations and possibilities of center life. There were fewer unfulfilled expectations and false starts.

IMPACT OF THE RELOCATION CENTERS

The new physical mold into which people had to fit was a rigid one. The relocation centers were built by Army engineers according to standard plans for housing a young, unmarried, male population. They were Army camps of a type called "theatre of operations," that is, temporary constructions designed for only a few years' use. They consisted of tar-paper covered, wooden barracks 100 feet long, grouped into what were called blocks. Each block was composed of two rows of six or seven barracks each, between which were a mess hall, a laundry room, latrine and lavatory buildings, and another barracks to be used as a recreation hall. Heart Mountain was a variant in that two such units composed a block of 24 barracks. The families were to sleep in the barracks, eat,

After claiming their baggage, evacuees were assigned to barracks such as these at Rivers, Ariz., June, 1942. Small buildings in the center housed laundry, latrine, lavatories. One barracks in each block usually was used as a recreation hall, another adapted for a mess hall.

wash clothes and bodies, go to the toilet, and play in the communal buildings in the center of the block.

At the start each block framed the life of 250 to 300 people. The usual center consisted of about thirty such molds into which the people were poured, busload by busload, as they came from the railroad stations to the centers. Lined out with precision, the blocks stretched in rows and cross rows, with dust and the debris of construction in the spaces between. At the edge of the outer blocks the view was of desert hills, sagebrush plains, or, in the Arkansas centers, of dark woodland. Emphasizing the newness and the isolation, roads from the railheads into the camps were still under construction when the evacuees arrived.

At one edge of the blocks, often separated from them by a broad firebreak, were a few more barracks or somewhat more solidly built houses where the WRA staff lived and where the offices of the agency were being established. Here, too, there was usually a common mess hall and laundry room. Some distance away, but in sight of the blocks, was another miniature Army camp housing the military police whose job it was to patrol the boundaries of the camp and supervise arrivals and departures.

None of the centers was finished when the first trainloads of evacuees began to arrive. Construction crews were still nailing on roofs, building more barracks, finishing up the water installations, or doing other jobs in the basic construction. At Minidoka the workmen kept just one block ahead of the incoming evacuees. At Gila, Heart Mountain, and Granada some evacuees slept in laundry rooms or recreation halls on the first nights after arrival, because of insufficient barracks space. Not even the latest occupied of the centers were thoroughly ready for their first arrivals.

There were a number of reasons for the unfinished condition of the camps—reasons which reflected the nature of the framework in which evacuees were to live and WRA staff were to work. In the first place, the whole movement was planned with the utmost haste. When the evacuation order was given, Army officials had not foreseen the need for relocation centers for all evacuees. It was only after opposition appeared to unpoliced movement of evacuees into the states east of California that the idea of relocation centers for everyone crystallized. Sites were selected, and work started on the first center only in early April, a few weeks before the last assembly centers were filled.

At once the problem arose of finding sufficient labor and materials for construction in a country that was gearing itself rapidly for wartime production. The scarcity of lumber, pipe, stoves, wallboard and many other essentials was from the first an obstacle and continued to be for months after evacuees had been moved into the centers. An important

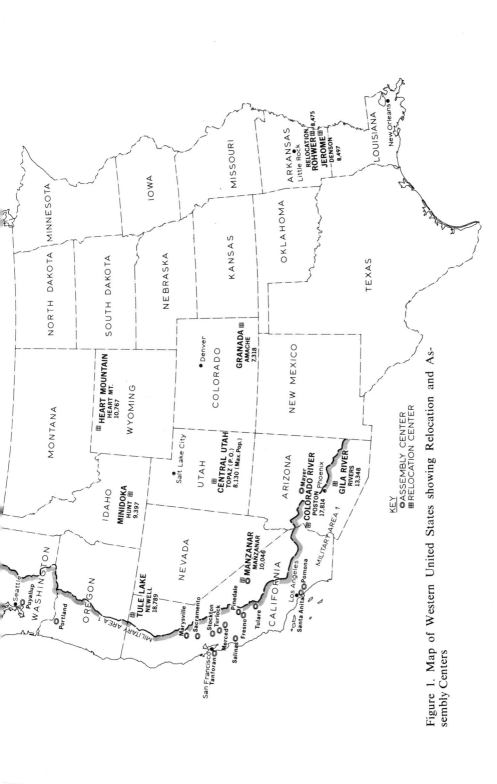

Figure 1. Map of Western United States showing Relocation and Assembly Centers

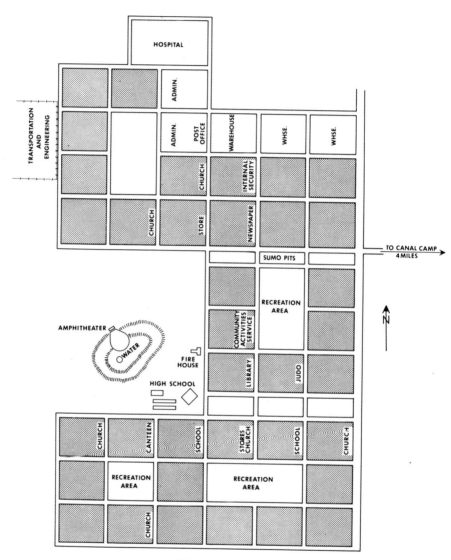

Figure 2. Plan of Relocation Center

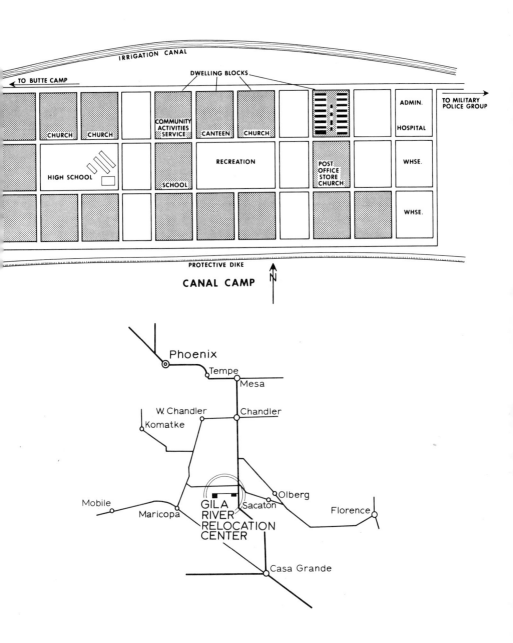

TO BUTTE CAMP ←

IRRIGATION CANAL

DWELLING BLOCKS

TO MILITARY POLICE GROUP →

CHURCH CHURCH

COMMUNITY ACTIVITIES SERVICE CANTEEN CHURCH

ADMIN.

HOSPITAL

HIGH SCHOOL

RECREATION

SCHOOL

POST OFFICE STORE CHURCH

WHSE.

WHSE.

PROTECTIVE DIKE

CANAL CAMP N

Phoenix

Tempe

Mesa

W. Chandler

Chandler

Komatke

Olberg

Mobile

GILA RIVER RELOCATION CENTER

Sacaton

Florence

Maricopa

Casa Grande

Rivers, Arizona

69

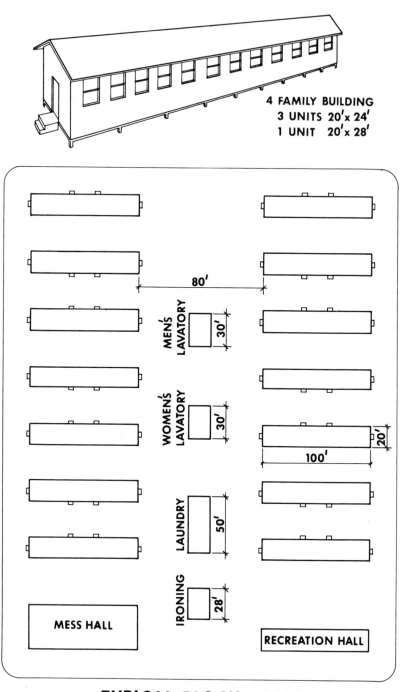

4 FAMILY BUILDING
3 UNITS 20' x 24'
1 UNIT 20' x 28'

MEN'S LAVATORY 30'

WOMEN'S LAVATORY 30'

LAUNDRY 50'

IRONING 28'

80'

100'

20'

MESS HALL

RECREATION HALL

TYPICAL BLOCK PLAN

factor was that the Army assumed responsibility only for getting evacuees into and out of assembly centers, while the civilian agency of the WRA had responsibility for receiving and caring for evacuees the moment the Army relinquished supervision. The plans of the two agencies were not always well coordinated.

Thus the evacuees were unloaded in the centers on the littered, bare ground of construction jobs yet in progress. Everywhere still fresh in the dust were the marks of the bulldozers, for the construction crews had cleared from the sites all brush, trees, and whatever greenery there had been. Only in the Arkansas centers were a few trees left in corners of the camps. The earliest impression of almost everyone who came to the

Curious, defiant, casual, and bitter evacuees gather behind a tense, uncertain military guard to watch arrival of more evacuees as Manzanar Center opens in April, 1942.

centers was of drabness and dust. The assistant project director at Minidoka described the opening of that center:

It was hot, dusty, desolate. Flat land, nothing growing but sagebrush, not a tree in sight . . . . Bulldozers were still filling in ditches
while registration went on; the air was choked with dust; so were the
people. The evacuees had gotten off a train pulled by a coal-burning loco-
motive, and were black with soot . . . . Next day the girls on the [ad-
vance] crew showed up, their hair grey from dust, but otherwise clean
and fresh; crisp, ironed blouses that were spotless . . . . [We] have never
understood how they managed.

A month after Poston opened a young evacuee wrote:

Our mouths are always gritty, and the rooms including the mess
halls cannot be kept clean even by closing all the doors and windows
because there are so many cracks in the walls and floors. From about
1:30 p.m. daily, the wind rises, and often we can't see half mile ahead
due to the dust cloud. Each step we take we stir up dust. Dust settles
on the typewriter and is noticeable even while writing a letter.

The reports officer described the early days of another center:

There was a dust storm nearly every day for the first two months
. . . fine, choking dust . . . swirled over the center. Traffic was
sometimes forced to a standstill because there was no visibility. Sometimes, standing in one barracks, another barracks 40 feet away
couldn't be seen. People devised masks and filters of various kinds
and plugged their ears and noses with cotton. The various devices made
people look weird in the blowing dust.

Staff and evacuees alike began their life in the new places with a sense
of desolation in the midst of isolation, but this was momentary as the
urgency of jobs to do gripped almost everyone.

In every center the unfinished condition of barracks and blocks was an
immediate stimulus to individuals to provide the basic comforts that were
lacking. There was a concentration for the first five or six weeks on this
sort of activity. The dominant mood was one of busy concern with straigh-
tening out the details of living. As families and individuals completed
the process of being unloaded with their baggage from the buses, registering, and signing the forms of induction they ultimately found themselves
in bare rooms about twenty feet square or in unpartitioned barracks.
There was nothing in the rooms but army cots and blankets, no other
furniture, no running water, nothing with which to prepare food or the
baby's bottle. Everything remained yet to do to make the places habitable.
Makeshift furniture had to be built if one could find the lumber. The
ground around one's barracks had to be cleaned up. The administration
was requesting workers for innumerable jobs. Generally there was little
time for talk or to get acquainted with one's neighbors; people were too
busy, too intent on fixing up their own rooms or on making some of the

urgent block improvements such as clearing away the debris of construction.

There was nevertheless another note in these first days of center life. It was a note of dejection and apathy present in many of the young men and women from the moment they stepped off the trains. As one young married man said:

We haven't fixed up our house any. You don't feel like it . . . . Some of the people have done very good jobs fixing up their places, the ones that have the carpenter knack, you know. They enjoy that sort of thing and the old people who don't have anything else to do. But I don't know much about that sort of thing. There isn't much incentive to impress anybody. Everybody's got about the same sort of place to live in.

Salvaging lumber from scrap pile to make furniture for barracks rooms, Heart Mountain, Wyo., Sept., 1942.

All we've done is just to figure that we needed something more handy for keeping clothes in, so we ordered one of those little chests of drawers from Sears, Roebuck . . . . We got tired of reaching into suitcases.

For him and many others like him—younger people who had been stopped in midcareer—the centers loomed only as a blank interlude in what had been up to then a purposeful life. For them there was no sort of incentive in any aspect of the relocation center. They fell immediately into a sort of waiting state, immobilized by lack of purpose and unresponsive both to the bright plans of the administrators for community development and to the more modest plans which older evacuees were beginning to work out for growing vegetables and beautifying the blocks.

For others who were at first stimulated to work a little for themselves in fixing up their rooms there was frustration—a new sort of frustration connected with living under Government supervision:

The administration told us to mop at least once daily and to keep everything off the floor at least six inches off the floor. Now, how were we to keep our belongings six inches off the floor if we had no lumber with which to build stands? Every time we mopped we had to put our belongings on top of the beds. We were told not to take lumber scraps or otherwise we would get into trouble. The administration promised us furniture at that time. I couldn't believe this promise so I gathered scraps of lumber from here and there and tried my best to build some crude furniture for the home.

This was a type of experience which was to encourage the growth of negative attitudes during the next few months.

There were also young men for whom the arrival in the unfinished desolation of the relocation centers was a last straw. The pent-up emotions of the uncertain period before evacuation and the restricted life of the assembly centers found vent immediately on arrival in the relocation center.

Last Tuesday we were suddenly ordered to this center from the Mayer Assembly Center . . . . Government showed poor judgment in sending clean-loving Japanese to this dump. The whole affair reveals lack of careful planning, lack of foresight, and utter ignorance of Japanese psychology. Authority are asking for cooperation and suggestion, I understand, but such will not be forthcoming . . . . I can see no evidence of the much vaunted American sense of fair play, sportsmanship, et cetera. The Niseis are sore because no distinction has been made between them and the Isseis, and grumble that citizenship doesn't mean a damn thing. The Isseis are laughing at the dumbness of the Americans in treating us this way. The whole mess is rotten, as far as we know.

This sort of bitterness was most characteristic of the younger men, college students or men just beginning their careers. Their feeling of rejection by the rest of the United States, provoked by evacuation, was deepened by the remoteness of the centers and the abundant evidences of hasty and inadequate preparation. Their bitterness was to increase and find channels for expression later on. Initially there were too many new and confusing experiences to assimilate and consequently too little clear grasp of the import of the centers for wide crystallization of such attitudes.

The full impact of the centers on the different segments of the evacuee group was not to appear for another month or two. People were too preoccupied with securing the elementary comforts and getting used to new climate, new diet, and new neighbors. It was not until these basic adjustments were well begun that people could start to measure the limitations and possibilities of the new way of life framed by the centers.

THE ADMINISTRATIVE SHELL

The physical framework within which life would be lived was quickly apparent. The blocks with their barracks and common buildings pointed to an inescapable patterning. Waiting in turn to brush one's teeth in the lavatory the morning after arrival, it was clear that neighbors would be more than neighbors. They would be encountered many times a day in all the most intimate operations of living. In one's room there was little escape; already the voices of the children through the wall on one side and the cough of the man through the wall on the other were becoming familiar. The view of wasteland or forest at the edge of the blocks gave a vivid feeling of the ultimate limits of the new world. There would be no coming and going. The life of the blocks would be the whole of life.

In contrast the social framework was not so obvious. It was clear enough to the newly arrived evacuees that they would be extremely dependent on other persons for everything they needed. One did not choose what he might eat at breakfast, but ate what someone else had ordered and the evacuee mess crew placed on the board table. One did not select a doctor, but went to the hospital and waited for whatever service was available. This dependence on people whom one had never seen before was definite enough from the first. It was clear that food, shelter, and medical attention depended on a group of Government employees who were to be found at the edge of the center in the administration buildings, but what kind of people they were and how they would use their authority remained to be seen. During the first weeks, the nature of these men and women was discovered by only a small minority of the evacuees, only those who went up to the offices seeking jobs and those whom the administrators sought out to take jobs. For the great majority there was little contact.

During the early weeks the WRA staff in the centers had more of a sense of unity of purpose and satisfactory relations with evacuees than at any time thereafter. This was true no less in the early centers than in the later ones. There was a spirit of pitching in together to do the innumerable jobs that obviously could not wait. Almost every evacuee was anxious to do whatever he could to make himself as comfortable as possible and, usually, to help others to do the same. There was unity of purpose in getting the mess halls into shape for serving food, in establishing the hospitals on a working basis, in cleaning up the blocks, in making the continuing flow of newcomers as comfortable as possible in their barracks. There was so much to do and everything was so urgent that a spirit of cooperation grew up promptly and continued for several weeks.

In meeting the recurring emergencies, the WRA staff were working chiefly with a very special group of evacuees in each center—the "volunteers." Young men and women came directly from their homes to the early centers, volunteering to help make them ready for the later trainloads. Advance crews volunteered from the assembly centers to the later centers to prepare them for the mass movements to come. They were generally young and vigorous with the determination to make the best of the situation and to do whatever needed doing. Their smiling acceptance of conditions, their industry and anxiety to help impressed the WRA staff. Working closely with them, the staff found their relations with evacuees smooth and pleasant.

Relying heavily on volunteers and those of the others who were aggressive enough to come up and ask for jobs, the WRA staff plunged into the task of building up an organization that would function. Particularly in the early centers organization grew out of the first contacts between staff members and volunteers. There was, for example, immediate need for some competent person who could understand English to carry out the distribution of food to the mess halls. There was no time to go over all possible candidates who might have had some experience of similar work before evacuation. Hundreds of people had to be fed promptly. An energetic young volunteer offered to do the job, or perhaps suggested a friend of his who he knew was "a good man," and he was immediately given the responsibility and began to work closely with the chief steward and the latter's assistants. He recommended others with whom he knew he could work well. They recommended others. In surprisingly short time, there were truck drivers, clerks to check the food into the warehouses and out to the mess halls, and people were getting the food.

There was only a small staff of WRA employees, less than a hundred at the beginning of each center, to handle everything for 5,000 to 10,000 evacuees. Hence there had to be swift recruitment from among the evacuees if the necessary services were to be carried on. Administrators chatted with individuals as they passed from the buses or trucks through the induction lines, learned that this one or that had needed skills, liked their looks, or consulted with a volunteer or some other evacuee with whom they were already acquainted, and so selected men and women to take over the urgent jobs. During the first week or two every administrator, by design or accident, gathered a number of volunteers or other evacuees around him who served as advisers in the selection of personnel. All came with suggestions, some inspired confidence in the administrator, and he took their advice. Through this process organization emerged in vital areas in the new community life.

Not only in supplying food and getting the mess halls running, but in manning the hospitals, in setting up a skeleton force of police to insure law and order, in securing typists and clerks for the indispensable paper work of the Government agency, men and women were selected and put to work immediately.

Out in the blocks away from the administration offices, it was quickly apparent that a special sort of service was needed. The newly created social units of the blocks were now full of people who were looking to someone to provide them with what they lacked or at least to answer their questions about what would and would not be provided. Brooms to sweep their dusty rooms, mops to clean up the mess halls, another blanket, soap to wash with—dozens of questions and requests were coming up every hour. Evidently someone was needed in every block to distribute and keep track of the mops, buckets, brooms, and soap—all Government property—and above all to answer the endless questions of the suddenly dependent people. The office of block manager was created and the administrators went about selecting evacuees for the jobs. Block by block, as each filled up, a person was chosen. The administrators asked their evacuee advisers about candidates, rejected or accepted some on their recommendation, or perhaps went ahead on their own judgment and chose men who seemed capable on the basis of a brief chat. Sometimes the people of a newly occupied block were asked to choose their own man. Sometimes a supervisor of block managers was appointed at the start from among the volunteers or other early comers and his judgments predominated throughout in the selection of other block managers.

By the end of the first month, in every center the framework of administration was formed. Essential services were proceeding and the life in the blocks was linked to the administrative offices—the source of all supply—through the network of block managers. Order had been achieved out of the chaotic swirl of human beings moving from train to bus to barracks. Truckloads of food were moving regularly through the dust from railheads to mess halls, doctors in clean white uniforms were making rounds through the hospital wards, typewriters were pounding in the still partially furnished offices. There were no serious breakdowns in any centers. It was an impressive piece of improvisation that quickly became organization.

Not only the basic immediate needs of the people were being met, but already the organization was being extended to take care of the longer range needs. Each center had its blueprint, for the earlier centers less clear and complete than for the later, but for all complete enough to exist as charts on the walls of the administration offices. There was provision for organizing almost every activity of a normal community as a part of the hierarchy of the Government agency.

There were plans at first in all the early centers for considerable agricultural production, fresh vegetables for the evacuees and possibily some contribution to the food supply of the nation as a whole. Small industries were planned. Divisions of agriculture and industry were set up in the early projects and long-range plans began to be worked out for subjugating land and bringing the centers as far as possible toward self-sufficiency. By August, Poston had an evacuee staff working intensively on plans for agricultural production. Stores where people could buy toilet articles, magazines, and the other little necessities that came through no regular branch of the agency were set up promptly in all centers. Store managers, buyers, and sometimes boards of trustees for these community enterprises, as they were called, were functioning within a few weeks after center opening. Through the summer teachers were recruited for the schools and the school buildings began to be built. Full-fledged school systems were organized at each center in the space of a few months. Recreation programs were planned, and quickly after each center opened men and women were found who could organize and instruct in baseball, dramatics, and many other activities. Within a few weeks the plans in regard to these broader needs were translated into at least a beginning of organization. A few men and women from among the evacuees had been selected to get them functioning and were hard at work building the elements of a community life. Each center was more than just a going concern; it was, through the hard-working staff and the evacuees they had so quickly brought into their plans, aspiring to an organized and rich community existence.

At the end of the first month or two after center opening, the staff were generally enthusiastic and hopeful of the future. Their success in meeting the first difficult problems and the response of the volunteers and others in making the unpromising camps habitable tended to create in the staff an attitude of hopefulness and expectation of better things to come. It was not merely an official attitude cultivated for the purpose of maintaining morale. It was something personally felt by a majority of

Land cleared of sage brush the previous fall and furrowed for early spring planting, Heart Mountain, Wyo., 1944.

Issei women harvesting daikon, a Japanese radish indispensable for pickles and used in various dishes common in the Japanese-Americans' diet, Gila River, Ariz., Nov., 1942.

Playgrounds for children were established as soon as possible in the bleak
new environment, Heart Mountain, Wyo., Nov., 1943.

staff members in the early weeks. A large number, especially among the top staff at each center, had come to their jobs imbued with a high purpose, sympathetic with the problems of the uprooted evacuees, and sincerely hopeful of building something meaningful out of the chaos into which they had been thrown.

In July at Poston the top staff were trying to orient themselves. In brief daily conferences in the rush of heavy duties, they were expressing to one another their views on the possibilities of the peculiar community that was growing up before them. One staff member wrote down his ideas in an effort to crystallize what he and the others were thinking:

> . . . the success of the Colorado River Relocation Project is dependent on [among other things the evacuees'] willingness, not only to cooperate, but to erect and activate a governmental, and a cultural structure of realistic democracy, of their own design within the community; sufficient not only to the present, but geared to the future as well . . . [and] the sympathetic, but necessarily realistic approach of the administrative personnel to the problem as a whole, as well as in individual contacts with the group . . . .
>
> . . . there is an opportunity to share in the accomplishment of a modern miracle . . . the eventual return of every member of the relocated group to their normal place as members of the American Community not only as loyal citizens or resident aliens, but as better citizens, more *realistically* democratic in principle, in thought, and in effect: tempered, perhaps even more keenly than the rest of us, to carry forward the living principles of democracy which all of us, in our fashion, are fighting for now, and for whose future all of us must share the responsibility.

This statement represents perhaps an extreme expression of the idealism that was current among the staff in the centers after the first flush of accomplishment in setting up the communities. The spirit was by no means uncommon, however. Every center had at least a small group among the staff who were looking at the still nebulous communities in this manner. It was a period when plans and hopes and some degree of this sort of idealism dominated staff attitudes.

At the same time, however, weaknesses were beginning to be apparent in the structure which they had already reared. Staff members began to hear complaints from the community about the rudeness of evacuees now employed in the offices and whom the staff regarded as very polite and respectful. There were complaints about block managers who were said to be ordering people around, complaints about evacuees in important positions who it was said were incompetent and yet whom the staff regarded as industrious and conscientious workers. These complaints multiplied after the first month or two and reached such volume, especially in the early centers, that there was no ignoring them. There were charges not only of rudeness or incompetence of dictatorial ways, but also much more serious charges. The staff began to hear stories of the dishonesty of evacuees they had placed in responsible jobs in the center organization. A manager of the community enterprises was said to have been known before evacuation for sharp practice and shady dealings. Another man known to the staff as a hard worker, cooperative and energetic, was said to have preyed on other Japanese in various ways in the trying period just following the attack on Pearl Harbor. The charges were not sufficiently clear cut to prove or disprove, but they circulated widely in the camps. Along with such charges usually went others, the full meaning of which did not become clear for several months. The labels "administration stooge" and "informer" began to be heard, words at first hardly intelligible to the staff. It was clear, however, that they embodied an extreme and widespread distrust toward many of the men and women who had been given places of responsibility in the center organization.

What had happened was that the administrative framework had grown like a shell over and above the mass of people. They had no sense of having built and sponsored it despite the fact that it was composed for the most part of evacuees. The evacuees who were part of it were the volunteers and usually the younger, more aggressive persons who were thoroughly at home in the English language, actually persons who were on the very fringe of the life in the former Japanese-American communities. As people got more settled and after the first weeks began to feel the administrative shell impinging on them in the form of a block manager or a supervisor of a work crew, they began to ask questions about how these persons had gotten the jobs they had. Here was a young man who as block manager seemed to antagonize all the older people in his block by giving orders and assuming an authority which they did not feel he had. Here was a young woman whose Japanese was wholly inadequate trying to advise people concerning changes in housing which they might or might not make. There was a young man set up as manager of the newly created stores who acquaintances knew had only a very limited business experience, while experienced older businessmen were acting as janitors in the mess halls. There was a young man who had earned a bad reputation in the county of his former residence who obviously had the ear of a top administrator and was presuming to advise about everyone's needs. People were beginning to say that it was bad enough to have WRA staff, who were not yet fully aware of what the people had gone through and what their problems were, in the ultimate positions of authority (that could not be helped), but why should the next level in the hierarchy consist of these young, untried, and sometimes downright distrusted persons from among their own number?

Not all those in what had come to be called the "key positions" were the targets of such disapproval and distrust. Many were thoroughly respected and their relations with other evacuees were good from the start. Particularly in the later centers the greater number of the first selections met with the approval of the community as a whole. Thus for example at Minidoka the staff held meetings with evacuee groups within a few days after arrival from the assembly center and were influenced by the discussion that was encouraged. They became aware of difficulties which had upset the people in the assembly center and accepted advice in their selections that originated not from among miscellaneous acquaintances of a few days but from groups and committees of both older and younger men who had gone through the experience of trying to work and live together for three or four months in the assembly center. In contrast, it was at Manzanar, Poston, and Tule Lake that an administrative shell was formed at first which consisted chiefly of WRA staff as yet with little knowledge of the people they were to administer and evacuees not only with similar lack of understanding but often also with definitely antagonistic attitudes to the evacuees as a whole.

The growth of antagonism from within the community to the rapidly constructed administrative shell was a source of conflict of far-reaching importance in the early centers. There were similar antagonisms in the later centers, but never quite so much feeling of distance and lack of participation on the part of so many evacuees.

EVACUEE AND CAUCASIAN

Tied up with the antagonistic reaction to the rapidly forming administrative structure was a sharp sense of a new status. As the uprooted people came into the centers they suddenly found themselves in communities organized on the basis of two distinct classes of persons—on the one hand "evacuees" and on the other "appointed personnel." Despite individual efforts of WRA staff to act as if distinctions did not exist, the basic fact was inescapable. At point after point the earliest experiences in the centers drove it home. Later, even though distinctions often became sharper, they also became customary and were accepted as a part of the scheme of things.

In the early centers, occupied by people with little or no assembly center experience, the consciousness of the new status was acute. Everyone old enough to understand felt it, the volunteers no less than the others. The first 11 volunteers to arrive in Poston were escorted after supper to the block farthest from the administration buildings. As they made ready to sleep on their cots, they saw military policemen preparing to stand guard over them through the night. The soldiers were friendly enough, but they had guns and none of the new arrivals could forget the fact. A few hours before, the young men and women had regarded themselves as loyal citizens of the country anxious to help out in an emergency. Now suddenly after pleasant chats with the WRA staff they found themselves unmistakably set off from those people and under guard. The close guarding was quickly eliminated and, at Poston as at other centers, the military police confined their sentry duty to the outside borders of the center, but other signs of the new status were just as vivid.

For those whose first confinement had been in the assembly centers, there was a feeling of some release; the military police were far less in evidence, the confinement was not so close, and fences surrounding the centers had not yet been built. There was consequently some feeling of relative freedom. Nevertheless the sense of restriction involved in being an evacuee quickly closed in on them. For fences and armed guards constituted only the more obvious forms of restriction. Every activity of daily life seemed at first to have some reminder of the new status and consequently of the old freedom that had been lost.

As evacuees looked at their barracks rooms they began to compare them with the homes of the WRA staff. At Manzanar and Tule Lake and other centers many of the staff lived comfortably in nearby towns and came and went daily to the centers. Those who lived in the centers occupied barracks little better in appearance than the evacuees, but they were supplied with furniture. At Poston top staff members had well-built little family houses also supplied with Government furniture. In the four centers within the Western Defense Command area, whatever evacuees ordered from Sears, Roebuck or elsewhere had to be opened for inspection in the presence of military police. No evacuee could have a camera, and hence the new babies, the children, and the brides could not be photographed. Although WRA staff came and went freely, no evacuee could at first leave the early centers, except for emergency family or business reasons and then only in the company of someone who was not of Japanese ancestry. There was no fence around Poston until November and there was some little freedom to take walks into the surrounding desert or river botton land. On the other hand at Manzanar which was originally an assembly center there were fences and watchtowers for guards from the first. It was, however, equally common for the young men of Poston as for those of Manzanar to speak of the centers as jails and prisons. The feeling of being prisoners permeated the centers from the first.

It was not only the restrictions, little and big, that defined the new status. Being an evacuee involved being in a subordinate position, a fact which became apparent as soon as one went to work in the center. At first there was uncertainty as to what the wages would be, but by June it was clear that so long as one was an evacuee he could get no more than $19 a month, whether he was a doctor in the hospital or a laborer on the farm. At the same time it was clear that white-skinned doctors and laborers at whose sides evacuees worked were getting regular wages for what they did. Moreover, in every job an evacuee found himself supervised ultimately by someone not an evacuee. Only the lowest level of supervisory jobs could be occupied by anyone of Japanese ancestry, regardless of competency or experience. The subordinate position of all evacuees in relation to the WRA staff was an inescapable fact of center organization and one which irked most intensely the evacuees who had professional training, long experience, or former positions of authority. The sense of subordinate status was aggravated at every point at which

Evacuee family spends a quiet evening in their 20' × 24' "apartment" with homemade furniture, shelves, and other conveniences at Tule Lake, Calif., Sept., 1942.

there was incompetence, lack of experience, or prejudice among the hastily recruited WRA staff.

The subordination and restriction of the evacuees inherent in the WRA organization not only antagonized evacuees, it also constituted a contradiction for the WRA staff itself. The national policy which was taking form was developing around the idea that the relocation centers should be "as nearly like normal communities as possible," that restrictions should be at a minimum, and that those which could not be eliminated should be de-emphasized. Many of the most flagrant and troublesome restrictions, especially those in the western centers, were insisted on by the Army. Others, such as the low wage level, seemed insurmountable to WRA policy makers because of the political pressures which were shaping the program. Accepting these as inescapable, the policy makers encouraged center administrators to promote a spirit of cooperation and equality in relations with evacuees in the centers. The attitudes of most top staff members were generally in line with the spirit of national policy, but such a spirit was contradicted at innumerable points by the actual facts of center organization.

In line with national policy, center administrators attempted to eliminate some sources of antagonism felt by evacuees. Thus the term "Jap" quickly became a taboo word among the staff. The Tule Lake project director became famous among evacuees for his vigorous condemnation of the word. Recognizing it as distasteful to evacuees and a source of bad feeling between staff and evacuees, he outlawed it in staff meetings. It similarly became taboo at other centers. Even the term "evacuee" was felt to be undesirable by staff members as calling attention to the evacuation and a reminder of the present status arising out of that event. They substituted various terms for it. "Residents," the official term at Poston, and "colonists" at Tule Lake were widely used at other centers. Nevertheless some staff members at every center continued to use "Jap" in referring to evacuees in conversations among themselves, and "evacuee" continued as probably the most generally used of all terms.

A need was felt by the staff also for a term by which to call themselves which did not emphasize their superior status. "Whites" in contrast with "Japanese" began to be used in the early centers, but quickly came into disfavor. In its place the term "Caucasian" steadily increased in usage. However, this was not felt to be in harmony with national policy since it emphasized racial differences. In August a memorandum was issued from Washington banning its use, and center staffs were instructed to use "appointed personnel" in its place. The latter was somewhat clumsy, and although its official use became firmly established, it never superseded "Caucasian." Both staff and English-speaking evacuees fell increasingly into the use of the two terms "Caucasian" and "evacuee" in referring to themselves and to each other. Japanese-speaking evacuees used the Japanese equivalents of the terms "whites" and "Japanese," namely *hakujin* and *nihonjin*.

At the same time staff members were attempting to find words which would minimize the existing differences, they were led by the nature of the situation into practices which emphasized them. In the early months in all centers there were either stated regulations or tacit customs excluding evacuees from eating in the "personnel mess halls." Some staff members objected to joint eating on the ground of racial prejudice, but to the responsible administrators it merely seemed like good organization. The evacuees, they felt, had their assigned places to eat and their food needs were taken care of by the systematic operation of the agency. If evacuees were invited by friends among the staff to eat in the personnel mess hall, the privilege might be abused or it might appear as favoritism to other evacuees who were not invited. At some centers the commanders of the military police announced that there was to be "no fraternization with evacuees." Some project directors also let it be known among their staff that they did not encourage close personal relations with evacuees. Such measures, which were not dictated by national policy and varied in interpretation in every center, arose from feelings that they were necessary for the good of the organization. Many staff members supported them, feeling that they were in line with the existing distinctions embodied in the national policies of different wage levels and Government provision of housing and other facilities for evacuees. A few on every staff, however, felt them as unnecessary, restrictive on themselves, and an obstacle to the development of mutual confidence and good working relations. Whatever staff members felt about it, there was no doubt that a real but varying line existed between the two groups based on the distinctions which had been institutionalized in the organization of the centers. The contradictions inherent in it were a source of minor but persistent conflict among staff members and of attitudes among evacuees which had far-reaching significance for the over-all program of the agency.

For evacuees the feeling of subordinate and restricted status colored the whole early experience in the centers, but it was felt differently depending pretty much on the age of the evacuee. The older men and women looked at the distinctions in the center more as a confirmation of old prejudices and discriminations which they had experienced on the West Coast for a generation. The sense of being up against a color line was hardly a new thing; it was only the definiteness and the official governmental sanction of it that was new. There seemed little to do but learn how to live with this latest manifestation of it. For the younger people, particularly those of high school and post high school age, it was hardest to accept. For them, catapulted suddenly out of school and college where they had seen nothing quite comparable to the discriminations their parents had endured, the organized discrimination of center life was an unforgetable shock. Most at first reacted bitterly. Young boys became cynical over night. A young evacuee in one center wrote:

In the warehouse . . . area . . . where maintenance construction and supply crews are headquartered, resentment is particularly keen against "obvious preferred treatment" of "whites." Typical comment: "You can't eat in the Caucasian mess hall;" they call this democracy where everyone is supposed to be equal; look at our housing . . . and the Project Director ordered his quarters completely re-made.

It was not only bitterness and resentment that the situation encouraged, it went further than that, stimulating a whole new mode of thought. The same young man wrote:

A perennial discussion topic among virtually all groupings of Manzanar residents is the "color line." There is common tendency to refer shortcomings or faults of individual administrators as attributes of the entire "white race."

WORK AND WAGES

The new way of looking at themselves and at their relationship to the WRA staff became quickly apparent as evacuees went to work. With arrival in the centers, making a living suddenly ceased to be a problem, at least in the sense of feeling any relationship between one's job and what one might have in the way of necessities and comforts. With shelter, food, and other needs taken care of, work promptly lost much of its old meaning. The artificiality of the new situation was enhanced by the early efforts of the WRA to provide jobs of some sort for everyone able to work. Original policy held that there was to be no scarcity of jobs in the centers. The agency began with a plan for a work corps in which everyone could enlist under an agreement that one would work on assigned jobs for the duration of the war and 14 days thereafter.

Evacuees coming into Poston in the first weeks signed agreements to join the work corps. At Manzanar and Tule Lake such agreements were not signed, but pamphlets distributed to the incoming evacuees described the work corps. The basic principle was that jobs would be provided for everyone who wished to work under whatever conditions the Government would stipulate. The Government's obligation was to provide jobs; the evacuees' obligation was to work in those jobs whatever they might be. The idea of the work corps involving the generalized agreement between evacuees and the agency was abandoned after a few months, but the concept of full employment regardless of the operations needs of the centers persisted for the whole first year. It contributed to a feeling of evacuees that they were in a make-work situation.

The work corps concept, despite its early abandonment, also created confusion in the minds of evacuees in the early centers. Many went on believing that the agreements they had signed in Poston were still in effect. As late as October some were still asking whether the "cash advance" mentioned in the agreements as monthly payment would ultimately have to be paid back to the Government. Employment was gradually put on an application-and-referral system in the early centers and was officially on that basis in the later centers from the start, but uncertainty about the conditions of employment persisted in Manzanar, Poston, and Tule Lake, and was also apparent in Gila. The confusion was added to by delays in paying the monthly wages in all centers. On

Relocation centers were built in so-called "wilderness areas" like this in southern California. Evacuees were organized to do whatever was necessary to keep the communities operating. This crew is clearing brush to enlarge the Manzanar Center, June, 1942.

into the winter of 1942 there were lags of several months, persons being paid for their first month's work two, three, or more months later. This added to the feeling for the majority of evacuees that the work situation was not a real one related to any economic necessities.

After the first burst of activity in making the blocks livable, lack of interest and dissatisfaction set in, especially among the young men. It appeared among volunteers who felt that agreements in regard to wages had not been lived up to at Manzanar. At Poston and Tule Lake, young men who had not been in on the early distribution of "good" jobs were bitter. In early June one such young man wrote:

[The WRA staff] don't know what our wages will be, how they are going to finance the project which they want to be (according to their interpretation) a cooperation or partnership with the Government. The whole thing stinks . . . . Fault probably not due to local authorities but to the system—the system starting with a bang on a grand idea without attention to details . . . . I am not working yet. I don't feel like working. If they force me to, I might have to . . . .

Young men in this mood were numerous in all the early centers. They were not in touch with even the partially formulated plans of the administrators at that time because, if they had decided to work at all, they were working in their block mess halls or elsewhere at some distance from the administrative offices. They and their associates were confused also because WRA policy on employment had hardly crystallized by June. They felt strong resentments against "the system" because they did not feel themselves to be a part of that system. When, in June, they did become aware of the fixed wage scale of $12, $16, or $19 a month, they became all the more resentful and cynical about work in the centers.

In strong contrast to the bitter young men of this type were a fringe of other young men and some older, including many of the volunteers who had secured better jobs at the start and who were responding eagerly to the opportunities in the centers. They took the attitude that the low wage was irrelevant. Some were anxious "to work for the people"; some were enjoying the new feelings of responsibility, prestige, or authority. They undertook assigned tasks and worked tirelessly, filling those jobs in the agency hierarchy next below those of the Caucasian staff. They remained more in touch with the plans and intentions of the administrators and tended consequently to move away from the intense bitterness and withdrawal of those who did not feel themselves to be participating in the development of the centers.

On the other hand, thousands of evacuees in each center were faced with the prospect of occupying indefinitely the routine jobs of center operation. Among them, as they tentatively felt out the new situation, a complete reevaluation of work and working conditions took place. The economics of center life became sharply different from the economics of normal life. The attitudes and relations which determined the new economics were not obvious to WRA staff at first and, when they were sensed, were often misinterpreted. The adjustment of staff to the evacuee re-evaluation of work was a slow and painful process never fully accomplished, but the adjustment proceeded, however erratically, as the months went by.

The determinants of economic life in the centers came into operation in the earliest weeks. They did not spring from embittered young men chafing at the injustice of evacuee status or the meaninglessness of center life so much as from the older, experienced men. The attitudes of the Issei toward work in the centers crystallized quickly and remained dominant throughout. As one of them put it in July:

Fresno was a sand-dune fifty years ago. Japanese turned it into a fertile land. The Issei pioneers made great sacrifice in human life . . . in developing Fresno. When I visited Parlier [near Fresno] recently, the driver told me that Japanese owned this and that land and it made me happy. "Let us make it a good place here [in the center]," someone is reported to have said . . . . But Poston is different from Fresno. For $16, we should not work like we did in Fresno. For $16 and $18, we should not work so hard. Of course, we should all work. But we must not think this place is the same as Fresno.

This statement was made in a public meeting in which leaders, both Nisei and Issei, were attempting to arrive at some common conception of the meaning of the centers as a guide for their behavior in working out community government. It expressed the feeling of the majority of the older people. The centers were not, in their view, places in which to turn their traditional industry into channels laid out for them by others. They should work to make the centers as comfortable as possible, but they were wary of the vague, larger plans in terms of which the administrators seemed to be talking. They were suspicious of the purposes behind such plans, but they could accept the objective of immediate comfort in the near-at-hand aspects of center life. Beyond that, the Issei generally did not feel any obligation, since they had been put in the centers against their will and were not participating in the formulation of further plans.

A young evacuee observed this approach in operation in his block during the first summer:

The biggest thing that has come up [in the block] was the Vegetable Committee. That started back in July. I wasn't on the Block Council then, but I thought that it wasn't the right thing for us to grow vegetables. The way I figured it then was that the Government had agreed to give us certain things like food, clothing, and shelter in return for which we agreed to abide by certain rules. I thought that the Government should live up to its agreement, and why should we be expected to furnish food for ourselves? . . . . Well, the Issei thought we should grow vegetables for ourselves from the first. They talked a lot about daikon [a Japanese

Nisei boys watching an Issei whittler at Rohwer, Ark., Dec., 1943.

type of radish much used for food], saying it was the ideal thing for us
to grow, because if you couldn't pickle it all then you could dry it, and
use it that way. They thought it was a sure food supply. I don't like the
stuff and wasn't interested. But they went ahead and got seed of *daikon*
and Chinese lettuce (*nappa*) and other things. Then they got to work on
it. I have to admire those Issei. They have been hanging back from doing
anything the administration told them to do. They would just hang back
and talk about the administration all the time. But when it came to doing

something like growing vegetables, they sure got out and worked. The city men worked, too, along with the Salinas farmers in our block . . . . The young fellows in the block would just work when their turn came. They only worked to save their face. But the old men were out there whether it was their turn to work or not. I have to admire them for that.

This sort of activity was typical of the older people. It evidently was unrelated to wage scales, but was guided by a purpose which the men felt strongly, in this case insurance against what they felt to be an uncertain food supply and need for types of food to which they were accustomed. The work was planned, managed, and carried out by themselves independently of the WRA staff. Similar attitudes were apparent in other work which the older people were convinced was necessary to their comfort and welfare in the centers.

There was, however, strong feeling about the Government's obligations which led to a good deal of division of opinion in regard to the types of work to which the people should apply themselves. In some blocks older men as well as younger objected to devoting their spare time to growing vegetables because of their feeling that the Government was obligated to provide food. There was also some objection to working on the construction of schools, even though the older people were deeply interested in the provision of good schooling for their children. Many felt that the schools should already have been built or that the completion

Among the more practical articles carved from scrap wood were getas, wooden foot gear to protect the wearer from dust outdoors and athlete's foot, a constant threat in the shower rooms. Manzanar, Calif., 1942.

of buildings should be carried out by laborers hired at going wages, either evacuees or others, and not at the center wages. There was even objection to the heavy work of hauling coal from railheads to the blocks on the ground that coal, as well as other necessities, ought to be provided by the Government at the point of use. There was thus at first no universal agreement on precisely where the evacuee obligation to work began or ended. The older people did agree that it was their duty to work at jobs which were clearly directed to fulfilling their needs and comforts in the centers. It was not their duty, however, to work at jobs the purpose of which was not fully clear to them, such as the long-term agricultural projects at Poston, the future benefits of which they did not believe would come to them. There was also rather general agreement that evacuees ought not to work on facilities for the WRA staff or on the basic facilities of the centers, such as the water-pipe systems, which they regarded as part of the Government obligation to provide.

The beauty of hard-carved name plates, some using both English letters and Japanese characters, did a little to alleviate the starkness of barracks entrances. Granada, Colo., 1945.

The re-evaluation of work was apparent in the feelings that developed in regard to the $12, $16, and $19 wage scale. Once it became clear that this was fixed, several views appeared among evacuees. In some centers there were proposals that the highest wage should be paid for the most disagreeable work, for example, $19 for garbage collectors and coal haulers, and lower rates for the pleasanter and easier jobs, such as office work. The prevailing feeling in all centers, however, was that there should be no differences in wages. Everyone should get the same, it was felt, because actually everyone was working merely for the welfare of all in the centers and differences in wages were irrelevant in such a situation. There was also a widespread feeling that especially responsible and important work such as that of doctors and nurses in the hospitals should be more highly paid than other types of work. Practice in the centers gradually fell into line with this prevailing feeling. The $16 wage became general, the $12 wage was abandoned (except for learners), and hospital and other workers whose service was regarded as especially important for the general welfare were paid $19.

Although they failed at first to understand the evacuee feelings about the meaning of different types of work and their whole evaluation of work in the centers, WRA staff were generally inclined to regard $16 a month as insufficient incentive for a good day's work. Some foremen were openly sympathetic with tendencies to work "not too hard." However, all foremen were themselves up against the standards of the Government agency of a maximum work output for an eight-hour day, and moreover were faced with getting specific jobs done. Many, of course, had no sympathy with any standard other than that set by the agency. As a result, there was persistent trouble as the evacuee standard of "let us work, but let us not work too hard" came into conflict with the standards which foremen and supervisers were attempting to live up to. Rigorous foremen found themselves up against a sort of passive resistance, as evacuee work crews quietly developed their system of rest periods and early quitting times. They found a general tendency on the part of evacuees never to allow themselves to be pushed too hard and to balk at any signs of inconsiderate handling or evidences of racial prejudice. Some foremen, accustomed to work situations where a man could be hired and fired, exploded and found that their crews walked out on them. Friction between work crews and foremen was persistent throughout the early months in the centers. Most foremen, however, found themselves compromising gradually with the standards set by the evacuees, and slowly the evacuee standard dominated the centers.

The sharp limitation on cash earnings gave rise to other important attitudes that shaped relocation center economics. In Manzanar and the other early centers there was a strong current of sentiment against setting up canteens at which evacuees could purchase toilet articles and other things. There was a feeling that the Government would, if it had to, provide these things. Many older people felt that, whether the Government should provide them or not, there should be a minimum of opportunity to spend money in the centers. Economic resources, they said, should be conserved for the ultimate return to the struggle for a living outside. Issei opinion rather generally held that spending should be discouraged at every point possible. At first people determined to lay away their good clothes for the duration of life in the centers. People were urged to curb the traditional giving of money gifts at funerals and other occasions. Despite such feelings, the canteens became an important part of center life, and the giving of gifts of money according to the old customs continued, though modified in various ways. Moreover, there were numerous collections in the blocks from the very first for improvements of the mess halls and other block facilities or for gifts to highly appreciated cooks or other block workers. Sentiment and action never coincided on these points.

A WORLD OF RUMOR

The administration areas and the resident or colony areas, as they came to be called, were places of contrast. During the first months the important difference lay not in the buildings or the physical appearance, but was to be felt rather in the prevailing atmosphere, the contrasting moods of the two areas. The WRA staff were preoccupied with difficult and unaccustomed jobs and most carried a sense of high purpose into their work. The frustrations and the inherent contradictions that were to dog them in later months had not yet touched them deeply. The mood was generally one of hopeful embarkation on an important task.

The life of the people in the blocks was taking shape in a different atmosphere. Even during the first weeks of busy effort to straighten out the disorder of the blocks, the dominant notes were uncertainty, anxiety, and even fear. Instead of abating after a short time as people settled into their "apartments" and moved into the routines of block living, the anxieties increased as the weeks went on. At Manzanar, Poston, and Tule Lake, tensions mounted steadily during the summer and reached peaks in October and November, five or six months after the opening of the centers. In the later centers there was never the same degree of tension and unrest, although all went through periods of mounting anxieties several months after the first arrivals. Even the three centers which both staff and evacuees generally characterized as "quiet"—Minidoka, Granada, and Rohwer—had periods during the moving in when tension rose and rumor and anxiety swept through the blocks.

The state of mind of the evacuees had its roots in the process of disorganization that had been going on among them ever since the attack on Pearl Harbor. Fear and uncertainty had entered the lives of many with the sudden appearance of FBI officers in their homes to take the family head away to internment. Anxieties had increased steadily in the following months centering on the question: Will we be evacuated and interned? In the assembly centers, with evacuation an accomplished fact, the questions of the future loomed in terms of: Will we be released somewhere outside the coastal states to re-establish ourselves? Will we be confined in other places? What treatment can we expect from the Government from now on? Now, with the relocation centers enclosing them, it was not yet fully apparent what treatment could be expected or whether the new situation amounted to internment. Each new event in the uprooting process, as it shattered long-established ties and old bases of life, created new questions about what the future might be. And these questions went unanswered for months, leaving the people in a sort of limbo between a shattered past and an uncertain future.

In the centers no evacuee could answer with authority the multiplying questions. Only the agents of the Government which had created the situation could be looked to for some word. While Manzanar was still an assembly center an urgent need developed for some means of getting whatever information there was from the administrators to the evacuees. In addition to the block managers, an information center grew up in response to this need. Composed of evacuees who were in touch with the administrators and the latest bits of information that came to the center, it worked long hours collecting questions asked by the incoming evacuees, compiling answers when there were answers, and getting these back to the people in the blocks. The information center quickly became an important institution and an influential one in allaying the anxieties which arose over and over again each day. In the early weeks of Poston many evacuees felt, as one expressed it, that "the authorities themselves are indefinite, and don't seem to know anything." Many questions could not be answered; they probed a future into which WRA officials could not yet see any more than could evacuees. By July, however, means were growing up for at least bringing evacuees in touch with what could be said with certainty by the staff. An evacuee-organized "Issei orientation group" arranged meetings at which WRA staff members talked, describing what each part of the agency organization was doing and planning in the center, and answering as best they could the never ending flow of questions about the present and the future.

In all the centers the questions came through block managers, through delegations waiting on project directors, or in meetings called for purposes of organizing the community life. How long would families have to live doubled up? When would partitions come? Were more blocks to be built? Why was the food not better? Why did the government spend money on shredded wheat and cheese which almost no one would eat? How much money was allowed for food? Was it all being spent? Why had two babies died in the hospital wards? Was it true that the Caucasian doctor had misdiagnosed a case? What would wages be? Why was no one being paid for work done? Who would ultimately get the benefit of land developed by evacuee labor? Could one visit a sick relative in another center? Why were incoming packages being inspected? Would books and phonograph records confiscated in assembly centers be returned? Was the mail being censored? Was it true that the center would be closed and the people moved somewhere else? Were evacuees in the status of prisoners of war? Did the provisions of the Geneva Convention apply to them? Would Nisei citizenship be fully revoked? Were Nisei to be drafted? Did the 4-C classifications Nisei were now receiving from their draft boards mean that they were officially classified as aliens now? Would all evacuees be deported after the war? Why were so many people receiving application blanks for repatriation to Japan? Were evacuees all to be deported during the war? Could they count on the centers as homes for the duration of the war? The questions ranged through every phase of life, and often the administrators had no answers. Frustrated themselves at failures to get needed materials, they became wary of any statements or promises that partitions or stoves or coal would arrive by a certain date. They fell back on expressions of hope and seemed to the evacuees to be side-stepping. They could be even less definite about the longer range problems: the policies of the agency were not yet established, the questions were being considered in Washington. But the evacuees went on wondering, seeking some sort of certainty on which to build their lives.

As the relocation centers filled up with questioning people, anxiety began to focus on the tangible and near at hand. The larger questions were still there in everyone's minds, but at least now in the centers the houses people were to live in, the food they were to eat, and the hospitals in which they were to be cared for were here before them. For the first time in months there was something definite to live with and plan in relation to. In each center, early or late, as evacuees reached the limits of improving their barracks rooms, their attention and concern became focused on these immediate tangible bases of life—the trinity of housing, food, and health.

No center escaped crowding in its early days. Manzanar, the earliest occupied, remained the most crowded on into the winter of 1943. Poston, the next occupied, regarded itself still in a housing crisis in December 1942. All the other centers suffered acutely from lack of space at least during the first months. Crowding meant, specifically, families of four or more living in 20' x 25' single rooms, couples unacquainted with one another living together in one room, a family of three or more sharing a room with one or more individuals, twenty or thirty single men living all together in an unpartitioned barracks. The plan of the administrators to have at the barest minimum one room per family was defeated at first by insufficient barracks and by lack of materials for partitions which would separate doubled-up families into smaller, but at least private, quarters.

The prevalence of crowding did not mean that every block and every barracks suffered from the extreme forms of it. There were many families from the beginning who had adequate quarters in the sense that they had a room to themselves. Crowding in the form of two unrelated families living in an unpartitioned single room was by no means universal, but it was common enough to be an important source of friction in many blocks. The crowding varied from block to block, depending on the manner in which the block was filled up at first, the desires of friends to remain near each other in the same block, and the efficiency of operation of the housing departments. Some blocks in each center were never crowded, but most were at some time during the early months.

For the evacuees who endured the crowding, it meant disorganization of family life, frayed nerves, friction, and discomfort from which there was no relief. A weekly housing report in terms of floor space per person could hardly convey the real meaning. A Nisei mother wrote in her diary in September, four months after the opening of the center:

We tried to rearrange the house today. I suppose not much can be done with 20' by 25', but we always hope against hope that we can. Goodness, we certainly could stand just another room. This being seven in a room makes privacy an unknown word. Finally we got it arranged so that we have at least room enough to walk around in. All of us were tired and out of sorts when we finished.

Another woman described the nature of "doubling up":

Apartment is shared by one married couple, age around 50 years, and our family of our, one girl just nine and one ten years old, my husband is out during the day on a job . . . . The heat is terrific and the lady in our apartment is very sensitive to heat, so whenever her washing and ironing is done she is always taking naps—makes it hard for children to run in and out—for fear it may disturb her. She is an understanding person, but still there is time she wished she could have slept just another ten minutes . . . . The cook [husband of the woman just described] takes a nap after lunch. Unfortunately a friend visits us so I must beg her to whisper in low voice. It is not very pleasant to whisper. I must ask my girls to stay outdoors as much as they can—but they complain the heat outdoors—they come in continually to get toys to play . . . I must ask them to be quiet. I feel sorry for the children and the cook . . . . Our roommate has eaten something disagreeable and is vomiting and she has loose stool—she hesitates to use chamber—and manages to go to latrine. She is really too weak to walk. I know she will use chamber if she was the only occupant of the apartment. I got some ice for her from the kitchen . . . . The lady [who shares the apartment] bought some candies —she will always share with us. In return I buy fruits and give them half. This goes on and on. I told them they need not do this. But being in the same room, this is impossible on both sides. I know we do spend more than we really should.

The tension created by the crowded living conditions increased through the early months and charged the atmosphere of many blocks with little antagonisms and personal conflicts. Rumors appeared and disappeared as staff members made hopeful statements that partitions would arrive on various dates. The staff worked desperately to shuffle the people to relieve at least a little of the crowding. Rearrangements of families were hindered by the resistance of people in less crowded blocks to giving up what they had. Eventually partitions did arrive and the housing departments worked constantly at the task of adjusting the space to the people.

The crowding was an important factor in the background of most that happened during the first months. It contributed to the prevailing state of mind and the mounting tensions in the early centers. It was, however, around the other two basic interests—food and health—that most intense feeling crystallized. At the roots of the anxieties lay the experiences of the months since Pearl Harbor. Most important was a deep distrust of the Government and of the Caucasians who composed it and in whose hands evacuees now felt themselves to be. If "they" had conceived and carried out the evacuation of families and children, if "they" had picked up and separated from their families the family heads who people knew were not dangerous, if "they" had conceived the relocation centers with their restrictions and subordinations, how much consideration could be expected from "them" now? If "they" had done this much, what more might "they" not be expected to do? All the necessities of life were now in the hands of the distrusted group, represented by the WRA staff in the centers. The relocation centers were in remote and isolated spots off the main transportation lines. Here was the perfect setting for harsh treatment, if that were in the minds of the Caucasians. If the war overtaxed the transportation system of the country, the relocation centers would be the first to be cut off. What would happen to the food supply then? Perhaps, some said darkly, it had been the intention all along to get rid of the evacuees in this way. These suspicions, not yet known to the staff and incredible if they had been, were deep and based on real experiences. They gained wide currency in the early centers.

Then there were the realities of the relocation center life—the adjustment to a new diet at first not well chosen to meet the food customs of the older people, various temporary shortages in a nation that was beginning to feed an army overseas, inevitable little inefficiencies in the distribution of food to block mess halls, incompetent cooks and stewards' assistants in various blocks, inexperienced WRA staff in the stewards' departments, all the weaknesses of new organization in a complex operation. Similarly in the hospitals, there was lack of equipment at first; there was inevitable poor management here and there; there was difficulty in rapidly getting a staff; there was the sense of dependence on doctors in whom one had not developed confidence, some of them of the distrusted group. Out of these conditions grew anxiety and fear, and out of the anxieties grew rumors, sometimes fantastic rumors, which increased the fears as they sprouted and grew in the laundry rooms and the bachelors' barracks where people talked and listened.

The anxiety about food rose and fell in relation to actual conditions in the various centers. A succession of relatively poor meals gave rise to rumors that the warehouses were empty. A shortage of meat or rice resulted in rumors that the whole American transportation system had broken down and the food supply had been cut off. A large number of Issei began to believe that they could not trust the Caucasians to supply them with food and that consequently they would have to depend on their own efforts to raise vegetables in the block gardens. Inequality in the distribution to mess halls of a particular shipment of food gave rise to stories on the one hand of favoritism and graft among the evacuees who had jobs in the stewards' departments and on the other hand to rumors of dishonesty among the WRA personnel. The atmosphere of uncertainty and distrust led cooks and individuals in many blocks to hoard what food they did get against the occasional lean days, or to provide for the imagined eventual complete breakdown in the food supply. The failure of an evacuee to receive a personal shipment of food from a friend in California resulted in a widespread belief that WRA staff members were dishonest and were withholding and probably selling for their own profit food that was rightfully intended for evacuees.

Intense anxieties about health and medical care grew up simultaneously with those connected with food. Like the rumors about food, those about the hospitals were usually based on some real event, the death of an evacuee in the hospital, a shortage of equipment, or an instance of poor ambulance service or discourteous treatment in the hospital receiving room. At Manzanar during the summer a large number of evacuees came to believe that a mother had died in childbirth as a result of incompetence by a doctor. At Poston similarly large numbers of evacuees believed that two babies had died because of neglect. There were rumors that evacuees were being used experimentally in the hospitals; that Caucasian doctors deliberately allowed evacuees to die.

The world of rumor that flourished in the blocks took into its purview the outside world as well as the centers. It took each instance of hostility to Japanese-Americans which was reported in a newspaper or a letter and dwelt on it, magnified it, and elaborated it into a new source of fear.

Thus at every center the uncertainties of the new life and the intense concern about present and future welfare led to the construction of a shifting and fanciful world of additional uncertainties and distorted human relationships, to more fears, and to further distrust.

THE BLOCKS: FOUNDATIONS OF COMMUNITY LIFE

From places of dust and bare barracks in May and June, the blocks in the first centers were transformed rapidly. By August, Manzanar and portions of Poston were no longer bare. Irrigation water, the heat of the summer, and the industry of the people had changed them. The streets between the blocks were still dusty, and the afternoon winds raised daily dust storms; but within many blocks there were already flowers, grass, and carefully planned little gardens and pools for fish. Arbors and shades of various kinds had appeared between the barracks rows. The blocks looked lived in and vastly more livable than they had two months before. In the midst of the anxieties and antagonisms, the people were making determined efforts. In September, between comments on the horrors of sharing a room with another family, a mother in one of the early centers was moved to write in her diary:

The water came in our block Wednesday evening—the children are excited catching perch and little bass. Our block resembles city of Venice. At night the sight is for supreme. The reflection of the moon is beautiful and serene.

Family efforts and cooperative work of the block people had wrought the changes wherever they took place.

The same urge that was creating order and harmony in the block landscapes was also at work in ordering the social relations of the people in the blocks, but it was working against greater odds.

The filling of the blocks as the train and bus loads of people poured into the centers resulted in a certain amount of sorting into groups who had been associated before. The fishermen from Terminal Island, on their arrival in Manzanar, were placed in a group of adjacent blocks. The people from Orange County arrived at Poston on the same day and filled up a dozen blocks in the western part of the center. The businessmen of Sacramento went into adjoining blocks in Tule Lake. In later centers people from the same assembly centers arrived together and occupied blocks set aside for them. This resulted in about the same thing, that is, the grouping of people in every center in terms of their former localities. The sorting often was carried a little farther. Families related to each other, or who had been associated with one another before evacuation, made efforts to remain close together. People not only from the same locality, but also members of the same church, the same *kenjinkai,** or the same business association had themselves assigned to the same trains leaving the assembly centers, and sought to be assigned neighboring barracks, or at least to the same blocks, in the relocation centers. If they failed at first in the centers, they often moved as soon as they found where their former friends or relatives were living. There was a great deal of moving and exchanging of rooms in the early days of the centers. The various sorting processes that took place served to lay some foundation for the development of orderly social relations. People often knew a considerable number of the others in the blocks in which they ultimately settled, or at least were acquainted with a small group in the same block.

Nevertheless, the people in any one block constituted a heterogeneous assortment. Although it might consist of 300 persons from Los Angeles, or Santa Clara County, or Fresno, or Seattle, and although it might consist of a dozen groups of families, each group of whom had known each other before evacuation, still the dozen circles of friends often had very little in common. A typical block of country people might contain eight to ten families of well-to-do farmers, fifteen or twenty itinerant farm laborers, a dozen or more families of poor tenant farmers, a few small-town shopkeepers, possibly a dentist and his family—people who had lived according to widely different economic standards, who had gone to different churches, and who perhaps belonged to none of the same organizations. No block had from the beginning a background of common participation of all its members in some former community. Every block had on the contrary a background of differing class, religious, and family behavior. Antipathies sprang up and adjustments had to be made, as they adapted the semicommunal framework of the block to their needs.

Moreover, there was no ready-made guiding pattern for this adjustment. The whole situation was new, not only the mess hall system and the other communal institutions of the blocks, but also the dependence on an as yet unknown administration, and the uncertainty of objectives to work toward in the relocation centers. What might a block be? No one knew the pattern in advance, and inevitably there were differences of opinion as the more dominant personalities sought to influence the block life.

---

*Association of people from the same prefecture in Japan.

The adjustment took place in different ways in different blocks. Here it went smoothly as people leaned on a few like-minded men and women. There personalities clashed, or divergent views resulted in persistent cleavages that were reflected in mess halls, block councils, and the whole spirit of a block. Nevertheless, out of the initial disorganization and uncertainty, a way of life steadily took form. It was a distinctive way of life molded out of the crisis of evacuation and the peculiar artificiality of the relocation center communities, as well as out of deep-rooted traditions reaching back to Japan and up through the thirty or forty years of experience in

Family solidarity was difficult to maintain in the enforced communal living, with all 250 residents of a block eating in the same mess hall. Customary family rituals often had to be abandoned unless the family were large enough to occupy a complete table. Discipline dwindled, and differing family standards merged into a common mess-hall behavior. This adjustment was most painful for the older generation. Manzanar, Calif., 1942.

the United States. What took place as people adjusted to one another in the blocks ultimately determined the nature of the communities which WRA staff and evacuees, in their different ways, had talked of building as the centers opened.

The basis of social life, as before, was the family. Here in the blocks, however, the family could not be precisely what it had been before. Dining room, lavatory, and recreation room were all communal, and hence every home was broken into three or four distinct places, with all but the room in which the family slept shared by sixty or more other families. Moreover the one unshared spot allowed neither privacy among family members or wholly from families on the other sides of the partitions. This division of the home and its lack of privacy had immediate effects on both parents and children. A young father described the situation during the early months of one center:

The worst part of it is not being able to bring up the baby right. He's just eighteen months . . . . Naturally he cries some. If you were living alone in your own house, you could let him cry when he did it and not spoil him. But here you've got to pay attention to it. You don't feel like letting him bother the people on the other side of the partition. They can hear everything that goes on. You've got to shut him up some way. So you have to fuss around with his crying and pay attention to him. That's not good for the baby.

Parents were feeling the impact of a new discipline, of having to manage their children more or less in public instead of in privacy.

In the mess halls the parents' problems often became acute. One mother said:

My small daughter and I used to eat at a table where two little boys . . . ate with their mothers. They had become so uncontrollable that the mothers had given up, and let them eat as they pleased. They behaved so badly that I stopped eating there . . . . But my daughter was fascinated. They would come running into the mess hall, and the first thing both of them did was to take off their shoes and stockings and jump up and down on the seat. Then they would start yelling for their food. After they were given their food they wouldn't eat it, but would just play with it. . . . They would often bring toy automobiles and trains, etc., with them, making noises as they pushed the toys in and out of food that was spilled on the table. . . . Now these little boys had older brothers and sisters, and if they had eaten at one table with both parents, things like that couldn't have happened, for the older children would have protested out of pride, and the father probably would have forbidden it.

Despite valiant efforts of women and others in the various blocks, most centers failed to work out systems for family grouping in the mess halls. Such a plan was worked out early at Tule Lake, and there were individual blocks in most centers which tried at various times to adopt family groupings in the mess halls. But in general, eating, under the influence of mess hall conditions, ceased to be a family affair. Mothers and smaller children usually ate together, but the fathers often ate elsewhere with other men, and the older children joined others of their own age. Thus family control in the basic discipline of eating changed character rapidly, and the differing family standards became merged in a sort of common mess hall behavior. Family solidarity ceased to have the re-enforcement of customary family rituals associated with the meal-time gathering of the group.

There was also some loss of control resulting from the crowded rooms and the proximity of large numbers of children in the blocks. With schools not yet open, the children seemed to the parents to be running wild with their playmates in the blocks. A constant refrain in the early days of the centers was that children were getting out of control, that family life was breaking down. The constant complaint reflected the anguish of the new adjustment more than any real breakdown of the family. The public display of parent-child relations, and the grouping of children around their age mates, rather than their parents, in the mess halls, were tending to break down the morale of parents to a greater extent than they were actually setting new standards of behavior for children.

The changes in family life affected not only the relationships of parents and children but also those of husbands and wives. The position of both was profoundly altered by the new framework. The husband was no longer in the position of principal breadwinner in many families, his wife and his older children often drawing the same monthly wage. There was an accompanying sense of loss of prestige on the part of the husband and of independence on the part of the wife. More important for the women was the real independence from housework. There was little floor space to keep clean and no cooking to do unless the woman chose to work in the mess hall. Work for the family was confined to washing clothes and tending children, and often there were women of both generations in one family to share in these labors. For many young Nisei wives, the new abundance of leisure resulted in loss of interest and boredom as one of them expressed it:

Today has been a rather peculiar day. I wonder if it's because I didn't have to wash. Funny how one begins to depend on routine work to pass the day. Mom says it's embarrassing for her to save a tub for me all morning. So she did the wash today. . . . The day ended, thank goodness. Reminds me of that dumb song: "Twenty-one years and ten more days and we'll be out of the calaboose."

Some older women also found time heavy on their hands and often sought jobs in the mess halls washing dishes, serving, and cleaning. Even such daytime activities, however, did not take their energies and hence there was a steadily increasing enthusiasm among the older women for new activities—classes in English, in singing, in flower arrangement, and even in writing Japanese poetry. The women began to enjoy the new freedom early, and at least the older ones began to find center life stimulating and interesting.

For most of the older established families, the new freedom of the women resulted in little disturbance of the relations of husbands and wives, but for many of the younger there were serious crises resulting from the demands of the new adjustment. The relations of the couples were not always threatened, but the new situation placed a heavy strain on the individuals as one man expressed it:

I get pretty blue sometimes. You can't help it. And my wife has changed. It's really tragic. Women look at the practical side of it more than we do, I guess. They don't have any philosophy about it. I can talk to her until I'm blue in the face, but it doesn't make any difference. She's losing weight. So am I. . . .

In other cases, the marital tie could not withstand the new strains and there were separations. An extreme example was analyzed by a neighbor:

Right in our block there is one middle age couple sharing room with a very young divorcee, her brother and father. She is very modern and sociable. She brings in her young girl friends and practice new Poston dance steps. The middle age couple are very quiet type and the husband is sick person. There is always a big fight and quarrel because the wife understands the younger set and is too lenient to her roommate. Now the wife and husband is separated just because of the roommate. It is not the fault of either side, merely because the extremes are put in same apartment.

The new developments in family relationships tended toward the disruption of established family patterns of behavior, but there were factors which threw the balance in the other direction. Most families had achieved a renewed solidarity in meeting the crisis of evacuation, and the attitudes stimulated by the crisis continued strongly during the months of uncertainty about the future in assembly centers and early relocation centers. Related families had, whenever possible, joined each other to go through the evacuation together. As the crisis developed and the uncertainty of the future deepened, the need for family support and family loyalties heightened. Older children began to feel increasingly that their parents needed their presence and support in facing the future. The parents, increasingly distrustful of the Government and often expecting ultimate deportation to Japan, clung to their children and emphasized the virtues of family loyalty. Thus, as the support of outside groups melted away from both parents and children, there was a general turning to the family group as the ultimate and only remaining source of support. Parents and older children throughout the first months of center life were closer to each other than they had ever been. The new patterns of living in the blocks constituted a threat to the newly achieved family solidarity, and for that reason were felt most keenly by the older people. They made, however, few real inroads on family solidarity until new events began to alter the outside relations once again.

The family controls merged gradually and almost imperceptibly with larger group controls, that is, the public opinion of the block. Everyone's life was lived in view of the block people. The communal facilities steadily drew people into intimate relations with one another. Did some women wish to make the mess hall pleasanter by putting up curtains? It had to be talked over with the mess crew and the block manager. No one could move to do anything until a large number of people had discussed it. Did a man become enthusiastic about building a little fish pond in front of his barracks? He had to discuss it with the neighbors across the way and at least the family heads in his own barracks, for they, too, had claims on the area. Moreover, such utilization of block space had to be considered in relation to the general plan of the block people for the use of the total space between the barracks. Block councils were formed, usually consisting of a family head elected from each barracks, to decide such questions as whether or not the block area should be devoted to the growing of vegetables or to recreation places for the children, or in what proportion it should be allocated to each of these uses. Actions which formerly required a brief family discussion at the most, now could be taken only after consultation, however indirectly, with 250 to 300 other persons. Through this process the blocks steadily grew into little communities.

Most of the block communities took form and achieved a real unity and integration within two or three months. Some foundered on obstructive personalities or factional disputes and remained crippled and disorganized for months. Almost universally, the first source of both organization and disorganization was the mess hall. Here took place the first systematic organization of any group within a block—that of the mess-hall crew. As soon as a block was occupied and its mess hall equipped for use, its operation required an organization of twenty-five to thirty people. How a mess hall became organized and the personalities of its top administrators, namely, the chef and the block steward (who served as liaison with the WRA steward's department), often determined whether or not the first four or five months of life in a block were peaceful or wracked with conflict. Chefs who were able to prepare edible food, to organize a mess-hall crew efficiently, and also to cope wisely with the suggestions, criticisms, and complaints of the miscellaneous block people, were not abundant in any center. The scarcity of even reasonably good chefs put those who cared to do so in positions to exercise a good deal of power. Block people usually did not care to risk the loss of a

competent cook by criticising or trying to control him. The often repeated reaction of chefs to any criticism in the early months was "All
right, I'll quit if you don't like what I do." In the face of such threats
people endured a great deal.

Many chefs proceeded to assume dictatorial powers, and the result
was usually conflict. Some gathered about them loyal crews of young
men who would do the chef's bidding, but recognized little obligation to
treat block residents considerately or courteously. The mess hall became
the regulator of life in the block, and people found themselves having to
conform to the chef's schedules set for the convenience of the mess-hall

Community councils were WRA's gesture toward democracy within the
relocation centers. Membership was at first restricted to Nisei, because they
were citizens of the United States. But each center worked out its own way
of bringing the mature Issei into the deliberations. Heart Mountain, Wyo.,
1944.

Dignity and formality characterize the Heart Mountain Court. The court was composed of seven judges selected from the residents and appointed by the project director; it heard cases of infractions of Center regulations. 1943.

crew rather than the people of the block. Suggestions from block residents became taboo, and offenders found themselves outlaws in the mess halls or threatened by the chef's loyal young men. Occasionally clashes between individuals in the blocks and members of the crew over some feature of service were prolonged into factional struggles with all the residents lined up on one side or the other. Block managers sometimes entered the lists and found themselves impotent in the face of the power of the mess crew.

Gradually, as the weeks went by, people in many of the blocks afflicted with mess-hall troubles learned how to control their chefs and mess crews. Chefs were sometimes allowed to make good their threats when they offered to quit, and it was found that some hitherto subordinate cook could handle the job just as well. Although this sometimes also resulted in the quitting of a whole mess crew in loyalty to their chef, block residents continued to exercise increasing control over their mess halls. Through determined groups of women, skillful negotiation by respected older men when trouble arose, and through the adjustment of the chefs themselves to their new roles as community dignitaries, the mess hall began to assume a position as the block institution of central importance, becoming the focus of interest, comment, and often block pride. In a sense it became the heart of each block, determining largely the well-being and tone of block life.

Some blocks found guidance for developing the pattern of block life in elected councils which were encouraged by the administration in most centers at an early stage in community organization. These were most often informal groups, but sometimes a systematic plan for organization was followed. In some centers each barracks in a block had its council,

Women seldom were elected to councils, but this one impressively makes her point as the group formulates a charter for the Topaz, Utah, Center, 1943.

consisting of the heads of all the families living in the barrack. The block council was then often composed of a head of a family from each barracks elected by the family heads of the barracks, constituting a group of about fourteen men. The group rarely contained women, since women were not regarded as family heads, and the great majority of the men were married men with families, although there was often a representative or two from a bachelor barracks, usually an elderly farm laborer. Councils such as these, where they were formed, usually met in response to specific needs felt by the block people, for example, to make a decision concerning the allotment of block land to recreation or food-growing purposes, or to organize a cooperative venture of the block people such as building an arbor. Sometimes meetings were called in response to a request of the administration for raising volunteer labor to meet some center emergency. Often, but by no means universally, the block manager was the chairman. After community councils were organized, the councilman sometimes served as chairman or as joint chairman with the block manager. A few blocks made efforts to have the young men, the American citizens, represented on the block council, for example: having both an Issei and a Nisei chairman, or equal numbers of Issei and Nisei on the council. But by far the majority of blocks in all centers allowed voice only to family heads who might be either Nisei or Issei, and to the elderly bachelors. This resulted in an inevitable domination of the meetings by the older men.

Fairly typical of the block councils was one described by a young married Nisei who as a family head was the representative of his barrack:

I just go [to block council meetings] because they want me to. I figure you can't do anything, because they are almost all Issei on the council. Most of what they talk about I don't care about the results. The only thing I'm interested in is getting food that is a little more in American style in the kitchen. But we can't do anything about that. The chef is an Issei, too. Two of the other Nisei on the council never say anything at all. I'm the only one [of the Nisei] who ever talks and I don't say much. We Nisei can understand the drift of what is said, but we don't get it all, and sometimes the other Nisei who talks, and I, can't express ourselves in Japanese and so we have to use some English.

. . . the married Nisei, like myself, are closer to the Issei than . . . [a group of young, unmarried college graduates in the block]. We learned before we came in here that we had to work with them. My business depended for the most part on the Issei and that's the way it was with the other Nisei who had got started in the world. So we are still closer to them. We support them more than the college people do. The college people don't have any representatives on the block council. Some of them [like one in a responsible position in the center administration] don't have much to do with the rest of us in the block. They are sort of by themselves. . . . It's the Issei who run the block all right. There are only

15 married Nisei in the block and most of them live with their parents. I guess that explains why the Issei run things.

The block council referred to here concerned itself, typically, with how much block land should be devoted to growing vegetables, the collection of funds from block residents for curtains in the mess hall, and other block improvements. The dominance of the older people in the discussions, the use of the Japanese language, and the sense of nonparticipation by even the oldest young men reflected the developing character of life in most blocks in every center. There was overt conflict between Issei and Nisei in very few blocks. Each block strove for unanimity in its councils and achieved it usually by the withdrawal of the younger men.

Block managers were the direct link between evacuees and the WRA administration. Young persons such as these, fluent in both languages, often served in the go-between role. This former medical research bacteriologist explains draft procedures to fellow block managers so they, in turn, can explain to center residents at Heart Mountain, Wyo., 1944.

Although councils were important institutions in many blocks, met regularly, and sometimes discussed current issues in center life, they were much less vital in block life than the mess halls. Most blocks achieved existence as the basic social units in the centers through less formal organizations. A few Issei gradually emerged in the majority of blocks as shapers of block opinion, arbiters of disputes that arose, and advisers on family and individual problems. Occasionally such a man might be block manager or a barracks representative in the block council, but more often he held no formal office. Frequently the men looked to for advice were parolees from internment camps and deliberately refrained from holding any formal position. Through position in the former West Coast community and through generally recognized soundness of judgment, they assumed positions of authority in the blocks and people looked to them for guidance. It was around them and their ideas that the blocks took form steadily as little village communities.

By fall in the early centers and by winter in the later centers, the blocks had crystallized as the foundations of the communities. Their unity began to be apparent in their attempts to control the block life by passing on the desirability of persons who wanted to move into them and sometimes in taking action to eject persons of whom they had come to disapprove.

COMMUNITY CROSSCURRENTS

The harmonizing of differences which people achieved in the course of adapting block lands, barracks, and mess halls to their needs was not sufficient to create communities out of the relocation centers. The adjustment of person to person in terms of these elementary needs resulted in the rapid establishment of working relationships and the creation of thirty or more little autonomous communities in each center. The integration of these into wider communities was another process which involved the adjustment of the people to divergent points of view among the center population as a whole. The process was relatively slow and sometimes tempestuous, especially in the early centers. Many of the tried and experienced leaders who might have given direction to this process were still in the internment camps. The leaders who emerged, although spokesmen for the dominant ideas within the group, too often carried insufficient influence and authority.

As the hot summer wore on through July in Manzanar, Poston, and Tule Lake, there was a growing uneasiness in the air. The atmosphere was charged with complaint and dissatisfaction. The anxieties about food and health were stronger than ever. But the uneasiness that became marked in August sprang from other sources. It arose in and spread from gatherings which brought together men from different blocks, meetings in which men who were emerging as spokesmen for different points of view among the evacuees discussed broader issues than mess halls and hospitals.

The uneasiness showed itself in different ways, but in all three of the earliest centers there was no mistaking its presence. Early in August in Manzanar some young men called a meeting to discuss a recent ruling of the WRA. A regulation had been issued from Washington excluding Kibei from the privilege of going out from centers to work in the harvest. The regulation reflected the suspicion of officials and others against Kibei as citizens who had gone to Japan for all or part of their education. Some Kibei in Manzanar wished to discuss this discrimination against themselves. Their meeting was attended by many Nisei who had never been in Japan. Quickly the meeting became heated, speaker after speaker arising to denounce the evacuation, the restrictions in the centers, the Army's discriminations against Nisei, the failure of Nisei to demand their rights, the "collaboration" of some Nisei leaders with Army and WRA. All the resentments that had piled up poured out now suddenly in the speeches. The regulation concerning Kibei and harvest work was forgotten. One speaker cried that Nisei were no longer citizens of the United States: "If anyone, any Nisei, thinks he's an American I dare him to try to walk out of this prison. This is no place for us. It's a white man's country." Efforts of a few to curb the denunciation and take a more hopeful view of their situation were booed into silence. Finally the meeting became so tempestuous that an administrator who was present requested the chairman to stop it. Later the project director pronounced the meeting "disgraceful," and thereafter the use of the Japanese language in public gatherings was prohibited. The "Kibei meeting," as it came to be called, was a manifestation of sentiments that had been steadily crystallizing ever since evacuation. The currents of emotion that it roused swept back into the blocks.

During August a series of meetings was held in Poston II, the second to be occupied of the three Poston units. A group of older men who called themselves the Issei Informal Representative Committee sponsored the meetings chiefly for the purpose of discussing a WRA memorandum of June 5. This memorandum, reflecting the desire of WRA officials to provide some recognition of citizenship in the center, ruled that only citizens might hold the elective offices in the community councils which were to be established, thus excluding all Issei from holding such offices. The meetings were conducted for the most part in Japanese. They were quiet as compared with the Manzanar Kibei meeting. Elderly men rose and stated quietly that they did not have confidence in the Nisei, that they felt the WRA ruling was creating a dangerous rift in the community, that in this crisis there was need for parents and children to stick together. Some spoke bitterly of the hopelessness of the whole situation into which Japanese had been thrown in the United States. Others spoke hopefully of making the relocation center into an ideal city if only fathers and sons would work together. One urged appeal to the Spanish Embassy (the neutral protective power for Japanese nationals) in case the United States Government did not show sufficient consideration for evacuees. For the most part serious and dignified, these meetings brought up into the realm of public discussion the basic issues which the older people felt faced them in the centers. Leaders not only in Poston II but also in the other Poston units were stirred and the several points of view became poles around which many of the leaders crystallized their ideas. On August 24 the major issue which they had set out to discuss became an academic one when the exclusion of Issei from elective office was embodied in an official administrative instruction of the WRA.

At Tule Lake on August 26 the center newspaper carried a headline and news story which began:

COUNCIL ACTS TO OUTLAW GANGSTERISM

Deeply concerned over the increasing instances of gangsterism within the colony, the Community Council last night took steps to formulate basic policies to preserve law and order in the community.

The account went on to say that the most recent in a series of assaults by unknown persons against other evacuees had taken place during the night in block 26. The persons assaulted had received threats beforehand and were said to be on a list of persons scheduled to be beaten. The young men singled out had been prominent in one way or another in activities of the Nisei organization, the Japanese-American Citizens League.

The Kibei meeting, the Issei discussions, and the beatings were manifestations of a fundamental adjustment that was taking place among the evacuees. The various segments of the Japanese-American population had reacted differently to the evacuation and the treatment since evacuation at the hands of the United States Government. Family unity had increased in the face of the attack from without. The old cleavages between American and Japanese citizens, children and parents, which had characterized the Japanese-American communities seemed to have been narrowed as all were subjected to the same treatment. Yet on a different level from the family the old cleavages widened. There were young men who refused to accept the treatment as final and spoke vigorously for their views. The ideas of young and old were now in ferment. There had been clashes of personalities and new alignments under the stress of adjusting to Government supervision. The attitude that the group as a whole should take toward this Government supervision was emerging as a crucial issue. What was the meaning of the relocation centers for the future of the Japanese-Americans? Around this issue, in one form or another, revolved most of the broader discussion of the summer, and closely related to it were the beatings which began to take place in all the early centers toward the close of the summer.

Steadily among the older men during the first months in the relocation centers, a conception of what life should be in the centers had begun to crystallize. It was a simple and practical approach to the new situation, strongly influenced by the years of experience with Americans on the West Coast. It dominated the cooperative efforts many had made to convert the blocks into livable places. The view was simply that the centers should be peaceful havens in which to wait out the war. The evacuees should work together to make them as comfortable and as harmonious as possible. There should be compliance with the United States Government's orders. At the same time, however, vigilance was necessary to see that Government treatment did not infringe the rights of interned enemy aliens, for it was obvious that whatever the Government might call the centers, they were essentially internment camps. The Issei in them, like the several hundred whom the Department of Justice had interned, had been involuntarily neutralized by the Government. The Government, having brought them against their will to the centers, had certain obligations, chiefly the provision for elementary needs of food, clothing, and shelter. Moreover, there must be no exploitation of their labor, and since the Government had for all practical purposes classified them as interned enemy aliens it ought not, in accordance with the Geneva Convention, make them do any work which would directly contribute to the war effort against the nation—Japan—in which they had legal citizenship. There was rather general agreement among the older men on this interpretation of their new status and the meaning of the relocation centers.

This view was to have far-reaching consequences in the adjustment of the evacuees to the centers. It was in conflict with the view which the WRA policy makers were developing in the very month in which the tensions of community adjustment intensified in the early centers. The WRA was reaching the decision that the centers should not be considered internment camps. They were to be, on the contrary, merely a stage on the way to new adjustment in American life for Issei and Nisei alike.

Moreover, this view of the centers as neutral, waiting stations was in sharp conflict with the view of another segment of the evacuee population. The citizen Nisei, more deeply shaken by the evacuation and its implications for loss of citizenship, were less able to reach a simple agreement on the meaning of the relocation centers. A majority of them were angry and resentful but unable to see any way out. As their bitterness increased through the summer, they were more and more inclined to listen to the view of the older men, to accept the centers (although more bitterly than the Issei) as places "to rot it out" for the duration of the war. Among them, however, there were leaders who were inclined to no such view. They vigorously opposed what they felt to be fruitless denunciation of the type that came out in the Kibei meeting and, as well, what they felt to be the sterile acceptance of the situation in the dominant Issei conception. Some of these young men were leaders in the Japanese-American Citizens League, although others were not. They had come to the camps with the conviction that although evacuation was misguided it should be complied with as a war measure for the benefit of the country as a whole. Once in the centers they sought desperately to make the situation have some meaning in relation to what other Americans were doing and to their own future in this country. Some of them joined in petitioning the War Department to open the armed services to Nisei. Some eagerly embraced the opportunity to join in the American war effort when the Army proposed to establish camouflage net factories in Manzanar, Poston, and Gila. Their conception was essentially that the relocation centers should be places in which evacuees could demonstrate that they should not have been placed there. Holding this view, they sought to cooperate in all plans of the WRA and inevitably looked to WRA for support.

There were thus two sharply opposed views in the early centers, one embodying a static view of center life aloof from the life of the country, and the other seeking some integration of the people in the centers with all that was going on outside. The first was primarily the view of the older people (although not all Issei held it), but the frustrations and restrictions of center life were drawing into its orbit a majority of the Nisei. The second view was held by only a small minority of the younger men and women, many of whom had participated far less in the former Japanese-American communities than in the wider community around them. Some had been actively antagonistic to most that the Issei leaders of the pre-evacuation communities stood for.

The dominance of the Issei view was fostered by the whole emotional aftermath of evacuation, while that of the Nisei leaders was one that had to be regenerated through acts of faith, once evacuation had taken place. The circumstances of center life, the discharge of many Nisei from the Army, the classification of Nisei by Selective Service boards as "ineligible because of ancestry," the growing evidences of hostility in segments of the American public, and ultimately the construction of fences and guard towers around the centers (Manzanar had been so fenced from the beginning)—all these developments gave an increasingly unreal aura to the Nisei leaders' views. The Issei view of the centers as a sort of temporary dead end, on the other hand, seemed to fit the facts both of past discrimination and present growth of restrictions.

Moreover, negative and static as the Issei view seemed to the crusading young men, it had many positive aspects which seemed obvious to most Issei and even to many Nisei who had spent formative years in Japan. It was a view which, equally with that of the Nisei leaders, related the relocation centers to the war. At the time it was being formulated in the summer of 1942, the Pacific war seemed to be moving steadily toward a Japanese success. Probably all but a handful of Issei believed that the facts indicated that Japan had permanently consolidated her position in the Southwest Pacific. If this were true and Japan should emerge as a real world power, then the position of the Japanese minority in the United States after the war could be expected to improve. Exclusion of the Issei from American citizenship and all the discriminations that accompanied and flowed from that might well be remedied, probably promptly through measures that would be taken at the peace table. In the light of these beliefs the enforced neutrality in the centers was a happy solution for families whose members' citizenship straddled the Pacific conflict.

The implications of the Issei view of the centers unfolded point by point as the evacuees came up against the frame which the WRA was designing for life in the centers. The most important implication of the view was the necessity for solidarity in the face of all that threatened the group. Most Issei felt that there was no intelligent view for Nisei to take other than that all had now been placed in the same position, that Nisei interests now coincided, as they never had before, with those of the Issei. The attempts of Nisei leaders to construe the centers as anything but internment camps seemed to the Issei both futile and contrary to the interests of the whole group. Many Issei were willing to admit that those Nisei who wanted to had the right, for example, to work in the camouflage net factories and so contribute to American war activities. So long as there was no attempt to bring all evacuees into such activities, it was proper for Nisei to engage in them. But Issei generally did not feel that they could rely on the Nisei leadership, which was so interested in relating itself to the American war effort, to uphold the interests of the Issei who were not, and had never been permitted to be, American citizens. They sought a solidarity of Nisei and Issei in the approach to life in the relocation centers.

The nature of the solidarity which Issei sought became clear in the discussion roused by the WRA ruling concerning community councils. This ruling, restricting elective office in the centers to citizens, was precisely in line with the view of the Nisei leaders that citizenship should be given some meaning in the centers. It was regarded by Issei leaders, however, as a profound threat. They felt that it presaged a rift in the solidarity of the group and thereby weakened their whole position in the relocation centers. In the meetings in Poston at which the point was discussed in August, the Issei viewpoint came out clearly. One view held that the Nisei had not demonstrated a capacity for sound leadership of the whole group:

Since the Niseis minds run in different channels, even though they have within their systems a part of our blood, we feel that we cannot entrust our future welfare to the Niseis. . . . We feel that after the poor job that the Niseis have done in California, we cannot possibly entrust our future welfare to that group.

Others were more conciliatory, but still insistent that Nisei not be mis-led into acceptance of the proffered status as official representatives of the whole evacuee group:

Our Nisei are gradually coming to the front and I am happy about it. We parents have had the desire to make them good American citizens and, therefore, we are greatly concerned about them. How can we be most helpful to the Nisei? We want to work together. We know the con-ditions are bad and so we want to make them pleasant. If we don't have equal rights, then there may be instances where we may not be able to work together. I hope the Nisei will understand how much we Issei are thinking and worrying about them.

The feeling that the Nisei did not understand fully what had happend to them was strong, and there were efforts to wake them up to the situation as many Issei saw it:

Will you look forward into the future a little? After peace, what is going to happen to the Nisei? There is no doubt in my mind that they will be kicked around like dogs, as witness the treatment of the Germans in the past post-World War period. I don't know if the Nisei realize the predicament they are in. What we really wanted to hear from the Niseis was a statement to the effect that they will work hand in hand with the Isseis . . . and fight any problems . . . which may arise from time to time.

The ultimate appeal was in terms of the family relationship:

The Issei and Nisei relationship is that of parent and child. It should not be disposed of lightly. Even if the government regulations make a distinction, we should all cooperate to create an ideal city. Your parents came as poor immigrants. They sacrificed a great deal . . . . You should have pride in your ancestors. I believe you who are wise will welcome the cooperation of all to create an ideal city here.

This last statement embodied the essence of the Issei approach to life in the relocation centers. It was a turning in toward the family group and a limiting of the horizon to the neutral haven of the relocation center which then might become "an ideal city."

Over and over again in the months since evacuation the Nisei had been hearing the refrain that all must now stick together. In the meetings discussing the WRA ruling excluding Issei from political office they heard it again in formal speeches:

In our block there is no Issei or Nisei. We only have Japanese in our block. . . . We will elect Nisei representatives. However, we want them to understand that they will be working for all the people as a Japanese and not as an American.

The Issei conception had become crystallized in all centers in the often repeated phrase: "We are all Japanese together." The evacuation had done its work. As nothing else could have, that attack on the basic security of the group was stimulating a solidarity which had not been there before. Most Nisei began to accept it wholeheartedly or else gave up as they had already done in their attempts to find a voice in the block councils. Those who still sought to equate citizenship with community leadership came into head-on collisions with the majority sentiment that had begun to dominate community life by the end of the summer.

The August beatings at Tule Lake constituted another manifestation of the drive toward solidarity among themselves as over against the Caucasians who had attacked the group through evacuation. It was a sinister manifestation outside of and below the political expressions and public efforts at persuasion. Gangs of young men who threatened, intimidated, and sometimes beat other evacuees formed in every center, early and late, some two to four months after center opening. In their first stages, the gangs did not operate at random. The men they chose to intimidate or beat up were carefully selected and for very specific reasons. The objects of their attacks were leaders of the Japanese-American Citizens League or like-minded Nisei. The reasons for selecting such young men were well understood by evacuees.

The leadership of the Japanese-American Citizens League, after initial efforts to forestall evacuation, had taken the stand that thoroughgoing cooperation in the process with Army and Government agencies was the only possible course. Public statements of JACL leaders urging cooperation and acceptance of evacuation as the Japanese-American contribution to the war effort earned the organization the reputation of having "collaborated" with the Government against the best interests of the whole group. Southern California evacuees were embittered against some JACL leaders because of what they felt had been efforts on their part to save the Nisei from evacuation at the expense of the Issei. Attitudes of antagonism towards specific JACL leaders were fostered by old, long-standing political conflicts in the California communities and by suspicion concerning activities they had engaged in just before evacuation. There was widespread belief that JACL leaders had turned over to the FBI for sums of money the names of Issei community leaders and that such information had led to the internment of the leaders. The sons of many internees felt bitterly over what they regarded as unjust detention of their parents and brutal treatment by the FBI agents. They sought someone to blame and the JACL leaders served the purpose.

The Japanese-American Citizens League during the months just after evacuation quickly became a scapegoat for all the misfortune of the evacuees. It was blamed for all that had happened and its leaders became symbols of betrayal. These feelings increased intensely when some JACL leaders in the centers began to take the position that the armed services should be reopened to Nisei. The petitions of Manzanar Nisei leaders to Washington officials became known and were interpreted as further betrayal of the group. To a majority of the parents the drafting of their sons after the family had lost its economic stake and was still in the re-location center appeared as the ultimate in injustice and a threat to the only security remaining, namely, the solidarity of the family. Feeling ran even higher against the JACL leaders than it had in the first months as evidenced by the organized gangs intimidating JACL leaders into silence and carrying out vengeance for the already accomplished acts of "informing" against their fathers to the FBI and "collaborating" in the evacuation.

The young men who carried out the beatings at Tule Lake were not caught. Similar attacks began to occur in Poston and Manzanar, and the undercover intimidation assumed a wider scope. Not only JACL leaders heard that their names were on "the list," but also individuals who were merely working cooperatively with the WRA administrators in the centers, particularly young men who had obtained good jobs during the early formation of the administrative shell. The terms "informer," *inu* (the Japanese word for dog), "administration stooge" began to be heard more and more frequently. Evacuees who had had no connection with JACL policies or organization were beaten or threatened. Fear and suspicion spread through the blocks. Individuals became fearful of getting on intimate terms with administrators or urging cooperation in some project suggested by the administration. Some evacuees who had been working well with administrators and accepting responsibility in center management withdrew suddenly. Fear was rampant in all three of the early centers. The technique of intimidation was enforcing a solidarity of evacuees as against Caucasians, based chiefly on fear. The result was a sharper separation of evacuees from WRA staff and a sense of tension in most relations between the two groups.

The two related trends in the evacuee communities (the Issei conception and the intimidation attempts) were converging by different means toward the same result—toward solidarity among evacuees and opposition to the Caucasians. They were, however, not compatible with each other. The Issei concept of an "ideal city" had to be built on law and order, and the Issei ideal was destined to triumph.

THE OUTSIDE

When schools opened in September high school boys in one center expressed their cynicism by scrawling in chalk on the black tar paper walls of their classroom: "Jap Prison"; and, like inmates of prisons, the evacuees generally fell into the habit of referring to the universe beyond the boundaries of the relocation centers as "the outside." It was a universe with which they had steadily lost touch from the moment they stepped into the assembly centers.

For many evacuees as they left the assembly centers, interest in the outside world focused down on the small towns near the relocation centers. Evacuees who went to Poston quickly became aware of the barber shop in nearby Parker, Arizona, which had in black crayon on its door the words: "Jap, keep out, you rat." People scheduled to go to Jerome and Rohwer speculated in the assembly centers and on the trains en route about racial prejudice in the Arkansas towns, whether or not Japanese would be equated with Negroes and subject to the same discriminations. Many of the older people expected extreme hostility in the small towns neighboring the centers and felt that the military police would be a necessary guard against attacks from nearby farmers and townsmen. Once in the centers, this interest continued, and the nature of prejudice and good will in the nearby towns became a basis for judging the attitudes of all Americans. Except with the WRA staff there was almost no other contact during the early months on which to base a judgment.

The attitudes of the people in the vicinity of the relocation centers turned out to be much like those of people in the West Coast communities from which the evacuees had come—a peculiar mixture of hostility and friendliness. There were shops in most of the towns which posted "No Japs" signs of one sort or another, but as shopping privileges were granted to evacuees and it became evident that there would be a large volume of trade such shops generally became a minority. Project directors worked hard to promote good feeling and tolerance and to break down the inevitable identification of the Japanese-Americans with the Japanese with whom the country was at war. Local people were invited to visit the centers and some made inspection tours of the centers, usually with the result of offers of various kinds to help the evacuees. The four western centers—Manzanar, Poston, Gila, and Tule Lake—remained the most isolated from local contacts and the most hedged about by minor local hostilities. The relations of the later centers with neighboring people were generally somewhat better.

Nevertheless there were "incidents" of various kinds. In Arkansas someone shot at a Nisei soldier in a town not far from the Jerome center. In Idaho the Republican Committee of the large town nearest to the Minidoka center paid for an advertisement advocating rigid supervision and detention of all Japanese-Americans. In every little town neighboring the centers from Cody, Wyoming, to McGeehee, Arkansas, some evacuees at some time or other during the early months encountered discrimination and prejudice in some form or saw evidence of it in a letter to the editor of the local paper. At the same time local ministerial associations or other groups were proffering aid in the form of contributions of shrubs or flowers to make the center more pleasant or gifts of books

Schools were in operation in the autumn months of 1942 at most centers. This group at Rohwer, Ark., showed exuberance as in any school, unmindful of equipment which was scant in the early months.

to the libraries or at least a gesture embodied in an editorial or a public statement of some kind. Such gestures received less attention in the centers than the evidences of hostility and prejudice. Each unpleasant "incident" was blown up in rumor to large proportions and discussed passionately by the evacuees. The news of a discrimination near one center went by letter to other centers. There was little balance, in the atmosphere of the centers, in the appraisal of the events. The conviction grew through the summer that the outside world was increasingly hostile and that evacuees would be better off to remain in the centers. This feeling was backed up in September by the news that Selective Service had officially classified all Nisei as ineligible, on the grounds of ancestry, to serve in the armed forces of the United States.

The conviction of increasing American hostility which settled over the

High school students changing classes in tar-paper covered barracks at Rohwer; it was young people like these who chalked on the school buildings such phrases as "Jap Prison."

centers was hardly touched by indications here and there of another trend. Almost at the same time that Selective Service was closed to all Nisei, the War Department began to recruit young men from the centers for special training in Army Intelligence schools. Then, as farmers in the West found themselves faced with a labor shortage at harvest time, recruiters for the big sugar-beet companies began to appear in the centers with offers to the young men of jobs throughout the western states at going wages. The cotton growers of southern Arizona also applied pressure to the Commanding General of the Western Defense Command to allow evacuees to leave the centers of Poston and Gila to pick cotton. These developments were interpreted by evacuees in different ways. A few welcomed them as opportunities to participate in the United States war effort, to demonstrate the loyalty that they felt to the country. To others the recruitment for Army Intelligence seemed a threat to family security, and in some cases young men who wanted to take the opportunities found themselves faced with parental opposition. The offers of outside work at going wages seemed to most not to be indications of any good will, but rather of the desperate plight of the farmers. The cotton picking was viewed in the same light by the majority and, moreover, seemed to be, with its offer of outside wages, a threat to the cooperative view of center life, with everyone on an equal basis, which some leaders were trying to develop. Nevertheless, young men did begin to respond to the opportunities in the beet fields to make something more than $16 a month. WRA began to issue "seasonal leave" for the harvest work and the young men flowed out of the centers by the hundreds. By late fall some 10,000 were out of the centers temporarily, making going wages throughout the western states. The centers, whether evacuees wished it or not, were linked solidly with the outside world.

As the pressures for harvest work intensified in the late summer, the WRA policy makers began to see it as a means for furthering the idea which had been developing among them that a way out of the centers for the evacuees should be found. They had already encouraged church and other groups to help college students among the evacuees to continue their education in colleges outside the exclusion zone. A trickle of students had begun to leave the centers for this purpose. Now, with the growing demands for evacuee labor in the harvest, the WRA developed a policy of "leave clearance" to enable evacuees to meet this demand. By October the National Director of the WRA was making a tour of the relocation centers announcing a general plan for resettlement of the evacuees outside the centers. At Topaz he said that he hoped to see 20,000 evacuees resettled in normal communities within a year and that he hoped everyone would be out and re-established before the end of the war. For the top policy makers in Washington this announcement marked the culmination of a serious weighing of the possibilities for the future of the whole Japanese-American group. It was a decision based on the feeling that people would deteriorate in the camps and that the best solution of the problems created by the evacuation lay in the quickest possible re-establishment in homes and jobs in normal communities outside the excluded zone. It constituted a rejection of the idea of internment for the group and an effort to link them again with the national life from which they had been isolated.

The different segments of the evacuee population reacted in different ways to the new prospect. For the majority the new policy was not so decisive as it seemed to the administrators. During the same period that the policy makers had been arriving at their decision, the majority of evacuees, and particularly the more thoughtful leaders among the older men, had been with increasing conviction arriving at the conception of the centers as quite tolerable havens for the duration of the war. Those who had spent several months in the early centers had been adjusting themselves systematically to this view. The whole trend, usually with the encouragement of WRA center staff, had been to regard the centers as war-duration homes and to find ways of making them livable and as self-sufficient as possible. This view was solidly rooted among the Issei by the time the National Director made his announcements. To them, therefore, the new policy seemed hardly credible; at least the plan for resettlement of the whole group did not seem really practicable. It disturbed them that the National Director should have such a view, but they had come to feel that "the Government" was capricious and that such an impracticable scheme as this probably would not be carried out. It introduced merely another factor of uncertainty for speculation and rumor. Moreover, at about the same time that the announcement was officially made, the Army began to build fences and watch towers around the borders of all those centers which did not already have them.

For many young people who had been bored and miserable in the centers and in active revolt against having to live with people with whom they felt nothing in common, the new prospect of leaving the centers was welcomed with enthusiasm. The young students eager to get on with their education and young Nisei families who had friends or relatives in Denver and Salt Lake City moved out quickly, as soon as they could get leave clearance. This trend made for a little more unity and harmony in the blocks as these people left during the fall.

For center staff members the new policy raised problems which they could see immediately. For those in the early centers it meant considerable reorientation of their thinking. They had been struggling with the task of laying the foundations for more or less stable communities. Most of their thinking had been in that direction since no other very clear prospect had been held out to them. Now they had to contemplate what seemed an even more difficult job, namely, the management of an unstable community which would be constantly losing population. There would be readjustments to be made constantly to the loss of individuals trained in some aspect of center operation, the need for constantly breaking in new persons in responsible jobs, as people should leave. To the staff in the early centers the readjustment was more difficult than for those in the later ones. In those centers opened after July—all but Manzanar, Poston, Tule Lake, and Gila—the staff were more or less aware of the trend in top policy. They were not already set in another direction.

Nevertheless all centers got some taste promptly of what the new policy would mean. New and old centers alike lost hundreds of young men from September to December as they responded to the recruiting for harvest workers. From Minidoka, 2,000 men went out within six weeks after the center opened. Almost as many left Granada, and all the other centers lost from 800 to 1,200 workers, mostly the more vigorous and able young men. Although in the later centers this probably made for a better long-term adjustment in the community, as the administrators fell back on the older men in organizing the centers, it also gave a foretaste of the difficulties involved in a resettlement program. There were shortages of labor in most centers, difficulties in getting persons to haul coal and do the heavy work of center operation. Then there were the problems of the return in the early winter of the young men after the seasonal work, men with money in their pockets who were not too anxious to work, and the upsetting of the adjustment that had been achieved in employment and center organization. What was to be an abiding contradiction—the crosspull of straddling the outside world and the economic vacuum of the centers—had entered center life.

CRISES

As the program of Government supervision unfolded, each successive development seemed to create a new contradiction in the lives of the evacuees. There were reasons—good reasons in Washington—for the features of policy, but that did not make them any less contradictory in the lives of the people in the relocation centers. The classification of people into evacuees and Caucasians struck at the roots of cooperation and laid the foundations for division of interest and mutual distrust. The leveled wages demanded substitution for economic incentive of community interest—in communities that did not yet exist. The isolation of the centers reared a bafflingly unreal world of rumor and fear which competed successfully for evacuee belief with a relentlessly real world outside the communities. The reality of Issei dominance in block life was faced by the unreality of Nisei dominance in community councils. The majority of evacuees, having progressively adjusted to the concept of "ideal cities," now were asked to consider the dissolution of the communities. Responsible staff members in the centers who had been struggling through the summer to achieve stability had begun to feel the contradictions as keenly as the evacuees themselves. In October, addressing a Nisei mass meeting called to discuss the most recent evidences of restriction on citizens, the project director of Tule Lake declared: "I have a thankless job as director of this project." The mood of hopeful community building in the early centers was giving way to one of frustration. The mood of the blocks had penetrated the administration area.

The later centers, settled in August and after, were still largely in the stage of development that had characterized the early centers in May and June. Moreover the evacuees who entered them were settling into a somewhat different mold. The basic living conditions and the fundamental restrictions were the same, but the framework of policy to which they must adjust was better defined. They had learned something about living with one another in the assembly centers, and they were to learn by proxy during the fall from what took place in the less fortunate early centers. In Manzanar and Poston the resolution of paradox was moving toward a climax which many evacuees sensed as early as September.

Crisis: Poston

In Poston I, after a brief and frustrating false start, a framework of community institutions designed to link evacuees and administrators in cooperative effort steadily grew up during the summer. In response to the WRA announcement that "It will be up to each community to plan its design of community life," administrators in May and June had stimulated leaders from among both Nisei and Issei to work out a plan of community organization. They organized a Civic Planning Board and by late June had prepared a constitution. Only then did they become aware of the memorandum of June 5 which ordered another form of organization and excluded Issei from holding elective office. The Civic Planning Board disbanded and discarded its plan. The project attorney of the center staff assumed leadership in carrying out the Washington plan. An election was called and thirty-six young men, all but one under forty, were chosen, one from a block, to form a Temporary Community Council.

There was little interest among evacuees as the council took office. Amid talk in the blocks about "administration stooges," the council began work. The chairman had been active in the Los Angeles chapter of the Japanese-American Citizens League. He had also been active in the Santa Anita Assembly Center as an outspoken critic of the food and mess-hall conditions. Sensitive to current dissatisfactions about food in Poston and aware of rumors that the project steward was engaged in graft at the expense of evacuees, the council formed a Food Committee. The committee promptly sought facts about the management of the mess division. In similar fashion, in response to the widespread anxieties and complaints about the hospital, a Health Committee was formed and proceeded to investigate the hospital. This exploration of the framework within which evacuees had to live was not taken in good part by the administrators. They talked of cooperation and of the council's function as getting the people behind the administration to support the administration's plans for community development. They did not see the council's actions as the real basis of cooperation which they were. They were convinced themselves that they were doing everything in their power to make the hospital and the mess halls satisfactory. They did not realize that suspicion and distrust was so deep, and that the investigations sprang from the real need of the evacuees for understanding just how the men in whose hands they had been placed were going about their business. They refused to let the Food Committee see the steward's books and thereby increased the suspicion. They also objected when the council chairman showed signs of carrying out a wider exploration of the framework in which evacuees were living. He wrote letters to Washington officials about conditions and needs on the center and sought to keep in touch with them personally and directly. The administrators began to write off the council as a group which could not be relied upon to proceed "constructively" to get the cooperation of the people.

At the same time that the young men on the council were incurring the disfavor of the administrators, hostility to them was growing up in the community. There was some appreciation here and there of their efforts to find out how the center was managed, but these efforts had not been successful and most of the older influential men were inclined to feel that this proved the ineptness of the Nisei leaders. The block managers, who like the council consisted of a group composed of one man from each block, had become an ever more important institution in the community. Through them the residents were constantly getting tangible results from the administration. When they wanted specific things, the block managers reported it and they either got them or got definite information that they were not to be had. The councilmen were a somewhat confusing element in block life. Sometimes their information about administration plans and activities did not gibe with the block managers' information. Some competition for prestige and position in the blocks developed between councilmen and block managers. Often from the point of view of the block resident the councilman seemed superfluous. The wider issues of center life with which the council attempted to concern itself did not seem relevant to the real and specific needs of the individuals. In addition to such criticisms of the council, active antagonism was developing to specific members of the group. The general hostility to the Japanese-American Citizens League played its part. The chairman and other councilmen had been active in that organization. One in particular had had a bad reputation before evacuation and was specifically suspected of having been an FBI informer. In the fall he was reported to be on "the list" scheduled for beating up by a young men's gang. His reputation colored the community reaction to the council as a whole. Thus despite the efforts of the council to do something about allaying the most intense anxieties and suspicions of the majority of evacuees, people came more and more to refer to them as "administration stooges" or as an ineffective "child council." The council was between two fires and was fast becoming a symbol of the evils of "collaboration," as anti-administration feelings focused on them.

The top staff was by no means unaware of the antagonism of the community to the council, nor of the dissatisfaction with the ruling against Issei office holding. The project attorney who organized the election of the council also encouraged the formation of a group of older men, called the Issei Advisory Board, which was to act in an advisory capacity to the council and the administration. This board, consisting of one Issei from each block, was formed in August, amid considerably more interest in the blocks than had attended the formation of the community council. It proceeded to hold meetings separately from the council. The chairman of the council, although he himself met with the board and listened to its advice, resisted the holding of joint meetings, fearing domination of proceedings by the Issei group if that were done. He made it clear that, although he would work with the Issei board, he nevertheless approved of the WRA distinction between citizens and aliens and would seek to maintain that distinction in the method of work of the council.

The Issei Advisory Board went on consolidating its position. Its members were in touch, as the Nisei council was not, with the deeper currents of community sentiment. Its members were in fact spokesmen of those deeper currents. They believed generally in the view of centers as neutral havens for the duration of the war and in the need for solidarity of all segments of the evacuees in order to insure making the center into what they felt it should be. They voiced the general distrust of the administrators, discussed unfulfilled promises such as the failure to relieve the

housing situation, and denounced the retention of unpopular and distrusted young men in key positions in the block managers' organization,
the community stores, and elsewhere. Feeling the council to be ineffective
and feeling lack of sympathy with their position on the part of its
chairman, the board became increasingly critical of the community
council.

In this atmosphere of competing political groups, intimidation by
gang elements increased through October and early November. Several
persons were beaten up in Poston I and the beaters were not discovered.
Nisei leaders became fearful, and the atmosphere of the blocks became
tense. The WRA staff felt their relations with evacuees becoming increasingly strained. Attitudes of suspicion grew on both sides. The
center seemed to be ripe for some sort of explosion.

It came on November 18. A few days before, one of the councilmen
was attacked and seriously beaten. While he lay in the hospital, FBI
agents came to the center to ferret out the perpetrators of the beating.
They followed leads to various barracks and finally, in an action that
reminded evacuees of the days following Pearl Harbor, they picked up
two young men as suspects and placed them in the center jail. One was a
popular judo expert; the other was a popular and civic-minded young
man who had been active in community affairs. For two days they were
kept in the jail and rumors spread that they were to be removed from the
center to the hostile "outside" for trial. Sentiment that the young men
were innocent became widespread and petitions were framed requesting
their release. Hardly anyone believed that they would get a fair trial in
an outside court. On the morning of the third day a crowd collected at
the jail and announced their determination to prevent the removal of the
young men. They refused to disperse at the request of the acting project
director.

Around the jailed men and their defenders community feeling crystallized rapidly. Members of the Issei Advisory Board, personal friends of
the young men, and others spoke to people in various blocks. Support
for the defense of the suspects was marshalled. Hundreds more people
gathered at the jail during the afternoon, men and women, whole families with their children. From somewhere the rumor spread that there was
to be a "strike," and by noon evacuees were leaving the offices in the
administration area. In an atmosphere of emotion running high, the
Nisei council met, passed a resolution urging the release of the suspects
for later trial, heard the acting project director reject the request, and
resigned in a body. That night the block managers resigned. As night
came on, in the increasingly determined atmosphere of the crowd around
the jail, an Emergency Committee of representatives from all the blocks
was formed and immediately dominated by leaders from the Issei Advis-

ory Board. A general strike of all workers in the center, except those in the essential services of mess, hospital, fire protection, and police was called. The community was in defiant demonstration against the administration and all official channels of communication between the two groups had been broken. The Issei Advisory Board was dominant.

This was no ordinary strike, such as had occurred with this work crew or that. It was a community upheaval and members of the WRA staff were well aware of it. Some staff members excitedly urged putting the whole affair down by force, calling in the military police and dispersing the crowd with tear gas or guns. The top staff rejected the idea, sensing that force could not solve the problems which lay at the root of the demonstration. They decided to find some means for negotiation with the strike leaders.

Meanwhile the consolidation of the community behind the strike leaders proceeded. Block managers or Issei advisers or others, no longer acting in administration-sponsored official capacities, organized their blocks for support. Regular shifts of men, women, and children from each block were organized to go and stand watch beside the little fires that had been built to keep the crowd warm. Flags with the numerals of the blocks were mounted on poles and rose over each group of block people around the police station. Pictures of "dogs" (informers) appeared on the walls of the police station and on placards among the crowd —symbols of betrayal of the group which focused the feelings of the crowd. As people relieved each other in continuous streams from the blocks through the night, the leaders held meetings in the adjacent mess hall. Speakers denounced "informers" of all kinds; all the host of grievances of the people were voiced again and again. Speakers who attempted to speak in English were denounced and booed to silence. Nisei on the outskirts of the crowd began to wonder if there were not something in all this. Maybe a solid demonstration was needed, and certainly there was a civil rights issue here since the young men were being held on suspicion beyond the legal time limit. Out in the blocks there were men and women who refused to participate, who resented and resisted the pressures that were applied to them, but they were in a minority. Community sentiments had crystallized in the demonstration, and for the first time since evacuation there was a sense of striking back at oppressors.

The existence of the crowd acting in defiance of administrative desires had a powerful impact on the WRA staff in their barracks and offices at the edge of the community. Fear, suspicion, and hatred sprang up among some of them. They could hear records of Japanese music played through loud speakers to the crowd. All were distraught and some began to identify the demonstrators with the Japanese enemy in the Pacific.

The majority, however, were anxious for some peaceful solution. Yet, even though they felt disposed to visit friends among the evacuees to talk and get at the roots of the demonstration, they found as the strike wore on for several days that there was an invisible line between them and every evacuee in the center. They sensed quickly that visiting an evacuee in his barracks might be dangerous to the evacuee. A friendly visit challenged the solidarity that the evacuees had momentarily achieved; evacuees indicated that they might be beaten if they had traffic with Caucasians. Still, there were evacuees who crossed the line to declare loyalty to a friend on the staff or even to offer to finish an urgent job. Such offers were quickly discouraged by staff members, again with the welfare of the evacuees in mind. No one crossed the line even for a moment without intense consciousness of it. A solidarity of the evacuees vis-à-vis the Caucasians had been achieved in part by force and intimidation, but for most through the opening of a channel for expression of accumulated resentments and frustrations.

The issue broadened as the rift widened between evacuees and administrators, while both sought a basis for negotiation. It was evident that the holding of the suspects was little more than the catalyst of community sentiments which arose out of still deeper issues. As representatives of the administration talked with the Issei leaders of the community, it became clear what the latter wanted: a real voice in the management of the community. Primarily, they felt that the wrong evacuees had been selected for responsible positions in the center organization; inexperienced and untrustworthy persons who did not command the respect of the community were in too many places of responsibility. They felt that a board, to be called an Honor Court, composed of elected persons with good reputations, should have the power to pass on persons in key positions. If this were done, there would be unity, and law and order would replace disorganization and gangsterism. They also felt that the administrators had not shown that they could deal effectively with the evacuees. The orders and desires of the administration should be passed down to the people through an executive board of elected evacuees who understood "the psychology of the people." This would produce smoothness and efficiency in the center operations. Finally they wanted really representative committees or councils, or whatever the administration wanted to call them, to discuss and work with the administrators. Negotiation went on over these points. The objectives of the Issei leaders—law and order, smoothness in center operation, and real community organization—were precisely what the administrators wanted. They differed on the nature of the institutions which could achieve these ends, and some administrators strongly distrusted the newly emerged leaders. At the end of the week of discussion, during which administrators and evacuees got in touch with one another as they never had before, the project director and the strike leaders reached agreement on the major objectives. One of the suspects had already been released for lack of evidence and the other was released for trial by the center Judicial Commission. The crowd at the police station listened to a friendly speech by the project director, disbanded, and went back to their blocks.

Crisis: Manzanar

Within a week after the settlement of the Poston strike, Manzanar faced an even more serious crisis. The background differed in many important respects, but the same crosscurrents of community life were present. Unlike Poston, Manzanar had never fully accepted the official framework of community organization as set forth in the WRA self-government regulations. The block managers, at first under the Wartime Civilian Control Administration while Manzanar was still an assembly center, and later under the WRA, constituted the single over-all community organization. At first they formed a body which was called the Block Leaders Council, consisting of both Issei and Nisei, with Issei predominant. There were members of the group who acquired the name of administration stooges, but for the most part the men were respected in their blocks and were in close touch with majority sentiment. The Block Leaders Council was to some extent reorganized at two different times, once in response to the WRA administrators' suggestion that the leaders obtain the approval of their blocks through election and again, in preparation for the election of a community council, to conform to the WRA regulation that block managers be appointed by the administration. The name was changed from Block Leaders Council to Block Managers Assembly after the second reorganization, but in the main, from April to December, it was the same institution throughout. In October the community voted against the institution of a Nisei Community Council, and there was no Issei Advisory Board. The political organization of Manzanar was, therefore, simple and existed more or less continuously as a body of leaders in close touch with the community and representative of the variety of opinion in the blocks. It was not from this source that conflict developed.

Manzanar differed from Poston in another very important respect: there was more spontaneous organization of groups not sponsored by the WRA regulations or the center staff. The discord that developed was expressed chiefly through these organizations. A number of vocal and active young Nisei leaders came to Manzanar from Los Angeles. They differed among themselves; some had been active in the Japanese-American Citizens League, others were known among the Japanese as *aka*, or left-wingers. They did, however, agree on the concept of making the centers into communities in which evacuees could contribute to the war effort and on the necessity for opening up the armed forces to Nisei. In July some of the leaders formed a Manzanar Citizens Federation which they hoped would escape the stigma of the JACL, but which stood for much that the JACL leaders had stood for. The famous Kibei meeting in August was in large measure an antagonistic reaction to this new group and its doctrines. The sort of young men who arose in the Kibei meeting to denounce the evacuation and the treatment of citizens in the centers had a vigorous spokesman in a Nisei who had fought in the first World War and had since the evacuation become intensely bitter against the United States. He and his supporters were in constant conflict with leaders of the Citizens Federation through the summer and fall.

There was another spontaneous organization in Manzanar not provided for in the WRA regulations. This was the Kitchen Workers Union headed by men who were antagonized by particular members of the Manzanar staff and who steadily developed a bitter anti-administration feeling. One in particular became convinced that there was graft among the WRA staff, that sugar and other food meant for evacuees was being appropriated and sold for their own benefit by members of the steward's department and others. The suspicion that developed around food anxieties was even stronger in Manzanar than in Poston. Kitchen workers' leaders opposed the Citizens Federation leaders less on the ground of their attitudes toward the war and the draft than on the ground of their cooperative attitudes toward WRA staff.

As in the other centers, gang intimidation grew up in Manzanar in August and intensified during the fall. When the issue of the establishment of a Nisei council came up in October, threatening notes and notices appeared urging nonparticipation in self-government, signed by "Blood Brothers." The block managers and Kitchen Workers Union in November pushed an investigation of the use of sugar in the center. Late in November a prominent JACL leader was beaten. He had attended a JACL convention in Salt Lake City and was believed to have presented himself as a representative of all the people of Manzanar in urging that the armed services be opened to Nisei. On his return he was severely beaten, and immediately a leader of the Kitchen Workers Union, who had been active in pushing the sugar investigation, was picked up as a suspect. He was lodged in the jail of a nearby town and then returned to the center jail, as feeling ran high in the community. A group of young men formed and they apparently quickly formulated two purposes: to beat up further the already beaten JACL leader in the hospital and to release the suspect from the center jail. Military police were called in to maintain order. One of them fired on the crowd that had formed near the jail, two evacuees were killed, and the center was shaken for weeks. Working relations were re-established and some community equilibrium restored only after long conferences between the project director and the block leaders.

Crises were common in all the centers. This one at Topaz, Utah, in 1943, arose from the incident of a sentry shooting an elderly man who merely stepped beyond the strands of barbed wire marking the boundary of the center. He had no intention of escaping. The funeral ceremony became a protest demonstration, the size of the crowd indicating the tension that lay just under the surface in the first year of impoundment.

Effects of the Crises

The effects of these crises within the two centers in which they occurred were very similar. They cleared an air that had become heavy with distrust on both sides. They brought the administrators decisively into touch with the evacuees' view of life in the centers. They revealed unmistakably to both evacuees and at least some administrators the crosscurrents in the communities. The specific effects in terms of influence on community organization in the two centers were quite different in detail, but in both they opened the way to foundations for sound working relations between staff and the evacuee community. In Manzanar, in line with the tradition already established, a simple community organization now took definite form. It consisted of a single group of block leaders, elected by the block people without reference to citizenship. They began to work directly with the top administrator and constituted clear-cut channels from their block people up to the top administration. In Poston, also in the tradition already established there, the strike resulted in an elaborate set of community institutions with many positions of status for evacuees. The Nisei council emerged again, but with new leaders and a close working relationship with the Issei Advisory Board. Other institutions, such as a Central Executive Board and a Labor Relations Board, gave wide opportunity for Issei participation in positions of influence. Both centers entered more peaceful periods, but through different means. In Manzanar, following the crisis, Nisei leaders of both clashing groups were removed from the center, and community life fell under the domination largely of Issei leaders. The chief leaders were not removed from Poston, but the strike had pointed the way to means for cooperation between Issei and Nisei in political life. New Nisei leaders emerged who had the confidence of the influential Issei leaders, and gradually accomodation of interests was achieved.

The crises also affected the other eight centers profoundly. Every center learned about them quickly and speculation grew as to the real causes. Staff and evacuees in the other centers knew that the materials for such explosions were present in their communities. The same dissatisfactions and anxieties were present. In some degree the same crosscurrents of community sentiment were recognizable. They had felt similar tensions to those which preceded the Poston and Manzanar incidents. There was a feeling that the same sort of explosion could occur in any center. Thus, although it was probably true that community or mob action could only be crystallized by direct attack on specific individuals as in the jailing of suspects in Manzanar and Poston, nevertheless the sense of being on the brink of similar crisis in the other centers served as a sanction on both staff and evacuee actions. Responsible evacuee leaders as well as staff worked more carefully to avoid the precipitation of similar incidents.

The repercussions of the crises in the outside world were far reaching. To most outsiders who read of them in the newspapers where they made front-page news they seemed to be evidences of subversive activities in the centers. The complexities of community adjustment that lay back of them were hidden from the outsiders. Particularly in the regions near the centers, the "riots" gave rise to rumors of dangerous action to be expected from the evacuees. Everywhere that the news penetrated, the result was increased misunderstanding of Japanese-Americans and more ammunition for the campaign to further restrict the evacuees.

2.

BEING SORTED

The decisive action of evacuation set in motion in the United States two currents of opinion towards persons of Japanese ancestry. On the one hand it crystallized suspicion of the group far beyond the borders of the coastal states. On the other hand it stimulated a reappraisal of the assumptions on which the evacuation decision seemed to be based. The two approaches to the 110,000 persons now uprooted in the relocation centers developed rapidly during the summer and fall of 1942. As the people themselves sought to work out some way of life in the isolation of the centers, the two forces that were shaping their fate interacted and clashed in state legislatures, in Government offices in Washington, and in the halls of Congress. There was less and less possibility that the evacuees could remain secluded from the national life. They were with increasing sureness becoming a national issue.

In September an American Legion Convention in Kansas City took up the issue of the Japanese-Americans. The convention discussed the admission of young men and women evacuees to colleges east of the evacuated zone, where certain church groups, encouraged by the WRA, had arranged for them to continue their education. The American Legion leadership took the view that the students threatened the security of the country. Like many others, Legion spokesmen interpreted the fact of evacuation as proving the disloyalty of the whole group. They protested the release of students and of harvest workers on the assumption that every Japanese-American was a potential saboteur. Not only the Legion leadership, but also influential newspapers here and there in the West and state legislators in states into which the student resettlers were going, took up the cry. They wanted the Japanese-Americans, all of them, kept locked up.

Simultaneously those who had been thrown into close contact with the evacuated people were reaching a different view. The WRA staff, various church groups who had come to the assistance of the Japanese-Americans during evacuation, and officials of the War Department had begun to see sharp distinctions among the group. They were steadily becoming convinced that only a small minority, if any, constituted any threat to the country's security. They were beginning to feel that opportunities should be given to as many as possible to demonstrate their loyalty and that this could never be done so long as they were penned up in the relocation centers. War Department officials, in particular, had been made aware of the large numbers of Nisei who were embittered by the denial of right to serve in the armed forces. They had received petitions from Nisei leaders to reopen Selective Service, and some officers had had close contact with Nisei in their efforts to recruit them for the Intelligence Service. By January, War Department officals were convinced that they should give Nisei a chance to demonstrate their loyalty.

A plan was formulated to call for volunteers for the Army from the relocation centers and at the same time to register all male citizens of draft age. The response to this program was to serve as a basis for determining whether or not to reopen Selective Service to all Nisei. Once the plan was settled, the WRA policy makers decided to take advantage of it by simultaneously conducting in the centers a registration of all adults. This would provide a basis for leave clearance for all those evacuees determined not to be dangerous to resettle outside the centers east of the excluded zone. For by this time the WRA had become convinced that the best solution of the problems of the evacuees lay in getting them out of the centers and reestablished in the industrial and agricultural life of the country. Only in this way, reasoned the WRA officials, could the evacuees take roots again and reintegrate themselves in American life.

At about the same time that the Army-WRA registration was being put into execution, the American Legion resolution protesting the WRA's leave clearance program and recommending transfer of the centers to the Army was embodied in a Senate bill which came up to the Senate Military Affairs Committee for consideration. The two forces that were shaping the evacuees' destiny—one working for tighter restriction and the other for restoration to a place in American society—thus found their ways to level of national action almost simultaneously. They were to clash for another twelve months and the conflict was to shake the lives of the people in the centers as deeply as had evacuation itself.

REGISTRATION—A NEW CRISIS

Early in February teams of Army officers flew to each of the ten centers to conduct, in conjunction with the WRA staffs, the registration agreed on by the War Department and the War Relocation Authority. They went into conference with the project directors and with the one member of each center staff who had previously been called to Washington for a hurried discussion of the meaning and procedures of registration.

To Army officers and many WRA staff members the registration appeared to be an important move on the part of the War Department to correct the discrimination against Nisei. It offered an opportunity to the young men to show their loyalty in concrete ways. There was to be a call for volunteers. The officers were to receive applications for service in Army combat teams composed entirely of Japanese-Americans. If many volunteered from the centers, that would in itself, even before they proved themselves in combat, indicate to the country the essential loyalty of the group. But even for those who might not volunteer there was another means of showing loyalty. Every man of military service age was to be asked to fill out a questionnaire which in addition to basic information about the individual would contain his answers to two questions dealing with loyalty to the United States. These questions, numbered 27 and 28 on the questionnaire forms, were conceived by the War Department as the general test of loyalty for the Nisei. They were worded for simple "Yes" and "No" answers:

No. 27: Are you willing to serve in the armed forces of the United States on combat duty, wherever ordered?

No. 28: Will you swear unqualified allegiance to the United States of America and faithfully defend the United States from any and all attack by foreign or domestic forces, and foreswear any form of allegiance or obedience to the Japanese Emperor, or any other foreign government, power, or organization?

To WRA officials in Washington who had been working with the War Department, the registration of the young men by the Army seemed to point the way to further reduction of the restrictions that had been imposed on all the Japanese-Americans. They had decided to extend the registration to all adults in the centers. The same questionnaires, with the same loyalty question concerning unqualified allegiance to the United States, were to be submitted to all female Nisei and to all Issei men and women. The questionnaires were simply labeled differently: Application for Leave Clearance. This embodied the basis for carrying out the plan of the WRA policy makers to open the way for all evacuees back into the productive life of the nation. As each person filled out the Application for Leave Clearance he would furnish information on which his eligibility to resettle from a center could be determined. Thus a basis would be laid for a general speeding up of resettlement, the people could move rapidly out of the center, and so return to a normal life free from the restrictions of the relocation centers.

Granada, Colo.

Dubious, defiant, or thoughtful moods expressed on the faces of Nisei as they are being asked to register for the armed services in February of 1943. Being asked to serve while one's family was being held in a relocation center was more than an ordinary sacrifice. The officer explains that if the young men join the special combat unit of Japanese-Americans, the way will be opened for other men and women to go out for defense work.

Army officers who came to the centers to conduct the registration knew that they had a somewhat delicate job before them. Each team had been instructed that it was no ordinary recruiting job in an ordinary American town. They had been told that they were asking young men to volunteer in an army which had already rejected them once on the vaguest suspicion. They had also been told that they should consider that they were asking young men to declare their willingness to serve a country which had placed them and their parents behind barbed wire. Every Army team captain soon after arrival in the center addressed meetings of evacuees and each gave a speech, prepared in the War Department, which contained these words:

Manzanar, Calif.

We are here on a mission . . . . The effort is not a campaign or a drive . . . . Its fundamental purpose is to put your situation on a plane which is consistent with the dignity of American citizenship.

You may object that this—your life here—is not freedom. The circumstances were not of your own choosing . . . . The only answer which needs to be made to such an objection is that if there were not many millions of Americans who agree with your point of view we would not be here and this statement would not be made.

The present undertaking is of itself an acknowledgment that the best solution has not been found for you during the present war emergency in your relation to the United States, which is the country of your birth and of your residence.

Your government would not take these steps unless it intended to go further in restoring you to a normal place in the life of the country, with the privileges and obligations of other American citizens.

Army officers were prepared not only with speeches and instructions which showed some knowledge of the attitudes of people in the relocation centers, but also with a set of carefully worked out questions and answers designed to anticipate the questions that would come up to them from the young men in the meetings they would address. The questions and answers dealt with the details of the Japanese-American Combat Teams, treatment of Nisei who had and had not been discharged from the Army after Pearl Harbor, and even went on to consider the problems of parents who would be left in the centers when their sons entered the Army:

Question: Will my family be permitted to return to the West Coast?
Answer: Not for the time being.
Question: What happens to my father who is not a citizen of the United States?
Answer: Like all other persons now in relocation centers, he may file an application for leave which will be acted upon by the War Relocation Authority. It is probably fair to say that his chances for favorable action will be better by reason of your going into the service.

In all there were forty-two prepared questions and answers. They indicated some awareness of the feelings and points of view of many bitter young men, as those views had seeped from the centers to Washington. They also indicated some awareness of a need for justifying to the young men the decision to place Nisei in separate combat teams apart from persons of other ancestry in the Army.

The center staffs were also for the most part aware that the task before them was not a simple one, although they were little prepared for the full complexity of the evacuee reactions. At Minidoka, the staff was not content to talk over only with the Army officers the best methods for presenting registration to the evacuees, they asked the advice of some of the older evacuees on whom they had come to rely in problems of center management. The Issei leaders worked out a plan for thorough discussion of the questionnaires and the purposes of registration in meetings in various parts of the center. The meetings were addressed not only by the Army officers and members of the WRA staff but also by some of the Issei leaders themselves. One of the Issei took it on himself to speak vigorously in favor of volunteering, saying in the course of the speech which he delivered at each of the discussion meetings:

Americans are not exceptions to the adage that "it is human to err and divine to forgive." But when they find they are mistaken, they have the courage to try to correct it. If they have made mistakes in the past, your children, as American citizens, should share the consequences of these mistakes. My advice to you is to forget the past and look to the future. Let the Nisei do their duty toward the country in which they were born and to which they have allegiance . . . .

The principle involved is that since our children were born here, they belong here. Morally speaking, they do not belong to us, but to their country. I believe our attitude towards this principle will be extremely important for the future welfare and happiness of our own race in the United States. We should look to our own moral code in this matter.

The Minidoka meetings resulted in informing the community widely as to just what the War Department intended in presenting the questionnaires. Hundreds of questions were asked and answered at each meeting, and by the time registration actually started most evacuees in the center knew at least how the War Department and the WRA conceived the purposes of registration and what the implications were of answering "loyalty" and other questions in various ways. At the other centers, with the exception of Tule Lake, there were similar detailed discussions and efforts, although often not so intensive, to answer the doubts and questions which registration raised in the minds of the evacuees. Most staff members had learned through frustrating experiences during the moving in that an administration program often did not get far unless there was opportunity to discuss it thoroughly on the part of the evacuees whom it affected.

The plans and preparations of the War Department and the WRA had not, however, taken fully into account the already deep emotional effects of evacuation and incarceration in the centers. They were not presenting a program to a people who could act as though such things had not happened. They had happened, and they had affected profoundly the attitudes of almost every adult evacuee concerning the Government and all its agencies. A new program of that Government could be viewed only in relation to what had already taken place. Confidence in the Government's newly professed intentions could not be built up in, at best, a few days of discussion and explanation. The evacuees were faced with being asked to declare themselves on paper for purposes which were by no means clear to them. The compulsory nature of the registration for all adults and the fact that centers closed down all activities for several days or a week in order to get everyone registered left no doubt of the great significance which the WRA attached to the program. What that significance was had to be discovered in part by hearing all that officials had to say about it and the rest had to be guessed at. All the suspicion and doubts of government intentions came up in the centers during registration. All the crosscurrents of community opinions and emotions came into play on one another, for every adult was required to make a decision of some sort. Every center was the scene of many meetings among evacuees, of impassioned speeches by evacuees stirred by one issue or another which registration raised. In some centers staff-evacuee relations were not disturbed, but in others the whole framework of the community was threatened. Whether or not the issues were injected into the structure of staff-evacuee relations, however, crises in blocks and particularly in families were widespread. No center, not even Minidoka where registration progressed most smoothly, escaped the turmoil and unsettling of families split and in conflict over the decisions of registration.

The extreme manifestation of the turmoil into which registration threw the evacuees took place at Tule Lake. Preliminary discussions of the sort that were carried out at Minidoka and Topaz and other centers were cut short. The Army team met with evacuees on the evening before registration was to begin, gave explanations of the program, and read some of the previously prepared questions and answers. No time was allowed for discussion from the floor. The morning following, when registration was to begin, found many evacuees unwilling to come and fill out the questionnaires. After attempts to persuade a group in one block to comply, it was announced that they would be compelled to register. There were persistent refusals and further passive resistance. Gangs formed and intimidated young men into not registering or into answering the "loyalty" questions negatively. A group of young citizens who had refused to register was picked up and removed from the center. Intimidation and passive resistance spread. The community council and Issei planning board, who had been attempting to find ways to break the impasse between administration and evacuees, finally resigned. Registration was never completed, several thousand evacuees refusing to comply. There were fifty-nine volunteers, a small number for such a large center, and a large number of negative answers to the "loyalty" questions. Moreover, the community organization was disrupted by the resignation of the council. Tule Lake, which had been well on the road to a stable community organization before registration, became the most disorganized center of all in the weeks following registration.

These reactions to what seemed a simple and clear-cut process to the administrators are understandable only in the light of what the various features of registration meant to evacuees who were asked on short notice to register. For them it was no simple process. It posed fundamental issues, some of which had been sources of conflict for years in the west coast communities.

The Real Issues of Registration

"Great chess game, government makes all the moves." This, reported the project director of Tule Lake during the first days of registration, was a typical statement of young men concerning the Army-WRA program. The mood of the statement was engendered by the whole set of experiences beginning with evacuation and even before. It was the mood of people who had experienced a progressive loss of self-determination, who felt themselves increasingly to be in the hands of a power over whose actions they had no control and whose purposes had consistently worked injury to the group. People in such a mood were suspicious of the motives behind registration. A majority in the centers lacked confidence in a Government that had conceived evacuation for 70,000 of its citizens.

Experience so far provided a basis for interpreting the new move of the Government as having behind it sinister motives. Were all the young men now to be drafted? Did "application for leave clearance" mean that all the fathers and mothers and small children were to be set down outside the centers, still far from their homes, to shift for themselves? There were no answers to these questions. Army officers could not say whether Selective Service was to be opened up or not; it depended in part, they said, on how people responded to the questionnaires. WRA officials did not make definite statements about the plans for resettlement; they only said they thought people ought to resettle. The Government kept making moves in the great chess game. It was now calling for moves from the evacuees, but the Government seemed to be making the rules.

The mood of the centers when registration fell on them was the mood of people who felt that they had already been well tested. They had been filling out forms and giving their life histories to various officials for months. They had bowed to evacuation and most had been striving to live peacefully with WRA staff in the centers. Most of those who had received applications (without having requested them) for repatriation to Japan from the Commanding General of the Western Defense Command had protested only mildly and sent the applications back without filling them in. The tests had been intricate and abundant. Now came another test. To an overwhelming majority of the evacuees, particularly among the Nisei, it seemed that the Government, rather than themselves, had to prove good intentions. Was opening up some segregated units in the Army to Nisei volunteers really a demonstration of any new attitude toward Japanese-Americans? Under the first sudden impact of the new situation the great majority of Nisei, as well as their parents, were doubtful.

It was in this atmosphere of distrust of Government intentions, of fear of further persecution, and of a pervading sense of helplessness and frustration before an impersonal and implacable power, that the reactions to registration developed. Yet generally, even at Tule Lake after a few days, the issues raised by registration were greeted by a majority of evacuees in a spirit of serious discussion. The meetings planned by the administration became forums where most evacuees tried honestly to present their points of view, the basis of their doubts, and their problems, as well as to probe as far as they could into what the WRA staff and the Army officers could present of the government's point of view. The questions were serious and searching more often than they were defiant or inflammatory. The spontaneous meetings of the evacuees in blocks and barracks were more emotional, but they also were the scene of serious weighing of issues and efforts of leaders to calm the more angry and to curb the hasty.

The issues appeared to the young men in various lights. There were a few who immediately accepted the War Department view that this was at last the test of loyalty for which Nisei had asked. "What we face," wrote a Nisei in Minidoka, "is the acid test. If we flunk it, we damn ourselves and our posterity." There were others who felt much the same way, but resented the separate Army unit and wished at least to register their protest against such "Jim Crowism." There were some who merely welcomed the opportunity to get out of the centers by volunteering.

It was quickly apparent, however, that the majority among Nisei of military service age were not ready to accept the War Department program as a proper test to be complied with uncritically. They felt that any test should carry with it some demonstration of the Government's determination not only to admit Nisei to the Army but also to restore the lost freedom of both Nisei and Issei. Willingness to submit Nisei to a new test was not enough. Meetings were called and discussion went on far into the nights, sometimes Issei and Nisei together, sometimes groups of Nisei alone. Talk rose to emotional heights over the questions: Why do we have to reregister? Didn't they register us all once? Doesn't the all-Nisei combat team mean just more discrimination? Do they expect us to volunteer while they keep our fathers and our brothers away from their farms in California? Why don't they undo evacuation and restore some rights to us? The Government was promising nothing. In Topaz, in Heart Mountain, in Manzanar, in Granada, in Jerome the discussion went on, while WRA staff and Army teams tried to secure more information and more assurances from Washington. Meanwhile the issue as most Nisei saw it sharpened into the question: Shall we go ahead and register under protest or shall we register only on condition that our full rights as citizens are restored? Very few were ready to register without at least a strong expression of protest against the restrictions which had been imposed on them.

At Heart Mountain a group of protesting Nisei formed a Citizens' Congress to discuss the issue. On the night of February 11, after registration had officially started there was still vigorous discussion and strong feeling that registration should be conditional. The point of view was expressed by one speaker:

The minds of many of us are still shrouded in doubt and confusion as to the true motives of our Government when they invite our voluntary enlistment at the present time. It has not been explained why some American citizens who patriotically volunteered, at the beginning of the war, were rejected by the Army. Furthermore, our government has permitted damaging propaganda to continue against us. Also she has failed to reinstate us in the eyes of the American public. We are placed on the spot, and our course of action is in the balance scale of justice; for our Government's honest interpretation of our stand will mean absolute vindication and admission of the wrong committed. On the other hand, if interpreted otherwise by misrepresentations and misunderstandings, it will amount to renewed condemnation of this group.

Although we have yellow skins, we too are Americans. We have an American upbringing. Therefore we believe in fair play. Our firm conviction is that we would be useless Americans if we did not assert our constitutional rights now; for, unless our status as citizens is cleared and we are really fighting for the high ideals upon which our nation is based, how can we say to the white American buddies in the armed forces that we are fighting for the perpetuation of democracy, especially when our fathers, mothers, and families are in concentration camps, even though they are not charged with any crime?

We believe that our nation's good faith is to be found in whether it moves to restore full privileges at the earliest opportunity.

Such speeches were being made in nearly every center. Conditional registration was still the considered reaction of many Nisei who were thinking seriously about the matter. The group at Heart Mountain who felt this way sent out telegrams to all the centers asking for cooperation of Nisei in a united stand on conditional registration. No concerted action was taken in response to the plea, but groups were acting individually at various centers. The Heart Mountain group framed resolutions asking for restoration of citizenship rights. At Topaz a Committee of Nine wired Secretary of War Stimson for assurance of restoration of rights before going on with registration. At Granada the WRA staff put a Nisei leader in communication with War Department officials to discuss the Nisei objections to registration.

The statement of the Nisei position did not fall on deaf ears in Washington. The Topaz telegram brought forth a response from the War Department:

The present program is not complete rehabilitation but it is the first step in that direction.

Steadily, finding WRA staff willing to listen and War Department officials concerned to reply to their protests, the current of opinion among Nisei began to shift. Many who had stood for conditional registration began to feel that the only course was to accept registration as presented. They had made their protests. They had not taken the new "test" lying down, and their protests had received serious consideration. A sufficiently strong presentation of the case had been made. A Topaz Committee of 33 Nisei on February 16 replied to the War Department:

We accept this registration as an indication of the Government's good faith.

The great majority of Nisei now proceeded to comply with registration and to answer the questions as presented in their original form. The organized consideration of the issue had focused Nisei feelings, articulated the basic resentments and protests, and, only after such expression, pointed a course of action which the majority of Nisei followed in all centers.

The path taken by the majority did not chart the way for thousands of other Nisei. There were hundreds who remained convinced, like the Heart Mountain orator, that further expression of loyalty should be made only after the Government should take action to restore full citizenship. There were still many who opposed on principle the segregation of the combat teams. There were more hundreds who remained uninfluenced by the discussions in the block meetings or, as at Tule Lake, who had not had any opportunity to attend such open discussions. There were many who remained sceptical and defiant in the face of the official assurances. There were some, as on the outside, who wanted to dodge the draft, as they had already dodged military service in Japan a few years before. There were a few also who quite definitely, as a result of long residence in Japan and education there, felt that they wanted to go to Japan and serve that country. There were many others who were confused when they were faced with the specific questions in the questionnaires and did not know how to reply. There were thousands on the wrack of the community crosscurrents—pulled this way by fearful or stern parents and pulled that way by friends and their own inclinations. As the concerted Nisei thinking crystallized toward acceptance of registration under protest, individuals continued to assert themselves outside the area of majority opinion. But each individual was a free agent only insofar as he could see his way through the medly of influences that played on him in each block.

The issues raised for the Issei in registration were not the same as those raised for the Nisei. The Issei were not directly concerned with the issue of military service on an equal basis with other Americans, nor were they in a position to suggest obligations to themselves of a country in which they had no citizenship. Nevertheless, citizenship rights of the Issei were at stake in the registration as first presented. Question 28 asked them to foreswear allegiance to Japan. As soon as Issei saw this question in their forms, it was obvious to them that the officials who had framed it were ignorant of the legal position that had plagued them for forty years in the United States. Regardless of how much of a stake in family and property they might acquire in this country, American laws had denied them the right to apply for American citizenship. The Government had forced them to retain their legal tie with Japan whether they wished to or not; all were citizens of Japan and no possibility of naturalization in this country had ever or was now being held out to them. To answer Question 28 with a Yes would make them men without a country; to answer it with a No would lead to no one knew what action by the United States: to deportation or to more severe restrictions?

In the very first moments of discussion in the centers the WRA staff were made aware of the impossible position in which the question placed all Issei. At Manzanar the project director, after calling Washington on the phone, changed the question to read:

Are you sympathetic to the United States and do you agree faithfully to defend the United States from any and all attack by foreign or domestic forces?

This involved some recognition of the Issei position, and the great majority proceeded to answer in the affirmative. At other centers the issue came up promptly also and WRA staff members wired Washington to do something about it. Soon they were authorized to change the question:

Will you swear to abide by the laws of the United States and to take no action which would in any way interfere with the war effort of the United States?

This gave full recognition to the Issei legal position, required no renunciation of the only citizenship which they had, and opened the way to an answer in line with all that they had been attempting to do from the start, namely, abide by the laws of the United States. With the change, Issei proceeded almost unanimously to answer Question 28 with a Yes. Like the great majority of Nisei, an even greater majority of Issei now went through with the registration, once their legitimate objections had been raised and they had met with some indication of understanding.

There was, however, another point of concern for Issei. This was the implication of the original title of the form for registration of aliens: Application for Leave Clearance. Few Issei wanted to leave the centers while the war was still going on. The general Issei attitude to the relocation centers as neutral havens was well crystallized by now. Yet since registration was compulsory, they felt that they were being compelled to make application to leave the centers. Their hesitation on this score also was quickly made known to the WRA staff, wires flew back and forth from centers to Washington, and the announcement was made in the centers that the title of the form could be changed to "Information for Leave Clearance." This was better. It was at least not an apparent statement of desire to leave the centers. Nevertheless, the intention behind the original title of the form could be guessed at. Most Issei felt that the officials who had planned registration must have some plan for getting everybody out of the centers. If not, why had they first asked everyone to apply for leave clearance? Who could tell now what was in their minds? The feeling of dealing with men who in the first place did not understand the simple fact of their lack of legal status in the United States and in the second place seemed to have some unstated purpose back of their actions colored the whole Issei reaction. It focused more sharply the feeling that had been growing since the autumn announcement of resettlement plans that the Government was deviously moving in a direction contrary to what Issei felt was in their best interests.

To the majority of evacuees it was clear enough, as a result of the widespread and sometimes passionate discussion during registration, where they stood. In general most Nisei wanted a positive move from the Government in the restoration of real citizenship status; the majority were willing, once they had registered their protests, to accept the re-opening of the Army as such a move. In general most Issei wanted to be left alone until the war was over and they could see their way to new starts in the country in which they had their roots of family and property —the United States. But in every center there was a minority who fell outside the general patterns of response to registration, who either took the opposite view of the issues as the majority saw them or were pulled now this way, now that. It was for this minority that registration constituted the most intense and unsettling crisis.

The Issei minority were concerned with the possibilities for return to Japan. Before registration those who had seriously considered return consisted of something less than 3,000. These were for the most part men and women who had been planning before the war to go to Japan and live out the last years of their lives. There were also some for whom evacuation seemed to wipe out any possibility for starting over again in the United States. They had relatives or they had property in Japan and they consequently made the decision to return and start over in Japan with this help. They had filled out applications for repatriation and were waiting for some word from the State Department as to whether they could be repatriated during the war. When registration was announced, WRA officials indicated that those, and those alone, who had made applications for repatriation would not be required to register. The reaction to this was prompt and definite at some centers.

At Tule Lake, as misunderstanding and antagonism grew in the first days of registration, WRA staff began to find evacuees in their offices asking for applications to repatriate to Japan. As the numbers increased, the project director stopped the issuance of such applications. At Manzanar, also, repatriation requests were not issued during registration because of the obvious demand for them as a way to abide by regulations and yet not go through with registration. The requests for repatriation increased at all centers, indicating that repatriation was a definite reaction to the stresses of the process. This did not mean that the Issei who were applying necessarily wanted to go back to Japan—it was a way to avoid registration. But there were also many who under the stress of registration made decisions hastily and thought for the moment at least that the best way out was to return to Japan. A request for repatriation meant at least that one would not be pushed out into the hostile United States. Chances for getting along in Japan that had seemed slim a few weeks before, now began to appear in a different light. Anything was better than the sort of treatment that was being meted out in the United States. Thus 3,000 more people, with various motives but principally as a result of resentment and fear, were moved during registration to apply to go to Japan.

The consequences for the children of the Issei who decided to repatriate under the stress of registration were serious. Some with great docility or with wholehearted sharing of their parents feelings proceeded to answer the loyalty questions negatively and to request that they be expatriated to Japan, to willingly go along with their parents. But for many more who had decided to register and answer Yes, there was intense conflict. Young men and women feared to go home at night because it meant painful debate with their parents or an hour of being browbeaten by parents who had decided to repatriate. The young people had no desire to go to Japan and often suspected that their parents' judgment in deciding to go was not good. Children and parents talked and pleaded with each other. Two sons in one center persuaded their father, a laundryman from San Francisco, not to repatriate before registration was over, but the whole set of family ties was threatened in the process. Generally the parents prevailed on unwilling sons and daughters, appealing to their sense of family duty. Hundreds of teen-age young men and women, in order to keep peace in the family and sometimes in hope that the Government would never really carry through on repatriation, gave in to parents and answered negatively to the loyalty questions.

Family pressures were not the only forces driving Nisei in directions which led them to classify themselves as "disloyal" in the eyes of readers of the questionnaires. Just as there were a minority of Issei who chose repatriation as against compliance with registration, so there was a minority of Nisei in every center who chose forceful No's to the loyalty questions as their means of protest rather than resolutions and subsequent compliance with registration. They remained defiant. The word No on the questionnaires stood for them as a symbol of protest—protest against evacuation, against compulsory registration, against all that had happened since evacuation. At Tule Lake, young men in large numbers refused to register at all in protest against the administration's arrest of a group of young men in one block who had refused to register. In Manzanar, hundreds went defiantly to the registration tables and wrote No on their questionnaires. Some said simply that it was protest, some said it was because they had given up hope in the United States and went on then to follow through with requests for expatriation to Japan, even though they had never seen Japan. At Tule Lake, and to a lesser extent in other centers, some of these defiant young men went about the centers warning other young men that a Yes meant disloyalty to the group, that it was cowardly, that it was taking mistreatment lying down. Far fewer than were affected by family pressures, but nevertheless a good many young men in the Tule Lake, Jerome, and Manzanar centers yielded to such pressures and, against their better judgment, put themselves down with No answers.

In some blocks young people remained confused in the welter of pressures, misinformation, and lack of information, and went to register in the mess hall with no clear idea of the meaning of either question. In other blocks older men carefully advised young men to answer Yes to everything. In others older men advised No answers. What block one happened to live in often determined his response to the loyalty questions: a No answer in one block obviously would have been a Yes answerer in another block. Some blocks held meetings and attempted to get unanimous agreement for the responses either one way or the other. Individual young men wrestled through the night with their decisions and came sleepless to declare themselves Yes or No, having in a few hours gone through the whole process of going to Japan or remaining in the United States, and then suffered the reality of block life again in the mess halls and latrines. One young man struggled with his parents' accusations of disloyalty (to them) for several days, when he indicated that he would answer Yes, then yielded and answered No and came back to feel that friends in the mess hall were now calling him disloyal to his country. It was a minority in every center who faced the dilemmas of family conflict and an even lesser minority who wrestled with the dilemmas of the symbolic No. But the agonies of the minority pervaded many blocks and wrought up whole centers. It was a time of testing, but less a testing of national loyalties than of nerves and family ties.

The Effects of Registration

What happened in the centers during registration could be stated in statistical tables, in a numerical analysis of the answers to questions 27 and 28, and in the figures summarizing the numbers of requests for repatriation and expatriation to Japan in the months immediately following registration. Thus out of a total of a little over 20,000 young men of military age in all the centers 5,000, or 25 percent, gave No or qualified answers or refused to answer the loyalty questions. Of the young women citizens about 2,500, or 13 percent, answered negatively or refused to answer. Of the older men and women citizens of Japan about 1,000, or 6 percent, fell into the same category. This made a rough total of some 8,500 persons who appeared to have behaved in the same way and made the same response to the loyalty questions, out of a grand total of something over 75,000 adults required to register. It might appear from looking at the tables that about 11 percent of the whole group had failed to meet what the government officials had presented to the evacuees as a test of loyalty.

As WRA officials looked more carefully into the table of returns, the figures alone, without the aid of their real knowledge of what had taken place, began to reveal peculiarities that challenged any simple conclusion in terms of loyalty. From center to center there were striking differences. For instance, at Minidoka and Granada less than 3 percent of the young men were No answerers while over 50 percent of the young men at Manzanar had answered No. And so it ranged through the centers. The conclusion was inescapable that the motives behind the answers depended on many things that the questionnaires had not taken into account. The WRA staff in the centers knew what these factors were because they had seen the process and they had begun almost immediately to interview the young men to get at the meaning to them of a No answer. They learned in the course of interviewing to distinguish between the No of protest against discrimination, the No of protest against a father interned apart from his family, the No of bitter antagonism to subordinations in the relocation center, the No of a gang sticking together, the No of thoughtless defiance, the No of family duty, the No of hopeless confusion, the No of fear of military service, and the No of felt loyalty to Japan. Dozens of men and women in the center staffs, like the evacuees themselves, began to realize that the numerical counts measured primarily the individual frustrations and the family confusions that had arisen in the wake of evacuation and subsequent events in the relocation centers including the registration crisis itself. They knew that registration had indeed sorted people, but not in terms of loyalty to the United States and to Japan. In terms of feeling about the United States Government, it had sorted people chiefly into the disillusioned and the defiant as against the compliant and the hopeful. As with any cross section of humanity, even while deep in a trough of bitter experience, the vast majority continued to be hopeful.

The experience of registration was as profound and disturbing for many staff members as for evacuees themselves. Some who embarked on their jobs in the centers with little sense of the meaning to evacuees of the experience of evacuation had felt that evacuees harked back to that experience unnecessarily and too often. As one project director said, "They have a persecution complex." What was a reality for evacuees was not a reality for staff members because they had not experienced it themselves. Now, after days of interviewing and intensive contacts in meetings, the reality of the evacuees' experiences was driven into staff members' consciousness. They were nearer than they had been to interpreting attitudes as normal reactions to the reality in which evacuees had been living rather than as delusions of persecution. Nevertheless, even though they were a little nearer to the reality, staff members were still confused by the injection of the emotionally charged word "loyalty" into center life. One staff member expressed a widespread type of reaction while still fresh from the experience:

My part in the show was organizing and running the machinery of block registration. I saw the whole show, backstage and front. Registration itself went off smoothly and quickly. The team captains and block managers did a good, businesslike job of lining up the residents and running them through on time. The interviewers were for the most part patient and fair and accurate. It was conducted on the whole with dignity and good feeling and an appreciation of the gravity of the issues . . . .

Now we're standing round looking at what we've dredged up. All of us I think have been startled by the sweeping repudiation of loyalty to this country, or of hope of any future here. You expected it among the Kibei, but not among the citizens. And to find, by the hundreds, products of our high schools and colleges who've never been in Japan answering No to the loyalty questions they gave, was shocking. Our first reaction, mine anyway, was anger, I wanted to wash my hands of the whole traitorous bunch and consign them to any concentration camp the public wanted to set up.

Now that I've had time to reflect a little, and have talked with well over a hundred about their attitude toward this country, and seen the real anguish that accompanied many of the decisions, and the fears that prompted others—well, . . . I want to see if anything can be salvaged from the wreck.

The current feelings of evacuees were real for the staff member, even if the feelings of the previous months were not quite so real. In every center some staff members at least came into touch with evacuees as they never had before. Issues and points of view which had been taboo ground had been brought up, and the staff and evacuees had met now on this taboo ground. Staff members had participated in aiding the serious Nisei who wanted to present their view of things to the War Department. A new respect for the Nisei position had spread among the staff in most centers, and in others, for the first time, staff members began to glimpse the position of the Issei as they transmitted to Washington their objections to signing away their citizenship. There was unquestionably, after registration, a larger area of common ground on which evacuees and the staff could stand to deal together with common problems in the centers.

Nevertheless, the feeling of the Manzanar staff member that something evil had been uncovered was also present in every center. The damning word "disloyalty," even to sympathetic staff members who had learned how to distinguish between the symbolic No's, was an obstruction. "The jungle depths" and "the dark, tangled conflicts," as the Manzanar staff member called them, which registration had revealed, were not easily understood. Staff members had suspected them before, but when they were able to look directly into the depths and conflicts they were still hardly understood and to some extent feared. To interpret them as the necessary and normal results of actions taken by our government and even by the agency of which one was a part required an aloofness and objectivity which life in the centers did not permit. Most staff members, then, fell into a certain pattern of attitude as a result of the new, but partial, insights the experience of registration had given them. They had more sympathy and a somewhat better understanding, but they needed some protection from the vision of "dark, tangled conflicts." They felt this evil should be got rid of. Even though they might use "disloyal" with quotation marks around it, in their awareness of the tangled motives, they still tended to use the term and to feel that the "disloyal" should be removed from the centers. They were the source of evil and should be put away. The "disloyal," thought of in a hundred different ways by staff members, but nevertheless spoken of by means of the emotionally charged word, became a scapegoat for staff feelings. Somehow they wanted "them" out and away, and then the evacuees and staff could work together and go on with the task of building center life.

To some extent registration, like the incident at Poston, cleared the air of unvoiced distrust in the centers. Insofar as it brought staff members and groups of evacuees into closer touch for honest exchange of views it did that but this differed from center to center. Much more than in Poston, moreover, it was a one-sided revelation, affecting staff members by bringing them onto common ground with evacuees. At the same time that it did this in most centers except Tule Lake, it also increased staff distrust for one segment of the evacuees. And for the evacuees generally there still lay behind the center staff the unplumbed intentions of "the Government."

Registration was comparable to evacuation itself in its unsettling effects on the evacuees. The chief difference lay in the fact that it did not involve any physical uprooting, that it fell on people who had some sort of home base in the relocation centers. But the expectation of further physical uprooting was the central fact in the new unsettling. The process injected three new sources of uncertainty about the future into the lives of the evacuees. In the first place it raised the question of the purpose of placing the "loyalty" questions in the registration forms.

What was the Government's intention in getting answers to these questions? Did they intend to make a separation of the evacuees on the basis of the answers? There must be some intention, evacuees reasoned, or otherwise why should they have included the questions in the forms for Issei and young women as well as for the men of military age? If there was to be some separation on this basis, then where would the two groups of Yes answerers and No answerers be sent? In the second place there was the question raised by the labeling of the forms as applications for or information on leave clearance. What did the WRA intend to use these for? Was it a plan to move everyone out of the centers? If not, why had they begun by requiring everyone to fill out the applications? If it was, whom would they send out first, where would they send them, and when would they begin? Finally, there was the question raised by the talk of the draft. Did the Army intend to draft all Nisei? When would they make their decision? How would they deal with the No answerers?

The questions raised by registration had to do with the two securities which had been achieved since evacuation, namely, the increased solidarity of the family and homes in the relocation centers. Both of these threats were strongest for the great majority who answered the loyalty questions in the affirmative and did not make application for repatriation or expatriation. For them the probability of the opening of Selective Service could be viewed as a threat to family solidarity, and the probability of resettlement outside the centers threatened the loss of homes in the centers. Thus it was those who had come through the Government's test with an official classification of loyal who faced serious uncertainties about the future. Speculation and rumors about forced relocation sprang up quickly and spread through the centers. They were based primarily on the anxieties arising out of registration concerning the Government's intention to resettle everyone. As the speculation increased through the spring of 1943 a sense of being at odds with the WRA policy makers crystallized. Evacuees referred back to the lack of understanding of the Issei situation as indicated in the first form of question 28. The older people set themselves to hold on as long as they could to the present security of the relocation center homes and most became convinced that the government agency did not have their real interests at heart. The reactions which a minority had had during registration—such as applying for repatriation as a means of settling the sense of insecurity about homes for the duration of the war— spread in some centers, particularly at Tule Lake, Jerome, and Manzanar. The psychological effects of registration were deep going and long lasting. They became increasingly apparent in their unsettling effects as the Government program unfolded during the spring and summer.

AN EMERGING FRAMEWORK OF COMMUNITY LIFE

Although registration planted a new cycle of anxieties deeply in the minds of the residents of relocation centers, it did have some constructive results. Most of the centers were more in the nature of integrated communities after registration than they had been before. The new fears, unlike the intense anxieties aroused by evacuation, were at work not on amorphous collections of individuals and families, such as had originally moved into the camps. Since their arrival, people had been forming themselves into groups in which individuals found strength and support. Every center had begun to shape as a community. The crises of the winter had generally given impetus to that development.

The growth of the communities was a process which had two aspects. On the one hand the people in each block had to get used to one another. They had not only to find ways for utilizing jointly the mess halls and laundry rooms and block lands, but also to discover how neighbors felt and thought about the things that were most on people's minds. How they felt about the Caucasians who had put them out of their homes, what they thought about the obligations of the government to them, what attitude they were taking toward their subordination in the relocation centers, how long the war would last, and how it would come out. On these and other fundamental points, a sense that one knew how one's neighbors were thinking was growing up in the blocks from the beginning of the relocation centers. The strike at Poston and registration at the other centers served to re-enforce the feeling of unity and of participation in a common approach to fundamental problems, not alone within individual blocks but on a center-wide basis as well. Important elements of the common approach were embodied in the majority behavior of both Nisei and Issei during registration. They had insisted on being heard, asserted the right to protest injustice, and objected to being pushed around. At the same time they had sought to find acceptable compromises so that peace and harmony could be restored.

As the sense of a common view of things increased among evacuees, there was a heightened awareness of those few persons in nearly every block who did not fit into the general pattern of behavior and feeling. Individuals who held that everything that had been done to the evacuees was all for the best, who were outspoken in urging acceptance of each new feature of the government program as presented, who wished to cooperate uncritically with center staff members in all they proposed—

such persons became marked. They were suffered in many blocks, but lived in a certain atmosphere of ostracism. In other blocks they found life actively unpleasant and, by the spring of 1943, they sought to get out of the centers. Some who had volunteered for the Army during registration found themselves so strongly disapproved that they were glad to leave as quickly as they could. The fact of having volunteered was not in itself the issue. It was rather the divergence of the person's whole point of view from the majority sentiment about evacuation and living in the centers. The response of neighbors depended to some extent on the individual's way of expressing himself and to some extent on the nature of the other people in the block. There were volunteers who found little antagonism and often a good deal of support. Every block overlooked slight variations of opinion and one block differed from another in what it approved and disapproved in its members. But a majority sentiment had crystallized by the end of registration, and the people were beginning to feel a sense of common agreement on what mattered to them most. The basis for an *esprit de corps* of blocks and of centers had emerged.

Somewhat less surely and progressively the other aspect of community growth had developed in the months since arrival in the centers. This was the process of evacuees and administrators getting used to one another. Up through the crises of the winter of 1942–43 the characteristic development in social organization consisted in the growth of block unity and community consensus. During the following year the characteristic development consisted in the growth of working relations between evacuees and staff. The stabilization of these relations could not be accomplished until the relations of the people in the blocks among themselves had reached some sort of equilibrium. Poston had an early start as compared with other centers as a result of the influence of the strike on the evacuee community. Immediately following that crisis, staff-evacuee working relations moved rapidly toward stability. The Manzanar crisis had similar effects at that center. Tule Lake, without the catalytic influence of a concentrated crisis, had been moving in the same direction. Unified sentiment in the other centers was still in the early stages of growth when registration fell on them. For some of them registration acted much as the Poston crisis had in bringing evacuees together and laying the foundation for stable staff-evacuee relations. Only Tule Lake was not affected in this manner by registration. And at Heart Mountain and Jerome three or four months were required to complete the unifying process registration had set in motion.

At Topaz during registration the nature of an evacuee organization which could express and focus community sentiment for action on important issues was clearly revealed. As soon as evacuees became aware of the WRA-War Department program, many among them realized promptly the serious implications for the future of the whole group. Quickly block meetings were held and each block elected two representatives, one Nisei and one Issei, to obtain information, discuss the issues involved, and attempt to arrive at some concerted approach to the problems. This Committee of 66 discussed among themselves and with members of the administrative staff and the Army teams every aspect of registration. They recognized that there were different issues involved for Nisei and Issei. And the Nisei members of the committee, calling themselves the Committee of 33, discussed the Nisei issues separately and prepared their resolutions to send to the War Department. The Issei members of the over-all committee considered separately the matters that seemed to concern Issei exclusively. Previously, in line with WRA regulations, a temporary community council of Nisei had been elected. Members of the council individually and the council as a formal body functioned in the discussions and played important parts in giving leadership during the crisis, but the reaction of the community as a whole in the face of what people considered a vital and crucial problem was apparent. They had not relied on a body formed for the purpose of dealing with the administrators in center management under the WRA regulations. They had proceeded to organize their own representative groups with direct sanction from block opinion. It was in the Committees of 66 and 33 that the sentiments of the people as a whole were expressed and that some sort of majority sentiment and approach was developed. They had quickly accepted the administration's statement that registration itself was to be an individual matter and that the exerting of group pressures could legally be interpreted as seditious. Nevertheless, it was the Committees of 33 and 66 that thrashed out the issues, explained the general viewpoints of evacuees to administrators, and reported back to their blocks for sanction on the resolutions framed. Called "rump" groups by the administration, they were actually the effective representatives of majority opinion during the crisis. When the crisis had passed, the Committee of 66 disappeared from administrative notice. It was never recognized under WRA regulations as having any existence. Yet not only in registration but also in subsequent crises which evacuees regarded as of vital importance to them, this type of organization, tied closely to current opinion in the blocks, rose again and offered leadership and means of approach to the problems. Meanwhile, in periods when no crucial matters were at stake, the council elected under WRA regulation continued to function as the organized body representing evacuees to the administration.

What happened in Topaz during registration was neither new nor was it to be exceptional in the centers. A very similar sort of organization took place in Poston during the strike there. After the Nisei council had resigned, an over-all Emergency Committee was elected with two representatives from each block, usually but not in all cases consisting of one Nisei and one Issei from each. This became the basis for an executive committee which gave leadership during the course of the strike. As a unified committee of Issei and Nisei, the over-all group disappeared after the immediate crisis, but the Issei half of it continued to function as an Issei Advisory Board, and most of the Nisei members were elected to a community council under the WRA regulations. The Nisei council and the Issei Advisory Board then proceeded to meet jointly, the chief difference from the emergency strike committee being that the Nisei instead of the Issei leaders maintained the formal and official relations with the administrators. The crisis at Poston had given rise to the same sort of over-all community organization that sprang up at Topaz during registration.

In one form or another this type of organization had begun to operate in all centers by the spring of 1943. In some centers it was not so clearly formalized as it had been at Topaz or Poston. But in all centers, whatever names the formal bodies took and whatever relationships they bore to WRA regulations, there were apparent four essentials in the functioning organization of evacuee-staff relations.

1. It was evident that Issei would not be excluded from places of dominance in the center organization by the regulation prohibiting them from holding office in the community councils. It was not only that Issei were the shapers of majority opinion in the blocks; it was also that they were unwilling to allow the younger men to monopolize the positions of liaison between staff and community. They did not believe that the younger men could interpret fully and truly the position of the Issei to the administration. They did not think that the younger men fully understood their problems as citizens of Japan with families and economic stakes in the United States. Lacking that understanding, the younger men could not work in their best interests for the future.

2. It was evident that Issei recognized some differences in the interests of Nisei and Issei. However much they might urge solidarity of the whole group in center life, Issei leaders had demonstrated through the months that they believed Nisei had certain special interests as citizens of the United States. The more responsible and influential Issei had insisted that Nisei have places on the over-all committees that grew up

in the Poston and Topaz crises. They had even worked for equal representation of the two groups. There was a segment of Issei opinion which tried to ignore differences of interest, but the dominant Issei opinion in every center recognized it as fundamental.

3. It was evident that certain types of men could not for long function in positions of community leadership. Men who vigorously pushed unconditional participation in the American war effort, who followed without question all the features of the program as laid out by the Government agencies, who attempted to take seriously the regulation excluding Issei from elective office, or who were insensitive to the Issei problems of status in Japan and the United States—men with such beliefs or qualities could not function effectively as leaders. It was not necessarily a question of being Issei or Nisei. True, a man holding such beliefs was more likely to be Nisei than Issei, but there were many Nisei who did not and there were even a few Issei who did. The capacity for effective leadership went deeper than the label of citizenship. It was a matter of feeling about the whole progressive loss of self-determination by the group and of sensitivity to the majority sentiment. Staff members in the centers, as well as many Nisei leaders, had realized well before registration that the centers could not be managed by individuals who were out of step with the majority feeling, and such individuals were to be found in greatest number among the Nisei.

4. It was evident that the councils could not do duty as representative bodies for the communities under all circumstances. Even though they might, through various adjustments such as cooperation with Issei advisory boards, function more or less adequately in conjunction with block managers in the day-to-day liaison activities with the administrators, they were not adequate in deeper crises. The issues of center management were on a plane of minor importance as compared with the issues of registration which involved the whole future of the group. Councils and block managers were elected by the people to serve a specific function of day-to-day liaison. The members were chosen for qualities, such as knowledge of English, which would be useful in the contacts with administrators. In times of crisis others, who were closer to the core of community sentiment, were looked to for real representative functions.

These four principles of community organization were expressed in various ways in the ten centers. The formulas for organization proposed by the WRA—the community councils and the block managers—were adapted to them in different fashions. All but three centers had proceeded to elect Nisei councils under the regulations. Then, by a variety of means they had brought Issei into the community organization. Three early centers—Poston, Tule Lake, and Gila—had elected Issei advisory boards which worked closely with the councils. Granada also experimented with Issei advisers, but finally worked out an arrangement whereby Nisei resigned from all block manager posts, and the two bodies, a Nisei council and an Issei block-manager group, functioned as the community representatives. At Topaz, Rohwer, and Jerome, although no such formal agreement was made, the arrangement was substantially the same. Nisei councils and Issei-dominated block managers divided between them the functions of liaison with staff. The later centers thus operated with somewhat less complicated organization, since they did not elect Issei advisory bodies. Three centers never elected Nisei councils. The people of Manzanar under the stresses of the early months refused, despite administration encouragement, to accept the WRA "self-government" regulations. After the December disturbance they continued, as before, to be satisfied with only a block manager organization, dominated by Issei. Thus, throughout the existence of the center they maintained the simplest sort of over-all organization. At Minidoka during the spring of 1943, largely through the staff's unwillingness to inject a purely Nisei body into the framework, there was no council. The administrators worked with a small predominantly Issei group (who had been set up originally as an organization commission to draft a charter for self-government) and the block managers who were also mostly Issei. Heart Mountain reversed the Granada arrangement by electing at the very beginning of the center a so-called temporary council composed of Issei which served until August, 1943. Nisei filled in the block-manager posts. At all centers with the possible exception of Heart Mountain the efforts to adapt the WRA formulas to the realities of center life resulted in some strain and complication of working relations. But by the time WRA, in April 1943, withdrew its prohibition against Issei sitting in the community councils, the matter of Issei participation had ceased to be a vital issue. The four principles of organization had been expressed in a variety of institutions which were answering the purposes of evacuees and center staff.

While a system of community-administration relation was being worked out, there was some pulling and tugging and sizing up of the respective roles of staff and evacuees. In January 1943, the young man who had emerged after the strike as chairman of the Poston Nisei council wrote a memorandum which he titled "One of Poston's Problems." In it he took up the question of the size and competence of the WRA center staff. He pointed out that there were evacuees capable of doing many things which were now being done by less competent Caucasians and that evacuees were excluded from those jobs by the rule that the Civil Service supervisory positions could not be held by evacuees. He took the position that fewer Caucasians were needed in the center and that evacuees could manage the camp if given the opportunity. The council had the memorandum mimeographed and distributed to the Poston staff, and copies were sent to community councils in other centers. Some staff members in Poston regarded the criticism as legitimate and felt much as the council chairman did. A few who saw the memorandum regarded it as insubordinate and insolent. Top staff members, responsible for administering the center under the agency's regulations, were a little annoyed by the outspoken approach of the council chairman, but they had been thinking along the same lines. They had themselves reached the conclusion that the center operated more smoothly if they gave evacuees maximum responsibility under the agency regulations and limited the official contacts of staff with evacuees to a small number of carefully chosen staff members. Poston had in fact already moved to keep the number of appointed personnel in Units II and III to a bare minimum and to concentrate as much as possible the responsibility for contact with organized evacuee bodies in Unit I to a single administrator. This was one way of resolving the contradiction of the evacuee-Caucasian classifications.

The chairman's memorandum was indicative of the process of adjustment of community to staff. It indicated most clearly the sort of qualities a person, and particularly a Nisei, must have to achieve any sort of real leadership in center life. The chairman, despite the bluff, facetious manner apparent in the memorandum, was deeply critical of the whole situation in which evacuees had been placed. Moreover, he was willing to express his conviction and to announce his criticism in terms of an evaluation of Issei and Nisei as persons at least on a level of ability and intelligence with appointed personnel and other Caucasians. Only if a man took such positions and kept such points in some way before the administrators could he operate as a community leader. True for Poston after the strike, this became increasingly true in all the centers as community organization developed.

The chairman's memorandum calls attention to another phase of staff-evacuee relations. As evacuees came into contact with staff, either through the over-all community organizations or as members of work crews under staff foremen, they made critical appraisals, not only in terms of competence and relative ability as compared with the evacuees working under them, but also in terms of attitudes towards evacuees in general. They were looking about, spotting the ones who seemed to them to be tainted with race prejudice and therefore unfair in their dealings with evacuees. By the spring of 1943 they had pigeonholed staff members according to their own classifications. The classifications were not always just, for work crews were often inclined to read prejudice into rigid adherence to agency regulations or to express purely personal antagonisms. But the judgments were there, and the prejudice and ill will toward evacuees that existed among some staff members in every center were a topic of evacuee conversation and a source of friction and difficulty in center operations.

The theme voiced by the Poston council chairman was to be heard at other centers as staff antagonisms to evacuees crystallized in the period of disillusionment immediately following registration. An Issei at Jerome said:

I heard [the project director] say that since registration he has lost faith in the Japanese. . . . I think it would be a good idea to get rid of most of the Caucasians here and let the evacuees run the center themselves. They have the experience of the Co-op and I am sure they could run the camp democratically. When this feeling of compulsion goes away then the people will cooperate more.

During the spring, work groups at Heart Mountain attempted to influence the project director to remove staff members regarded as prejudiced. Their efforts ran up against the stone wall of the director's determination to do his own hiring and firing and assigning of personnel to jobs.

There was no doubt that evacuees were to have no voice in that function and that they were going to have to find ways of getting along with many kinds of staff members. In May at Granada an evacuee leader summed up the situation at his center:

Most of the appointed staff are all right. They try to do the right thing. Many times they don't understand the psychology of the Japanese-Americans and consequently make mistakes, but they are honestly trying to help the evacuees. . . . We have only two or three Hitlers among the staff here, and while they make it hard for us sometimes, we know we can trust and work with most of the appointed staff.

Project directors everywhere were affected by evacuees' attitudes toward staff members and concerned with staff behavior toward the people. Poston sought to channel contacts with representatives of the community through carefully selected appointed personnel. On other projects the problem was dealt with in different ways and with varying degrees of effectiveness. Staffs were adjusting to evacuees as well as evacuees to staff.

The adjustment process was aided by what had become a consciously formulated aim of the evacuees who had emerged into positions of leadership. When evacuee leaders organized an assembly immediately on arrival in Granada in October they stated that:

The chief concern . . . was the preservation of harmony among the center residents and the administrative staff . . . .

The objective of "maintaining harmony in the centers" was more and more on leaders' tongues as the months went by and disharmony and conflict developed. The serious breakdowns in staff-evacuee relations at Poston and Manzanar loomed as threats in other centers. Steadily the councils and the various over-all committees began to see their function as harmonizers of differences among evacuee groups and as go-betweens in the relations of administration and community. They had learned that the agency under whose supervision they had been placed would continue to operate relentlessly like a government agency, controlling its personnel, financial, and other policies with its own hand. There was then the problem of interceding between the agency and the people so that there might be a maximum of harmony in their relationships. The councils and other representative bodies were rating that function as important.

THE SORTING

During the spring of 1943, as "harmony in the centers" became the watchword of evacuee leaders, the eyes of most evacuees were turned outward to a series of events which intensified their anxieties about the "outside." The majority of the Issei, who shaped public opinion in the centers, saw the outside world beyond the neighboring towns chiefly through three Japanese-language newspapers published in Denver and Salt Lake City. Primarily concerned during 1942 with reporting developments in the Pacific war, these papers in 1943 began to give increasing amounts of space to events in the United States. The reason was the emergence of Japanese-Americans as a national issue and the consequent abundance of statements by congressmen and senators and other public officials concerning them. Committees of both the Senate and the House were investigating the relocation centers. In May, Senator Chandler, chairman of the Senate Military Affairs Committee, publicly announced his interpretation of the committee's investigation into the results of registration. The Japanese-language newspapers gave space to his statement that 20 percent of the evacuees were disloyal to the United States and, with the exception of the *Rocky Shimpo* of Denver, heaped scorn on the estimate. Their estimates varied from 2 percent to 11 percent. Senator Chandler went on to say that the disloyal evacuees should be separated from the loyal. Meanwhile the House Committee on Un-American Activities went into action to investigate the extent of disloyalty in the relocation centers, and western newspapers gave wide publicity to charges and speculations of the committee members.

Through May, June, and July the Japanese-language papers faithfully reported the whole burst of antagonism and suspicion. Evacuees in the centers read the stories carefully, discussing the misinterpretation of registration figures, ridiculing the wild fears of congressmen that the unobtrusive neighbors in the next barracks could be dangerous because the sons had answered No in protest and the parents had asked for repatriation out of fear for their security in the United States. Nevertheless, as the attacks intensified in June, most evacuees expected that something would be done about the registration figures. They had expected it ever since registration and now the public clamor seemed to make it certain.

At the same time they were seeing confirmation of the other expectation to which registration had given rise. Many had concluded then that the WRA was getting ready to resettle everyone who had answered Yes and had not asked to be repatriated to Japan. They knew that the WRA had established field offices in Chicago, Spokane, Kansas City, St. Louis, and other places for the purpose of finding jobs and paving the way for evacuees to resettle. They knew also that young men and women had been leaving the centers in some numbers during the spring. By June 1 nearly 9,000 had gone out to settle in the Mountain States, Midwest, and East. More important than these developments, however, for the people who were settling into the centers were certain features of WRA policy. In June the Washington office announced a tightening up of employment policy in the centers. Specifically this was to be a correction of the "jobs for everyone" policy which had obtained in the early months. The purpose was greater efficiency in center operations and the means was reduction of working forces to a minimum designed to eliminate overstaffing. This was generally regarded by evacuees as being aimed at stimulating them to resettle. Employment curtailment was immediately interpreted as a move toward forced relocation. The anxiety had been growing steadily in the weeks since registration. When the project director at Minidoka announced in June that movies were to be discontinued in the center for the summer, this confirmed evacuee fears that they faced indirect pressures and that there would be efforts to make the centers less pleasant places in which to live. Other centers did not follow suit, but the feeling of impending pressure in them was strong.

By late May, as a result of the news of the congressional committees reported in the Japanese-language and other papers, the expectation of some move to separate persons classified as "loyal" and "disloyal" was intense in all the centers. Rumors increased during June and by the end of the month persons in some centers who had requested repatriation to Japan were packing their belongings in preparation for some sort of move. On the sixth of July the Senate passed a resolution urging the separation of the people in the centers on a basis of loyalty. About two weeks later the WRA announced plans for what it called "segregation." The Tule Lake center was designated as the place of segregation. All persons from the ten centers who had asked for repatriation to Japan and all American citizens who had applied for expatriation to Japan were to be sent to Tule Lake. In addition all American citizens, men and women, who had answered the Army registration loyalty questions with No would also be sent there. The WRA policy makers recognized that both these classifications would cut across some family lines, despite the efforts evacuees had made to maintain family solidarity in their answers and requests, and so the provision was made that family members could accompany other members of the family to Tule Lake. These were to be classified as "voluntary segregants," and their going to Tule Lake would not be considered an expression of disloyalty. The WRA policy makers, well aware that the categories of persons they had set up included many who were not disloyal to the United States, did not emphasize loyalty and disloyalty as the basis of segregation in their announcements to evacuees. They presented it as a move to separate those who "wanted to live as Japanese" from those who did not. This, it was felt, was more in line with the evacuees own feeling about the separation. The removal, WRA officials explained, of certain groups to Tule Lake was not a punishment for past acts or expressions but rather a move toward establishing more harmony among evacuees in the centers by placing like-minded people together. There would now be one center in which people could live peacefully according to Japanese ideals and way of life and nine centers in which they could live in the American way. However, many staff members in the centers did stress loyalty. The official Washington interpretation was known chiefly to a few evacuee leaders and did not penetrate deeply to the people in the blocks.

With the announcement of segregation the tensions of April and May resulting from the unanswered questions about the future were somewhat relieved in all centers but Tule Lake. The great majority of people in the other nine centers would be little affected by the transfer itself. Only a thousand, more or less, in each were faced with an immediate move; only for those in the segregated categories and their relatives did important problems arise. At Tule Lake, on the other hand, the great majority of persons were faced with moving to some other center unless they were on the lists of persons to be segregated. Tule Lake consequently was thrown into a new turmoil, and signs that people would put up some resistance to being moved again began to appear immediately. It meant for them the third move within about a year and they did not wish to undergo it, particularly since they were classified as "loyals." Tule Lake was thrown into a turmoil which no other center experienced.

In the other nine centers the majority of people accepted the new development very quietly. There were a few in each, particularly among those who had emerged in positions of leadership, who regarded segregation as a desirable thing. They were convinced that among the repatriates and expatriates there were some who were too antagonistic to the WRA administration to make peace possible so long as they remained in their centers. These few leaders wanted to see the strongly disaffected men eliminated and felt that harmony in the centers then could be more easily achieved. Such feeling among leaders was particularly strong in Jerome. There a group of young and older men had advised people strongly to ask for repatriation and expatriation during registration. They were convinced that there was no future for Japanese in the United States, believed that Japan would win the war, and that Japanese-Americans would be wise to prepare to live somewhere in the Japanese Empire after the war. The first step toward this, they argued, was to declare oneself for Japan.

The relatively few leaders who thought this way in Jerome, some of them from among a deeply bitter group evacuated from Hawaii, had met determined opposition from other evacuee leaders. Three of them had been expelled from the board of the Young Buddhist Association, and the expulsion resulted in a split in the Buddhist Church of Jerome. The smaller, avowedly pro-Japan faction formed its own Buddhist Church, called the *Daijo* Buddhists, while the majority, opposing their point of view and advocating a future in the United States, continued to maintain the Denson (named for the Jerome post office) Buddhist Church. There were similar small groups in other centers—at Heart Mountain where a similar conflict played a part in the splitting of the Buddhist Church there and at Manzanar where there was considerable sentiment during and before registration for preparation to live in Japan after the war.

Following registration the factional antagonism in Jerome was strong for a time, but had died down to some extent by July. Elsewhere the few strongly pro-Japan individuals had never figured prominently in community life and did not seem very dangerous to other evacuees—even in connection with preservation of harmony in the centers. There was, nevertheless, a little sentiment here and there that segregation would contribute to more peaceful living in the centers. This was in line with widespread feeling among WRA center staff, who since registration had tended to magnify the disrupting influence of the "disloyal" among the evacuees. Even staff members, however, by the time segregation came were beginning to be doubtful as to whether the removal of anyone would do much to promote the harmony that was already being achieved. The processes of community organization had already begun to produce a workable cooperation in all centers.

If the move to separate the loyal from disloyal had come immediately after registration, it is likely that there would have been much more feeling among evacuees that it could serve some useful purpose. The feeling was stronger then that there were some sharp differences of viewpoint among evacuees and that the differences might lead to disruption of center life. By the time segregation came, however, the most widespread feeling was that, except for a few queer people who did not fit into block life very well, the majority of those who had answered No or asked for repatriation were not essentially different kinds of people from the rest. They fitted into block life better than did those who thought in terms of unprotesting acceptance of the Government program. The tenor of majority opinion in regard to segregation was that it was probably a waste of Government money to have such a large number of people shuttled back and forth between Tule Lake and the other centers, that it was an unnecessary move for those directly affected, and that it was too bad to force friends to separate once again. The program for separation was accepted in the nine centers by the majority as one more indication of the government's lack of understanding of the group and one more arbitrary vagary to be endured and made to go off as smoothly as possible.

For the small minority in each of the nine centers, however, the meaning of segregation was quite different. For those classified as "segregants" it meant moving again, an upsetting and tiresome business of which there had been too much already. For some among them, particularly the older people who had even before registration decided to go to Japan, the move was welcome because it seemed to lead to definite security for the duration of the war in a center where no more moves of any sort would have to be faced. There was a similar welcome security involved for the several hundred young men who were interested primarily in avoiding the draft. Also, for the few who were devotedly patriotic to Japan, Tule Lake seemed to hold forth the opportunity of a place where they could live uncontaminated by the loyals and begin to prepare themselves for a future in Japan by studying the Japanese language and practicing pure Japanese customs. For such persons, wholeheartedly devoted to Japan or perfectly clear in their minds that their economic security ultimately lay in Japan, the move to the segregation center could not come too soon. But they constituted a minority of those scheduled to be sent there.

Most of those classified for Tule Lake fell into other categories despite labels which lumped them together. There was the large class of defiant and protesting young men whose original motive in saying No had been criticism of the United States Government but not expression of loyalty to or even interest in Japan. Many were holding to their No answers despite opportunities given by the WRA to reconsider. Some of them were beginning to find reasons, which they had not dreamed of at first, for building their No's into reasons for going to Japan. Others still remained uninterested in Japan and were harried by the idea of being placed with Japanese patriots at Tule Lake, but their defiance was also still strong and they were ready to go through with it and let their future unfold as it might. For these No answerers segregation was further evidence of their persecution by the Government and they greeted it with further defiance and cynicism.

By far the deepest problems were for the families whose members fell into different classifications—sons who answered No and parents who answered Yes and hoped to stay in the United States; parents who asked for repatriation and sons and daughters who were determined to stay in the United States and had answered Yes; brothers, some of whom answered No and some Yes, and parents who did not know which way to turn; parents who asked for repatriation and under-age children who had not been required to answer anything, but had been going to school in the United States for years. Many families, feeling from the first the implications of the registration decisions, had tried desperately to get all their members on the same side of the fence, but many had not been able to agree. Now they were faced all over again with the same struggles they had gone through during registration. In every center, segregation was a time of family conflict, for there were roughly 100 to 150 families in each center who had to decide whether to go to Tule Lake as a group or to separate, some going to Tule Lake and some remaining in the relocation centers. A partial way out was provided in the WRA regulation that family members could go to Tule Lake without being branded as disloyal, and for the most part family loyalty prevailed so that families did go or stay as groups. The question mark of the future hung heavily over thousands of young people who obeyed the family will and went to Tule Lake as a postponement of the ultimate decisions.

The dilemmas of segregation were not confined to the determined young men and women already down as No answerers and the parents already down as repatriates. On the margin of the 4,000 to 8,000 majority in each center who were down on paper as "loyals" and faced no official compulsion to move, there were hundreds who were tempted by the possible securities of Tule Lake. If Tule Lake was to be the one center where one could look forward to no more moves for the duration of the war, why not go there? Why not change one's answers to No or why not ask for repatriation or expatriation and so get sent to Tule Lake? Then the fear of forced relocation would melt away. One could be sure of not being pushed out into hostile Chicago or Detroit where they had just had a race riot. Perhaps one could wait quietly until the war was over and then slide back into the old place on the West Coast.

There were rumors that Tule Lake was an unusually pleasant center— the name indicated that there was a lake there, photographs and description sent around to the other centers by the WRA indicated that it was no worse at least than where one was, and WRA officials were emphasizing that it was not a place of punishment. People decided to ask for repatriation or expatriation since that was the means by which one could gain the *security* of Tule Lake, not in terms of any ultimate future in the United States or Japan. Families settled their differences in the

A new category of persons was created as the bureaucratic machinery ground on: "voluntary segregants." These were the children in no way considered disloyal who must accompany their parents who, for a variety of reasons, had been classified as disloyal and must be sent to a newly created segregation center. This situation was as incomprehensible to many Caucasians as to these children at Jerome, Arkansas, September, 1943.

compromise of security for the duration, friends influenced friends to come along with them to avoid separation and to live quietly at Tule Lake. For some in the far eastern centers, like Jerome and Rohwer, it even became a way of getting back to California; their decisions meant no more than that. Steadily the numbers of those scheduled for Tule Lake increased—families successful in getting their adult members all classified together, new applicants for repatriation, "voluntary segregants" by the thousands accompanying their parents or even parents accompanying their eldest sons. Tule Lake had become a temporary escape from what the WRA policy makers conceived as freedom in the resettlement program, a cynosure for people seeking immediate security.

The segregation process in the nine centers moved smoothly, very smoothly as compared with registration. People had been prepared for months; it was no surprise. The majority had to make no new decisions even though tempted sometimes by the apparent securities of Tule Lake. There was elaborate preparation for the processing and movement of people by the WRA staffs who had been instructed from the start to encourage participation of evacuees in making the transfer arrangements. Evacuee committees were encouraged to gather information about the details of the segregation center, the status of the segregants, and the steps necessary for those who were to be moved and to pass the information back into the blocks. One project director insisted on eliminating the word "segregation" from all center announcements and bulletins. The process at his center was merely called "transfer," which well fitted the majority evacuee conception of what it was. Pleasing cooperation was shown in every one of the nine centers, cooperation on the part both of persons scheduled to go and those remaining who did everything they could to help the process go smoothly. Through September and October the trainloads left the centers amid farewell parties and little gatherings of friends saying good-bye for the duration, while from Tule Lake came new trainloads to fill up the barracks again in all the eastern centers. At Poston, Manzanar, and Gila it was a one-way process, with segregants leaving but no one coming in from Tule Lake.

At Tule Lake the process was not at all smooth. The burden was lightest for the "disloyals"; they had no move to make and were established now for the duration. But for all the others, the great majority, segregation meant breaking up the household and going to a strange place all over again, a sort of second evacuation. Most eventually chose centers from those available where they had friends or acquaintances. But several thousand were not ready to accept the move so easily. Where in the other nine centers the temptation to go to Tule Lake had been felt by hundreds, at Tule Lake itself the desire to remain was strong for thousands. For them, unlike the majority in the other centers, segregation was as much a peremptory order to do something they disliked and feared as had been registration. And there was a tradition of widespread refusal to comply, represented in the 3,000 at this center who never filled out registration forms.

A large number had refused early in the program to choose centers to go to and more pleaded in interviews that they could not move because of illness or other reasons. Passive resistance developed in solid units in the blocks which had also resisted registration. In the discussion of the older people the Japanese word "to move again" was used both for "segregation movement" and for "resettlement, or relocation, movement." The two things, distinct in the minds of the WRA staff, had identical meanings for large numbers of Issei, and they were reacting to segregation as they would to forced relocation, which had become as widely talked of here as at other centers. A rumor spread through the center that those who remained at Tule Lake would have prisoner-of-war status and would receive $50 a month for the duration of the war. This was real security and many were acting on a belief in the rumor.

The WRA staff were forced to take steps which did not enter at all into the segregation process at the other centers. Speakers went out to the "wards" as groups of four blocks were called at Tule Lake, to try to correct the effects of the latest rumors and to carry on educational campaigns to counteract the resistance. The project director read carefully prepared speeches to mass meetings, and interviewers worked intensively on persons reluctant to make their family plans. Early talk among older people of sit-down resistance to any movement gradually became restricted to certain blocks and wards. Ultimately, however, 6,000 people remained at Tule Lake, and only 2,000 of these were in the categories of segregants defined by the WRA regulations. The other 4,000 were "unauthorized"; they had decided to remain at Tule Lake not because they had any particular sentiments of loyalty one way or the other but because they did not like to be pushed around, or they did not want to leave California, or they did not want to be sent too far away from home, or because they just did not want to move again.

The sorting of the people was accomplished by early November. All had been classified; all who would go had been transferred from Tule Lake to six other centers. All but 3,000 of the 12,000 scheduled to be sent from the other centers had been transferred to Tule Lake. Only 2,000, for whom there was no room at Tule Lake, still remained at Manzanar to be sent at a later time as soon as sufficient barracks should have been constructed at the segregation center. Another major movement of the evacuees had been carried out without serious incident. The meaning of the sorting to the people who had undergone it was quite different from what it was to the people on the outside who saw it in terms of the labels of "loyalty" and "disloyalty." The sorting had little important effect on people in the nine centers now designated as "relocation centers," but to those segregated at Tule Lake the effects were almost immediately cataclysmic.

FRUITS OF SEGREGATION

The trains moving westward from Arkansas, Wyoming, Colorado, Idaho, Utah, and Arizona carried evacuees back to California, but there were fewer from Granada and Minidoka than from any of the others. After a year of processing since evacuation, nearly 9,000 were headed back to their home state to live in the segregation center. This was the third uprooting, once from their homes, once from the assembly centers, and finally now from the relocation centers. No one was precisely sure what "segregants" and "voluntary segregants" meant, but all were hopeful that it meant no more uprooting for some time. Most arrived at Tule Lake in September, the others (except for those from Manzanar who were to be transferred later) during October. After further processing and fingerprinting down to the youngest, they settled into the strange blocks with the 6,000 "Old Tuleans" who had remained in the segregation center.

They were a more heterogeneous group than had entered any of the original relocation centers. They came from nearly all the counties of California where Japanese had formerly lived. There were 656 Hawaiians who had been in Topaz and Jerome, and there were a few hundred evacuees from Washington and Oregon. An expatriate wrote back to a friend:

This center compared to Topaz is a center from all parts of the West Coast—not just the East Bay Region of California. You always had some former friends around at Topaz. But here it's very hard to get to know people. In my particular block, there are people from almost every center and every part of California.

You just can't make friends with just anyone without knowing a little about their background. Thus it's hard to get the least bit congenial with your block people, ward people, center people. One noticeable thing about the Japanese here, though, and that is if the Issei came from the same "ken" in Japan they were more apt to become friends.

The new population of Tule Lake was different in other ways from the people left in the nine relocation centers. There was a greater proportion among them of poorer, rural people. A large number of unmarried farm laborers who had never made any success of life in the United States and who had no stake in the country in the form of family or property had come here, many of them with the idea of ultimately getting their way paid to Japan where they could live out their last years. There were also poor farm families, often large ones, who had not been doing well in the United States and were ready to give up. The WRA staff felt that this center was noticeably different from the others in the relatively large numbers of such people, less well off economically, less courageous, less confident in their ability to make a living for themselves than the average of the evacuees. "People with problems," as staff members phrased it, seemed to have come to Tule Lake.

If they had not been extremely different in their feelings about the possibility of a future in the United States when they left the relocation centers, they quickly became so. As the trainloads came in, there was no mistaking that the United States Government regarded them with intense suspicion. The little camp of military police at the border of the center grew steadily into a large garrison. Barracks for 1,000 officers and men were constructed. Army engineers went to work on a new fence surrounding the center—no simple affair of a few strands of barbed wire such as had been put up around the relocation centers the year before, but an eight-foot, heavy wire mesh, man-proof fence with barbed wire at the top sloping inward. And as the final trainloads came in, evacuees saw small tanks armed with machine guns lined up in the military area. The Army was ready for action against someone whom they evidently regarded as dangerous. The third uprooting had piled people into a place far more remote from the world of normal human relationships than anything they had experienced so far.

As soon as they entered the center the peace and the security that most had hoped for seemed to fade farther away than ever. The center was more bare and brown than any of the others except Topaz. The lack of irrigation water and the tension and confusion through the spring since registration had kept the people from giving it the greenery and air of being lived in that characterized almost every other center by this time. It was crowded, as crowded as had been any of the early centers. Recreation halls were turned into barracks for the bachelors. The whole atmosphere pervading the place was a repetition of the distraught early days in the relocation centers. But Tule Lake was even more upset, even less of a community of like-minded and congenial people than had been any of the early centers. The blocks were more heterogeneous, and the community crosscurrents swirled more rapidly and with greater intensity through them.

The majority of people who had got on the trains at the relocation centers were, as those had felt who gave them farewell parties and waved good-byes, much like all the other people in the centers. They had gone through the settling processes that took place in the relocation centers during the first half of 1943. They had learned to accept the centers as peaceful havens for the duration of the war and differed chiefly in their decisions to seek even greater security at Tule Lake. But from the moment they stepped into the trains and then as they stepped out into the segregation center an unsettling process had begun. They became aware almost immediately of a minority among them who were determined to give the segregation center a special meaning. This group, like the minority of Nisei leaders in early Manzanar, were determined to bring center life into some direct relationship to the war outside the center, but unlike the Nisei leaders of Manzanar they wanted to give it meaning in relationship to the Japanese war effort.

The conflict between conceptions of the segregation center held by the majority and by the active minority was clearly revealed in the plans for Japanese-language schools. As soon as the new people arrived a group of older men from various centers got together and organized a Japanese-language School Board. Their position was that the majority of people who had come to Tule Lake ultimately intended to go to Japan and that the WRA had said that they would be free here to "live as Japanese." Some felt strongly the need for preparing their children to live in Japan and recognized as most important the need for learning the Japanese language. Others felt that whether they ultimately went to Japan or not, speaking Japanese was essential for living like Japanese. The young people had merely a smattering of Japanese or an imperfect knowledge picked up in the pre-evacuation Japanese-language schools of the West Coast communities. The board therefore worked out a plan for schools which would be operated entirely independently of the WRA administration and would maintain class hours which did not conflict with the WRA English schools. There was wide support among the people for this plan. It became apparent immediately, however, that there were several Japanese language teachers who wanted their classes to be places for intensive indoctrination of the children in the current Japanese political propaganda. One group set up a private school and called it the Greater East Asia Co-Prosperity Sphere School and posted such a sign on the door. They were vigorous in their attempts to make their classes into active schools for the furtherance of Japanese mannerisms. Board members expressed disapproval. Moreover, as soon as the schools were established, it became evident that strong pressures were being applied to get students into them. Voluntary segregants who still had no interest in Japan and did not want to attend Japanese-language schools found themselves under pressure not only from parents but also from young men who wandered about the blocks checking up on attendance and seeming to threaten the stragglers.

This phenomenon of pressure from rough young men who took it on themselves to get people "into line" in one way or another was the first and most vivid expression of the working of the community cross-currents at Tule Lake. Young men moved about the center in groups, bursting in and breaking up Nisei dances, denouncing the style of dancing as "not Japanese." Others appeared in women's shower rooms, announcing that "This is Japan and here men and women bathe together." Still others slapped and insulted Nisei girls serving as clerks in the housing office, asserting that they were not helping the newcomers sufficiently with their housing problems. One night in October a gang of young men systematically smashed all the windows in the housing office. This was an unleashing of rowdyism, somewhat reminiscent of the gang activities in the centers during the moving in. It was a different rowdyism, however, aimed not at the beating up of Nisei leaders who stood as symbols of the miseries brought on by evacuation. It was more random and undirected, and to a greater extent represented merely youth running wild in a totally disorganized community. Nevertheless, there was some purpose in the activities of the gangs of young men. The new Tule Lake population differed from that in the nine centers now in the greater proportion of young men who had received some schooling in Japan—the Kibei. Disapproved by the majority of Nisei in the centers

The confusion that led many perfectly loyal Japanese to sign the Army-sponsored questionnaire in such a manner that they were classified "disloyal" resulted in the separation of families and friends. Many sad farewell parties were held, such as this one at Heart Mountain, Wyo., Sept., 1943.

because of their imperfect English or lack of familiarity with American ways and etiquette, they now found themselves in a majority in the segregation center. They took as license the designation of the center as a place where people could live like Japanese. Their treatment of Nisei girls, their objection to American dancing, their support of Japanese-language schools were all expressions of their newly found status, and they were busy trying to pull into line the "voluntary segregants" and the other Nisei who knew little Japanese and had been in the habit of looking askance at Kibei. As a Nisei girl said shortly after her arrival at Tule Lake:

Anything can happen in this dump. It's almost as bad as being in Germany. You wonder why you were born. No fooling, these guys have no respect for women, and boy, do they believe in Gestapo methods. You can't use your own mind. You gotta be on the alert of what you say, and on top of that you gotta respect the Kibeis.

The Nisei who had yielded to family sense of duty in going to Tule Lake were even more unhappy than they had expected to be. They were encountering pressures now not only from parents but also from young people of their own age group to "behave like Japanese." The formerly disapproved Kibei were in the saddle.

Crosscurrents which had largely subsided in the relocation centers as moderate Issei opinion had become dominant were set in motion anew in the segregation centers. Little groups of men from Jerome, Heart Mountain, Poston, and Topaz began immediately on arrival at Tule Lake to seek positions of leadership—men who had been relegated to positions of unimportance in the relocation centers, leaders of minority factions in the Buddhist churches, or discredited political leaders. Like the Kibei they felt that here in the segregation center their view of things could become dominant. There were many of their kind still in the relocation centers who had not come to Tule Lake for various reasons. Those who did come were the most determined and vigorous. They were angry about evacuation and subordination in the relocation centers. A few of them were seriously interested in getting to Japan, but for most of them the dominant interest was in asserting themselves and their dignity in the face of mistreatment. Groups of leaders determined among themselves quickly on plans for organizing the people in the upset center. There were little struggles for position among themselves, with a group from Jerome, with support of Poston and Heart Mountain men, emerging as dominant. They raised issues which had general appeal for the incoming segregants—dust control, better block facilities, improvement of food—all projected against the better conditions in the centers from which people had come.

Before many people had got their bearings in the new center, the new leadership was organized with a Negotiating Committee and picked spokesmen for dealing with the administration. Late in October they sought to develop popular support. The death of a farm worker from Topaz in a truck accident became the occasion for a public funeral which was utilized to rouse and focus public opinion against the administration and conditions in the center. Trouble developed between the farm crew and the administration. The crops lay unharvested in the fields. An issue grew. The leadership maintained that the people of Tule Lake did not want to harvest crops part of which would be sent for use in other centers. They wanted, the leaders maintained, Tule Lake labor and produce to be used only for Tuleans who had determined to be Japanese and not for other evacuees who had determined to be Americans. The administration proceeded to recruit evacuees from other centers to harvest the Tule Lake crops. The gulf between the administration and the suddenly risen evacuee leadership widened.

Finally the leaders decided to make a real show of their strength. On November 1 the National Director of the WRA visited the center. The Negotiating Committee went up to the administration building to present their points to him and the project director—and behind them came thousands of evacuees from the blocks to stand through the afternoon surrounding the administration buildings while the leaders presented their case. Young men worked at the edges of the crowd keeping the people there and, at the doors of the buildings, keeping WRA staff members inside the buildings. The crowd, estimated as high as 10,000, stood and sat patiently, men, women, and children, for three hours. It was the biggest and best organized demonstration of evacuees that had taken place in any center.

It was also the most premeditated and least spontaneous demonstration. The new leadership had worked out the details carefully. They had planned it as a peaceful show of strong popular support for their program, but few in the crowd knew all that was being presented to the National Director. Many had come up as a result of announcements in the mess halls that there was to be a protest over the "bad food." Others had not even as definite an idea as that for their coming, but had simply been told to appear. The leaders began their presentation with a request for some definite statement as to the legal and international status of evacuees at Tule Lake. They wanted to know whether they were prisoners of war, aliens, or what. They presented their criticisms of living conditions in the center and ended with a demand for the dismissal of six top staff members at the center, including the project director. This last was the most positive effort of an evacuee leadership to assume some control of the staff under whom they had to live that had appeared in any center. It represented the sort of feeling about center life that had been steadily submerged during the previous year in the relocation centers. In a sense it was the final direct and organized expression in any center of the rebellion against Government supervision which most evacuee leaders felt but had learned to express less directly and sweepingly. The aggressive expression of the demands for removal of personnel did not have popular support from the thousands of evacuees who came up to the administration buildings. It was not ordered by them but was the expression, as one evacuee said, of "a few leaders who had more push and 'guts' than common sense."

Planned as a peaceful demonstration, the gathering of evacuees did not go off entirely quietly. While the crowd was gathered around the administration buildings, some young men entered the hospital, sought out the very unpopular chief medical officer, and gave him a severe beating. This and the pushing back of a few staff members who sought to leave the administration building during the afternoon, together with the whole spectacle of the evacuees surrounding the administration building, had effects which began to work even more strongly after the crowd had peacefully retired to the blocks with the National Director's assurance that he would study the Negotiating Committee's points. Fear grew up and spread among the staff. There was a demand from some that a fence be put up between the administrative and evacuee areas. False rumors spread that there had been knives and other weapons among the demonstrating evacuees and that there had been attempts to set the buildings on fire. Many members of the staff were terrorized and their stories got to newspaper reporters who publicized the incident throughout the country as a dangerous attack by the evacuees of Tule Lake on the WRA staff and as a threat to the nearby towns.

In the atmosphere of tension immediately following the demonstration more happened. Some evacuees who had participated or watched the demonstration were pleased with what had happened. One who saw it from the hospital wrote to a friend:

There exists within the center a common idea of unity that no other center can achieve. The leaders are all men of ability, high caliber and possess diplomatic talents. [On Monday, a crowd went to the administration building] similar to the crowd that occurred during the Santa Anita riot. During the three hours 20,000 of us waited eagerly, as from time to time one of the representatives would state, "Now's the time for united spirit; we must not fail or else the whites will take advantage." We should be proud of our race. He sure brought up the morale. At the end, the results were presented by the Japanese leaders and the [National Director]. It seems that our committee of eight had won the first round.

The sense of triumph expressed itself in several ways. On November 3, the anniversary of the birthday of the Emperor Meiji of Japan, a small celebration was sponsored by a group of the leaders, and pressure was applied to workers in the administration offices to leave their jobs during the morning and attend the celebration. This increased the fears and distrust among the staff.

Then on November 4 violence broke out on a small scale. A group of young men who had heard that trucks were to leave the warehouses during the night to take food to the evacuees recruited to harvest the Tule Lake crops determined to stop the trucks. There had been a notice after November 1 that no evacuees could come to the administration area without passes. In their efforts to locate the trucks (which were actually bent on another task) the evacuees were intercepted by internal security officers and a fight took place. The movements of the gang and the officers in the administration area roused other staff members and there was a brief period of excitement. In the midst of it the internal security chief called the commander of the military police and a contingent of soldiers with guns and tanks came into the center. Some of the young men were captured after one internal security man had been badly beaten, and the captured men were in turn beaten by the internal security officers.

The Army came in to stay for several weeks. The center was placed under military supervision: jeeps and command cars began patrolling the center, a fence was put up between the administrative area and the blocks, and soldiers placed on guard at the gates. A curfew was instituted. The whole center was systematically searched for weapons (which were not found) and for the leaders of the demonstration. The leaders were placed in a stockade and some were held for ten months. The military police maintained control over the center for about two months, and the basis for working relations between evacuees and WRA staff was upset. The segregation center had become a place of real repression. The peace that people had been looking for had receded farther away than ever. The future loomed dark and the present became plagued with community crosscurrents far more complex and far more destructive to security and individual balance than had ever existed in the darkest moments of the first months in the relocation centers. The forces that made Tule Lake what it became had been present in the other centers, but there they had been channelized and brought back under control by both the character of administration and the stabilization of the people under their leaders. At Tule Lake they had been stirred into motion again and were not to quiet down until the final weeks of the center—almost two years later.

The incidents at Tule Lake in November provided the last real material for the movement to bring all the evacuees under a regime of greater repression—the movement that had begun with evacuation and had been largely responsible for the program of segregation. Tule Lake immediately became the focus of investigations by the California State Senate and the Dies Committee. The WRA and the evacuees were attacked again. Pictures of a threat to the whole nation were conjured up out of the demonstration. Newspapers everywhere headlined the incidents, stirring excitement from one end of the country to the other and particularly on the West Coast. The Dies Committee carried its investigations to Washington, but in the face of the facts the attack and the charges gradually petered out. Steadily, as the evacuees of Tule Lake took up their new life under Army control, what national interest there was in the evacuees turned to the resettlement plans which the WRA now had for the 73,000 left in the nine centers.

3.

SETTLING DOWN

The process by which a few hundred of the most bitter and least well balanced of the evacuees had been skimmed, along with thousands of other average people, into the segregation center was only one aspect of a sorting which had begun in the early months of the relocation centers. The moment that the rich and poor farmers, established and struggling businessmen, students, housewives, and fishermen had entered the centers they sorted themselves into congenial groups. The voices of the bitter and the unbalanced steadily became submerged—as they do in ordinary communities which are not unbearably oppressed—in those of the sober, the practical, and the experience-wise ones.

During the process individuals emerged in every center who could find no peace or satisfaction in the developing center way of life. As soon as the doors of the centers were opened a little in August 1942, a sorting began into those who could adapt themselves to the centers and those who could not. The young men and women who had never been a part of any Japanese community on the West Coast in any real sense began to leave the centers in the fall of 1942. A few hundred had left permanently even by January 1943. Young people who had been straining against parental controls for years broke off and went out. In the spring of 1943 about 7,000 left the centers. Some were young people responding to the situation in typically American individualistic fashion, some were the children of parents who did not feel themselves part of the Japanese community in the United States. They were people whose identifications were so completely with the majority group that life in the centers was painful. There were others, too, who began to leave in the spring and early summer of 1943. Some of these still felt some identification with the Japanese community, through intimate bonds with parents who were much a part of the community or through a good understanding of and sympathy with the problems of the group as a whole. But despite such feelings (and some of those who left had begun in the centers with a desire to "serve the people" and help them in the crisis) the framework of center life had defeated them. As the meaning of government supervision closed in on them, as they encountered the frustration of sharply limited leadership in the framework of life under an agency, or as they felt the impossibility of solving the problems of the group so long as the group clung to the centers, they gave up and moved out.

The spring of 1943 was characterized by the disappearance from the centers of many young men who had emerged as leaders of the Nisei councils or as vigorous community organizers. They were not men who had rejected the Issei or who had antagonized the Issei by any lack of understanding of the problems of the group as a racial minority in the United States. They had worked hard and sympathetically with the center communities as wholes, but they began to feel that there was nothing important they could do from within the centers. They saw their base of operations as on the outside and they went out to Chicago, Cleveland, Minneapolis, and elsewhere. By no means all such persons left the centers during 1943, but many did. The centers were well sorted in this respect even before segregation took place.

The solid core of the former West Coast communities were the ones who remained in the centers at the beginning of 1944. . . . The nine centers—now called "relocation" centers with a new emphasis by WRA to contrast them as bases for resettlement with the segregation center— were thus purged largely of the extremes which had lived at their edges in the years before. The people in them were the people who had made the Japanese-American minority what it was before evacuation. They were the old communities, peculiarly refined, set down under the circumstances of government supervision in strange places. It remained to be seen in what manner the people and the government program would adapt themselves to each other.

PROGRAMS—GOVERNMENT AND EVACUEE

For more than a year prior to December 1943 two programs for solving the problem of the future of the evacuees had been developing in considerable isolation from each other. In Washington a group of men who composed the top staff of WRA had long since reached the conclusion that the problem of economic rehabilitation of the group would best be solved by beginning that process immediately without waiting for the war to come to an end. Only, they believed, if evacuees moved out of the centers and took up life promptly in normal communities could they establish a base for meeting their individual problems in a postwar United States. The whole conception of the program of resettlement, or relocation as these men called it, rested on this belief. The quicker evacuees moved out of the restricted and dependent status of the relocation centers, the better it would be in the long run for their morale and their economic future. These men knew too much about the people in the centers to accept the easy interpretation of segregation as a separation of the loyal and the disloyal. But they were convinced that if there were any dangerous persons among the evacuees, they would either have gone to Tule Lake or would be sifted out in the processs of leave clearance for those in the nine other centers. Now with segregation completed and the demands of Congress and segments of the public for a separation met, the men in Washington felt that they could move more vigorously to carry out their plan for general resettlement.

To this end they had set up in October, while segregation was still in progress, a special division of the WRA to coordinate the whole program of resettlement—the Relocation Division. Field offices to find jobs, houses, and public acceptance for evacuees had been established in cities all over the United States outside the prohibited West Coast zone. WRA officials had been pleasantly surprised to find an abundance of requests for evacuees to fill available jobs and also to discover that there were citizen groups in many places not only willing to accept evacuees in their communities but also to aid them actively in getting reestablished. In Cincinnati, in Cleveland, in Chicago, in Milwaukee, and elsewhere it was evident that there were more places for evacuees than there were evacuees willing to take them.

The attention of the men in WRA therefore turned to the centers. They felt that their big task was one of informing evacuees adequately of the many jobs, the acceptable living conditions, and the good community acceptance which they knew existed, but about which evacuees did not know. They were well aware of the evacuees' small knowledge of any parts of the United States except the West Coast and their fears of the areas outside. To inform the evacuees, leaflets were written and distributed to the centers describing cities and regions where evacuees were resettling successfully, movies of resettlers were made and shown in the centers, and in the winter of 1944 "relocation teams" of WRA field office staff began to visit the centers to tell evacuees directly of conditions in their areas. The WRA policy makers were aware that their program depended on patient persuasion as well as simple providing of information. Plans included formation of committees in which leaders of the evacuee communities could participate in furthering the program. In the winter of 1944 every family in every center was interviewed to encourage and assist them to plan for resettlement. The Relocation Division's vigorous action was begun almost simultaneously with the completion of segregation.

The people in the centers had expected an intensification of the resettlement program and felt that they saw it in the tightening up of center employment which was announced in June and carried out in following months. They were, in accordance with their distrust of WRA policy makers, looking for evidences of the "forced relocation" which they expected. They began to see what they felt were signs of it in developments during the winter of 1943-44. This belief was strengthened with the appointment of the relocation commissions composed jointly of staff members and evacuees. Two centers already had such commissions—Rohwer and Gila—and most other centers proceeded to form groups, so that councilmen and other evacuees appointed to the commissions or boards became aware of Washington's interest in more intensive organization for stimulation of resettlement. In addition, bulletin boards in the centers were posted with pictures of happily resettled individuals, offers of jobs, and information concerning various parts of the United States. Relocation teams came and went, showed movies, talked to mass meetings and

A massive persuasion program was set up to convince Japanese-Americans that it would be to their advantage to leave the centers and relocate in the Midwest and the East before the end of the war. The faces of these men, listening to a Japanese-speaking relocation officer at Rohwer, Ark., register the difficulty of making a decision. Dec., 1943.

Some traces of home and comfort appeared at Rohwer, Arkansas, center when trellises, walks, and gardens blossomed at barracks doors.

individuals about opportunities outside, and interviewed families concerning plans for resettlement. There was therefore no doubt in the centers that the WRA was working hard to persuade people to leave and resettle. Evacuee leaders in constant contact with staff were well aware of the emphasis on resettlement. The people in the blocks were much less so, but many got glimpses of it in block bulletin boards, or in the movies and talks of the relocation teams, or eventually as a result of being called in for a family interview. Some were quietly considering jobs and making their decisions to go out. There was a constant trickle of persons through the relocation offices every week. But for the great majority in the centers consciousness of the resettlement program amounted to an awareness that the WRA staff in the administration area and the WRA in Washington wanted people to leave the centers—which was something they did not themselves want to do.

The WRA program was impinging on another program which had been developing over the same period. In the minds of the evacuee leaders was a program for holding on to the security that the centers offered until the war should end. The main features of this program had been formulated many months before and the majority in every center had steadily accepted them as the most practical and realistic approach to the ominous problem of their future. In isolation from the policy makers in Washington the influential Issei in each center had been weighing their losses, what they knew of the attitudes of Americans towards them, the extent of the government offer of financial aid in resettlement, and the possibilities for any future assistance. Most had decided that the best course was to hold on to the centers for as long as they could, a popular program in the centers where people had grown accustomed to the restricted life, shrank from moving again, had many immediate securities, and were fearful of the outside.

In December at Minidoka, where the project director had taken various actions which led evacuees to believe that he wished to force them to resettle, a group of leaders presented a statement of their position to the Spanish Consul for submission to the United States and Japanese Governments. In a section entitled "Spiritual and Mental Welfare of Evacuee Residents," the statement set forth the reaction of the leaders to the resettlement program:

Relationship between WRA and Residents

The evacuee residents of this project with a sincere desire to abide by the laws of the United States, to preserve peace and harmony within the project, and pursuing a policy of patient forbearance, have at no time resorted to improper conduct. It is fully realized that in view of war conditions, our feelings of dissatisfaction and uncertainty are to a certain extent unavoidable. But it is indeed regrettable that certain segments of the American people, press, politicians and government officials have deliberately and maliciously fanned the flame of anti-Japanese prejudice. We in these relocation centers have been used by them as a "political football," and to spread false and inflammatory reports designed to harm us. Within the center itself, the overbearing attitude of racial, social and intellectual superiority assumed by most of administrative officers, high and low, in violation of the announced WRA formula of mutual cooperation, has undermined the morale of the residents. All of these factors have severely tested our confidence in American justice and our sincere desire and willingness to abide by its laws. With a view to removing these and other causes of our feeling of uncertainty from our daily existence, we earnestly desire a clarification of our wartime status and in particular our relationship with the WRA administration.

WRA Relocation Policy and the Residents' Reactions

Early in the evacuation stage, the Government announced that for the protection of the evacuees themselves, it will retain them in relocation centers for the duration, and guarantee them food, clothing, shelter, and also recreational and educational facilities. Despite this promise, the Government abandoned this original policy, and began to enforce a policy of persuading evacuees to leave the centers and resettle in American communities. The existence of intense anti-Japanese feelings and its threat upon the personal safety and livelihood of the evacuees are well-known to the authorities in charge of the evacuees' welfare. Despite those and other unfavorable circumstances, the Government, acting through the WRA, has undertaken to impose upon the evacuees a policy of sprinkling them unnoticeably across the length and breadth of the country.

This statement was signed by a group of sixteen Issei leaders in the community. Several were men who had been serving the project director as advisers on community organization. Several were men who were shortly to emerge as the most prominent and effective community leaders after Minidoka finally established a community council. They were not extremists, but representative of the sort of men who were regarded by evacuees as responsible and capable leaders in dealing with the administration. Their statement to some extent reflected special conditions at Minidoka, where the approach used by top staff members in promoting resettlement had more than anywhere else roused evacuee opposition. The statement however may be taken as reflecting the state of mind of majority leaders in all centers concerning the resettlement program. It was more than that. It presented what were coming to be the accepted points of argument in all centers on behalf of the evacuee program. Broken promises in regard to the security of the centers, the impossibility of the situation on the outside for persons of Japanese descent, and the intention of scattering evacuees far from each other through the country—these became central points in the statements of evacuee leaders everywhere as they opposed, either in discussions among themselves or with WRA staff, the government program. As the weeks passed and the evidences of intensified WRA effort increased, reactions such as these by the Minidoka leaders also intensified. It was program against program. The WRA policy makers and the evacuee leaders had not worked together in the development of their programs and now they had moved very far apart.

The resulting impasse was felt most keenly by the WRA staff in the centers. So long as "forced relocation" did not actually appear, the evacuee leaders could simply withdraw. The Washington staff worried about low resettlement figures, but they were not faced with daily frustration as were center staff members at work on the job of furthering the WRA program. To some extent, however, the staff also withdrew from any head-on conflict with the evacuee program. Aware of the active antagonism of evacuee leaders, staff members at Topaz, for example, followed the tradition of that center by steering clear of using the word "relocation." The reasons were indicated in the statement of a staff member:

> Careful observers in camp have long been aware of a strange paradox in resident thinking, namely, that almost one hundred percent of the evacuees express themselves as opposed to relocation in theory, 'though in practice a sizable minority obviously approves the policy since hundreds actually join the "immigrant train." Thus, even the very mention of the word "relocation" makes residents resentful and makes some bristle with indignation.

It was evident that the evacuee communities were setting themselves against any general acceptance of the WRA program. Leaders were formulating their position, the majority of people were simply ignoring resettlement as they went about their affairs in the blocks, while a few made plans and went out. It seemed to Washington authorities that center staff members were not pushing relocation vigorously enough. Staff members did not see how it could be pushed without rousing more intense opposition. Some were already convinced that there was "organized resistance," mistaking the solid pattern of community sentiment for a sort of underground movement designed to sabotage the plans made in Washington. Staff members settled down to chip away at the edges of the community attitude by helping those who voluntarily came to the center offices to ask for aid in reestablishing themselves outside. Steadily during 1944 the mass approach of the relocation teams gave way to the individual approach of the family counseling program.

To some extent the predictions that evacuees had made during registration were coming true. First had come segregation with its separation of the No and the Yes answerers. Next had come an intensified resettlement program, which if it was not forced relocation was at least motivated by WRA's desire to see everyone leave the centers. Now in January came the draft; the War Department, like the WRA, was following through on its program. Nisei, it was announced, were to be drafted as replacements for the Nisei combat teams which had been giving such good accounts of themselves in the Italian theatre of war. At Poston, at Heart Mountain, at Topaz, at Granada, at Minidoka, at Rohwer, at all the centers there were meetings. Block representatives were elected to a citizens committee at Topaz to thrash out the old issue: conditional or unconditional acceptance of the draft. A "Voice of

Nisei" anonymously posted signs in Poston urging young men not to report for induction until all civil rights had been restored, and almost immediately a counter "Committee for the Restoration of Civil Rights of United States Citizens of Japanese Ancestry" was organized to urge acceptance of induction but at the same time to petition the President for restoration of rights. At Topaz, as the citizens committee worked on petitions, a committee of mothers from the blocks also struggled with a decision between a strongly and a more mildly worded petition to the President. At Heart Mountain the strongest organization against unconditional acceptance of the draft appeared—the Fair Play Committee—and speeches were made which echoed those of the year before at registration. Feeling at Heart Mountain was if anything more intense among the Nisei than it had been before. Rumors grew up in the centers that the draft was to be called off, that all Nisei who reported for induction were being turned back, that nothing would be done to any who did not report for induction. Through February the centers continued to be stirred, as young men reported. In Poston III and other centers there was a mounting pile of requests for repatriation by parents and new requests for expatriation by sons and daughters. People were resisting the drafting of their sons by finding a way to go to Tule Lake where they did not face the threat to family solidarity. Apparently some who had not gone to Tule Lake before were merely waiting to see whether the threat of the draft would materialize. Now it had come and they were ready for Tule Lake. More than 200 from all the centers refused to report for induction or for physical examinations, and United States marshals were beginning to come and take the boys away for hearings or to jail. But, as in registration, the majority had signed up and now they were leaving the centers in little groups. The War Department program, like the resettlement program, was draining off the young men from the centers. As spring passed the communities increasingly became places of the old and the very young.

Resettlement and the draft were two facets of the same program. The policy makers in Government offices were carrying through on the plan which they had conceived in 1942 for bringing the evacuees back into the mainstream of American life. The program struck at the roots of the security which had been achieved since evacuation—the unity of families and the shelter of the relocation centers. The resistance which the Government program inspired reflected not only the desire to retain this security but also the whole history of the minority group. Voluntary relinquishment of the centers seemed to them a further loss of autonomy. What they phrased as refusal to be further "pushed around," the policy makers regarded as short-sighted "resistance to freedom."

EVACUEE ORIENTATIONS

The various processes of sorting had, by the winter of 1943–44, resulted in the achievement of a high degree of common sentiment and opinion among the evacuees in all the nine centers. The differences between early and late centers had been largely leveled. All had now gone through their crises of growth. Every center, particularly as regards the evacuee community, was very much like every other center. The sense of solidarity and agreement on fundamentals reached its peak in the winter of 1943–44.

Coming into the centers from the farming communities, the cities, and the small towns of the West Coast, the Japanese immigrants and their children had found themselves for the first time in their lives facing a common problem on common ground. Domestic workers, farm laborers, produce merchants, shopkeepers, students, Buddhists, and Christians had been funneled by evacuation into an identical situation. Momentarily at least they had felt the same about evacuation: the dismay, the anger, the sense of unjust treatment, the distrust of Caucasians— all these feelings they shared in greater or less degree as they moved on into the relocation centers. The cry, "We are all Japanese together," had risen quickly out of these emotions, but once the phrase had been formulated, the variety of meanings which people attached to it revealed the differences which during thirty or more years had crisscrossed the clusters of Issei and Nisei in West Coast communities. Volunteering, resettlement, and segregation removed from the nine centers most of the people who held variant interpretations of the phrase, "We are all Japanese together." The nine centers were now dominated by heads of families who had some common understanding of the expression. It was heard much less than it had been in the early months, because people did not need to use it so much.

A staff member at Poston wrote in January 1944:

In a recent conference which I called to consider child welfare and youth guidance procedures, the familiar dilemma became evident: whether the project services should stand back to be called upon by the residents, or the professionals in the project administration should reach down into the blocks to direct the living of the residents along the lines which we approve. In the discussion several interesting observations were offered by a young, Japanese-born, American-educated Block Manager who has had social work experience in connection with a California Juvenile Court.

He agreed that the life of the project is now sharply separated in its orientation around two opposite poles: the California Japanese culture, which, as he reminded us, is at least 20 years behind the social progress of the Mother country which these people left at least 20 years ago; and the professional Americanism of the schools with their curricula, their recreation and activity programs, and their appointed teachers from all over the country. The first pole represents the orientation of what he called "the core of the community." To belong to this core, one must have been for years a member of one of the Japanese cultural clusters from which the residents came. The process of relocation, he said, has simply drawn off the individuals who were farthest from the core—like molecules escaping by evaporation from the surface of a liquid. . . . The young people who are left . . . are increasingly reabsorbed into the culture of the core. They are learning more Japanese—with or without Adult Education's sanctions; are conforming more closely to family expectations; are marrying rather unexpectedly with non-English speaking Kibei; and for the most part, are "postponing" their plans for relocation to some indefinite date.

Most staff members were not so clear in their understanding of what had happened in the postsegregation communities, or did not have such articulate interpreters of the situation. For the majority there was merely increasing awareness that they were now dealing with Issei to a much greater extent than Nisei and that the blocks seemed farther away, more remote from the administration buildings. There was a consciousness of people "out in the blocks" or "up on the hill" going their way in a world that staff members were inclined to describe as Japanese.

Few would have understood the emphasis of the block manager when he said, "California Japanese culture." What he meant was that the men and women who now dominated the life of the centers were as much, if not more, Californian than Japanese. They had left Japan, as the block manager insisted, twenty, thirty, or forty years before. Japan had been for them, before evacuation, more a memory than a reality. The reality of which they bore the marks in the seams of their faces was Fresno, San Francisco, Hood River, Imperial Valley, Seattle. They had struggled to make their livings in these places, adapted themselves to Irish section-gang foremen, Italian merchants on the produce market, old American vegetable ranchers, and more recently farm laborers from Oklahoma, and had schemed to get their children through the city and country schools and on to the universities in Berkeley and Seattle. Although they bowed endlessly when they met one another, got together for picnics with Issei from the same Japanese prefecture, drank sake with relish, and ate raw fish when they could get it, the values around which their lives had shaped were California and Oregon farms, houses in Los Angeles and Sacramento, American ranchers and produce buyers, and American schools and children. For a generation since putting on American clothes they had moved along roads and streets which had led them far from Japan. The core of their experience had been in America. The Issei world was not a Japanese world.

The minds of the family heads in the relocation centers were oriented to a constellation of values which had ruled their lives for thirty years.

These values were not different in outline from those of any other group that one might pick in the United States. They were deeply interested in their homes, property, and businesses, their friends and business associates, their children, their immediate families, and some of their remote relatives. But almost every one of these values with which they felt such deep concern was involved in a complicated milieu lived in by no other group except the Japanese in the United States. Their homes and property and businesses were, or had been, in states which maintained laws against their owning land and in a country which prohibited them from assuming the obligations and privileges of citizenship. Many of their business associates and even friends were unpredictable in their behavior and often maintained peculiar barriers and attitudes towards them. Their children frequently could not communicate with them very well and obviously looked askance at some of their ideas and customs. Their brothers or sisters or cousins lived in a nation with which the United States was at war. The complicating factor in connection with all these values was, of course, being Japanese—being Japanese in America. From the deep-going and pervasive insecurity arising out of denial of citizenship to the little daily frustrations of being unable to communicate with children, the fact of being Japanese was central and inescapable. It was intertwined with everything of importance in the lives of the Issei.

Being Japanese in the United States, then, had very real meaning for the family heads who now dominated the nine relocation centers, a meaning not to be explained in the simple concepts of loyalty and disloyalty used by nations at war. In the first place there was the feeling of being Japanese which had nothing whatever to do with Japan's place in international affairs. Pride in being Japanese was something which every Issei had. It was a feeling embedded in each, permanent and unchanging, independent of distance from Japan or rises or falls in the fortunes of the Japanese nation. It was the sense of pride of being some sort of human being, the sort of human being that one was. It was a simple and basic fact for Issei, but it was also one of the most difficult spots in the relations between Issei and Nisei. Few Issei had escaped the sharp disappointment and dismay of finding that their sons did not have a simple pride in being Japanese. The gulf between Issei and Nisei on this score was great. Issei were dismayed and exasperated although sadly sympathetic, to find that Nisei had no bulwark against American prejudice and discrimination, such as they did in the rocklike pride of being Japanese.

Being Japanese had other meanings for Issei which were connected with Japan, the country. Most had come to the United States with some idea of returning to Japan eventually. Steadily, however, during the 1920's and 1930's as their families grew and their economic stake in this country became more solid, the idea of return faded. They still talked about it—it had become a sort of habit for some through the years, but the talk had more the character of recalling a pleasant dream or plan that one had once had. The interest in Japan and the possibility of returning there was, however, kept alive to some extent by the sense of insecurity in this country. Even though a man knew in his heart that he no longer had any real intention of returning, he still felt that something could happen to force him to take his family back. The impossibility of attaining any legal status in this country, the recurrent rises of hostility between Japan and the United States, the persistent discriminations against Japanese by Americans—these things kept alive for Japanese a somewhat more vivid interest in the Old Country than for other immigrants. It was a practical interest which nourished the fading sentimental interest.

This interest during the 1930's became an issue in all the West Coast Japanese communities. Nisei who were maturing in the United States rebelled against it. They felt some sympathy for their parents' nostalgic indulgence and for them as aliens. But they felt that the turning toward Japan endangered the future of the whole group in the United States. Able to think of Issei merely negatively as aliens, Nisei had little or no understanding of what was to the Issei a very positive side of the matter, namely, that though they might be aliens in this country they were also citizens of Japan. After the Manchurian invasion in the early 1930's Issei began to make contributions to Japan and to send soldiers' comfort bags. Some Nisei leaders and a few Issei protested. But the contributions went on. The China "incident" did not seem to be an issue which particularly involved Japanese interests in the United States. Japan was a good country, the Issei had relatives there, and they would like to help out. Only in early 1941 when, as Issei interpreted Matsuoka's foreign policy, it began to seem as if the Issei stake in America might be involved, did they stop.

Once evacuation had taken place and the Issei, together with their children, were in the relocation centers, being Japanese began to have additional meanings. They had been attacked by and cut off from the United States. The evacuation capped a long series of discriminations against Japanese in America. Now it had been extended to their children, despite the fact that they were American citizens. With heavy property losses and the prospect of having sometime to start at the bottom again, Japan began to appear as a hope. The Issei were still Japanese citizens; that was now the only clear-cut status they could see that they or their children had; nothing had happened to that. During the first months in the relocation centers Japan seemed to be winning the war and people talked a great deal about what it would mean if she should. Some merely took out their aggressive feelings about evacuation against the United States Government in hoping for a Japanese victory. Others thought about the situation a little more carefully. The important thing seemed to be not that one or the other should win. The important thing was that if Japan should emerge as a strong nation, either through victory or a negotiated peace, then the Japanese minority in the United States would have a strong nation at its back. Japan could protect their interests here as she had never done before. They might hope for pressure to repeal the alien land laws, to permit Japanese to become citizens of the United States, to lift the restrictions on immigration. The whole accumulation of discriminations which had handicapped them might be eliminated. A strong Japan would mean greater security for the Japanese in the United States. A few even went so far as to hope for funds for rehabilitation from Japan after the war, but this seemed doubtful to the more sober. The hope for a strong Japan loomed large in the centers during 1942 and early 1943, a hope tied in closely with the general desire to remain in the United States and to continue the lives they had been building without Japan's aid in Oregon, Washington, and California. This attitude toward the war, rather than the first burst of identification with Japan in evacuation-inspired feelings of aggression against the United States, was the one that had grown and brought people under its sway after two years in the centers. The majority had come to regard Japanese success as the best basis for their future in the United States.

As the war developed in the Pacific, the people in the centers began to realize slowly that Japan was not so strong as she had first seemed. The possibility that she might not win began to be accepted here and there. The sense of insecurity in this country was increased by such a possibility. There had been present among the Issei from the moment of evacuation the feeling that evacuation might lead to stronger measures by the United States. Deportation after the war was felt to be a real possibility. Had not congressmen and California legislators brought up such a possibility? There had been deportation of aliens after World War I. It was necessary to plan for such a possibility. For most it seemed merely to reinforce their feeling that they should remain in the centers until the war was over and it was clear what course of action the United States would choose. For some it seemed to call for a more positive attitude about remaining in the centers. At Heart Mountain and elsewhere there was talk of the Japanese criminal code. Someone dug up the fact that the code provided for two years' imprisonment for any Japanese citizen who voluntarily aided an enemy nation in time of war. Resettlement, it was reasoned, involved a voluntary decision to go out and contribute to American manpower. That would make one liable to imprisonment if he were ultimately deported and, if it became known in Japan, might result in harm to one's relatives. This highly refined argument was not taken too seriously be very many, but its currency in the centers indicated the nature of the approach to the issue of resettlement.

Being Japanese in the relocation centers in wartime thus had very definite meanings for the Issei. The end of the war was a key point in their program in relation to the centers. They could not accept the view of the policy makers in Washington that the war was irrelevant to their future in the United States. Too many elements of that future were bound up with being citizens of the country with which the United States was at war and with the ultimate outcome of that war. In one center where the composing of three-line poems, called *senryu*, flourished, an Issei put into a poem what he and thousands of others felt about it:

Balancing the war news
With his own future—
Dilemma of dilemmas!

The aspect of being Japanese, apart from legal status and the place of Japan in international affairs, also took on new meanings in the world of the relocation center. As it had always been a source of strength in the milieu of prejudice and discrimination on the West Coast, it was now more than ever a bulwark in the restriction and subordination of center life. It flourished in the blocks, where the Issei pitied the Nisei a little in their lack of it and tried to build it up in them. It nourished old prejudices against the hakujins and was expressed in many ways in center life. There was much talk in the centers about the spiritual greatness of Japanese as compared with the mere material greatness of the Americans. The spirit of the Japanese —*yamato damashii*, or *seishin*, according to the more new-fangled usage—became a sanction for many kinds of behavior. It was in this spirit that people urged one another to stand up against the administration in the Poston strike. But it was also in this spirit that they controlled themselves in the face of injustice and obeyed the laws of the country in which they were living. An Issei used it to encourage volunteers for the Nisei combat teams in Minidoka. Buddhist priests invoked it in honoring Nisei dead in the service of the United States. It was also in this spirit that people urged one another to present a solid front against being pushed around any further and to maintain their right to remain in the relocation centers.

The program of the Issei for their future was built solidly on their stake in the United States. The outcome of the war was a factor, and therefore Japan was a factor. But the war was an unknown in the equation. All of the known quantities were in the United States, and the Issei viewpoint was tied solidly to these. Their program was built on America; Japan was merely a hope and possibly a necessary last resort. America meant homes, property, business, children, and Issei and American friends. All of these except the children and other Issei were in California and the other two states of the West Coast. When they first came to the centers, almost universally Issei had expected a short war. The centers were to constitute a short vacation and then they would be back in California. The nostalgia for the Coast during the early months in the dusty centers was intense; it had not really been left behind. The idea of moving on somewhere else hardly crossed an Issei mind. Through the months two trends appeared. The West Coast faded a little for a few, particularly for some who had not been very happy there. The tie weakened a little, and here and there decisions were made to have a try at life somewhere else for a little while. Then the belief grew that it would not be a short war. After the first predictions of peace in April 1943, and again in August 1943, failed to materialize, people began to think that it might turn out to be a long war. A very few responded to this belief by planning for a temporary start somewhere to the east.

The overwhelming majority of Issei in the centers by 1944 were still looking back to the West Coast. Their roots were there. They had property stored there. They knew their way around. They were in touch with friends in the former communities. Many still had property there which they had rented out for the duration of the war. The ties of thirty or forty years had not melted away. Chiefly only the young or the formerly less well established looked eastward. Moreover there was, beside the emotional and economic ties, another point to be considered. So long as the West Coast remained closed, there was not a free choice about going somewhere else. They were being forced, they felt, if they chose Chicago when San Francisco was not a possible choice. Until the Coast was open, they said, the government had no right to send them elsewhere. Thus California and the other Coast states were more than home. They were also a symbol of the government's unfulfilled obligation to restore their freedom of choice and movement. In this the thinking of the men in Washington coincided with that of the Issei; the relocation centers should be available until the right to return to their homes should be restored.

One feature of the former stake in the West Coast was not there any longer—it was now in the relocation centers. This consisted of the other Issei on whom Issei had depended in their businesses and farm production. Every Issei who had been a part of a Japanese community at all felt strongly his dependence on other Issei. It was not only the very important matter of association in churches and other organizations, but also in financial support, in organization to meet competition and withstand discrimination. Few of the Issei left in the centers felt able to go out and start anew without the long-standing mutual support of other Issei. A large part of what had made life both possible and worthwhile on the West Coast had depended on the relations among Issei. This was in the minds of the Minidoka leaders when they wrote the Spanish Consul that WRA had plans to scatter the Issei over the length and breadth of the United States. To them it seemed on the very face of it an unfair and destructive plan. It did not even seem necessary to label it as such. In Rohwer, during 1944, plans grew for what certain leaders called "colonization." This meant resettlement in large groups in the farming country of Louisiana or elsewhere. In following months in other centers the idea began to be talked of more and more. It was an expression of the deep desire to hold on to that part of the stake in the West Coast homeland which Issei still had with other Issei in the centers. It was not a feature of the most widely agreed on Issei program in all centers, but it indicated one of the essential points of disagreement between the Issei and the WRA. It was part of the determination to hold on to the West Coast stake.

The other major value in Issei life which was solidly a part of America were their children. They had placed an unusually high value on education in American schools and colleges and had more consistently than any other immigrant group seen to it that their children finished high school and went on for higher instruction. Only a small proportion, less than 13 percent, had attempted to have their children also educated in Japan. The trend among the Issei who were in the United States in 1942 when evacuation came was to provide their children with the most possible American schooling in order to help them combat the discrimination which existed on the West Coast. They were, through their children, planning for a future in the United States, and recognized that their children's future was in this country. As one father in Topaz put it, when he sent back unsigned an application for repatriation which had been sent him: As the proud father of nine children—all Americans—I would like to stay and see what their fate in their own native country will be.

The Nisei were a value for the Issei, but the Issei generally did not believe that the Nisei were capable of taking care of their rights in the American milieu. Many professed to be disappointed with what they regarded as the Nisei leaders' too easy acceptance of evacuation. Issei groups attempted to inject themselves into the discussions of the reopening of Selective Service in Topaz and other centers. Everywhere they felt that although the Nisei had interests distinct from the Issei in this country, they needed their fathers and mothers to guide them and stand up for them. Moreover, Issei also felt that they now needed the Nisei in their declining years to take care of them, and they urged family solidarity in the face of possible deportation to Japan or "forced relocation" from the centers. The Issei feeling about Nisei and the relocation centers resulted in constant and persistent conflict. The parents repeatedly expressed fears of what living in the artificial communities would do to the young peoples' morale and initiative. They decried the tendencies in the centers to misbehavior and "delinquency," and yet they felt that more was to be lost by breaking up the family through resettlement than by keeping the young people in the centers with them. All the other points in connection with their program for remaining in the centers for the duration of the war were clear and certain. Only the future of the Nisei bothered them in the relocation center setting.

The outcome of the war, the West Coast stake, the Issei community, and family solidarity were the fixed points on which was reared the Issei program for their future. The weighing of these values over two years had resulted in a common agreement: they should hold on to the centers for as long as the war lasted. The point was clear. But the WRA did not agree. The plan of the men in WRA was not taking into consideration the main factors which had made the Japanese-American minority what it had become over a period of forty years. The WRA therefore loomed as an antagonist in the sentiments of the community leaders. They had settled down to a fencing match with the WRA as the year 1944 began.

STABILIZATION OF STAFF-EVACUEE RELATIONS

In the year since registration, people had settled deeply into the blocks. The coming of Tuleans to the eastern centers during segregation had briefly stirred the calm of block life, but since then they had merged with the older block residents. The daily round of getting up, going to the mess halls for meals, going to a job somewhere in the center, gossiping or playing baseball or Japanese checkers in the evenings had become routine. The pattern of living in the limited world of the blocks while waiting for an unknown future to unfold seemed to be set. A former WRA Washington staff member wrote in February, 1944, after a visit to Topaz:

The most striking impression on revisiting Topaz a year after registration is the remarkable sameness, a sameness in the black tar-paper barracks, the lack of trees, the biting frosts, and the isolated circular thinking of the residents.

Topaz, in common with Heart Mountain and Minidoka, had changed little physically. Because of poor soil or long winters the transformation from bare camps into tree- and garden-studded spots which had taken place in Manzanar and the Arkansas and Arizona centers had not been possible. But what the outside observer charac-terized as "circular thinking" was just as apparent in the other cen-ters as in Topaz. To outsiders, evacuees seemed out of touch with reality, ingrown, nursing ideas which had no relation to what was taking place in the world around them. Washington staff members of WRA felt it every time they dropped in on a center. Evacuees seemed perverse to them, and they devised plans for informing them of current events and bringing them out of the isolation of the relo-cation centers.

The people had settled deeply into the blocks. A relocation center now consisted roughly of 9,000 evacuees or, if it were one of the smaller units, of 4,000 evacuees. At its edge was a newly constructed unit of "personnel housing" into which staff members who had been living in neighboring towns or in barracks were moving as fast as they became ready. In these, depending on the size of the center, lived 100 or more Caucasians, men and women who ran the offices in the administration buildings, supervised the work crews in the ware-houses and on the farms, and struggled to carry out the plans and regulations that came by teletype and mail from Washington. The social life of the majority of staff members was confined to their own group. Every staff had a small group who mingled socially with some evacuees, but the majority who maintained strictly business relations with evacuees looked a little askance at such persons. They were marked as a special group, and conflict and little rifts developed occasionally as when they attempted to make an issue of opening a personnel recreation hall to evacuees as well as Caucasians, or spoke in favor of "fraternization." Thus, although there were friendly and even intimate relations between Caucasian and evacuee office work-ers and some development of visiting back and forth between a few evacuees and a few Caucasians, the staff in general constituted a segregated minority living at the margins of the relocation center

Enforced isolation only intensified the awareness that the cycle of life is perpetual here as elsewhere. The lonely first grave in the Manzanar cemetery, July, 1942.

communities. They were walled off by a recognizable line between them and the people who had now settled so deeply into the blocks.

Relatively few evacuees came over to the administration area at all, except for an occasional visit to the post office, the hospital, the lawyer's, or some other office. A couple of hundred evacuees, mostly young women and men, came to the administration buildings daily to work in the offices, went back to their block mess halls for lunch, and came again to work for the afternoon. They came to know a few staff members, but generally learned little about what was going on outside their own offices. From almost every block a few young men went out daily to work in the warehouse area, a little removed from the administration buildings, where they saw the supplies come into the center and got to know a supervisor or two. Older men went out, often with no Caucasian supervisor, to work in groups on the farms. The children in the schools were in daily contact with several Caucasian teachers and often the teachers became friendly not only

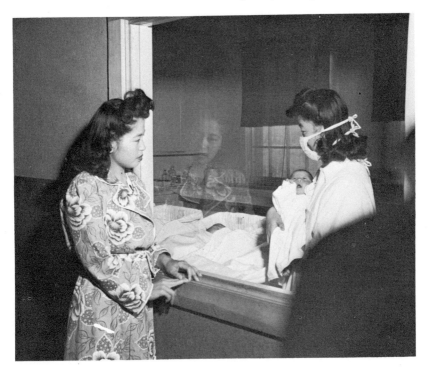

And the pendulum swings to the other extreme—the proud and contented face of a mother as she views her baby through the nursery window at Heart Mountain, Wyo.

with the children but also with their parents. Aside from such contacts there was little association between the evacuees and the Caucasians in the centers. They were living in worlds which were intermeshed at only a few points where younger evacuees and a few older made contact during office hours. However, the consciousness of the evacuee world, massive and solid around them, loomed large for staff members who rose every morning to see it stretching out before them and whose daily work dinned some aspect of it into them constantly. The staff world, on the other hand, had faded into vagueness for most evacuees, as they moved out of sight of it in the blocks.

More than half the adults lived almost wholly in the little rectangular communities of their own blocks. The older people and some of the younger Kibei who lacked confidence in their English sought jobs within their blocks. They worked in the mess halls, as block janitors and gardeners, or in the block manager's offices. Nearly a third of the working adults were so employed in a block. They left their blocks

Every center had its newspaper, and at Heart Mountain, Wyo., the *Sentinel* is being folded and wrapped for distribution, Jan., 1943.

only for a visit to the community store, for an evening of entertainment at one of the stages or athletic fields set up in the center, or for visits with friends or relatives in some other block. They might go for weeks on end without even seeing a Caucasian. By 1944, after two years, there were hundreds of people in every center, particularly in the larger ones, who had not even walked through the administration area after their arrival. They lived in a world of Japanese faces, makeshift barracks quarters, and opinion and attitudes which had been formed in that milieu. What they knew of the busy little hives of activity in the administrative areas came through comments of block managers or block councilmen, an occasional announcement in Japanese posted on the mess hall bulletin board, the center newssheet, or gossip or rumor based on sources even father removed from contact with administrators than the block officials. Their world, however, extended out beyond the center, skipping over the administration area as it were, through the Japanese-language newspapers and some English-language papers and through correspondence with old friends on the West Coast and with evacuees who had resettled or sons who had gone into the Army. This was the link with the outside world on which they chiefly relied. The general tendency was to discount all that they heard about resettled evacuees and about attitudes towards them on the outside that came through the WRA offices. It was colored, people felt, by WRA's anxiety to get them out of the centers and therefore unreliable.

There was nevertheless a bridge between the center communities and the peripheral segment of the administration area, a bridge wrought from the WRA blueprints for "community organization." Out of the 9,000 evacuees in a large center there were seventy or more men, usually two from each block, who came into contact at least weekly with some of the top administrators. These men were the block managers and the members of the community councils. Every center except Manzanar (which had only block managers) now had its two groups, and the three units of Poston and the two units of Gila had in addition over-all organization at least formally linking the units. At Heart Mountain the council, which had always been composed of Issei, was the more important, and the block managers, chiefly Nisei, served more or less as assistants to the councilmen. At other centers both groups served as important links with administration, and dominant personalities emerged at different times from among either the block managers or councilmen and guided staff-evacuee relations. There were manifold differences from center to center in connection with the esteem in which either councils or block managers were held at different times by either the evacuee community or the administrators. There were differences in operation between the two bodies and differences in conception of function and division of labor. Except at Heart Mountain, the block managers had, through the nature of their duties as dispensers of supplies, better understood and more stable relations with people in the blocks, and their clear-cut and immediately useful activities generally gave them a stronger position with both evacuees and administrators. The significant feature of councils and block managers, however, was that they were both performing the same important function—that of liaison between the two groups, administrators and evacuees, who made up the center communities.

Individual administrators here and there had a good understanding of the dominant sentiments and motives of the people in the blocks and had developed techniques for getting along with those segments of the community with which they had some dealings, but the majority of staff members in every center had only a superficial or partial understanding of the evacuee community. They were, moreover, constantly beset by frustrations arising out of the failure of evacuees to behave as they thought they should and therefore their vision was often clouded by at least latent antagonisms. The evacuee community, on the other hand, was out of touch with the administrators and the sentiments and motives which produced the regulations from Washington and determined the relations of the administrators with evacuees. Among the evacuees there was also a persistent current of antagonism to WRA which interfered with their understanding of the administrators. In this situation there had always been an explosive potential in the centers. The evacuees who served as liaison between the two groups were therefore in difficult and vital spots.

The evacuees who assumed these positions were not all the same kind of men. Some were quiet, unobtrusive men who were serving unwillingly because their block people could find no one else. For such men the job was routine and they did not make much of the liaison function. But in each group there was always a small core of men who took the job seriously and gave leadership to their council or to their block manager group. Such men had been elected to office (in the case of the councilmen) or selected and recommended for appointment (in the case of block managers) by block people for the express purpose of dealing with the administrators. They were chosen because they could speak and understand English and because people felt they had qualities for getting along with the administrators. They had also been selected because they had demonstrated over a period of months that they could get along with people in the blocks, which meant not only that they were regarded as fair minded and personally pleasant but also that they were sensitive to block opinion in issues of center life.

The men who fulfilled these qualifications and emerged to dominate the councils or block managers were very much the same sort of people in all centers. They were men who had formerly maintained numerous contacts with Caucasians. They were usually insurance agents, storekeepers, hotel keepers, businessmen, doctors or dentists rather than farmers, laborers, or fishermen. They were men who had gotten around more than others in the wider communities in which Japanese lived, who usually had a better than average education and who had some ability to express themselves both in English and Japanese. They were not, therefore, necessarily men who had been most prominent in the affairs of the Japanese associations and other purely Japanese community organizations. Many of the latter were still in internment camps and others, although now in the relocation centers, were in the status of parolees from internment camps. The parolees were not inclined to emerge in prominent positions in the relocation centers. They were not sure it was safe, feeling that there was danger of being sent away from their families back to interment.

Thus the men whom the administrators met with as the leaders of the evacuee communities were not usually men who had been the molders of public opinion in the Japanese communities before evacuation. Nor were they now necessarily the molders of public opinion in the blocks. Some were actually the most influential men in their blocks, but most either looked to one or a few other men in the blocks or were merely one of the several men who determined block opinion. When issues arose block managers or councilmen discussed them with the two or three most influential men in the blocks and determined their own position only after such discussion. They were in a real sense go-betweens, mediating between the blocks and the administrators.

The sphere of activity of the liaison men had been pretty clearly mapped out by the time segregation was over. They had tried and found that they could not directly influence the hiring and firing of appointed personnel in the centers. One council had felt that it had influenced at Heart Mountain the removal of an unpopular Caucasian chief of police, back in 1942, and there were efforts even in 1944 to get hospital personnel removed or transferred, but generally it was recognized that project directors would maintain control of hiring and firing. The evacuee leaders also knew that they could have no influence on the budget and expenditures in the centers. These limitations were quite clear by 1944, but there still remained a sphere of action which seemed to them of great importance. This was bound up with the conception of "peaceful centers" or "harmony in the centers" which some leaders had formulated at the very beginning and had come to seem more and more important after the crises in staff-evacuee relations at Poston and Manzanar in the fall of 1942.

The guiding idea of most of the more prominent liaison men was that the people in their blocks wanted peaceful centers. What was involved in maintaining peaceful centers had become clearer through the months of dealing with administrators. First there was the matter of harmony in one's own block. Most blocks at first had at least a few outspoken men or women who were vigorously anti-administration in attitude. In block meetings they urged resistance to building school buildings, to registration, to Selective Service, to reduction of janitor forces, to most things that the administration wanted done outside the routine of center operation. They urged flat resistance and always found some support from among block people. Such thoroughgoing noncooperation seemed unrealistic and dangerous to the most influential men in the majority of blocks, to the majority of people, and to the sort of men who had assumed the liaison jobs. Ways had to be found to influence people against acceptance of these uncompromising attitudes. Part of the liaison men's job was to bring anti-administration spokesmen into line by persuasion, by pressures within the block, and by maneuvering in block meetings. Block managers and councilmen who were emerging in center affairs spent a great deal of time in adjusting the attitudes of block people to what they had come to regard as the realities of government supervision.

The other aspect of their job, as they saw it, was the adjustment of administrators' approaches to the people to what they were convinced were the realities of block life and opinion. They sought information from administrators about new regulations and order so that they could formulate plans for presenting them to block people in such a way as to arouse a minimum of resistance and opposition and misunderstanding. They tried to persuade administrators to adjust their plans or the wording of administrative orders so as to make them more acceptable to block people. At the same time they attempted to weigh and phrase complaints of the people so that they would not antagonize administrators and yet might most likely result in action. Maintaining peace in the centers thus had two sides as the block managers and councilmen saw it, involving a continual vigilance to avoid unnecessary and useless conflict between the two groups who had to some extent come to regard themselves as pitted against each other.

In order to be able to operate at all in this situation the liaison men had to be sound, from the point of view of block people, on a few fundamental points. They must be aware of the people's general attitude on work in the centers, fundamental because it was the most recurrent source of conflict between administrators and evacuees. A block representative had to understand that the people regarded work as something for the welfare of the community and nothing more. Working in the center had nothing to do with an eight-hour day or any standards of efficiency in terms of which the agency operated; the vital point was that a certain amount of work had to be done to keep the people reasonably comfortable. The monthly wages were token payments designed to fulfill some of the government's obligation for having cut off normal sources of income. Work that went beyond the routine needs of the center residents was the administrators' interest, and evacuees had no particular obligation in connection with it. Basic construction such as the replacement of the corroded pipe lines at Topaz involved no evacuee obligation; the Government had originally set it up and should replace it as part of the basic facilities. A block manager or councilman had to evaluate unerringly the administrators' requests for aid in getting jobs done, evaluating them in terms of what the block people felt it was their obligation to do and not to do. He must not go wrong on this point very often.

A block representative also had to make judgments as to what the block people regarded as moves which meant loss of ground for evacuees. This was especially important in the winter of 1944, when labor reductions were being pushed by the administration. The reduction of janitors in the mess halls at Gila, of block employees generally at Poston, of boilermen and other block employees at Minidoka were administrative moves which had deep repercussions in the blocks. To block people, they stood on the one hand for the disruption of work routines they had grown accustomed to and presaged longer hours and harder work for the employees retained. On the other hand, there seemed to be moves aimed toward making the centers less pleasant places to live in and therefore part of what they felt was the WRA campaign to force them out of the center. The council at Gila understood the significance to the people of mess hall reduction, attempted to work out a compromise, failed, and sank low in community estimation. At Poston the block managers retained face with evacuees and also gained a minor concession from the administration in the reduction of block employees. The liaison man had constantly to be aware of the need for obtaining some concession from the administration, however small, in any moves that threatened the stability evacuees had so far attained in the centers.

Finally, especially during the winter of 1943–44, block representatives had to let the whole issue of resettlement alone. They had to understand that people did not want to resettle and that they must not transmit back to their constituencies any sense of the urgency which WRA staff felt about the matter. They must deal gingerly and not become identified with the staff efforts to persuade people to resettle. It was all right to help in posting notices for a relocation team meeting, if the administration wanted that done, but it was not all right to urge people to go to the meeting or to accept the picture of the outside which the relocation team presented. A representative had to maintain a constant awareness that no one felt that everyone should resettle, even though he might maintain that it was anyone's right to resettle, if he wanted to.

If a liaison man was sound on basic points such as these—did not urge on people work that was the administration's obligation, worked for the maintenance of the status quo, and ignored the resettlement program—he could count on support in his block. If he were suspected of being out of line on such points he became, or ran the risk of becoming, an "administration stooge" to his block people, and therefore without influence. The realization of this by the men who had emerged in positions of influence among block managers and councilmen by 1944 provided the basis for stable staff-evacuee relations. So long as they remained sound in the block people's estimation, they were in a position to work out compromises with the most unpopular administration measures and hence contribute to the maintenance of "harmony in the centers."

To the administrators, the evacuee communities had become something they had to live with. They wanted harmony as wholeheartedly as did the evacuees and boasted about it when they had it. From the lowest paid foreman up the hierarchy to the project director they had been learning how to get along with people under relocation center conditions. After two years many had developed their rules of thumb for getting a maximum amount of cooperation in the jobs the agency set them to do. A foreman in one center summed up the fruits of his learning as follows: "You've got to treat them all as if they were volunteers. If you do that everything is all right." What he meant was that crews who worked under him persistently set their own work periods and rest periods. They, rather than he, determined the amount of work they would do. He had found that there was no conflict if he accepted their standards and adjusted his own to theirs. And what is more, he also found that if he acted according to this rule consistently, his crews would help him out in an emergency by temporarily working according to his, or the agency's, standards in order not to let him down personally.

Project directors and higher officials, not working so directly with individuals but rather with the communities and the public opinion that dominated them, had a harder job. They chafed at the differences between running communities and running an organization of government employees. They looked for the same sort of obedience and respect for regulations and were frustrated when they found that their hierarchy often broke down at the point where an administrative instruction had to pass from a civil-service employee into the community. All recognized from the start that they must deal with the community through some chosen group of evacuee advisers. Some welcomed the idea of the councils and tried hard to work with them. Many had learned by the time of segregation to rely heavily on their councils, on their block managers, or on other specially created committees in accomplishing programs that affected or seemed likely to affect the whole community. In the winter and spring of 1944 they were especially beset, as were the evacuee communities, with the problems of manpower shortage. The resettlement and draft programs were drawing off the able-bodied young men. Retrenchment and readjustment had to take place all through the center organizations. Little strikes, resistance to labor cuts, and resulting evacuee dissatisfactions were constantly up before the project directors. They dealt with the liaison men, whether block managers or councilmen, who in turn dealt with their communities. The project directors who maintained the most harmony in their centers were the ones who learned to prepare the communities first through discussion with the liaison men, to bargain a little with them by beginning from a position from which they could concede a little, and to let the liaison men handle the presentation to the block people. This did not always yield results the administrators wanted because something often happened in the course of the step that they left up to the liaison men, namely, the presentation to the blocks. They felt that the whole of what they wanted said to the people was not said, but they nevertheless were tending more and more to trust the judgment of the liaison men in that step which remained out of their hands. The stability of staff-evacuee relations depended heavily on project directors' willingness to rely in this way on the liaison men. Through 1944 most of the directors of the nine centers learned more and more to do so.

In the midst of administrators' impatience with the system and a pervasive belittling of both councilmen and block managers on the part of the evacuee communities, the liaison functions assumed increasing importance. Block representatives themselves laughed at their own powerlessness to deal with basic issues and painted word pictures of themselves as "administration messenger boys." Nevertheless they knew, as did the wiser administrators, that the liaison functions they had learned how to perform were of solid importance in the maintenance of peaceful communities.

THE CENTER WAY OF LIFE

As compared with the distraught, angry, and fearful agglomerations of people who came into the relocation centers during the first summer of the war, the 70,000 people at all the centers except Tule Lake two years later were settled and calm. They were so, however, only by comparison, and moreover chiefly by comparison of the external features of daily life. The anxiety about the future was as strong as it had been before, but the future had been set a little distance away. The antagonism to the Government was only a little weaker, but it had been channelized into set phrases and attitudes. The peacefulness of center life was based on a postponement, not on a resolution of the questions which had remained unanswered since 1942. The surface calm overlay thousands of individual and family problems with which men and women went to sleep at night and with which they woke up in the morning.

Life in the centers had been accepted by the majority of older people as an interlude. It had become more than bearable. For many it had become pleasant as it took on meaning through association with other Issei, but it was still felt to be an interlude between acts in their real lives. This sense of its unimportance, of its lack of meaning in relation to real life, colored most of the activities in the centers. People tried not to take events in the centers too seriously. The leaders and the liaison men increasingly took this attitude. They had moved from the ideal of "model cities" to the conception of "play-toy councils," as the realization of the artificiality of the communities grew more clear. Life in the centers led nowhere in particular; it was a waiting, but nevertheless a time that could be passed pleasantly.

One of the early doctrines which Issei men had enunciated when they first came to the centers was that they had come "for a vacation." In the first months they stated this view repeatedly, and as the months went by it became evident what they meant. They tried to do what people do on vacations: they put worries into the backs of their minds; they let themselves go; they shunned discipline; they indulged suppressed fancies; they took it easy. For the first year and a half it had not been easy. The issues among evacuees were too urgent; the problems of getting along with the Caucasians were too insistent. But by the winter of 1944, issues seemed to have been settled and the government program had become less insistent. Older people who were still in the centers were taking, or trying to take, their vacations.

A small number of men and women in every center found that vacations were impossible. Their training and experience was needed by the people. Doctors, dentists, and other professionally trained persons in the hospitals found themselves under a constant heavy load of work. Few refused to accept the responsibilities. Men who could cook and manage the mess halls were in similar positions. Ministers, both Buddhist and Christian, found demands on them heavy. Others felt deeply the needs of young people or of the women for guidance and leadership and worked ceaselessly organizing and guiding their activities. For such persons life in the centers was the most intense period of their lives, and satisfactions came chiefly from the respect which the evacuees accorded them. They were a group apart, and periodically the communities became concerned about them, presenting them with gifts, raising community funds to add to their $19 wages, and otherwise making it clear that their services were valued and appreciated.

Other persons found that they were incapable of vacations. Although there was no particular social pressure on them, they found that they had no resources to develop outside their old business or other workaday interests. Despite original intentions of taking vacations they found themselves getting more and more deeply involved in various aspects of center operations. Former businessmen took increasing responsibilities in the community stores, keeping abreast of the markets and learning new fields. Farmers got themselves involved in the chicken farms, the hog ranches, or the center crop production and found little time for loafing. Councilmen and block managers sometimes found themselves too deeply involved in the politics of center life to have much leisure or time with their families.

The great majority of older men, however, did not have such opportunities or shunned them deliberately when they arose. They stuck to original plans and gradually found their vacations satisfying and worthwhile. They took little jobs that carried no responsibility and demanded a minimum of time such as janitors or helpers in the mess halls. Successful businessmen and farmers puttered around their blocks a few hours a day for their $16 or $19 and felt that their duty in behalf of the welfare of the people was fulfilled. Farm laborers and others took jobs outside their blocks on the farms or in the warehouses or elsewhere, worked not too hard, and enjoyed their evenings and Sundays. In their abundance of free time many merely sat around the "bachelors' barracks" or the laundry rooms and talked, speculating on Japanese and American strategy in the Pacific war, discussing bits of news from the outside, or spreading rumors about what WRA was

The game of *go* ("Japanese checkers") was a popular pastime at Heart Mountain, Wyo., and all the other centers.

going or not going to do. Some spent a lot of time carving wood, especially in centers where wood was to be had easily in the country near the center.

A majority of older men spent most of their time playing *go* (a Japanese checkerlike game), cards, or baseball. Every block had its little groups in the evenings and afternoons, in laundry rooms, in barracks, or under the trees in the southern centers, devotedly playing *go*. For hours the men sat poring over the boards with their black and white counters and 361 squares. Interest in the game deepened steadily. Men who had rarely played learned the game; organizations grew up for the purpose of ranking players and determining handicaps, arranging tournaments, and even putting out little booklets diagraming strategy and classic moves and games. The game became an obsession with many.

The chesslike game of *shogi* had relatively little vogue, but *go* claimed more and more devotees. The *go* clubs became the focus of the social life of the older men.

Card games also flourished—the Japanese game of *hana* (flowers) and the American game of poker and others. As gambling had been a major interest of a large number of men before they came into the centers, it continued to be inside the centers. There were small friendly games and there were organized "rings" of gamblers. Some blocks became known as "Chinatowns," ususally where a card-playing group had hollowed a little room out of the dirt under a bar-racks floor where they conducted their games. Farm laborers coming back from seasonal leave had money to gamble. Young and old joined in the games and much money changed hands. Public opinion rose now and again against the gambling, and community councils sometimes joined the protest and made efforts to curb it. An evacuee chief of police in one center was ousted from his job because of talk linking him with the gambling. But, as on the outside, the games went on in the midst of the rise and fall of public disapproval.

The older men also went in for baseball. Every center had block teams composed of Issei and most centers had "Old Men's Leagues." Through the summer they played or went to the several diamonds in the centers and watched and rooted in Japanese-English for their teams. Whole Sundays were spent at baseball and whole evenings de-voted to discussing the games. Between *go*, cards, baseball, and woodcarving, probably a majority of older men in every center passed their time. It constituted their vacation.

In every center there was a smaller group of older men whose inter-ests ranged more widely. Although enjoying an occasional game of goh, they devoted most of their time to indulging interests for which they had never before had sufficient leisure. They took advantage of the concentration of men like themselves and of Japanese books in the centers to read widely, their interests turning to Japanese history, and Japanese-American international relations. Some became inter-ested in group activities such as singing and the composition of poetry. Classes sprang up in *utai* singing, where men and women practiced the intoning of classical poetry—an accomplishment important in social gatherings of the more highly educated people where persons were often called on to make impromptu recitations. Groups got together in every center for the purpose also of composing poetry. The most popular forms were *Tanka* and *senryu*. *Senryu* are lyrics three lines long, each line consisting of a fixed number of syllables, five in the first, seven in the second, and five in the third. The group of amateur poets worked with a leader, or critic, who gave instruction and graded the compositions. Each week a number of themes were submitted by members of the group, one was chosen, and the whole group came together to write their poems on the same chosen theme.

In the formalized *senryu* the relocation center poets expressed vividly and succinctly the meaning of center life as they felt it. The greater number of poems produced had nothing specifically to do with life in the centers, and many felt that the composition of poems should be a deliberate escape from the centers. Nevertheless almost every theme suggested to a few some aspect of center life. Thus the theme "Acclimatization" moved a member of a poetry circle in one center to write:

> Inured to penury,
> The sixteen dollars
> Is more than sufficient.

The Theme of "Service" led another poet to write:

> At the hospital—
> An angel of mercy
> At $16.00 a month.

While "Arms" inspired:

> Every arm
> Evaluated—
> Sixteen dollars.

The *senryu* poets ranged through every aspect of center life:

> Now, after two whole years,
> Everyone can distinguish
> The sound of his own mess hall gong.

> Tomorrow in some other form,
> A piece of scrap lumber
> Is laid away today.

> Manpower shortage—
> Again today wearing
> The shoes of Service.

> The cooperating block
> Rings harmoniously
> With laughter.

The war, both as thought of across the Pacific and as they knew it through their sons in the American Army, was a recurrent theme. "All-Out Effort" inspired one group to write many poems on the theme of Japan gambling her national existence for a place in the sun in Asia, while "Worry" moved a poet to write:

> Trembling hands,
> As the mother opens
> The V-Mail

Enforced idleness nourished revival of another tradition—*Shibai* Theatre at Poston, Ariz.

and "Wrinkles" gave rise to:

> The cream of the crop—
> Nisei soldiers—raised
> By wrinkles on the parents' brow.

Less frequently the poets wrote of the outside and even of resettlement. One poet, letting himself go on the theme of "Numbers," wrote:

> Endlessly,
> Japanophobes
> List of their grievances.

and "Arms" gave rise to:

> "Relocation—
> To the east, to the west?
> Folded arms.

Kabuki, Japanese traditional drama, was revived at the Topaz, Utah, Center, July, 1945.

Senryu poets, men and women, became well organized during 1944 and got in touch with each other in the various centers. On January 15, 1944, the results of a Continental United Senryu Mutual Selection were announced in the Japanese-language section of a center newspaper, the *Rohwer Outpost*. There were contestants from most centers and also from outside the centers. The best poem submitted was written by a *senryu* poet at Tule Lake. The five next best, in order of excellence, came from Manzanar, Santa Fe Internment Camp, two from Rohwer, and Poston. A July 1944, mutual selection on the theme "Smoke" again resulted in a Tule Lake poet in first place and a Poston one in last. Rohwer and Santa Fe were again in the top selections, but now poets from Minidoka and Heart Mountain had also placed as third and fifth respectively. The *senryu* art continued to flourish on into the first six months of 1945.

As some of the more highly educated turned to poetry, others turned to drama. Dramatics groups were organized, with the aid of the WRA recreation staff, in every center. Sometimes a small, exclusive group ran them, but at the Canal unit of Gila there was camp-wide organization with representatives from each block participating in the planning and policy making of the organization. Most of the groups set as their aim the production of entertainment which would appeal to the wide variety of tastes among the center people. They secured the elaborate costumes for and trained young and old in traditional drama of the feudal period—*kabuki*. They arranged vaudeville dialogue called *manzai*. They worked out musical programs in both classical and modern Japanese music. In their productions there was what often seemed to outsiders a peculiar hodgepodge and medley of things Japanese and things American. In March, 1944, at Minidoka, for example a *fujiyose*, or variety show, was given. The program, with program notes by a Nisei spectator, follows:

1. Vocal solos entitled "Cucaracha" and "El Rancho Grande." (These songs were sung in Spanish by a Kibei.)
2. A Japanese modern comedy entitled "Borrowed Wives." (This is the story of two men who made a wager that the women he married would be better than the other. In order to win the wager, both men substituted good-looking women, to pose as his wife. The climax of the play was reached when it became known both had borrowed wives.)
3. A modern dance by a Kibei. (A Kibei dressed as a Chinese girl danced to the tune of a recording entitled "A Flower-Vendor of Nanking.")
4. The Star Band composed of Kibei boys.

Japanese wrestling—*sumo*—was revived at several centers. Tule Lake, Calif. 1944.

(There were saxophone, harmonica, guitar, and vocal solos which were extremely popular with the audience who applauded loudly for an encore.)
5.   A classical drama "*Komamonoya Hikobei.*"
(This is the story of a young man who went through much hardships to acquit his father's innocent crime.)

The whole program except for the Spanish songs was in Japanese. The audience in the mess hall where it was held consisted almost wholly of Issei. The mixture of new and old, of Japanese, of regional West Coast, and of general American traditions was fairly typical of relocation center entertainment interests. This sort of variety show flourished. In the southern centers, as a Rohwer *senryu* poet wrote:

At an outdoor theatre—
Craning necks
One behind the other

became a characteristic feature of center life.

The women in general were having the best vacations. For the first time since arrival in this country most of them were experiencing an abundance of leisure, less isolation in their own homes, and opportunities for daily association with other Issei women. For most their lives had steadily become richer and fuller than they had ever been. Women's clubs of various kinds grew up in the centers. Their interests turned to sewing, the making of artificial flowers, flower arrangement, and learning to read and write English. The last was important for writing letters to sons in the Army, and many mothers learned in the centers for the first time to write letters that their sons could read in English. The groups interested in sewing and flower arrangement met frequently and filled the need of long-starved women for social contacts with persons of their own kind. As one wrote in a *tanka* poem:

Fortunate me! Indifferent
To the fierce fighting
All over the world,
Here I am, learning
Flower arrangement, writing, and embroidery.

The meaning of the centers to many of the older women was summed up in this verse. Later, as they left the centers to return with a feeling of deep loss to lives of work and relative loneliness, many found themselves weeping.

The vacation in the centers was for the Issei a vacation in a deeper sense than they had at first conceived it. Their satisfaction in it did not derive only from the release from work and the constant press of problems in making a living, it was also, as one center observer phrased it, a vacation from assimilation. Placement in the relocation centers among thousands of other Japanese-Americans had resulted in an enforced retirement into Issei communities. This meant, except for a few, no daily adjustment to *hakujin* customers, *hakujin* business competitors, even *hakujin* friends. However small the contacts with Caucasians before, there had always been some, especially for the men. There had always been the consciousness of language, the effort to speak and to understand, the consciousness of not fully understanding. There had always been the caution, the need to act and express oneself in ways that would not be misunderstood, even for the most "assimilated." The relocation centers meant relaxation from this constant, however slight, strain of being regarded as—and of feeling—a little different. In one's block there were Issei all around, Issei of different backgrounds and views to be sure, but Issei whose words and whose thoughts were part of the continuum of one's own. In their presence it was possible to lower the guard, relax, and expand. The older people were, however unconsciously, taking the most thoroughgoing vacations that they had ever had since coming to the United States.

Renewed interest in traditions included instruction in the Tea Ceremony.

For the younger people the relocation centers had no such meaning. They had not wanted or needed vacations. Through the spring of 1944 more and more of the older boys and girls left, many of the young men to the Army, the young women to take jobs in midwestern and eastern cities. Graduation from high school in the relocation centers meant prompt resettlement for many. But many stayed on, unwilling to leave parents whose oldest sons had gone into the Army or unable to persuade parents to let them leave. Although the oldest stratum of Nisei, and particularly of the males, were gone, the boys and girls of high school age and younger were still in the centers. A large number of the oldest ones were unhappy and dissatisfied. They blamed their being in the centers on their parents and withdrew from their fathers. They drifted about the centers in little groups, not tak-

Honors awarded at the first high school commencement since segregation, Tule Lake, Calif., June, 1944.

ing their classwork seriously, and developed a sense of futility. When asked, they said they had no plans for the future, that they could not plan, that they did not know what to plan for. They loafed about when not in classes, and some of them began to get into trouble, stealing a little money somewhere, breaking up a recreation hall a little, or beating up another boy. They were aimless and up a dead end, and the people in the centers, both staff and evacuees, began to feel that they had a considerable problem of "juvenile delinquency" on their hands. The internal security officers thought it was pretty mild delinquency as compared with what was going on in normal communities outside the centers.

The younger boys and girls were getting along better. They formed innumerable clubs, the Starlites, the Bombadettes, the Exclusive Blues, the Jayhawks, the Whizzers, the Sagebrush Clan, and carried on their interests in groups, with the help of older people as advisers from both staff and evacuees. The WRA staff encouraged all possible organization to tie in with national groups—the Girl Reserves, the Girl Scouts, the Boy Scouts, the Brownies, as well as the YWCA and YMCA. Baseball and basketball teams sprang up by the dozens; at first they had been organized on a basis of the former locatities, now it was usually on a basis of blocks. Participation in athletics became wider and wider. Similarly more and more young people learned to dance. As they said, the shy ones were "coming out in the centers." Dances, parties, picnics, and hikes were frequent. There was a wider participation in social life among younger Nisei than there had ever been before coming to the centers. They had more time for it, they were living in much larger communities, and they had no complications with a color line. It was their own social life. Farm girls and boys liked the new life.

Although the flowering of social life among the younger Nisei was carried on in concentrated Issei communities and many people talked of the Nisei becoming "Japanicized," there was little real evidence of such a trend. Their radios were on full blast in the evenings and the songs they listened to were the latest hits. The magazines they looked at from the community stores were what all the other young people in the United States were looking at. The movies they went to provided by the WRA or the community stores, although often a little old, were the usual American movies. They were hearing more Japanese spoken than they had ever heard before and were using a little more of it than they had before. But the major effect was merely to produce a peculiar set of dialect terms, combining Japanese and English, characteristic of the relocation centers. Many still protested that they couldn't understand "that lingo" of Japanese. They scorned the Issei entertainments

Nisei social life followed American patterns. The swing band (above) is strictly in the groove for the jitterbugs (below) at the school dance in the gym at Heart Mountain, Wyo., 1943.

and even the Kibei who went to them. If they were influenced by the Issei, it was chiefly to accept their resentments against the government and government supervision. Their world was still the world of American schools, movies, comics, radio, sports, and socials—not the world of the Issei.

The center way of life—in family, block, social club, and church—was a quiet one, rather richer in many respects than life had been in the pre-evacuation Japanese-American communities. At its core, however, lay insecurity. By the summer of 1944 the people who had adopted it were ceasing to find satisfaction in it. The first burst of interest in things Japanese was fading a little. Issei and Nisei were becoming restless, and a new orientation toward the outside was slowly asserting itself.

TULE LAKE

Living at Tule Lake during the year following segregation was a very different experience from living in any of the nine relocation centers. The evacuees found no points of orientation on which the majority could agree as a basis for life in the center. No way of life developed for a peaceful accommodation to the meaninglessness of the interlude and the wait for the future to unfold. With no real community life among evacuees, the relations of staff and evacuees could not be stabilized. In short, the people in the segregation center did not settle down during the year as those in the relocation centers had settled down. They were, on the contrary, more at odds with one another and with the center staff by the end of the year than had been evacuees in any center at any time.

The differences between Tule Lake and the other centers arose less from the nature of the people who lived there than from the nature of the government supervision and control which they experienced. Most of the people, up to the time they arrived at Tule Lake, were much like the people in the other centers. Moreover, their reactions to what happened to them at Tule Lake were different in degree rather than in kind from the reaction of people in the relocation centers.

The conditions of life at Tule Lake constituted extreme developments of the most disturbing features of life in the relocation centers. The line between evacuees and Caucasians was much more sharply drawn, not only by the manproof fence around the center, but also by the manproof fence between the "colony" and the administration area through which an evacuee could go only with a gate pass and after being individually checked. It was drawn in the first weeks following the incident by supervision by soldiers in uniform, at the gates, and in charge of work crews. At all points the line was tangible and unyielding and gave rise to attitudes of antagonism and suspicion on both sides. The world of rumor throve on the extreme isolation of the people behind the fences, out of touch not only with the outside but even with the center staff. It battened also on the new anxieties of being segregants, of not knowing whether that meant deportation or what. The correctives for rumor in the other centers through the coming and going of resettlers hardly existed, although a few Tuleans were cleared and resettled. The community crosscurrents, brought into adjustment under Issei leadership in the other centers, were in motion again with an intensity greater than in the first months of the most disturbed early centers. No leadership arose that could adjust and control them. The desire for harmony in the blocks was just as strong as it had been in the relocation centers, but under the conditions of life in the segregation center no leadership could come forward effectively. The reasons for this were complex.

Following the November demonstration and the military control imposed at Tule Lake the first response of the people was withdrawal and passive noncooperation. A few days after the Army took control, the commander of the military police announced that he would address a mass meeting of evacuees for the purpose of informing them as to what would be involved in military supervision. When the day came for the meeting, the commander and WRA officials drove into the center, went to an open-air stage in the main firebreak, and prepared to address the evacuees. A cordon of soldiers with drawn bayonets formed a ring around the space in which the evacuees were to assemble. On schedule the commander of the military police proceeded to give his speech through the loud-speaker, but no evacuee came near the stage. Evacuees in nearby blocks could see and hear that something was going on, but none came over. As the speech continued, evacuees went on with their daily affairs. A few young people gathered some distance away and looked curiously at the soldiers, while the speakers addressed the empty firebreak. The military police were being ignored by everyone in the center.

This pattern of behavior in relation to the Army occupation continued on a wider basis. People made no resistance of any kind when military police carried out an intensive search of the whole center for weapons and for those leaders of the demonstration who had not already given themselves up. A general strike, stimulated by the leadership of this demonstration, had begun after the first pickup of leaders. It continued now. No evacuees went to work except in the few essential services necessary for the welfare of the community. Army officers acted as foremen over evacuee crews hauling coal and distributing food to the mess halls. Otherwise people sat in the blocks and waited to see what would happen. The strike went on for over two months.

The passive noncooperation was a reaction to the curfew imposed after the incident, to the patrolling of the center by armed soldiers in jeeps and command cars, to the rigorous search of everyone's apartments, to the mere fact of Army control itself. But it was a great deal more than that. It was a demonstration against the holding of the men picked up by the military police. These men were the leaders of the November 1 demonstration and several hundred others who had been picked up on suspicion of implication in that incident. At first they were placed in tents in the administration area and later in a group of barracks surrounded by a manproof fence in another part of the area. Their place of confinement came to be called "the stockade." Pickups continued during the months of Army control of the center. The original group of leaders of the November 1 demonstration were men whom many in the center regarded as their duly elected representatives who had championed their interests against the administration. Others regarded them as self-appointed and not proper representatives. Whether or not people thought of them as authorized representatives, however, large numbers felt some loyalty to them as evacuees who had stood up for evacuee rights. Consequently, like the men who had been picked up in Manzanar and Poston at the time of the crises there, they quickly became symbols around which large numbers of evacuees could rally. The strike at Tule Lake during the period of Army control was basically a demonstration like the general strike at Poston.

The chief differences from the Poston strike lay in the lesser integration of the evacuees and in the protracted length of the demonstration. The fact that evacuees were not unified in their attitudes towards the holding of the men was apparent in the failure of the community fully to back representatives picked by the men now in the stockade for dealing with the administration. These men urged continuance of the strike until the stockade should be liquidated. In January the Army sponsored a center-wide vote on the question of continuing the strike. The results indicated that the community was deeply split on the issue. The vote was in terms of maintaining the status quo, that is, the strike, or abandoning the status quo, that is, discontinuing the strike. Almost as many voted one way as the other, but a slight majority favoring the end of the strike led to the formation of a group of evacuees, called the Coordinating Committee, which undertook to restore the center to normal. Shortly after, the military police withdrew from direct control of the center. As this took place, people gradually went back to work, indicating in part that they had felt the strike to be directed against Army control and in part that they could no longer bear the lack of income and disruption of center life that the strike entailed. The issue of the stockade nevertheless remained, and the large numbers who had voted to continue the strike still maintained a position against cooperation with the WRA administration so long as the stockade existed.

The coordinating committee attempted to work with the WRA administrators. The position that they assumed was that if the community should abandon the strike and get things back on a normal basis, repressive measures might be reduced and existence in the center would be easier and more pleasant. They also felt that a normally functioning community would provide a better basis for negotiation for release of the men in the stockade. The administrators wanted a return to normal in center operations and encouraged the coordinating committee to enlist the cooperation of evacuees who held or formerly had held key positions in the center organization. The administrators, however, were not ready to negotiate the release of all the men in the stockade. Their view was that the release of the leaders who had organized the November 1 demonstration and others whom they regarded as trouble makers or potential trouble makers would result in new disturbances. Their retention in the stockade was designed as a measure for promoting peace in the center.

The stockade was not easily forgotten by evacuees and remained as the major source of disharmony in the center. Months after the November incident it stood, with more than 350 inmates, fenced within the administration area but in plain sight of center residents. Watch towers were erected at its edges and soldiers guarded it day and night. Wives and children of the family heads held within it came to the center fence daily, looking across the administrative area and waving or calling to their husbands or fathers. The waving and signalling between center and stockade became a prominent feature of Tule Lake life. As time went on some men in the stockade broke down. One morning a young Kibei was found weeping on the wire gate of the compound. Some let their beards grow as a gesture of anger and defiance. Some kept the fires in their barracks banked low so as to emit no smoke, which, it was said, signified a cry for help. Some of the men in the stockade wanted desperately to rouse the people in the center to some sort of demonstration that would result in their release.

The stockade was not forgotten. The coordinating committee, on shaky ground at the very beginning of its negotiation with the administration, found itself in an increasingly bad position with the evacuees as the months passed. It had tried to take leadership in

the unpopular cause of establishing working relations with administration. It had made no important headway in the matter of liquidat-
ing the stockade. From time to time a few inmates of the stockade
had been released, but all the formerly important leaders were still
there. In the center, the coordinating committee members were widely
spoken of as administration stooges and *inu*. Most of the members
of the committee were prominent in the cooperative community stores.
Criticism had been leveled at them at the start as persons who wanted
the stores to operate so that they could make money from the evacuees.
Their work to return the center to normal operation was regarded by
many as playing into the hands of the administration. The release of
a few from the stockade was regarded as evidence of playing along
with administration for the release of some of their personal friends.
With the stockade continuing on through the spring after the Army
had relinquished control to the WRA, it seemed to those who regarded the stockade as the paramount issue that the coordinating
committee had sold the evacuees out.

Yet, except for block managers and others employed by WRA in
the routine operations of the center, the administration had working
relations only with the coordinating committee. The administrators
were therefore not working with the community in any real sense.
They were working with men who had no recognized status as representatives of the people in their blocks. They could not function as did
liaison men in the relocation centers, because they had no solid
base in the community. They were not a product of the adjustment of
person to person in the blocks. They represented only a small group
in the center who believed that evacuees would suffer less if there
was some show of cooperation with the administration. They had not
worked to coordinate the sentiments of the people in the center, where
blocks were split over the issue of the stockade and where no settling
down process had yet taken place.

In this atmosphere there could be no stabilization of staff-evacuee
relations. The relations of the coordinating committee members with
the people in the blocks became more and more difficult. The routine
activities of operating the center went on sufficiently well to keep
evacuees housed and fed, but there was no leadership effectively relating the center residents as a whole to the administration. Eventually
the coordinating committee resigned from its impossible situation. The
evacuees had withdrawn to the narrow life of the blocks with a com-
pleteness unmatched in the relocation centers, and the center staff
had withdrawn to confine itself to the business of routine center operations. Neither group any longer seemed to have a program, so far as
the other was concerned.

Life in the blocks at Tule Lake bore much superficial resemblance to life in the blocks in the relocation centers. Men passed the time with games, the women went in for flower arrangement and sewing, and there were poetry circles and *utai* singing groups. Everyone found something to do, and in general the patterns of behavior were much the same as they were in the relocation centers, with a similar mixture of Japanese and American customs. But even these externals of life were roiled by the crosscurrents which arose at Tule Lake. Pressures of various sorts had developed from the time of the arrival of the first segregants in the center. Early efforts of rowdy youths to break up Nisei dances and to force attendance at Japanese-language schools continued with increased intensity. Nisei felt pressures against their speaking English at any time. Here and there all through the center there were little groups who were taking very seriously the revival of Japanese customs and activities. They did not regard the turn to Japanese games, dances, and entertainment as merely a pleasant relaxation —to them it seemed that such things should be cultivated with a purpose. Children must be trained for a life in Japan and adults must return to ways of behaving that would make them acceptable in Japan. Nearly every block had its residents who adopted this serious approach to the revival of customs. They were emotional about it. Under their influence more and more people were coming to regard as a discipline such activities as people had turned to for pleasure in the relocation centers. A program was steadily developing with preparation to live in Japan as the basis for unity in the segregation center.

As the months went by, the program was pushed with increasing vigor. It became more and more obvious to those who pushed it, however, that a majority of the people at Tule Lake were not disposed to take it up. Some Nisei tried to rebel, or at least did not respond to the pressures. Parents of many Nisei clearly did not take the program very seriously either. Attitudes towards activities designed to prepare for life in Japan became tangled with attitudes towards center issues. On the one hand were the people in every block who urged preparation to live in Japan, no cooperation with administration, and the liquidation of the stockade. On the other hand were the many in every block who seemed largely indifferent to both matters, who seemed not to care much about the stockade and even said that they had never really supported the men in the stockade, and who did not take Japanese customs with much seriousness. Harmony in the blocks began to seem impossible to the people with the program, and to the others seemed to be fading farther and farther away as they felt the insistent pressures.

The Ground Swell of Discontent

As the sense of differences increased and factionalism sharpened in the blocks and all through the center, an organized movement developed. It was not wholly new, for it had been suggested in the program of the leaders who organized the November incident. But now in the summer of 1944 it grew to proportions which steadily overshadowed the stockade and every other internal center issue. It took the form at first of the circulation of petitions for a new segregation. Its spokesmen took up the point raised on November 1: what is the status of evacuees at Tule Lake? They had wanted as soon as they got here to know what their legal status was in relation to Japan and to the United States. Some had asked then whether citizens of the United States who had asked for expatriation could break their ties with the United States by renouncing their citizenship. Now they urged that the people at Tule Lake should be separated from each other on the basis of whether or not they really wanted ultimately to go to Japan. They had recognized increasingly that many of the people at Tule Lake were there for temporary security from the draft or from hostile wartime feeling in the United States. They recognized that a great many had not declared themselves once and for all for Japan, but were waiting things out. The spokesmen for resegregation wanted to be separated from all such people. They wanted to be in a separate center where they could take seriously the preparation for living in Japan and where they could live uncontaminated by the people who were not really interested in Japan as a place to go and live.

A small group at first, the spokesmen for resegregation circulated petitions among the evacuees in an effort to find out how many people at Tule Lake were ready to go all the way to Japan. They claimed 10,000 signatures on the first petitions requesting a resegregation. People in the blocks began to feel a new pressure. Spokesmen of the program went about talking with Nisei and their parents, urging them to think of a corner of the Japanese empire where they could go and live as real Japanese after the war. They denounced the "fence sitters" who they said were merely waiting out the war. They shuddered at being contaminated in the center with men who were merely dodging the draft, the No-Yes-No men who had wavered since registration. They spoke of "purity" of race and of intention to serve Japan. More and more persons listened to them, as the outside world receded farther and farther away on the other side of the fences and life in the blocks seemed more and more sterile and empty. The new current—the movement for resegregation—was growing all through the summer at Tule Lake.

There was no leadership for any counter trend. The most vigorous Nisei and Issei who had, like the liaison men in the relocation centers, been concerned with center issues were still in the stockade. Others who had tried to establish "harmony in the center" by negotiating with the administration had run up against the stone wall of administration determination to keep the stockade. They were now generally branded as inu in the center and were even becoming fearful for their safety. Early in the summer the manager (Hitomi) of the cooperative stores, which had all along been associated with the coordinating committee, was murdered with a knife thrust. His murderer was never found. Former members of the coordinating committee, and others who had been prominent in cooperation with administration, sought shelter with the administration in the hospital and some left the center. Dealing with the administration had become impossibly dangerous. The field for leadership was left open to the men with the program for return to Japan.

By the end of the summer the issue of the stockade within the center had died down in the face of the larger issue of the future in Japan. Even the administration had come to feel that the stockade was not so important. Besides, the men in it were becoming troublesome. Some attempted a hunger strike. The administration sat out the hunger strike, which fizzled, and then decided to release the men who had been held for ten months. Their return to the center caused hardly a stir. A few who had been most active in the leadership of the November demonstration felt that the growing influence of the "Back-to-Japan" movement was bad and attempted some organization against it. But they had no following after the months in the stockade and their activities did not stem the tide.

By September the movement for resegregation had become a well-organized affair. It was not unified at first, but gradually became so. Spokesmen organized several hundred young men in a group called "Society for the Study of the Customs of the Fatherland." It drew more and more young men and some women into its influence during the fall. The young men cropped their hair short and began to appear in the firebreaks with headbands with Japanese emblems on them. There they marched and drilled and carried out exercises under the command of leaders. By November the organization had altered its name to "Society to Serve the Emperor on Speedy Repatriation." It had a membership running over a thousand and its activities were more and more prominent in center life. Every morning groups of young men marching and drilling, and now with plastic bugles announcing the formations, came out and went through their maneuvers. In every block the young men were feeling the pressures of the organization. And for many it seemed to offer a path to something meaningful in the aimless dead end of the segregation center. They were joining up, in many cases, out of a feeling that here was something which led somewhere. Others were joining up because their friends and brothers did. It was a movement that was sweeping confused young men along who had had nothing worthwhile to do since evacuation, men who had begun with a No at registration which meant defiance at mistreatment and who now were saying Yes to something which seemed to have more meaning than anything they had encountered for two and a half years. It was much more than something to do in the center; it was action toward what seemed at last a clearly defined goal.

As the year 1944 drew to an end it seemed possible to distinguish three quite different systems of sentiments, or orientations, among the people of Tule Lake. A Nisei observer summed up the situation in a description of one block, which seemed to the Nisei to be fairly typical:

This block, like all the others, has a few people who might be called relocation prospects. Because people are loyal to the United States, have property or other holdings "outside," or believe that democracy is the proper form of Government, they will eventually desire to relocate and start life anew. Now they are waiting for the present war hysteria and racial prejudice to subside or be controlled. They are a minority group in the block, but so far as their loyalty is concerned, there can be no doubt. Many of these families have already given their sons to the war effort of this country. They are willing to fight and stand by their principles. . . . Some are bachelors and have relatives elsewhere. These people are cool towards all actions aggressively aimed at the WRA, and they consistently follow the group that is conservative, if "political" pressure makes it seem necessary to follow a given course. Sometimes these people are referred to as the fence-sitters, who are waiting for the clouds to clear.

Then there are the two groups, called "disloyal," which consist of people who have expressed their desire to repatriate or to expatriate to Japan; the majority of these desire to be included at the earliest possible date in an exchange if possible. These two groups do not under any circumstances desire to relocate. Because they fear forced relocation and compulsory draft, they are taking whatever action they believe helpful to prevent such situations. They frequently state that such action on their part is necessary because of inconsistencies in the policies of the U.S. Government which they claim to have experienced. They will probably continue to be distrustful of future policies of the U.S. Government. Though both groups have similar ideals in mind, their means of attaining their goals are altogether opposite. These two elements constitute the majority who command the respect of the people of the center. Of the two, one is radical in its views and actions, while the other is conservative and law-abiding.

Radical Group. These people show their complete hate and distrust of the U.S. Government by drastic actions which are both detrimental to other law-abiding Japanese within the center and also undesirable from the point of view of the rules and regulations of the WRA. . . . Although it is the minority group when compared with the "conservative" disloyal group, the individuals are highstrung and uncontrollable. Their stock remark is that they are the only "true Japanese," although the great majority of the residents hardly agree. The radicals even go to the extent of using force and violence within their own group to hold it intact by putting pressure upon its members. They seem unreasonable and "one-track" and appear to care not in the least for the welfare of their fellow-residents. They further exhibit hostile and disagreeable attitudes which make social functions impossible in many blocks. The majority of the membership in the radical group consists of mild country folk who respond to the pressure of a few extreme leaders . . . who seem to be immune to common sense and gentlemanly ways, but who, in some cases, carry the country people along with them. . . .

Conservative Group. In this group are the people who have requested repatriation or expatriation to Japan. They would prefer an exchange, if possible, at the earliest date. About three-fifths of the people of the center fall in this category. Although there is no question of their loyalty to Japan, they feel that the countries involved are at war and that people are sacrificing their lives to protect their respective nations. While many were evacuated from their homes in a sudden action which often resulted in losing practically everything they had, they figure that this is now so much water under the bridge and that it's too late to do much about the past. Now that they have chosen to become Japanese subjects, they believe it is up to them to comport themselves in peaceful and law-abiding fashion. Being thankful for the shelter and food provided by the Government, and realizing that the tax-paying citizens of this country are being deprived of many luxuries, this group is anything but wilfully antagonistic. As long as the policies of the WRA make for livable conditions here, this group sees no reason why they should act in a manner hostile to their guardian. They ask no favor but to be left alone to pursue their ambition of returning to Japan. But should the attitude of the WRA or the Justice Department change in such a way as to interfere with their possibility of remaining in the center as disloyals waiting for exchange, they will no doubt respond in a manner of utmost hostility to whatever administration exists at the time. These people are complying with every request which is reasonable. They are "taking their medicine" quietly. But if aroused by unfair treatment, they will certainly respond. If this law-abiding, conservative group is aroused, it would easily enlist the sympathy of the center.

Because of their desire to be pleasant and understanding, these people keep the block on an even keel and earn the respect of all concerned. They desire to aid the majority of their fellow-residents and at the same time wish to respect and be respected by the people of this nation and its administration. These people want to say when they do go to Japan that they left friends in the United States who regarded them as decent, self-respecting individuals. They think hopefully of a better future abroad, but do not turn away from this nation in hate and passion.

The orientations at Tule Lake could be duplicated in the blocks in the relocation centers. The extremes of opinion and behavior present here were present also in the other centers. An important difference lay in the "conservative" groups. In the relocation centers the conservative group which stabilized block life was oriented not towards some concept of Japan but towards the relocation centers themselves. The security they sought during the war period had come to be identified with the relocation centers. At Tule Lake there was a similar orientation to the center as a place of greater security than the outside, but the repression, the disharmony, the general unsatisfactoriness of the segregation center, together with the steps already taken toward disassociation with the United States, had led the conservatives to identify future security more and more with a present orientation to Japan. That seemed still to be the path away from forced relocation and the draft. Consequently conservative opinion at Tule Lake had moved steadily toward the very definite identification of security with a future in Japan. This was the chief point of contrast between the majority at Tule Lake at the end of 1944 and the majority at the relocation centers.

The other major contrast was the role of what the Nisei observer called the radicals. In some blocks in every relocation center there were people of a similar kind, who upset the harmony of block life from time to time by uncompromising anti-administration expressions and actions. They were, however, generally submerged in the dominant conservative opinion and kept under control in various ways by the liaison men and other leaders among the evacuees. At Tule Lake, on the other hand, the influence of such persons had thrived on the succession of events which had upset the equilibrium of the center. As the Nisei observer indicated, they found support from the considerable number of people who had no stake in the United States, largely poor and unsuccessful farm workers. Anti-administration attitudes had spread widely and been encouraged by the strike following the incident and the constant agitation of the stockade issue during the spring and summer. Such attitudes had become set and crystallized in the center and formed a matrix in which spokesmen could continue to operate in almost every block. Instead of becoming submerged, as in the relocation centers, they had grown all through the year.

At Tule Lake, then, there had been no smoothing of differences among evacuees. There had been rather a sharpening of differences, and people in the blocks stood aligned against one another, uncompromisingly antagonistic and anxious to be separated from one another so that some sort of harmony might be achieved. It was this condition that produced support for the idea of resegregation which ultimately took the form of organized groups in the fall of 1944. In the basic conception of resegregation the conservatives and radicals of the blocks were at one with each other. They did not want to be associated with people who could look favorably on resettlement, who had no orientation toward Japan. But the conservatives did not want to be associated either with the emotional spokesmen of the "Society to Serve the Emperor on Speedy Repatriation." As the Nisei observer wrote:

Though they believe themselves to be the only "true Japanese" in the center, this claim is received with skepticism on the part of the residents who believe their actions to be contrary to their words. Indeed, their antics are frequently contrasted with the ways of the old Japanese *samurais* (warriors) "who kept their word once it was spoken, and never drew a sword unless for a purpose." Parading and flag-waving in a center still under a lenient care is looked upon as cheap exhibitionism and a disgrace to the Japanese people. The majority believe in working things out in a gentlemanly fashion "as proud people of a first-class nation."

In December, events moved to bring large numbers at Tule Lake under the sway of the extremists who had built up the Society to Serve the Emperor on Speedy Repatriation, called *Sokuji Kikoku Hoshidan* in Japanese. Congress had passed a law permitting citizens of the United States to renounce their citizenship if they wished to. The *Hoshidan* adopted the renunciation of citizenship as its own program. To them it seemed to be the fulfillment of the steps that many Nisei had already taken: first, the No at the time of registration, then the decision to go as a segregant to Tule Lake, then the request for expatriation to Japan. The renunciation of United States citizenship now seemed to leaders of the Hoshidan to be the necessary final act in the dissolution of ties with the United States in preparation for the ultimate identification with Japan. Their viewpoint during the fall did not seem realistic to most people at Tule Lake, but by the time representatives of the Department of Justice arrived to hold hearings for those who had applied for renunciation of citizenship, events had taken place which gave new meaning to the program of the Hoshidan.

About the time that the Justice Department representatives came, the Army announced that the mass exclusion of evacuees from the West Coast was lifted. The WRA simultaneously announced that all the relocation centers would be closed within a year. Renunciation of citizenship began to seem to the young men the only means left to avoid resettlement and the draft. The stage was now set for a widespread acceptance of the *hoshidan* program. Promptly with the inauguration of the Justice Department hearings an hysterical movement began for renunciation of citizenship. The movement was backed not only by the organized leadership of the *hoshidan*, but also by the conservatives. As the Nisei observer had pointed out, the threat of forced relocation could easily lead the majority at Tule Lake to act in extreme ways.

Thousands of young men flocked to join the *hoshidan* and to declare to the Justice Department representatives that they wanted to renounce their citizenship. The *hoshidan* flourished. What had seemed curious antics and exhibitionism a few weeks before now began to have meaning for an increasing number. The fear of the outside led parents and sons to actions which would have seemed hysterical to them in the months before—and which did seem so again a few months later. Well organized now, the *hoshidan* worked hard to bring the young men into line with its program. Renunciation hearings were called for by more and more young men.

DISINTEGRATING FACTORS—THE WAR AND RESETTLEMENT

Meanwhile, during the year 1944, the nine relocation centers had been undergoing changes. Even as sentiment in them had crystallized in the winter of 1943–44 behind the evacuee program, the communities from which it sprang were changing. The basic feature of the program—retention of the centers for the duration of the war—continued to have general acceptance in all the centers. It continued to be the basis of group relations with staff and the guiding principle of block life and politics. For more than a year after it attained its position of highest ascendancy in center life it continued to dominate majority action and thought. Out from under it, as it were, people nevertheless were moving into the world outside the centers. From month to month the population of each center declined just a little. The changes were small, but the cumulative effects were profound. Moreover, the significant effects had little or nothing to do with the numbers of persons who left. It was the kind of persons and what they were doing on the outside that was important. By the summer of 1944 it was evident that the process that was taking place had begun not only to affect physical conditions in the centers, such as the easing of crowding in the blocks and the creation of manpower crises, but also to alter in far-reaching ways the community sentiment on which evacuee solidarity had been based.

The movement of young men out of the centers into the armed forces was numerically small, but by the summer of 1944 it had been going on for one and a half years. About 1,200 had volunteered from the centers at the time of registration and shortly after. Since then there had been a few more volunteers, and with the reopening of Selective Service in February the numbers of young men in the uniform of the Army had steadily increased. In the single month of June, 1944, 166 Nisei left the centers for Army service. Every month

An Air Force Sergeant autographs for Nisei admirers at Heart Mountain, Wyo. Sent on tour of the United States by the Air Force, Sgt. Ben Kuroki contributed much to the better understanding of Nisei loyalty as he told Americans of the outstanding war records of Japanese-Americans.

there were some from each center. By December, 1944, the total number who had been accepted for service and were on active duty somewhere was not large, amounting to only 1,543 individuals, ranging from less than 100 to nearly 300 from each center. These men, however, by that time had been coming and going from the relocation centers for more than a year. While undergoing training at Camp Shelby, Mississippi, or Fort Snelling, Minnesota, they had been coming back to the relocation centers on furloughs for visits with their families and friends. They had come back in uniform, and portions of barracks had been set up in all centers as USO entertainment centers. Thus there was a feature of life in the relocation centers linking them with all the communities of the United States. Soldier sons and brothers and friends were going and coming. Parents, sisters, and friends in the centers busied themselves making the visits of the soldiers pleasant. Women worked on 1000-stitch belts, in the Buddhist tradition, for the protection of the soldiers on the battlefields. Mothers spent time preparing food for parties and their daughters arranged dances and other affairs. Young people clustered around the USOs and talked with the soldiers. The *senryu* poets, beginning in 1944, began to write of the uniformed Nisei and the feelings of their parents about them.

At first the coming and going of soldiers affected only relatively few persons in each center, but many of those affected were parents who had themselves accepted the centers as war duration homes, men and women who belonged to the core of Issei who had formulated community sentiment. With reopening of Selective Service in the spring of 1944 more and more began to be affected as sons of parents who had opposed volunteering were taken in the draft. The activities of the USOs were increasingly participated in by at least mothers and sisters of families who had steadfastly kept their attention averted from resettlement and the outside. Farewell parties for drafted young men increased, sometimes merely family affairs, but more and more whole blocks became interested in the outgoing young men. The recurring farewells became a more and more prominent feature of relocation center life, and to a greater extent than in outside towns of similar size the whole community began to be affected and to give some recognition to the departing young men.

Inevitably casualty lists began to have some meaning for people in the relocation centers. By early 1944, Nisei in the combat teams in Italy had been in action and there were dead and wounded. The news came back to the parents in the centers. Here and there the feeling developed that the communities as wholes should pay tribute in some way. At first there was resistance to such ideas. Then gradually as the

WRA administration encouraged the erection of honor roll tablets listing all the men in the armed forces in each center, sentiment swung behind the idea of community ceremonies. Buddhist and Christian ministers and community council chairmen and other evacuee spokesmen arranged ceremonies in honor of Nisei who had been killed. Memorial services became more and more frequent during the year and interest in them became wider. The relocation centers were now like normal outside communities with their honor rolls, and memorial services for war dead were an even more prominent feature of community life.

By midsummer of 1944 the effects of the Nisei soldiers on the people in the centers had become marked. An Issei mother in July said:

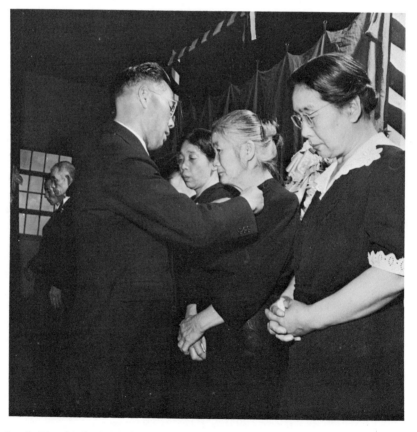

Inevitably, death claimed some Nisei soldiers. An official presents gold stars to mothers at Granada, Colo., Apr., 1945.

You know things are a lot different than they were a while ago. People really rebelled at the time of registration. They said awful things about the government, and they spoke of the boys who volunteered almost as if they were traitors to the Japanese for serving a country that had treated the Japanese so badly. When Selective Service was re-instituted all one heard was that the government had no right to draft men out of a camp like this. At first when the boys left, their mothers wept with bitterness and resentment. They didn't think their sons should go. This week five have gone from our block. I tell you I'm surprised at the difference. Wives and mothers are sorry and they weep a lot. But now they really feel it is a man's duty to serve his country. They wouldn't want him not to go when he is called. When they talk among themselves, they tell each other these things. They feel more as they did before evacuation.

Women in the laundry rooms were talking less now about the discomforts imposed on them by the government and the stupidity of arrogance of staff members they had encountered or heard about. They were talking about the casualties in Italy and about their own sons training somewhere or about to go overseas.

Block sentiment was changing in response to this impact of the war on parents. A block leader described what had happened in his block during the spring of 1944:

At first our block was a little slow in giving some recognition to the boys who went for induction. Then we started giving $10 to each inductee, provided they left from the block. But many of them took indefinite leave after they passed their physicals in order to get the cash grant and trip somewhere at WRA expense. These youngsters are smart boys. Last week we held a block meeting to decide if our policy was right. There were a lot of women present. They were interested in this question. We voted that all boys should receive a block present whether they went out on indefinite [leave] or not. After all, they were going to the Army. So now, before a boy leaves for induction or goes out of the center on indefinite after passing his physical, five or six leading men of the block dress up in their good clothes and call on him to present the gift and the best wishes of the block.

By no means all blocks acted in this way, but it was becoming less and less popular for anyone to suggest that Nisei who had gone into the armed forces were foolish or were being hoodwinked by a basically antagonistic government. The feelings of the mothers were more and more a factor to be reckoned with in block opinion. At Heart Mountain, parents who had encouraged their sons a few months before to resist induction in the Army were confessing that they felt differently and that they had advised their sons wrongly.

These changes did not mean that there had been any universal alteration of opinion about the war in general. The general feeling persisted that the end of the war was a key point in the evacuee future and that Issei generally could not make a decision about their future until the war should have ended. There was still widespread expectation that the war would end in a negotiated peace with neither Japan or the United States wholly broken and defeated. It was still impossible for an Issei who had become convinced that Japan was destined to lose decisively to say so in the centers. One such Issei who had re-settled in Chicago and wished, as he said, "to reorient Issei thinking" about their future and their clinging to the centers, wrote a series of articles for a Denver Japanese-language newspaper, the *Rocky Shimpo*. He wrote that the future of the Issei was in the United States and that they would be wise to leave the centers promptly and begin to reestablish their economic foundations before the end of the war. A group of Issei in one center wrote to the *Shimpo* protesting the articles and they were discontinued. When the man himself visited Heart Mountain and Granada in August to express his views from the platform, he found that only a tiny minority of Issei were ready to pay any attention to his ideas. The interest in and concern about the Nisei soldiers had by no means resulted in a complete reorientation of thought in the centers.

Nevertheless the course of the war was also having a subtle effect on community sentiment in the relocation centers. As a poet wrote:

The colors of the war maps
Having lately changed,
No longer can we smile.

The news of the war came into the centers in various ways— from letters from sons in the Pacific and in Italy, from the official communiques from both Washington and Tokyo which were selected and published in the Japanese-language papers, from materials sent to the centers by the Washington WRA office. There was no real lack of information in the centers. There was a difference, how- ever, between center and outside interpretation of the war news. Tokyo claims were generally discounted less as propaganda than Washington claims. Even with such interpretation, however, doubt was growing about the possibility of Japanese success, and as this happened the need for waiting to see how the war came out was less important for a growing number of Issei. Here and there a few began to make plans for leaving the centers without reference to the outcome of the war. Very slowly the turn of events in the Pacific was affecting the views of influential men. It was still not popular to say that Japan could be defeated and very few talked that way, but some were acting nevertheless as if they had accepted that probability.

An even more powerful and subtly working influence on attitudes in the centers consisted in the resettled individuals. The flow of individuals out of the centers which took place during early 1943 had little effect on community sentiment. The people who were leaving were for the most part those who were not participating in the process of formulating community sentiment, nor were they intimately related to those who were. But those who left later, and particularly those who resettled during 1944, were persons who had either accepted for a time the dominant orientations of the postsegregation communities or were children, relatives, or friends of those who had. Their movement out, however small in volume, had a profound, cumulative influence on the whole system of community sentiments built up in the winter of 1943–44.

By the end of May, 1944, more than 20,000 people had left the centers on what the WRA called indefinite leave. Some of these were the men, and a few women, in the armed forces. The great majority were persons who had gone out to take jobs with no intention of returning to the centers. More than half had left the centers since the first exodus of persons who had no sense of identification with the majority. Even though from 100 to 250 were leaving each center every month during the spring, center staff members did not feel that resettlement amounted to much. They felt the scarcity of able-bodied young men to do the heavy work of center operation, but the blocks seemed almost as full of people as ever. Evacuees in the blocks were able to spread out a little more as some rooms became vacant, but by the end of June there was even a little crowding again. The Jerome center was closed and people were transferred from there to Gila, Rohwer, Heart Mountain, Granada, and Minidoka, thus filling up much of the space gained through resettlement. To people in the centers it did not seem that there had been much reduction in population. It was not the numbers of people who had resettled from the centers that influenced the attitudes of the people, it was the kind of people and what they were doing outside.

At Manzanar by midsummer one or more members of about 25 percent of the families still in the center had resettled or were in the armed forces. At Minidoka, which had been maintaining the highest resettlement rate of any of the centers, one or more members of nearly 50 percent of the families were outside the centers. Somewhere between this range fell the other relocation centers. The families in them were tied in with the outside world in an intimate way. Letters were coming in constantly from the resettled people, telling of conditions both bad and good. Families in Manzanar or Gila were in

touch with their family members in New Jersey, Chicago, and elsewhere. Many of the resettled people were advising against resettlement for various reasons; others were working out plans for bringing out other family members. Whether the letters brought good
tidings or bad, they were an increasingly important link between the
people in the centers and the outside world. Moreover, almost daily
in each center there were a few people departing. Friends and relatives went down to the departure stations to see them off. The farewells for soldiers and for resettlers were more and more a characteristic feature of relocation center life during 1944. Then some resettlers
began coming back for visits, and their new clothes and possessions
looked good to the people in the centers. All of these developments
had begun to have an effect.

In June a staff member at Poston wrote:

There is a growing feeling in some Issei circles that there's just a
little something wrong with a young person who is still in the center.
The time may come when speculative gossip will surround most . . .
able-bodied people who are still in Poston.

Prestige had once been attached to making a successful adjustment to center life. People in good, but not conspicuous, center jobs
were admired, as were those who had made great improvements in
their apartments and yards. Community leaders universally advocated
remaining in the center. In fact, a "leader," from the vantage point of
the administration, seemed to be definitely definable as a man who
had committed himself publicly against relocation.

There have been more and more older men who were considered
leaders—men who had advocated remaining in Poston—who have
departed. Some of them were leaders of Issei cultural activities;
they were most improbable candidates for relocation. Their departure
may well make their admirers question the wisdom of staying.

Not many months before, people who had decided to resettle had
been leaving quietly. They had said nothing to anyone about it, because they felt that their action would be unpopular, and slipped out
of the centers as unobtrusively as they could. Now it was a little
different. People were less fearful of incurring disapproval and shared
their plans with friends, evidence that public opinion had changed.
Most evacuee leaders had earlier decided that anyone who wanted to
resettle had the right to do so, that no one should be forced to remain
in a center any more than one should be forced to leave. The fruits of
that decision were being reaped as community sentiment toward leaving steadily changed. The departure of some who had publicly opposed resettlement was, more than anything else, working changes in
general acceptance of the program against resettlement.

A year before, in the spring and summer of 1943, there had also
been an interest in the outside world on the part of evacuees, but it

had been totally different from that that was now developing. It had been an interest in the statements of public officials and others antagonistic to Japanese-Americans. People had read them and they had been an important factor in the consolidation of evacuee opinion against resettlement. Now the interest was in specific individuals, family and friends, who were outside the centers, in the visible evidence of advantages that they were enjoying, and in the possibility of enjoying similar advantages. It was an interest with direct reference to oneself and possibilities for oneself. It was working deeply against the vision of the outside world as an implacably hostile one on which much of community sentiment had been built. It was being fostered by contacts with friendly and interested center staff as well as with evacuees who had resettled.

In late 1944 the relocation center communities were still fundamentally what they had been a year before. The forces for change were working deeply, but community sentiment was still oriented around the end of the war, the West Coast stake, and the security of the relocation centers. What was happening was that the meaning of two of the points of orientation to many people in the communities had changed during the course of the year. For an increasing number of parents "the war" had begun to be felt as "our war." Their sons were in it. That fact, together with the increasing difficulty in interpreting the war as going well for Japan, was opening the way for more persons to think about the future without reference to the outcome of the war. The changes were not decisive, but the feeling about the war was changing. Then the West Coast stake had slowly broadened. Sons and daughters resettled in the Middle West and East had extended the stake in America beyond the old limits. The orientation to the West Coast was still strong, but for many, economic security was no longer necessarily centered there. They were looking both there and to family members who were trying to get reestablished elsewhere. Some in the centers even had a few Issei friends and associates who were outside the centers somewhere to the east. The West Coast communities and the stake of friends and families formerly in them had spread beyond the narrow strip of coast. The old orientation was changing. The war and resettlement were subtly at work influencing the whole framework of community sentiment which had been reared the year before.

4.

GETTING OUT

The three years following the attack on Pearl Harbor had been a period of recurring crisis for the 30,000 families of Japanese–Americans. At intervals of four to six months had come successive decisions by the government, each of which demanded sweeping new adjustments for every family. The evacuation decision in March, 1942, and the swift transfer from homes to assembly centers; the movement in the summer of 1942 from assembly to relocation centers; registration in February, 1943; segregation in the fall of 1943; the reopening of Selective Service in January, 1944—relentlessly one official decision led to another and each meant crisis, reorientation of plans for the future, and new decisions for every family.

For three years the group had been acted on by the forces determining official policy; for three years, as the evacuees themselves said, they had been "pushed around." The settling down in the centers, when the chance seemed to come, had been one reaction to the successive upsets of equilibrium in the wake of previous government actions. The period of settling in the centers during 1944 had been the longest period during which there was no decisive Government action pushing the thousands of families in some direction in which they had not planned and did not want to go. For almost a year those who stayed in the centers had been free to respond to the currents of opinion among themselves, to proceed from a relatively stabilized base of known government policy. An adjustment was being worked out both to the relocation center way of life and also to the outside world as contacts with it redeveloped.

The expectation of further government action during the period of relative calm had, however, continued. People had been conditioned during the previous months to expect not to be let alone. The presentiment of forced relocation had never died since registration. People felt that at any time the WRA would make a new move to get them out of the centers. In the late spring of 1944 there were rumors that the Army would lift the exclusion orders which kept evacuees out of the West Coast defense zone. The rumors grew, then died down. As the Jerome center closed in June, rumors began to appear concerning the closing of other centers. Dates and the order of closing were discussed, with rumors differing from center to center. But nothing happened.

The rumors reflected not only the state of mind of people living under government supervision. They reflected also the actualities of policy formulation in Washington. For many months the men who made WRA policy in Washington had held the view that the key point for their program would be such time as the War Department decided to lift the exclusion orders on the West Coast. In contrast with the majority of evacuees, who held that the existence of the relocation centers should be assured until the end of the war, they believed that the liquidation of the centers could be planned promptly with the lifting of exclusion. As soon as evacuees should be free to move back to their home localities, the men in WRA believed, dates should be set for the closing of all centers. They were convinced that living in the centers was doing no evacuee any good and that the continuance of segregation in center life complicated rather than aided the solution of the ultimate problems of the minority group. Consequently they had been planning a course of action during 1944 in the event that the exclusion orders should be lifted before the end of the war. They had expected that exclusion might be lifted in June, at the very time that rumors were thickest in the relocation centers.

It was not, however, until December that the key event occurred. The War Department announced on December 17 the lifting of exclusion orders to take effect on January 2, 1945. Almost at the same time a Supreme Court decision was handed down ruling the detention of citizens in the relocation centers to be unconstitutional. The policy basis for setting definite closing dates for the centers had been established. The WRA proceeded to announce simultaneously with the War Department announcement that no relocation center would be maintained longer than a year following the effective date of the lifting of the exclusion orders. The date for the dissolution of the centers was no longer indefinite. The government agency was clear in its program, now had a goal, and had already begun to gear its organization to meet the deadline a year hence.

HOLDING THE CENTERS

The simultaneous announcement of the opening of the West Coast and the closing of the centers fell on people partially prepared for both. They were prepared in the sense that their anxieties about the future had kept both possibilities before them for many months. They had wanted the opening of the Coast. Some were already prepared to go back immediately and take over their farms or resume old jobs. But the closing of the centers had been something that the great majority who had remained in them had faced only in the curious world of relocation center rumor. For a few days after the announcement there was little apparent reaction as people struggled to put the official phrases into everyday words and to grasp the significance in terms of their own lives. Then slowly opinion in the blocks began to crystallize as the meaning of the new government action sank home.

On the one hand there was disbelief. As a high school girl in one center said: "This is a town. You can't close a town." The people who talked together in the laundry rooms of the northern centers and under trees in the southern centers did not feel that the centers could be closed. They were too solid a reality and also too necessary for one's security. They were still full of people and, moreover, just those people who could never resettle—the older persons over 50 and the children under 17. The long-nourished attitudes toward the Government and the WRA came up. This was a scheme, people said, to frighten into accepting resettlement those evacuees who so far had resisted the program. The Government wouldn't really carry through; they couldn't. They might close some centers, but they could never close all of them. Some said that the Japanese translation of the WRA announcement indicated that Gila and Poston would continue their agricultural program. Obviously then these two centers would stay open. Rumors began to appear concerning which centers would be closed and which ones would be kept open indefinitely. People even talked about which centers they would ultimately transfer to.

On the other hand there were people who began to react as if the announcement were true. Men sitting in the block managers' offices became angry as they talked about the possibility. They called center closure another evacuation. The thought of being forced out made men bitter. Old feelings rose again and some declared that they would not be pushed around again. A man in one center who had been planning to resettle suddenly cancelled his arrangements; he was determined not to go out if the Government was going to force people out. He would stay and at least be the last person to be "shoved through the gate." The feeling grew that the evacuees had "a right to the centers." The Government had put them in the centers after taking away their homes and therefore the Government was obligated to maintain homes for them.

There was talk here and there of a sit-down movement to retain the centers, if the Government turned out to be really serious in its announcement of center closure. Men listened to speeches in block meetings at Heart Mountain and Topaz. Speakers called attention to the WRA folder issued in 1942 describing the centers as war duration homes. They became more angry; in a block meeting a man said:

If the evacuees would just stick together, if nobody would budge out of here, we would get somewhere. We could force the government to keep the centers open or give us some real assistance . . . a lot of softies leave here for railway fare and $25. And now that WRA has said it is going to close the centers, probably more will crawl out of the place like beaten animals.

The sanctions of block opinion were being applied. A few months before, it had become possible to plan resettlement openly. Now in the face of the new program for center closure there was a sudden, although brief, revival of the antiresettlement sentiment of the winter before. The Topaz and the Heart Mountain block meetings were tempestuous, and the new program was denounced as brutal and inhumane.

At the same time that the majority of people were taking refuge in the idea that center closure could not happen and others were angrily planning resistance, the block managers and the councilmen were in constant contact with center staff. They were reading the administrative instructions and the information bulletins from Washington designed to acquaint evacuees with the nature of the resettlement assistance offered by the WRA. They were talking with the administrators and coming into direct contact with the plans that were emanating from Washington for an all-out resettlement program. They were not able to take refuge in the disbelief of the majority and they were convinced, as they had been for many months, that organized resistance could lead only from bad to worse. Many of them during their months of contact with center staff had come to believe, even though they had not voiced such sentiments to the people, that everyone who could ought to resettle as soon as possible. They were sure that the WRA meant what it said and felt a responsibility to help people face a serious problem realistically. They began to take leadership in the formulation of community sentiment in meeting the common problem.

The community councils of Granada and Topaz suggested to the councils of the other centers that a general conference be held at which representatives from all centers could meet and discuss a course of action. The Heart Mountain councilmen joined the proposal enthusiastically. The Poston Community Council had already made a similar suggestion, and other councils agreed to send delegates. Only the Manzanar block managers declined, saying that WRA had already considered the whole problem and there was nothing to discuss. By the end of January it had been agreed to hold an All-Center Conference in Salt Lake City on February 16.

During the period of discussion in the councils and block meetings concerning the conference, groups with differing opinions became distinguishable among the block representatives. At first the meetings were dominated by those who categorically refused to accept center liquidation as a possibility. Issei who wanted to petition the Spanish Consul to intercede to keep at least one or two centers were told by other Issei that it was better to remember that their children's interests and future were in America and should come first. Some representatives talked in terms of accepting center closure conditionally, declaring that the WRA policy might be carried out in part, at least, if the evacuees were indemnified for evacuation losses or were given enough financial and other aid by the agency to see the resettling people through one year of outside life. Such representatives regarded the conference less as a medium of protest than as a pressure group to win concessions from WRA and to present constructive criticisms of the resettlement program.

The various proposals that came up in the meetings in each center were passed on to the other centers to be digested for the conference agenda. In the end those who advocated general resettlement on condition of more aid from the government assumed dominance and leadership among the center representatives. Time worked for them because it was only as time passed that center residents slowly came to realize that WRA fully intended to try to close the centers within a year. When the delegates met in Salt Lake City, there was a strong minority who wanted to sit tight on the proposition of retaining some centers. The delegates who finally dominated the discussions, however, drew up a long list of the needs of evacuees for more assistance than they were getting from WRA—a list which was formally presented to the National Director of WRA. They had adopted the course of channeling evacuee opposition to the whole program into the form of specific proposals for increased assistance in reestablishing themselves outside the centers. The WRA replied that the agency had gone the limit and that there could be no significant modification of the program as already outlined.

The All-Center Conference delegates returned to their centers to find people largely indifferent to them and what they had done in their meeting. Interest had not been very intense among the majority of evacuees even before the conference. Moreover before, during, and after the conference the National Director of WRA had visited the centers and addressed mass meetings. He had told people that WRA was indeed in earnest about closing the centers, that he did not believe it was good for anyone to remain in the centers, and that there was no other course except to close them. His visits and personal assumption of responsibility for the program had influenced many people. The belief that WRA would really try to close the centers now began to spread and increasing numbers of people were beginning to act on the belief.

The organized effort which began in the emotional reaction against being pushed around again had moved, under the leadership of the liaison men, from a desperate movement to hold on to the security of the centers to a strong statement of disagreement with WRA's methods of closing the centers. The liaison men now took the view that WRA's methods would not work to the end that WRA wanted. They maintained in every center that with the amount of assistance that WRA was giving, only a portion of the people in the centers could ever reestablish themselves. The idea developed and received increasing expression from evacuee leaders that there would inevitably be a residue of people in the centers at the time of WRA's deadline. Most of the liaison men began to work hard to assist all who wanted to leave the centers, but they were confident for the most part that a large number would be ultimately left.

Once accepted, the idea of the residue led necessarily to further questions. During the spring the matter of the final closing of schools was raised as an issue with the WRA. Closing them by the end of the summer was regarded as a broken promise and as unjust to those "who couldn't relocate." The Minidoka council sought legal grounds for requiring WRA to continue the schools. The Parent-Teachers' Association and other groups in various centers protested and cast about for means of continuing the schools under evacuee management. In most centers, groups of parents continued through August to make plans for giving their children schooling in the centers.

Another important question on everyone's lips was "What will be done with the residue after WRA closes out?" Speculation developed along innumerable lines: Gila and Poston would finally remain open; Manzanar would be retained as an old people's home; the Justice Department would take over remaining centers; a new agency would be created to provide for the "unrelocatables." The feeling was strong that WRA had some undisclosed plan for taking care of the residue. This feeling grew and the issue was taken up in some councils. WRA's refusal to admit a residue was called unrealistic. As discussion continued, feeling against WRA hardened. Councilmen in Topaz held that it was inhumane not to reveal the plan for ultimate disposal of the people who could not resettle. WRA, they said, should let people know their fate. If, on the other hand, there was no plan, that was even more inhumane, for it would mean that the residue would be forced out at the end with nowhere to go. Feeling of this sort was strong all through the centers by the end of July.

The residue had become an unanalyzed stereotype which for many was something to lean on in their search for the security which the relocation centers offered. Liaison men and others did not think of themselves as members of the residue. They felt that they would ultimately be able to make the new start, but they saw large

The evacuees never ceased to work at plans for making the centers into "ideal communities." A dream of those in the hottest and dustiest center— Poston, Ariz.—was for a swimming pool and park. This model was made and exhibited at the Poston Center Fair in January, 1945.

numbers as being unable to do so. The relocation centers had, during the course of the previous three years, become a fixed point of orientation in the thinking of evacuees. They were real and tangible before them. They had become, for those who had remained in them, the only security in a world that had been made completely insecure as a result of the evacuation. The conviction that they must continue to exist had become a fixed and settled belief in the minds of almost everyone. The concept of the residue was the ultimate form taken by the relocation center value in the orientation of community sentiment which had crystallized in the winter of 1943–44. If there had been complete isolation in the centers, it is likely that the residue viewpoint would have been the only one of any consequence, and the overwhelming majority would have settled back to regard themselves all as members of the residue. There were, however, other forces working against any universal acceptance of the idea, and these gathered momentum during June and July.

THE STAKE IN AMERICA

Although the majority of evacuees during the spring of 1945 were clinging in desperation to the relocation centers, for many the opening of the West Coast was an immediate impetus to action. A nurseryman who had been biding his time at Manzanar was back in Los Angeles promptly the first week in January taking up the reins of his nursery business. A Nisei fruit rancher from Heart Mountain was back on the Coast within a few weeks, reestablished in his orchard, and a few months later calling for laborers from the centers. All up and down the Coast evacuees were moving back quickly to take up their interrupted lives. In numbers they were small, and many hung back to wait and see what would happen to the most adventurous, but those who still had their homes, their farms, or their businesses were at least planning definitely how to go back and when. The small minority who moved out during the late winter and spring had little effect on community sentiment in the centers.

The experiences of some, however, immediately had repercussions which temporarily consolidated opinion against leaving the centers. During the first months after the lifting of exclusion there was a series of attacks by West Coast people on evacuees who had returned. In Placer County a barn was burned. Near Fresno and in other places night riders shot into the homes of newly returned families. The American Legion of Hood River, Oregon, erased the names of Nisei in the armed forces from the town Honor Roll, and anti-Japanese organizations sprang up in the Northwest and in California. With such facts to go on, the world of rumor in the centers flourished anew. Evacuees who had just left a center for the West Coast were said to have been murdered. The number of real incidents was multiplied into a host of imaginary incidents. Fear grew in the centers. The existing hostility outside was magnified many times. People imagined what could happen to themselves if they should go back to the Coast. Even if no evacuee had yet been killed, the first to be killed might be oneself. Each new incident increased the fears, and many who had thought of going back to the Coast decided against it. Most who were going out continued to follow the lead of family members and friends and left the centers for the East rather than the West. By the end of February about 700 had left all the centers for the West Coast, while three times that number had gone East since the lifting of exclusion. The orientation to the outside was still predominantly to that portion of the outside not in the formerly excluded area.

With the coming of spring, however, it was apparent that old contacts with the West Coast were being renewed in ways that the volume of permanent resettlers to the region did not reveal. Many more persons were going out for the purpose of exploring and looking around than were going back to already secure places on the Coast with homes and businesses ready to walk into. As spring wore on these "scouts," as they had come to be called, increased in numbers. They were men who wished to explore for themselves and others the nature of their old communities, the possibilities for housing, the attitudes of friends and competitors. They went out for a week or two, looked over their old towns, interviewed many people, canvassed the possibilities for renewing their old lines of activity. They came back to the centers to add to the store of information that evacuees had been accumulating through correspondence with friends on the West Coast and through reading the home town newspapers. They came back with good and bad stories of their reception and of the possibilities for getting started again. They came back with accounts of their own experiences which people felt could be relied on. They had known the scout for a long time; they could accept what he said more readily than the information supplied by the workers of the agency.

Slowly the rumor world began to alter. The intense fear inspired by the shooting and arson on the West Coast began to die down by June. There was still fear, but too many evacuees had got reestablished and too many had been able to go about unharmed, meeting only friendly receptions. It was no longer possible to believe the wilder rumors of hostility. People had facts about their own communities, details about what it was like back there. A basis for distinguishing rumor from actuality had grown up. All through the spring and early summer people gathered around returned scouts and listened to their stories. A solid contact was being built up which rested on all the old memories and was tied in intimately with one's past life.

Not only individuals were beginning to be affected here and there. Groups of people from the same former locality on the West Coast were beginning to think and plan together for the best way to proceed in returning. Such groups, which had been largely in suspended animation as groups during the life in the centers, now began to emerge as units again. They were assessing the chances in the old localities, mobilizing their resources as a group, and planning to go back together or at least relating individual plans to one another. The Buddhist Church organization, centered at Topaz, began to urge and plan for return. The lines of action within the centers were slowly changing in response to the new stimulus. The relocation center community organization still rested on the program that centers must be retained—at least for the residue. The old, temporarily submerged former organizations were beginning to operate again largely outside the center structure of leadership and in terms of the orientation to the old West Coast stake.

In May the shift in attitudes about the West Coast was striking. A minister who had returned to his former locality in Washington state came back to his congregation in the centers and urged prompt resettlement on the ground that hostility could thrive in the old community on imaginary, suspicion-inspired pictures of the evacuees, but that the presence of some real former Japanese residents would work to dispel the hostility. He wrote letters recounting his experience and distributed them widely in the centers. Some evacuees everywhere were now out of the world of rumor, and back in the world of reality, but it was still a minority. Some were working outside the lines of action or inaction still stimulated by the center organization and sentiments. The West Coast stake was no longer merely an abstract value in the center system of sentiments. It had become an increasingly concrete reality.

Toward the end of May enough evacuees had re-established their old lines of contact in the West Coast communities to make it possible for the WRA to arrange for whole carloads of returning people to go back together. Railroad coaches were chartered to take the people back home. At Rohwer, Granada, Heart Mountain, and the other centers the coaches were filled with evacuees, amid the farewells of the hundreds who had come to see them off. Through June and on into the summer the departing cars and the crowds waving good-byes became a more and more prominent feature of center life. The large-scale embarkations for the homeland were viewed nostalgically by those remaining. There were many questions of "When are you going?" as people stood around waiting for the cars or buses to pull out. The reality of large numbers actually returning to the Coast had materialized. Not only had the homeland become concrete through the stories of the exploring scouts, but also friends and neighbors were really going there, and the people who were remaining in the centers could see it with their own eyes. In the midst of the still widespread conviction that most people could not go out, the orientation to the Coast was becoming more and more definite.

DISINTEGRATION OF THE CENTERS

All during the spring people had been worrying, and thinking, and planning. The wave of solidarity behind the idea of holding on to the centers had lasted for hardly two months after the lifting of exclusion. The worrying and thinking began to swing between two poles—between the relocation centers as places of known security and the outside as a place of increasing reality. More and more people swung to the latter pole and attempted to transform their worrying and thinking into planning. By summer the population of any center could be divided into four groups. At one extreme were the people whose plans were all made, with dates set for departure. At the other extreme were those who were determined to sit tight, some of whom were telling others to do the same. Between these extremes were the majority of people, some with plans that were not yet definite as to date of departure, but most of them, as a center observer said, "sitting, worrying, hoping for a miracle that will either save them from relocation or make relocation a less difficult undertaking." The state of mind of the majority by this time was described by an Issei women:

When WRA announced that the centers would close, a lot of people said they didn't want to go out, some of them said they wouldn't. During the next two months, many, many of them changed their minds. They decided they did want to go out and they thought they could. They talked this way more a little while before my husband left [in late March] than at any other time. Since then, what they have heard about the Coast has made them change their minds again. They still want to go, but they say they can't. And . . . they don't just say this. It is true. They really can't. They want to go, but there is no place to live and jobs are hard to get. Employers are afraid to hire Japanese.

She could have added that lack of housing in the places where people wanted to go had almost completely replaced the earlier fear of violence as an obstacle to making any sort of decision about a return to the West Coast.

The desperation of people who could not see, from the distance of the centers, any way to move back home was now steadily increased by the crumbling of the relocation centers. The security of the centers had not, since 1942, been merely the security of shelter and three meals a day. It was in a much more important way the security of other people to live with. The association of Issei with one another, the solid routine of block life, the indulgence of submerged interests with like-minded men and women—these constituted the meaning of the relocation centers. When people had formed their ideas about staying in the centers for the duration of the war, they had done so in the context of the warm social life of the centers. Holding the centers had meant holding that. But the relocation centers were now becoming, almost imperceptibly at first, something different.

The changes that were transforming the centers had set in months before. Early in 1945 they were accelerated. The WRA had adopted the policy of closing mess halls in blocks in which the population fell below a certain figure, usually 125. The closing ordinarily meant the consolidation of the mess halls of two blocks. At first people stubbornly resisted merging as though aware that it spelled doom for the centers. They resisted for more ordinary reasons, too; they did not want to eat the cooking of another chef or go through the process of getting used to some other block's mess hall after spending three years getting used to their own. Inexorably, however, the administrators negotiated the closing of mess halls as people went out to resettle and block populations dropped. They met the resistance by postponing dates of closure, making minor concessions on methods, and finally getting agreement to this plan or that. By the end of April people in every center had experienced the process. Once adjusted to the idea, they tried to make it as pleasant as possible. Usually the merging of two mess halls became the occasion for a little ceremony, with welcoming speeches and a special meal. The closing, like the farewells to departing carloads of people, was becoming a part of center life. In the process, as in the departures, the people remaining in the blocks lost something: the block with a closed mess hall was not the same. There was a different, empty feeling about living in such a block. The heart of the block had faltered.

Also there was now a great turnover in block personnel. Block managers here and there were packing up and leaving. Other block workers were dropping out. People filled in to do the necessary work. Block organization was beginning to give way to miscellaneous volunteering to do specific jobs. People began to feel that the substance of block life was disintegrating. It was not only the closed mess hall and the vacant apartments; much more important in the effect on the people was the growing sense that block affairs were being taken care of in a makeshift way. There was a feeling of decay and decline in the air that weighed more and more on people through the summer. Although the barracks and the block manager's office and a good many people were still there, the block as a social group was crumbling, and as they crumbled, the relocation centers began to disintegrate before people's eyes and under their feet.

Despite the changes in thinking about the war since the first entry into the relocation centers, the end of the war as a key point in planning for the future had persisted even into 1945. With Allied victory in Europe in May and the progressive loss of ground by Japan in the Pacific during the summer of 1945, attitudes to the war underwent further changes. The scouts who had been bringing people back into touch with the reality of the outside also began to bring them a new point of view to the war. An Issei woman in one center said as early as May:

When Mr. X came back from Spokane, I was talking to him one day. I wanted to find out what he thought about the war. I had to go carefully, because I didn't want to start an argument, and I knew how he used to think. So I just asked him if the people in the center had the right idea. "They don't know what is going on," he said. "In Spokane I was in just a little pin point of this country. But what I saw changed my mind. Trainloads of war material, week after week, all of it on the way to the Pacific. Then I realized what Japan was up against. The industrial power of this country is too great. If Japan is not beaten down, if peace comes in some way, we can be thankful. But we must expect the worst and act accordingly. We must go out and re-establish ourselves. Japan can never help us."

As the realization of the way the war was going grew stronger in the centers, many Issei were growing sad and gloomy, as this writer expressed:

It's hard to tell you how an Issei feels. I have a line that runs through me. On one side are my feelings for this country. It has done a lot for me. My kids are all-American and I want them to be. I have enjoyed my life here. On the other side are my feelings about Japan. Before the war, it was all right. I never thought of it. After Pearl Harbor, I felt pulled apart inside . . . . Now I feel awfully sorry for Japan. If I am truthful, I must say that I feel more for Japan than for this country. Not that I want or ever wanted Japan to win. . . . I wanted nobody to win; I wanted the war to stop; I didn't want it to start in the first place. I would feel terrible if this country was in danger of being crushed down. I guess I feel most for the country that is going to suffer most.

The hope for help through the country of their citizenship in the road ahead to rehabilitation had faded far. Even the few in some blocks who clung to a belief in Japanese success talked little about the aid to themselves, as they nursed their fixed idea. As the summer wore on, it became possible to speak freely of the few of this sort in the blocks as the "lunatic fringe." Their views could be doubted with impunity.

Thus the points of orientation of community sentiment had shifted sharply. The end of the war was less significant because so many people had begun to feel, whether they admitted it or not, that they already knew the outcome. The relocation centers were still a vital point of reference, but not the same thing to which people had oriented themselves two years before; they were fading slowly, but nevertheless unmistakably, as values to hold on to. The West Coast stake had risen as the dominant point of orientation in the constellation. People were responding all through the centers to the new alignment of values. Center relocation officers could operate as they never had before. Their interest in getting people out was beginning to be matched by people's desire to get out. Moreover, those of the liaison men who were left were responding to the shift in community sentiment, working hard from late spring on through the summer to assist, and even at times to urge, people who they thought could go out to do so. They worked more and more closely with center staff in helping people to get information, to make their plans, and to find their way out of the centers. They were still convinced that ultimately there would be a residue, but were also convinced that it was their civic duty to help resettle everyone who could be at all expected to make a go of it outside, before the gates of the centers closed on the "unrelocatables."

A councilman in one center expressed his point of view:

Many . . . of my block people have asked me if I thought the WRA would really close the centers. I always tell them the same thing—that the future of the centers and of the evacuees is no longer under the control of WRA. WRA itself is being abolished by the Government. It can't help what it is doing. It is actually a peewee organization—set up by the President and Congress to take care of the evacuees, now to be wiped out. It may be that WRA had more to do with closing the centers than this indicates. I try to protect WRA a little. I do not do this because I like WRA or because I think it has done all it could or should for evacuees. But I don't want people to blame WRA too much. WRA can do some things to help, and it will work out better if people do not hate the administration too much. I don't know what other councilmen tell their block people.

In July and August the agency moved inexorably toward its deadline. Closing dates, ranging from September to December, were set for all the centers except Tule Lake. Then in early August came an announcement that a few weeks in advance of those dates all persons still in the centers who had not already made their departure plans would be scheduled for departure by the project directors. Almost at the same time came the end of the Pacific war with decisive American victory. By some stroke of fate, the application of pressures to meet the deadline had been geared almost precisely to coincide with the disappearance of what was left of one of the old points of reference in the evacuee program to hold the centers—the end of the war.

Goodbyes are said as the final break-up of the centers take place. Friends and neighbors again separate to pick up their normal lives in different locations—some to their old homes, some to other parts of the country.

By the first of September the movement outward from those centers nearest to their closing dates was reaching great volume, evacuees leaving at the rate of more than 2,000 a week. The facilities for processing people in the centers were heavily taxed. Blocks were piled with packing crates. Few people were thinking of anything beyond the immediate steps to get out of the centers. The administration offices were full of people getting information and filling out forms. The sit-tighters who still announced intentions to stay were ignored or laughed at by the busy people in the blocks.

In the final weeks the centers more and more took on the character they had had three years before when people first moved into them. There was no real community organization any longer; it was organization for getting little things done promptly, not for the expression of anyone's feelings about things. Organization was temporary and improvised. More than ever councilmen were errand boys, running about seeing that this and that got done. Many block managers, out of a sense of duty to the people, had decided to stay and help to the last. Others left, and volunteers in the blocks undertook their work. Lines between staff members and evacuees broke down. The distance between administrative and evacuee areas became narrower. The two areas were merging and center staff found themselves able to perform liaison duties. This had begun to be apparent even before the August accelerated disintegration of the communities. In late July an assistant project director said, describing a morning session he had held with the community council:

They [the councilmen] were more relaxed, more at ease. Before, they seemed always on the defensive, sort of lined up against me. They watched what they said, tried never to commit themselves, and appeared interested in me mostly for what they could get out of me. This morning a bunch of men sat down to talk things over. I was one of them.

In the face of disintegration the centers had made the complete circle back to improvised teamwork to meet the basic individual needs.

As the centers emptied they became bleakly dismal places. People, as they left, some tearfully, talked a little nostalgically of coming back some time. The communities they were thinking of, however, were no longer there. The places were still there, but the communities they had clung to now existed only in their minds and memories. The vacation from assimilation was over. The rows of barracks in the moonlight seemed to one departing man to be hardly real. Had this been the place where so much agony had been endured, where so much of the spirit of a people had been expressed, where communities had been built and torn down?

Systematically, center by center, the people met the deadlines for the agency. By mid-December only Tule Lake remained to be closed. Manzanar, Poston, Gila, Minidoka, Heart Mountain, Granada, Topaz, Rohwer, Jerome had become names on the land, to crop up here and there on beauty parlors, social clubs, barber shops, and cafes all over America.

CONFUSION AT TULE LAKE

At Tule Lake the period to November, 1944, had been one of warring factions and sharp conflicts. Each in its turn, at first the stockade faction and then later the coordinating committee, rose to ascendancy and influenced center thinking only to be swept aside. The year 1945, by contrast, was to belong wholly to the re-segregationists, who by November had settled into an extremist position consistent with the war fever, the exaggerated consciousness of discrimination and race, and the boundless distrust of the Government which had grown up in 1944.

Although the transition to extremism was in this sense impersonal and inevitable, the control over and pressure upon center residents to conform to the tenets of resegregationist thinking was in the making. Yet the real or original background of the movement was to be found in the conflict which developed in the segregation center, a conflict which marked the period of settling down, of November incidents, of ten long months of the stockade during part of which the stockade following and coordinating committee supporters stood face to face in open opposition in the center.

The main fact of importance about this conflict was its confinement to a square mile of fenced-in area. Here babies were born, people married, others died, meals were prepared and eaten daily, wood was carved and gardens were planted. But the conflict, like the factors making for stability, ran through every ward and block, sometimes even through a family group. There was consequently no way of escaping it. The fence afforded no outlet for mass emotions, but rather leveled the responses to administrative handling and governmental programs to a few simple stereotypes. One opened the door to his barracks apartment—too small for retirement or solitude—and immediately felt the limited horizons, the magnified gossip and the uncompromising line-up of opinion.

Since there was, in addition, no outlet for conflicting responses to Governmental controls, it seemed to many that the conflicting groups had, to date, won nothing. It was known that without final center unity in the face of a unified administration and policy, murder had been committed, and reputations ruined; lost causes were everywhere, and futures remained indeterminate. Besides this, it seemed to any bystander that the coordinating committee, in overstaying its welcome, had served to show that there was no middle ground in dealing with administration, no escape for the "dog" or "informer," real or putative, no further point in maintaining disharmony, and no real safety from the relocation channel so quickly arranged for the men of allegedly unsavory reputation who fled the project and their coordinating committee group once Hitomi, manager of the cooperative store, was murdered. With the man-proof fence for a sounding board, and the least whispers of dissatisfaction echoing back from four walled-in sides, the reaction against relocation and disunity— or obversely, the cry for center security and harmony—reverberated through the blocks.

It was in the resegregationist camp, of course, that the cry was loudest, for there unity and harmony were linked with the widely accepted theme of escape from America, a program of organized cultural revivalism or a design to study and promote the customs of Japan. This retreat from defeat and frustration into the romantic world of the Issei was launched under the banner of unity, faced away from American soil for resettlement, and provided the solace of fighting against repression with the only weapons available, namely the world of custom. The objective of a future abroad was, in the final analysis, one which transcended the war of cliques, the fear of the government, and the immediate, dull concerns and monotonous gossip that hemmed in center life. So said the resegregationist and so echoed his following.

The escape motif of *senryu* poetry and *utai* singing associations could help to solve the problems of the Issei bachelor, or language schools and Japanese checkers, respectively, take up the time of perplexed Nisei and simple, common men. But the majority of families, poised between dissatisfaction with center life and future uncertainty, were for the most part willing to cast their lot with the organized resegregationists who provided the bulwark against relocation, championed the cause of harmony, and arranged the speeches and meetings promoting their study of custom. The speeches on Japanese customs and affairs were, to be sure, reassuring. "We are Japanese together." "Our customs are worthy of respect." "Our ideals are ideals of unity and progress." By August of 1944, the tight and fast-moving central organization claimed it had garnered 10,000 signatures for resegregation. The hopeful, but not actively participating, multitude of 7,000 was being towed in its wake.

Three months later, however, the program for the removal from the center of pro-American, "unsympathetic" elements reached a new peak. New leadership, pushing ahead from cultural revivalism to patriotism had taken hold. Unity became a phalanx of marching youth, harmony became intimidation or fervor in winning recruits, customs became uniforms of a sort—emblems on sweatshirts, a shaved head for boys and braids for girls, the red-bordered *hachimaki* or sweatband worn for drill. The aim was physical preparation of the male youth, and to warp determination into a new and defiant attitude. As time passed, a bugle corps intoned the foreign anthem, a mimeographed paper sang the praises of the Japanese spirit, cabinets were developed to guide physical, social, and cultural training with Issei advisors in the background prodded by Kibei drillmasters menacingly in front. Defiance of a relocation program of the government had by now changed qualitatively, becoming an organized request for speedy repatriation to serve Japan. There were thousands who quietly backed out before the next sign-up or petition for resegregation went the rounds. But others fearfully rationalized their continuing membership by convincing themselves that these objectives were good and proper so long as violence was visited upon Japanese relocatees outside, and so long as a secure future lay nowhere on this soil.

In December, events moved swiftly in the other centers with the lifting of rescission of mass exclusion on the West Coast by Army order. At Tule Lake a stable minority welcomed the opportunity to appeal status, or if cleared, to escape the rising tide of hysteria by relocation outside. The bulk of Tulean males and heads of families fell, by virtue of registration answers, into the excludee or segregee status, the former able to go out to eastern and midwestern areas, the latter having some chance to relocate through the appealing of status to the Western Defense Command. The process was slow and tedious, appeals always outstripping clearances, and the new factor, the resegregationist clique, was now sufficiently entrenched to menace the application of rescission to Tule Lake. Most important, by January, the Department of Justice had instituted two programs: first, the renunciation of citizenship and second, the counter attack on resegregationism. In a letter addressed to the *hoshidan* (serve-Japan) group, a representative of the Attorney General attacked the organization, insisted that it must cease activities, remarked upon his doubts as to the true measure of its patriotic motivation, and ended, after noting the violence and pressure employed to force loyalty to Japan upon residents of the center, by promising that the "intolerable" activities of the organization "will cease." A pattern of removal of renunciant and Issei members to internment was inaugurated. Nisei, again under the banner of harmony and solidarity, were swept into the renunciation program. The rumors of draft and forced relocation for nonrenunciants were broadcast. And as trainloads of men and youths left for internment centers, hundreds were coaxed, wheedled, or coerced into filling the ranks, renouncing citizenship, drilling, and entraining for internment in their turn. To prove the pattern of defiance to the Attorney General's representative in the center, the drill and exercise of the boys and then the girls was moved to the front area of the project and on Sundays moved back to 9 o'clock for his "benefit and edification."

To the lifting of exclusion, to fears of relocation and the draft, to insistent pressures of hysterical men, must again be added the isolation of the center. It was now a center not simply fenced off from contact with the outside and from Governmental personnel, but one in which the ordinary community sanctions of the outside were choked off. Issei, listening to short-wave radio in hundreds of apartments, suffered a deepening horror of resettlement in America with its inevitable breakup of the family, and magnified to dreamlike proportions the vision of a future elsewhere. There were now the blood-and-bones justifications of the order to children to renounce and to find a future in supporting parents in an Orient among "their own kind." The burning of the Doi barn in Placer County, the Hood River racist rejection of Nisei heroes, or the newspaper clamor about "disloyals at Tule Lake" turned the argument away from the theme of escape to Japanese culture to one of escape from American soil. To the Nisei the statement: "Renounce because you are Japanese," replaced the earlier: "Remain in Tule Lake because you will be drafted or menaced on the outside." The typical Nisei response in renunciation hearings, over 6,000 strong, was: "I renounce because I want to be Japanese." The Kibei version: . . . because I am Japanese—with Japanese face and hair." The Issei wishful thinking back in the center included a fund-raising campaign to buy a *nanyo* or island in the South Pacific pending the outcome of war. Leaders of the *hoshidan* promised a continuation of group enterprise and esprit de corps, long into the future. Nisei, perplexed by the magic ritual of drill, language class, and renunciation argued that if parents—ineligible even to American citizenship and excluded by the taint of race and foreign language from equal participation in American life—had succeeded against odds in building a life here (although it was now destroyed), then could not the Nisei of acceptable race and language in Japan achieve far more?

To summarize, Tule Lake residents were still moving in a framework of cultural revivalism. This trend had developed from, or at least could be traced back to, its first phase in the assembly centers from which it had been transplanted to all relocation centers and, of course, to Tule Lake as well. It was initially a type of cultural revivalism which could be duplicated among any American Indian ghost-dance cult in the early stages of reservation life, the first manifestation, from instance to instance, being the revival and preservation of arts, crafts, folkways, and mores, and the refurbishing of the habitual stock in trade of a defeated or frustrated older generation. In this case the patriachs—confined and in a sense imprisoned by governmental action—were the Issei bent upon preserving, in the face of disappointments and anxieties occasioned by evacuation, all things culturally Japanese which they felt were threatened in the war-conscious outside world. Included were poetry, music, wood carving, flower arranging, and possibly even the Japanese-style dance. Theirs had been in the nature of a social response to the hysteria, racism, and prejudice which backgrounded evacuation. It was, indeed, their first real answer to the reported taunt of the Commander of the Western Defense Command, "A Jap's a Jap."

At Tule Lake, even after segregation, this romantic dalliance with Japanese customs continued in such forms at first as *senryu* poetry clubs, *utai* singing societies, and in the Japanese-style theatricals of the Issei. But such clubs and associations as were devoted to these and similar interests were scattered throughout the project, limited in space and membership, and circumscribed in interest. In the face of the sharpening up of postsegregation conflicts, it was hardly such typical group activity which could conceivably bring about center harmony and unity vis-à-vis administration. And now, as the outside receded more and more into the past, local administration became America, "the Government," and "the General" in their modern form.

As we have said, it was the study-of-customs group which first suceeded in providing unity and harmony by offering a refuge from fears of relocation and inu and by providing an escape from boredom, defeatism and frustration in the hoped-for revival of Japanese customs. Of course, private classes in Japanese musical instruments, tailoring, painting, etiquette and calligraphy continued and associations for *senryu, utai, go, judo, kendo* and *sumo* multiplied. But from ward to ward and group to group there was no constant mechanism, except for the study-of-customs group, to challenge local administration and the government. Only here, with its 10,000 signatures representing more than half the population, were the most deep-seated fears, wishes, and responses to Governmental handling effectively expressed.

Up to the November period of reorganizing in the study-of-customs group, one could notice that something was happening in the extreme wing of the organization. Those who had been extremists in the prostockade faction, the aberrant Kibei wing who had been labeled "trouble-makers" in other camps, and persons who had figured prominently in the Poston incident, all lined up with Terminal Island boys headed by a former leader of the Fisherman's Union there, a man who happened to be a most disgruntled veteran of World War I. The five-man Issei top committee of resegregationists now appeared to be following their lead. While successive signups or petitions of the resegregationists netted fewer and fewer signatures, the extremists were mobilizing to take over the organization, a step which they managed to accomplish in the November election of cabinets.

At this juncture the change was felt up and down the line. New hoshidan headquarters were set up. Drill became more prominent. The theme of "preparation through study" gave way to the hysterical one of "speedy repatriation." The above-mentioned hair styles, some new signaling devices, and a bugle corps appeared. The tightly organized minority agitating for resegregation shifted to repatriation as a prime objective on the basis of two programs: the lifting of exclusion which of course opened the door to the possible relocation of Tuleans, and the renunciation program which sounded much as if it guaranteed a means for Nisei as well as Issei to adopt a status which ruled out the draft, forced relocation, family separation, or the much-abused stigma of loyal-*inu* or fence sitters, as the case might be. Since the renunciation law as first written did not even contain age limitations, whole families were swung very early into the program on the basis of the fears and motivations listed above. It is curious that as the government's program became resettlement, the residents' reaction favored renunciation and repatriation.

While resegregationism (and even renunciation of citizenship) was not clearly or simply a matter of loyalty, the lines were again being drawn in the center between resegregationist and antiresegregationist. Consistent with the program of resettlement, repatriation and expatriation requests were being cancelled by a few people, in this case through the instrumentality of a staff welfare office located in an unadvertised and undesignated barracks room in Ward III. Those antiresegregationists who could do so, relocated in the course of time, leaving the stragglers among the Nisei to be caught up in the renunciation program. A resettler was said to be a loyal administration man. A resegregationist had the courage of his convictions. Obviously loyalty lost any generally significant meaning.

One Nisei, not in the resegregationists' camp, later wrote retrospectively of the renunciation program:

It was funny, the mentality of the people in here then. I mean both Issei and Nisei. The Army, by lifting the exclusion order, had opened the door to relocation. You remember how people relocated then. The camp, however, wasn't ready for it, so people went out practically in the dead of night. Two Niseis actually did this. Remember? Anyway, the Justice [department] gave the hot-heads their reason for defiance when they began sending hundreds of renuncees to internment. To defy that, internment became an honor. Anyway, it meant no relocation and no draft.

There was, moreover, a qualitative difference between going to a place of infamy like a jail and being sent to an internment center to which many well-respected community leaders among the Japanese had been sent and released from over a period of wartime years. The formula of transfer to internment was apparently too simple. Handled by the Department of Justice and applied to an organization of 6,000 persons at Tule Lake, it brought together two factors which had hitherto been important in the community but which had, up to then, been fortunately unconnected: (1) the importance of cultural revivalism, now in its third or patriotic phase of escape to Japan; and (2) the desire to exhibit open defiance to the Government by accepting renunciation and internment as escapes from the intolerable conditions of center life, possible relocation, and the draft. Since the transfer of literally thousands to internment was obviously wedding these two psychological and mass responses, it was toward the end of this process, but as soon as feasible, that local administration intervened. The process of splitting families by interning hundreds of Nisei renunciants and Issei hoshidan members had, it seemed, gone far enough. Unfortunately, hysterical or coerced renunciations had been accepted by the Attorney General, in many cases contrary to the recommendation on the scene of the Justice Department's own hearing officer. It was further unfortunate that the Tule Lake ghost-dance cult of revivalism had been taken as *prima facie* evidence of disloyalty without proper investigation into individual cases or into the bases of renunciation or resegregationist thinking in the center. It therefore seemed important to administrators at Tule Lake to present to evacuees a clearer picture of the consequences of their action, using as a frame of reference one which would broaden the picture beyond the repression and defiance.

Administrative Regulations Imposed

With only a remnant of the hoshidan left, and before further contingents were "honored" by internment, administrative officials decided to deal directly with the organization, first through a set of special project regulations, and later by means of a series of logical proposals. The regulations interdicted marching, bugling, the wearing of emblems, the attendance at organizational meetings, and coercion upon youth to take part in organizational activities. This notice, or proscription, led to many withdrawals from the organization, but, as was expected, no slackening of resistance to the ultimatum on the part of those remaining—a situation which differed from defiance of the Department of Justice only on one important respect: loss of membership in the group.

The next step, therefore, following court trials of dozens of violators of the special project regulations, was to propose three logical alternatives to the organization, the proposals called propositions. Proposition No. 1 was to cease all prohibited activities and remain at Tule Lake without further family separation. Proposition No. 2 was to cease violations of the regulations pending an attempt by WRA to arrange an internment trip of eligible males. Proposition No. 3 was to continue the pattern of defiance and take the consequences. As was anticipated, the first proposal, although attractive to many personally, could not be fitted into the ghost-dance pattern of defiance to "white officialdom." The second, a compromise, fared better.

In the organization, a split occurred as between Groups 2 and 3. Since splits had already occurred in the contingents already in internment, this particular one destroyed finally or completely the unity and harmony which had been the main asset of the organization. Perhaps most important was the amount of administrative contact developed with the aggrieved and confused hoshidan in the presentation of these points. Unlike the tactic of the Department of Justice in simply arranging transfers to internment, the new method was one of attaching conditions of compliance with administration, while at the same time arguing against family separation. This new tactic produced immediate and visible results. Group 2 withdrew from morning drill. Without fanfare, they left the project after individually and collectively signing to comply with these special project regulations. Their bugles were turned in to internal security. Their more radical confreres in Group 3 were left in a ridiculous position at Tule Lake except for a top leadership forcibly ejected.

The importance of this action, the fact that administration had broken the front of unity and shattered the code of defiance cannot be minimized. From then on, defiance and unity were again disconnected and the hoshidan dwindled in size. Unfortunately, this was not the result of earlier Department of Justice transfers to internment.

Following a few months after the renunciation program of January, withdrawals from the hoshidan and a countermovement against unreasoning fanaticism were begun. The long road back to center normalcy had reached its second and final cycle. Administrative contacts with the center were again multiplied. Restrictions were loosened and shopping passes issued. For once, resettlement became the program both of the authority and of the center residents.

An analysis of this last trend is important since Tule Lake as a community completely reversed its character. A portion of the Proposition 3 group, once their confreres of Group 2 had left dejectedly for internment, managed to gain control of the business enterprises cooperative which the organized resegregationists, long before Hitomi's death, had originally hoped to close. Moreover, the language schools not only cooperated with officials of the American public and high school administrative system, but willingly curtailed activities and curricula as the latter system grew in enrollment. The Greater East Asia Language School became the Tule Lake Language School. The wards which originally opposed the institution of American nursery schools now disbanded their Japanese nurseries in favor of the administrative system. In activities, Japanese movies gave way to the familiar Hollywood type, the project director was invited to throw in the first ball of the baseball season, and shaved heads and braids gave way to usual hair styles. Nisei dances were again arranged. Renunciants, in some instances, attempted to join the Army before final victory was assured, their Nisei soldier friends, on furlough, being feted in the blocks. Resettlers were given farewell dinners. The Issei began to relocate in advance of their children, and there were no more *sumo* tournaments, *kendo* practices, or *judo* clubs. The recoil from relocation fears and escapism was complete. The center ceased to be a walled-in place of confinement. Except for the stalwarts who repatriated, there was no longer any alternative choice for the future other than on American soil.

In keeping with the swing in sentiment at Tule Lake, the reaction against renunciation was complete and final. On November 1, 1945, approximately a year after the *hoshidan* reorganization, steps were taken by outside individuals to mobilize approximately 1,300 Nisei into a legal suit against the Department of Justice renunciation program. At this time the feeling was that all renunciants were slated for deportation, and on November 14, when the original suit was filed, it appeared that: (1) the suit would attempt to prevent deportation; (2) win release from the confinement of Tule Lake; and (3) restore citizenship. The only major reason given by nonmembers for remaining outside the legal group was that the government would brook no further defiance even in this legal form and would place the blame for any coercion which entered into the renunciation program on the gullible followers of the hoshidan. This final phrasing of the theme, "We are Japanese together," died out as fear of deportation and continued confinement became the final fears of Tule Lake.

By the time the Justice Department instituted mitigation hearings designed to release renunciants through a rehearing process, the confusions at Tule Lake—between cultural and political affiliation, between government and racism outside, between unity which spelled progress and unity which spelled defiance—were not clear. The final months at Tule Lake were a counterpoint of detention, resettlement, and release. While many repatriated through a feeling of helplessness, in general most energies were now bent toward achieving self-preservation through a concerted effort to obtain a future in America. The "disloyal" center, its residents now facing only concrete and realistic alternatives, once more became a relocation center. The fears attached to the status of economic and social refugee no longer had meaning. A final contingent of over 400, mostly renunciants, was taken involuntarily to internment. And after a few final resettlers heard of their releases in the eleventh hour, the perimeter lights went out on a refugee world which had begun its pilgrimage for security in Fresno, Salinas, or Los Angeles, and traveled far in dreams and hopes only to return.

EPILOGUE

Almost from the beginning of the relocation centers people were leaving to resettle "outside" away from government supervision. While this was happening, the camps continued to exist and to function as communities until they were actually depopulated. The outward movement is significant in the account of the centers only as the departure of the resettlers and the reports that came back from them affected the organization and attitudes of those who remained. When a person went through the gate for good, he was off the stage. This epilogue will follow the resettlers.

THE JOURNEY CONTINUED

When the policy makers in WRA began to formulate the relocation program, they redefined the function of the centers. Instead of serving as war-duration homes, the camps were to be temporary stopping places. As soon as eligibility for release could be determined, WRA would urge and assist in resettling all who were free to go. The journey the evacuees had started on the West Coast when they were moved to assembly centers and then to relocation centers was to be continued until as many as possible were established in normal communities outside of the area of exclusion.

In administrative thinking, resettlement would bring many obvious benefits. Not the least of these was that it would disperse persons of Japanese ancestry throughout the country. It was recognized that their concentration on the West Coast was a factor back of the decision to evacuate them. If they could be widely scattered, they would become integrated with the American majority more rapidly and more fully. The prevailing national prejudice against Japanese-Americans as a collective abstraction would decline as Americans in many different communities saw them in the flesh and came to know

277

them as persons. So the relocation program really had three objectives: to get the evacuees out of the centers, to disperse them, and to integrate them into the communities where they settled.

It may be hard for the peaceful citizens of Colorado, Ohio, New York, or other states to imagine themselves and their communities as the evacuees saw them in late 1942 and during 1943. Sitting in the relative safety of the camps, center residents relived evacuation, read the newspapers (mostly West Coast papers), and recounted the occasional unpleasant experiences of early resettlers. Innumerable conversations re-enforced the fears they felt and strengthened their impression that America was almost universally hostile toward them. It seemed to them that most of the public had interpreted evacuation as tantamount to a declaration by the Army that all Japanese-Americans were guilty of potential sabotage. While this was the prevailing tone of thinking and feeling in the centers, evacuees understood that many Americans were friendly or neutral toward them. This was comforting to know but not too reassuring to a would-be resettler. He had no way of telling in advance what attitude a particular individual might take toward a person who had been ordered from his home and confined in a camp due to military necessity. Even if no outright hostility were encountered, there might be special difficulty in obtaining a suitable job or housing.

The journey out into America, therefore, was considered quite hazardous. The sense of uncertainty was increased by reason of the fact that the territory open for resettlement was strange. Few evacuees had ever visited the Middle West or East; fewer still had lived there. The Intermountain Region appeared a little more familiar. It was nearer the West Coast both in miles and in social and economic conditions. A fair number of the evacuees had resided or worked in the area at some point in their careers. Moreover, there were small communities of Japanese in several of the cities and Japanese farmers in some rural districts who had been affected by the war in certain ways but not evacuated.

The earliest relocation tended to concentrate in the Intermountain Region. The Japanese communities in the cities—especially in Denver and Salt Lake—expanded greatly. Farmers and farm workers sought out the rural sections where Japanese were already established. Denver and vicinity, for instance, had had about 800 persons of Japanese ancestry before the war. Between Pearl Harbor and the Army-directed evacuation, some 800 voluntary evacuees from the West Coast came in. Relocation from the centers added approximately 1,800 more within a few months. The influx stirred up so much local antagonism that by the summer of 1943 WRA was taking steps to curb the flow.

It may be noted in passing that the established Japanese residents shared the local antagonism toward the incoming evacuees to some degree. They were afraid that the newcomers might upset the relatively good relations with their Caucasian neighbors that had continued in spite of the war. Then, too, people from the centers bid up the price of land and leases and increased the competition in all lines of economic activity in which Japanese customarily engaged. It is true that many of the old-timers helped their friends in the camps to relocate, but they felt differently toward the strangers who were arriving from the centers.

While the majority of the early resettlers were limiting their attention to the Intermountain States, the more venturesome were going farther from home. They survived and others took courage. The setting up of Relocation Field Offices helped to instill added confidence. By mid-1943 Chicago had surpassed all other cities, including Denver and Salt Lake, in the number of resettlers. Smaller contingents were to be found in dozens of communities in the Middle West and East.

With the lifting of the exclusion order in December 1944, it became possible for resettlers to return to the area from which they had been evacuated. Instead of continuing their journey, they could retrace their steps. By that time more than 30,000—over a quarter of the total number of evacuees—had left the centers. The path of relocation to points outside the West Coast was quite well worn. There were friends the resettler could join. Public sentiment was known to be favorable and jobs were abundant. Housing was still a problem, but a practical and tangible problem now. Although cutting loose from a center remained something of an adventure, it was not a hazardous undertaking, at least for an able-bodied person with no or few dependents.

All this makes it understandable that many center residents did not return to the West Coast during the period the centers were being closed. About a third of those who left the camps in 1945 decided that resettlement elsewhere offered fewer difficulties than reestablishing themselves where they formerly lived.

The objective of WRA to disperse the Japanese had been partially realized by 1946. There were some in almost every state. But the dispersion was not as complete as this statement suggests.

Chicago and vicinity had about 20,000 resettlers, almost a half of those outside of the evacuated area. There were lesser concentrations in a few other cities and in some rural districts of the Intermountain Region. Moreover, during the three years relocation was taking place, concentration tended to increase. It was common for a person to go first to Omaha or Milwaukee and then move on to Chicago after awhile.

What kind of people resettled away from their former homes? Before the closing period, relocation was a highly selective migration. Until the end of 1944, 31 percent of the relocatees were 20–24 years old and 61 percent fell in the age group 15–29. Most were single. Married persons were usually men who left their wives and children in the centers or young couples with no or very few offspring. In view of the age distribution, it is obvious that Nisei constituted the great majority.

The selective character of the migration went beyond these demographic matters. Individuals who relocated while relocation was voluntary had motives for doing so. Most adolescent and adult Nisei were not satisfied in the centers. They had grown up on the periphery of the West Coast Japanese communities, dividing their participation between the life of the minority community and the life of the larger society. When they arrived in the centers, the minority community was there. True, it had been disrupted in transit, but Nisei associates and familiar Issei faces were present. In the centers, Issei proceeded to develop communities, resting on their past common experiences, that provided them with a rather full and pleasant day-by-day existence. Nisei could not build a corresponding Nisei society. Too much had been left behind at evacuation. They were too dependent on the larger community.

Relocation offered them a way out. They could leave the centers and participate again in the life of the American majority. But this raised another problem. They had to give up the Nisei-Issei world which had furnished a part of their social and emotional "home" since birth.

The adjustment to the "new outside" was least difficult for a very few people who previously had lived largely or completely independent of the Japanese community. Such persons generally left the centers as soon as they could since the center communities offered them almost nothing. Except for the possibility that they might meet some anti-Japanese prejudice, relocation meant little more than it means to a member of the American majority to move into a strange town. A young man who went from Heart Mountain to Atlanta soon had a good job and a circle of friends. He liked the city. The fact that he did not see another Nisei for months on end disturbed him not at all.

His case is unusual. Most Nisei missed the association of Japanese-Americans. Even one who resettled in the Intermountain Region had his troubles. The Japanese he met, both the established residents and other resettlers, were strangers. In the getting acquainted process he did not have the social and moral support of his family. What his life experience had really fitted him for was participation in a particular West Coast community—a familiar system of relations in which he had status in a family, in friendship groupings, in a minority society, and in a more inclusive society.

Nevertheless, the adjustments in Denver or Salt Lake were easy compared to the adjustments faced by those who went out early to the Middle West and East. Most of them felt acutely lonely, out of place, and self-conscious. They tended to contact the Relocation Office quite frequently during the first few weeks. It was one known item in their strange new environment. They obtained such solace as they could from companionship with other Nisei. The convention of formal introductions was generally ignored. Two resettlers who had never seen each other would exchange greetings. Soon would come the questions, "What center are you from?" and then "Where did you live before that?" Thereafter, there was a reciprocal search for common acquaintances. "So you're from Gila. I knew a few people who went there. Did you happen to meet . . .?" Or, "San Jose. I was there a couple of weeks once, visiting my uncle. You probably know some of the fellows I met . . . ." They were trying to establish quickly some common ground so that they could relax with each other and reminisce together about the old days before evacuation.

Even after Nisei had found some friends, they could not do things the way they used to on the West Coast. There were few places they could go where just Nisei would be present; where they could be natural and have a good time. Always, other kinds of people were around, making them feel conspicuous and at least a little uncomfortable. They were inclined to feel this way even if other people paid no attention to them. If they attempted to gain reassurance by seeking entertainment in fairly large groups, then they were conspicuous.

Nisei were helped and their troubles were increased by their friends and well-wishers. WRA, local resettlement committees, religious groups, and other organizations welcomed them, aided them to find housing and jobs, and attempted to integrate them into the life of the community. Nisei appreciated these efforts. At the same time they found it hard to behave the way they were supposed to or were expected to. At the time when public relations were still delicate and adverse reaction easily aroused, the word was passed around in some cities that no more than three Nisei should walk along the street together and that no more than five should be together in a restaurant. They were urged to avoid all-Nisei gatherings. Now was the time for the Japanese to integrate with the larger society and get away from the subsociety in which they had lived.

Nisei responded in differing ways to these suggestions and efforts. Those who relocated early generally tried to conform. They deliberately denied themselves Nisei company they longed for. They attended mixed-race parties at which they were inwardly ill at ease. Some of them became quite well adjusted to this sort of participation after awhile so that they continued it from choice. Others grew discouraged and turned again to other Nisei for social satisfactions or found some compromise acceptable to them. Quite a few never made any serious attempt to integrate. They simply ignored the program and associated with non-Nisei or Nisei as practical expediency or their personal inclinations dictated. Usually this meant work relations were with the former, leisure-time relations with the latter.

It sometimes happened that integration became an issue. The word acquired emotional connotations and was even used as a label for classifying Nisei. One girl said:

For awhile in Cleveland it was really funny. Integration was the subject of no end of arguments. One girl would say of another, "Oh yes, I know her. But I don't have much to do with her. She's not integrated, you know." Or, it might be the other way. One group of girls seemed to be the pride and joy of some Cleveland people who wanted us to integrate. These girls got along all right with each other but they avoided the rest of us. They always went around with Caucasians.

For a great many early resettlers, the first weeks or months were an uncomfortable period. Their lack of adjustment was expressed in numerous ways. They did not like their jobs. A large percentage had had little or no work experience. Even those who had worked for some years usually found themselves in jobs different from any they had held. But their criticisms of their employment went beyond what would have been evoked by the employment itself. Their reactions in that field were a part of their total reactions to the difficulties of adjustment. It was the same with other aspects. Housing was terrible. The climate was awful. The city was noisy and dirty. The local people were quite nice, many of them, but they did not understand. Conversations among Nisei tended to be gripe sessions. Many longed to return to the center. Few went except for visits.

They knew that would not satisfy them either. Some, especially boys, flitted from job to job, even from city to city, trying to locate a better situation. Other Nisei heard that this behavior was giving the Nisei a reputation for instability and affecting employers' attitudes adversely. So they determined to stick to their jobs tenaciously and work diligently, partly to establish a good record for themselves and partly to improve the reputation of the Nisei group. There were those who sought to make themselves feel better by earning and saving all they could. Others spent all of their wages in expensive and exciting entertainment and sent "home" to the center for more funds.

Most of these responses seem to have been symptoms of the big thing they missed in the new environment. They missed the old Japanese-American community—their families, Issei support and direction, Nisei groups with established organization and ways. To a degree they even missed the discrimination they had lived with and under on the West Coast. Now they were free to do many things they could not do before but they did not know what they could and could not do. The limits and restrictions they met seemed ill defined and inconsistent. They felt uncertain.

The process of adjustment was probably made more difficult by the sense of temporariness most resettlers felt. The West Coast was home; they intended to return someday. There was no use going to too much bother to make life more satisfactory. The outside was just a little better, or less bad, than the centers as a place in which to put in time until they could go home.

Conditions changed a good deal during 1944. Resettlers became quite numerous in New York, Cleveland, and Minneapolis. Chicago was the mecca. The early resettlers grew accustomed to the places they lived. They not only had objectively better jobs and housing, but their jobs and housing seemed better. There were Nisei clubs and meeting places where they could be by themselves. The natives got used to seeing them, even in fairly large groups. Among some Nisei and local people, there was still talk of the need for integration. But the program was no longer pressed with the urgency it had been.

As Nisei societies emerged, less assimilated Nisei left the center and were able to get along. A few Issei parents joined their children. They wrote back to their Issei friends and one now and again decided to come out. In 1945 this movement continued with increased volume. At first it was mostly more adolescent and adult Nisei. Then, as the closing dates of the centers drew nearer, wives and children, parents and whole families swelled the migration.

As of the spring of 1946, in the points of concentration in the middle western and eastern cities there was no lack of Japanese-American associates. Even Issei could find friends with whom they could relax. It was not as easy to get together as it used to be on the West Coast. That is, although there had been a tendency for Japanese to congregate in certain sections of cities they were not compact settlements of the sort characteristic of pre-evacuation California. In spite of the presence of a fair percentage of Issei, such organization as was developed by local Japanese populations reflected the Nisei rather than the Issei. Clubs abounded. For the most part their membership expressed sorting on the bases of income, occupation, sophistication, degree of assimilation, and so forth. Relocation center background was manifested weakly in social participation. Whether one's pre-evacuation home was California or the Northwest made more difference, but this factor appeared to be of declining importance. There was no formal over-all organization of the minority. JACL, where there was a chapter, spoke for the minority and was allowed to do so. But its membership was small and many Nisei were not very well posted on its program.

In economic matters, in matters of survival, the Japanese were a relatively undifferentiated segment of the population of the cities in which they had settled. True, there were some Japanese stores, restaurants, and professionals that catered to the Japanese. But the income that supported these services to consumers was derived from diversified kinds of activity carried on in many different lines. There was nothing comparable to the well-knit complex of growing, wholesaling, and retailing produce that the Japanese had built up on the West Coast. Probably the lack of common interests in income-getting activities was a factor in absence of formal over-all organization.

There was an over-all collective sentiment. Japanese-Americans felt they were a kind of people, and they recognized that members of the larger society thought of them as a category. The public behavior of any Japanese was of concern to all Japanese. They were interested in protecting and improving their status as a category. Not many persons were interested enough, however, to devote much time and effort to an organized program to that end. Those who were very interested composed JACL.

Formal organizations, except for JACL, existed for recreational and religious purposes. They divided the minority along many different lines.

Japanese-American communities in the Middle West and East soon had a fairly settled air about them. Nisei were not changing jobs rapidly; Issei and Nisei were buying property. Adjustment was still going on and there was much adjusting left to do. There remained some vital unanswered questions. One of the biggest was what will happen when and if depression comes. Would they meet discrimination and find themselves in a more vulnerable position than when they had a strong minority social-economic organization? There was much looking toward the West Coast. Issei talked about it more, but many Nisei thought they might go back someday. Individuals and families were leaving all the time, and others, more commonly, were disposed to wait and see how those who were there got along. If the reports were favorable, maybe then they would return. But perhaps by then many of the relocated Californians and Northwesterners would have become Middle Westerners and Easterners—no more likely to migrate to the Pacific Coast than their nonevacuated neighbors.

THE JOURNEY BACK

"When the West Coast is open to us again" was a frequently repeated condition to resettlement. The people who said it composed the core of the center communities. What they had in mind primarily was the possibility of going back to their old localities and reconstituting their former communities. When the exclusion order was rescinded and the closing of the centers was announced, they were deeply disturbed. At first it seemed that West Coast hostility might continue to keep them out. After the hostility began to subside, another problem became uppermost. They often spoke of it in terms of survival. They just couldn't live. But most persons were not really afraid of failing to survive. They figured they could be domestics, work on the railroad, be farm hands, or resort to casual labor. They could manage to eat all right. What troubled them most was how they could re-establish the broken economic systems on which their old communities rested. The systems and the communities would not have to be exactly as they used to be—everybody knew that was out of the question. But Issei especially felt that the main features would have to be restored before they could have anywhere near adequate economic security and a satisfying way of life. To a much greater degree than the Nisei who resettled eastward, their sense of belonging, of fitting in somewhere, depended on being able to participate in a Japanese community. Moreover, a good many knew that their standard of living would be definitely lower if they could not operate in a Japanese economic system as well. Produce wholesalers had both bought from and sold to Japanese. They and some other businessmen and professionals saw no substitute for their previous economic roles that would not involve a sharp decline in their economic status or, at best, expose any savings they had to great risk. They had "know-how" within the old framework; outside of it they were less sure of themselves.

How even the main features could be rebuilt appeared to be an insoluble problem. In the centers there was much discussion and many expressions of discouragement. As time passed and the agency reiterated its intention to close the camps, an increasing number of people concluded they would have to relocate, accept what they could get, and work toward the conditions of existence they wanted.

Characteristically, those who left the centers for the West Coast early in 1945 were persons who felt they could get along without other Japanese. They were not like the assimilated Nisei who fled from the centers to the Middle West and East as soon as they were allowed to leave. These 1945 resettlers who were going back home were emotionally tied to the Japanese community, but they could live without it. They had farms or businesses that could function as part of the general West Coast economy. Their sense of responsibility to the group seemed to be weak. They were concerned primarily with themselves and their own futures. Other Japanese would have to take care of themselves. An Issei stated before he left Heart Mountain for his orchard in Hood River, Oregon, that he did not intend to employ Japanese on his place. Their presence might damage his relations with the Caucasian community, already stirred up against the return of evacuees. A similar assertion was made by an older Nisei who was going back, with his Issei parents, to his farm in Santa Clara Valley. The Nisei went on to add that he hoped no returning evacuees would settle on his side of the river. There had been none there before evacuation and he thought his own situation would be easier if none came.

This individualistic thinking which abandoned the idea of the Japanese community and economy, though common at first, was not universal. In March, Hollywood evacuees held meetings in one center. Two successful contract gardeners offered to go back to see if they could get started again themselves and to develop opportunities for others. In the months that followed they called out many of their friends who in turn helped their friends.

During the mass exodus of the summer and fall, collective sentiments were reaffirmed and cooperation became marked. The journey back, as thousands joined the movement, created what amounted to a protracted crisis. People with nowhere else to go jammed temporarily into hostels—churches, former Japanese-language schools, and similar buildings filled with row on row of cots. For a short period in one hostel, 300 men, women, and children were fed out of a single kitchen and depended on two small bathrooms. Housing was tight, the search for it frantic. Jobs were needed, too, and in a hurry since subsistence was no longer furnished by the Government except in cases where eligibility for welfare assistance could be established. WRA did what it could, other federal and local agencies generally cooperated, and interested private groups and organizations lent their aid. But perhaps most of all, the returning evacuees helped each other.

This crisis, like others in the past, served to call attention to the common problems of the Japanese. But unlike evacuation or registration, the concrete and specific problems posed by resettlement were extremely diversified. Different people in different places faced a wide variety of situations. There was a general spirit of mutual sympathy and mutual helpfulness, but active and sustained cooperation tended to be limited to groups living in the same locality who had a particular set of practical and immediate needs. The whole locality group was too disorganized to function very effectively.

What happened was that people who owned houses or were able to get housing shared their space with those who came later while they hunted for a place to live. Japanese did give employment to other Japanese. This was true of the Hood River orchardist and the Nisei farmer in Santa Clara Valley. Of course, they needed labor and labor was scarce. But that was not the whole story. When the pinch came, as people poured back to the West Coast, they were "all Japanese together." Some individuals who were well fixed themselves devoted much time to finding opportunities for resettlers. In March 1946, a prosperous man in Palo Alto said jokingly: "I'm still working for WRA helping relocation. I've been doing it all along since I came back last June. The only difference is that when I was in the center WRA paid me $19 a month for my work. Here I get nothing," Nothing, that is, except the gratitude of his fellow Japanese.

Not all of the assistance resettlers gave each other was motivated by good will and the cooperative spirit. Everyone felt a sense of urgency to get started again, to obtain some income, to build up a reserve. Strategically placed individuals were under strong temptation to seek economic security for themselves by exploiting the often desperate needs of others. Among the resettlers bitter complaints were heard against certain Japanese who made a lucrative business out of "helping" their fellows.

The adjustments imposed by the journey back were too diverse and complicated to be described very well in general terms. Most Hood River Valley Japanese had been allowed to own their farms. Their chief problem was opposition to their return on the part of some of the inhabitants of the Valley. A vigorous campaign to scare them away was launched as soon as the West Coast was opened. Even their friends in Hood River feared for their safety should they come back. The pioneers, three Nisei who returned to widely separated farms in January 1946, recalled their sense of isolation, their feeling of being in hostile territory. A strange sort of homecoming! One Nisei told of the long quiet evenings, too long and too quiet, as he lived alone in the house where he grew up. It helped when a stray dog joined him. He named the dog "Friend." It also helped when the man representing WRA in the Valley called to give him encouragement and assure him that the agency was doing what it could to improve public sentiment. Some of the neighbors he had known all his life treated him all right. But they seemed a little self-conscious, as if they behaved cordially toward a Nisei. After awhile the scare campaign subsided. More neighbors seemed to accept him. He notified the rest of the family to come on out of the center. Other scouts reported and other families arrived. Almost all who were evacuated came back, plus a few more who were there as farm workers. According to one man speaking in February, 1946:

We are getting along. Some of the orchards are not in very good shape. They weren't taken care of right. Everybody is working hard trying to get them fixed up again. As long as prices stay the way they are, we'll be able to make money. We have trouble getting equipment, but so do all the farmers I guess. It isn't the way it used to be though. The people of the Valley don't treat us the same as before evacuation. But it's a lot better than it was a year ago and is getting better all the time.

Incidentally, the dog named "Friend" stayed with the family whose relocation he aided, a tiny factor in the readjustment of the Japanese in Hood River.

In no other place was ownership as general as in Hood River. An older Nisei, a block manager in one of the centers, stated:

In Santa Clara Valley very few owned their farms. Mostly they leased on a cash basis, but some share cropped. A few of the Japanese were pretty big operators. More of them worked on a smaller scale and there were a lot of little places. The important thing to remember is that, big or little, almost everybody had a farm which he operated on his own account. I would say no more than five percent worked for somebody else as farm workers. Maybe not even that many.

Except for those who owned their places, now we are all farm laborers, working for somebody else for wages. A few have been able to buy land or get leases. But the prices are high. And if you sold your equipment at evacuation the way I did, you're stuck. So here I am. The wages I get are good and the people I work for treat me well. But I don't like it. I would sooner be on my own. But what else can I do? I have a family and we have to live.

Another Nisei of about the same age expressed many of the same attitudes and gave some of his views of the future:

I am doing the kind of work I hadn't done for 15 to 20 years before evacuation. I used to hire other men to do it for me. But I'm not proud. I'll do anything that comes along. The only thing is that I want to be paid for it. I want all I can get. The whole family went out into the orchards and fields when we first came back. For five months starting in July, we averaged a thousand dollars a month. Of course, we couldn't keep on doing that well. That was the fruit-picking season. The girls kicked at doing farm work. I guess I spoiled them before evacuation. The relocation camp spoiled them too. They got ideas there about white-collar jobs. A girl can make more picking fruit and there is no question about her being hired even if she does have slant eyes.

Right now there is no chance of getting back into farming on my own. The way I figure is that there won't be a chance until we begin to get a depression. Until then, those who have land will hang on to it or boost the price sky high. As soon as the selling price of fruit and vegetables slips a little, you'll see. The way some people farm these days—just a little fall and they'll start to lose. Then they'll be glad to sell or lease. That's why I want to get as much money as I can now. I want to have a little capital for when the chance comes.

In Santa Clara Valley public sentiment toward the returning evacuees was consistently better than in many areas. There were more Japanese than there were before evacuation. Their predominant economic adjustment was to become farm laborers. The adjustment was accepted by them as a temporary expedient.

In several other rural sections where evacuees used to operate as tenant farmers, only a small percentage returned. Local hostility during the main exodus from the centers or the kind of agriculture carried on limited their opportunities even as farm workers. They had to look elsewhere. Some went to places like Santa Clara Valley; others to cities; still others to the railroads, where they worked chiefly in section crews or extra gangs.

In the cities, the first and biggest problem was housing. Returning evacuees had to have somewhere to live before they could begin to adjust in other ways. Most of them, through diligent search and much mutual aid, found living quarters of some sort in districts where the Japanese were allowed to live. Their distribution was similar to the pre-evacuation pattern, though they were somewhat more scattered. Many who were unable to locate a place solved the difficulty by taking jobs where housing was furnished—jobs as domestics and gardeners who lived in. Sometimes this meant the dispersion of families. A couple lived and worked at one place, their daughter at another, and their son had a room downtown near the shop that employed him. The pay was good and expenses were low. But Thursday family reunions were a poor substitute for having a home where the family could be by itself. Even when there was no family split, there was the matter of isolation. Domestics worked mostly in the "better" sections where Japanese could not have homes. On Thursdays Japanese resturants were crowded with people visiting with their friends and perhaps, eating their first Japanese food since the previous Thursday. Living in as domestics and gardeners was as much a temporary expedient to many urban people as farm labor was to rural people.

Another solution to the housing problem was provided by WRA in cooperation with Federal Public Housing Authority. A number of temporary housing projects were made available to returning evacuees. "Resettlement camps" they might be called. WRA considered them to be an emergency solution; they would afford living quarters until resettlers could find something else. It proved difficult to carry through with this conception. The camps, though definitely makeshift in most cases, were places to stay. Faced with the difficulty of finding anything else, people tended to settle down. Since the projects were generally situated at some distance from the main areas of employment this often meant that they took inferior jobs nearby or were unemployed. That is, the emergency solution as regards housing frequently interfered with adjustment in other fields. By the spring of 1946, practically all of the projects were closed and the remaining ones were fixed up so as to be less makeshift. For the occupants of the camps, this was the final "pushing around" they suffered at the hands of WRA.

The re-emergence of Japanese communities and the economic adjustment in cities can best be seen in Los Angeles. The former Japanese business district was taken over by wartime Negro inmigrants. Little Tokyo became Bronzeville. The central part of it rapidly became Little Tokyo again. Resettlers themselves were astonished by the speed of the transformation. An Issei said in April, 1946:

When I came back in January last year, it was solid Negroes around here. I wondered if this would ever be Japanese town again. Nothing much happened for quite awhile. Even during the summer, there were just a few places opened by Japanese. I figured it would be at least three or four years before we could take over. Then during the late summer and fall, they really started to come back.

Soon there were more Japanese than Negroes, and Japanese businesses all up and down the streets. I was surprised.

He told this in one of the several Japanese restaurants that were then operating. If he desired to do so, he could obtain from other Japanese most of the goods and services he would ever need within three blocks of the intersection of East First and San Pedro Streets. Resettlers also pointed out that the district was far from being what it used to be. But it did contain much that was familiar and gave people a sense of being home. In other areas of the city where less compact settlements of Japanese existed the same process went on. The wartime occupants were displaced and some of the former businesses were established.

But it was not in stores and restaurants that the main business comeback was staged. Japanese who had some capital to invest seemed most interested in small hotels and apartment houses. This was an important economic activity before evacuation. Now the preoccupation with the field was intense. Quite a number of men made their living lining up deals for others. Hotels and apartment houses were acquired not only in and near the old Japanese district but all over the deteriorated area of the city.

Two factors account for this extraordinary interest. It was one way to obtain both housing and income, and no insurmountable legal or customary obstacles were encountered.

The usual method of getting hold of hotels and other business property was to buy up leases. The prices that had to be paid were high. In the case of hotels and apartment houses competitive bidding by Japanese themselves doubled or tripled the prices during the previous year. Resettlers explained that this was another chapter in the losses that evacuation caused them. A number of small hotels were thrown on the market all at once when operators had to leave in 1942. Now resettlers were in the market again trying to buy them back. Men who sold the furnishings and lease of a hotel for $1,000 to $1,500 had to pay about ten times that much to get control of the same business.

Even at such inflated prices, hotel and apartment men made money. They admit it was a risk. Unless Los Angeles maintained its present level of prosperity for two more years, they would lose. But they must take the chance. The faith they shared with other Los Angeleños in the bright future of the city helped buoy their spirits.

Hotel men and other downtown businessmen called attention to the difference in their customers before evacuation and now. Before, the customers of restaurants and stores were chiefly other Japanese —city people or farmers from the outlying districts. This was less true of hotels. They were patronized by Caucasian transients and pensioners, mostly single men, as well as Japanese. In 1946, customers were predominantly Negroes. After some initial hesitation, Japanese businessmen concluded that Negroes were good customers. Some of the resettlers talked of a new economic role for the Japanese. Maybe, they said, providing goods and certain kinds of services to Negroes would be a new field that should be developed.

So far, the really big pre-evacuation business—vegetable marketing—had not been mentioned. For many months after the opening of the West Coast, the interests that controlled vegetable marketing maintained a solid front against returning evacuees. It was the original intention to exclude them entirely. Not only would they be kept out as dealers, but they would not be bought from, sold to, or employed. This extreme position broke down. Resettlers worked in the market. Farmers had no trouble selling their crops and retailers could buy produce. But they did not get far in the field that interested them most—wholesaling, shipping, and working as buyers and salesmen on commission.

Re-entering the produce market, of course, was more than a problem of overcoming the organized opposition to Japanese by those who controlled it. There were few Japanese farmers and few Japanese retailers. The whole complex of relations that used to exist was gone. Even if there were no opposition, this fact would be an effective obstacle. As Japanese succeeded in being admitted to the more lucrative aspects of market operations, they had to do business within a new framework.

The circumstance that the returned evacuees were still largely outside of the produce market had repercussions on many phases of their economic adjustment. It was partly responsible for the concentration on hotels and apartment houses. The interest in providing goods and services for the Negro community reflected a search for substitute business opportunities in another direction. Contract gardening was a profitable occupation before evacuation; now it was even better. The field was not crowded yet, but only the limitations of skill, housing, and equipment kept it from being overcrowded. The situation with reference to the produce market reenforced the housing shortage as a factor in inducing people to accept jobs as domestics. With reference to the Nisei, many who would formerly have been working for and with other Japanese, processing or selling vegetables, sought and found employment here and there in factories, shops, and offices that did not hire Nisei before the war. A few obtained white-collar positions of a kind that were definitely closed to them before evacuation.

There was a Japanese community in Los Angeles again. Only a few of the early resettlers had the experience of living in isolation from other Japanese. But the community was not the same as it used to be. Nisei complained during much of the period of moving back that there were not enough Nisei. Too many had relocated to places outside of the West Coast and were staying there. The complaint lessened, partly because a considerable number of Nisei returned from the East. A more important factor was that the Nisei who were back in Los Angeles all along became acquainted or reacquainted, developed some organization, and found places to go and things to do. They did not feel life was as it should be yet. Too many girls were domestics who lived in. Their hours and scattered location interfered with their contacts with other Nisei. Many boys were so preoccupied with their jobs and with helping their families that they had little time to mix with their friends. And there was something rarely known before evacuation—quite a few Nisei did not like Los Angeles. Some came back at the urging of their families to find that they had to take employment that was inferior to the jobs they had in Chicago or Cleveland. They were pleased to be reunited with their families, but they missed the Nisei world they had been living in.

When Issei had time, they could go to a Japanese restaurant to eat and talk with their friends, also to visit each other at home— providing the home to be visited was not too crowded. Ordinary casual social satisfactions with other Issei were there to be had. There was even an occasional dinner arranged for some special purpose. At least two *utai* groups functioned and there was talk of trying to get up a Japanese drama group. But life was too busy and too confused to do much that required time, money, or organization. In the course of visiting, the kind of organization that should be worked toward was considered. There were differences of opinion. Some held that something comparable to the old Japanese Chamber of Commerce—predominantly or wholly Issei—was needed. Others were afraid of its possible adverse influence on public relations. Such persons advocated staying in the background and letting Nisei do the organizing. The distrust of Nisei leadership and especially of JACL came up. But the question was discussed more calmly than it was in the centers. In spite of the inadequacies of Nisei leadership, maybe it had to be depended on. Maybe JACL should be supported more. Almost everybody agreed on one point, "We should wait and see how things turn out before we do anything." Then someone usually added, in one way or another, "We are too busy and our resources too limited to do anything now, anyway. Now what we have to do is to plan and work and try to rebuild our economic foundation."

More than 50,000 evacuees made the journey back. They relocated from the centers, but they could hardly be said to have resettled. Both their spatial and their occupational distribution had been profoundly altered. They were still largely outside of their two major pre-evacuation economic pursuits—farming on their own account and the marketing of vegetables. It follows that relatively few arrived at what they would be willing to consider a permanent or fairly permanent adjustment. Not many, on the other hand, still floundered around as far from an adjustment as when they left the center. Most people accepted some expedient which provided them a living and often permitted them to save. They viewed the expedient as a temporary base from which they could work toward the economic position and the kind of life they wanted.

The three most common of these expedient adjustments were employment as farm laborers, railroad laborers, and domestics. The direction the farm laborers wanted to move and how they intended to do it is quite clear. They came to the unhappy conclusion that most of them would have to work for someone else as long as profits in agriculture were high. When a depression approached, they would be able to get back into farming on their own account. In the case of the Issei, there was a chance that they might not be able to do this. Laws against leasing land to Japanese aliens were being enforced more vigilantly than before evacuation.

What would happen to the domestics and the railroad workers as they tried to leave their temporary bases was not so plain. Both of these expedients were chiefly the result of a pervasive factor in the situation—the housing shortage. The people in these groups had rather diversified backgrounds and probably equally diversified goals.

The returned evacuees did not proceed very far in rebuilding their economic system. There were businessmen and professionals who made their living dealing with other Japanese. But most income-getting activities on the West Coast, as elsewhere, go on with reference to the larger economy. The hope of recreating something along the line of the former produce marketing complex was not given up and persistent efforts were continued. The immediate economic objective was to accumulate as much as possible in any way that presented itself. People felt that while they were in the camps they missed a good opportunity to improve their fortunes and that now they must get all they could before a postwar depression set in.

Japanese communities in cities and towns all up and down the

Pacific Coast had not taken on much organization. The relations between Issei and Nisei, the kind of formal organizations that should exist, and the sort of orientation that should be maintained toward the rest of society were subjects for discussion. Action, it was generally felt, should wait.

In every way things were in a state of flux. Few people were satisfied with their own situation; nobody satisfied with the condition of the group. Many changes were expected in the next few years. Some persons were much discouraged, others saw possibilities for something better than used to be. Meanwhile, almost everybody planned and worked.

DISCONTINUITIES AND CONTINUITIES

As they sat in the centers and looked at the past, Issei reviewed evacuation in the perspective of their history in America. Their interpretation reflected their own biases in some degree. "After a half-century of discrimination and persecution, this came," they often said. That is, evacuation was just the last and most drastic thing that had been done to them. They found it all very hard to understand. Their labors had helped develop the West. They had tried to be good residents—to obey the laws, to be self-supporting, to take care of their own economic failures, to keep all members of the group in line. Especially after they got American children, it seemed to them that they had gone out of their way to do what they should. They sacrificed to educate their children and trained them so well that there was very little juvenile delinquency among Nisei. Issei organizations always had as a part of their program the promotion of friendship and understanding with the American public.

Still, year after year, some of the newspapers spoke of them as a menace. The land laws made their life difficult. They were considered unworthy to become citizens. Politicians occasionally "shook them down" as a price for not increasing the pressure. Worst of all, they saw the attitudes toward them being extended to their children. For all they could do to shield them, they noticed that many of the Nisei were growing up to feel inferior because their parents were Japanese.

When the war started, Issei soon found themselves viewed as being really dangerous, or at least potentially dangerous. And under the simple formula, "Once a Jap, always a Jap," their children and grandchildren were included with them. This, too, was hard to understand. Said an Issei earnestly: "We aren't dangerous. Really we aren't. I know. As for the Nisei—if it wasn't so tragic, it would be funny. Couldn't the Government find out how we were before they did this to us?" There was a feeling that the Occidental mind was a little inscrutable.

In the centers, the war had been followed with intense interest. Maybe it would make a difference in the life of the Japanese in America. If the United States could not win, if a stalemate and a negotiated peace were the outcome, perhaps Japan as a clearly recognized first-rate power could intercede regarding the land laws and the denial of citizenship. Even ordinary Americans might have more respect for persons of Japanese ancestry. Issei had not wanted the war. The growing possibility that it would come had filled them with dread. But now that it was here, they hoped that it might improve their status and make the future of Issei and Nisei in this country less difficult.

This was not to be. Japan was defeated. Back on the West Coast they had to face the same land laws and the same anti-Japanese prejudice. There were even some new things. Oregon had established a more stringent land law. The mechanisms of evasion that had been developed to permit leasing and ownership were under official scrutiny. California carried on a campaign to escheat land already held. The city of Portland would not issue business licenses to Japanese aliens. And until a new trade treaty with Japan was negotiated, Issei felt that their business operations were vulnerable to attack at any time. Moreover, they took up the struggle with depleted resources and without the economic strength they used to derive from their well-organized system for growing and distributing produce.

Most of the core of the Japanese community accepted this prospect. America and the West Coast was home to them and they would make the best of it. Some Issei and many Nisei, who at first perforce and later by choice, settled away from the West Coast, encountered some new problems and avoided some old ones.

A very few evacuees sought escape into unreality. They could not resume the struggle under the conditions that existed. There were persons—a few hundred, with rare exceptions Issei—who persisted in believing that Japan was not defeated. They resettled and lived on in a dream world, waiting for the truth about how the war ended to be made known. A large proportion of those who requested repatriation from Tule Lake had similar ideas at the time they left. This was the obvious human wreckage that the war and evacuation produced among the evacuees. To be added to the account was a small percentage of resettlers who were oriented in reality but who were so overcome by the difficulties of the struggle to get started again that they floundered about ineffectually or put forth only feeble effort.

Most of the evacuees came through the experience with surprisingly undamaged personalities. Issei especially seemed to be the same kind of persons they used to be. In a sense, they had had some preparation for evacuation. It was expected that something might be done to them, not because they were dangerous but just because such things are likely to be done during a war. Then, the communities they developed in the centers helped them. They were able to maintain a certain degree of self-determination and to fill their time with satisfying activities. Through their social solidarity they gave each other support and strength. Evacuation, life in the centers, and resettlement were shared experiences. This does not mean that there were not some persistent inward hurts and some bitterness. It was their children, and Nisei in general, that affected the Issei most. An Issei woman said:

We worked hard all our lives so that we could leave the Nisei a good foundation for their future. Now it is mostly gone. No matter how hard we work, we can't rebuild it. There just isn't time in the years we have left to live.

An Issei man expressed a more fundamental worry:

We Issei used to talk among ourselves and say that if war ever came with Japan, the Government might do something to us. But we didn't think our children would be touched. My two sons were bitter when they heard they had to go. One of them refused. He said the Government could put him in prison or shoot him. Almost all night I plead with him. The next day I went to see his teacher in college that he liked and respected most and asked the teacher to talk with him. They were together for several hours. After that he said he would go. That was all he said. The look on his face made me afraid. He behaved strangely in the assembly center and in the relocation center. The other boy was not himself either.

I sent both boys out to college as soon as possible. They have been outside for three years now. The older one, the one who refused to be evacuated, is in medical school. They are better, but it seems to me there is still a little warping in them. Maybe they will get over it sometime.

The Nisei were definitely more vulnerable than the Issei, but the effects which persisted were hard to measure. There were instances of marked cynicism regarding civic and social obligations which seemed to date from evacuation. There were also some overaggressive tendencies and some tendencies to withdraw readily from any situation where expressions of prejudice were encountered. For the most part, though, Nisei as well as Issei lived and worked and

approached problems generally like normal people. Of course, the results of evacuation were not all apparent at once. Getting started
again took its toll. Experiences in this phase were not shared as
fully as were the experiences in the camps. The situations faced by
different families and individuals varied a good deal.

Nobody recalled the actual evacuation—the moving out of
homes—with pleasure. Memories of the relocation centers evoked a
considerable range of emotional responses. Many Nisei and a few
Issei spoke of them as places of confinement. A resettler in Arizona
who visited Los Angeles reported that she had seen "many former
inmates of my camp." The majority of Issei, on the other hand,
remembered some of the favorable things and showed signs of nostalgia. In either case, the memories were of an interruption to the
rest of life.

There had been almost no carry-over of the community organization. Liaison men—block managers and councilmen—were just
some more returned evacuees working hard to get on their feet again.
A few who attempted to turn such prestige as they gained in the
centers into leadership on the outside were received with indifference.
All that persisted were some friendships and a vague bond of sentiment among those who were in the same camp.

Resettled Issei manifested a new orientation toward Japan. In
the centers they had tended to think of how Japan might be able to
help them after the war. Now they considered how they might help
Japan—by relief shipments as soon as possible and by trying to promote better understanding between the United States and Japan in
the years to come.

Issei also had a new orientation toward the United States. For a
time in the centers, the value that was Japan, their stake in this
country, and the security and neutrality of the centers were balanced
against each other. Even before the war was over, their stake in
this country—represented by their children, their property, and
their long experience here—had emerged as dominant. This dominance was now so complete in fact that it was a change from the pre-
war situation. Before the war, Issei weighed continued residence
in the United States against eventual return to Japan. Anti-Japanese
campaigns periodically made them wonder if they might be forced to
go back. So the question was kept open.

The experiences of evacuation and the outcome of the war settled
the question once and for all. The great majority of Issei concluded
they were here to stay. From Seattle to Los Angeles, one heard
such statements as:

Things are different now. People have made up their minds. They may think of taking a trip to Japan sometime to visit their relatives and to see how conditions are. But this is where they are going to live. They are more settled on this than they have ever been.

This settling made a difference in the way they approached the problems of readjustment. Before, many preferred to keep such assets as they acquired in easily transferable form. Now they wanted to buy fixed property. Before, it was common for them to plan their economic lives in terms of a number of years. Now their planning was for an indefinite future.

The settling modified views in other directions. Said an Issei:

Maybe we made a mistake before the war trying to make too much money. We should have taken some of the time we spent working to visit our neighbors. I hope that we have learned and that we do this in the future. That is the best kind of public relations.

In the centers the legal action Issei had appeared to want most from the United States was provision for compensation for their losses at evacuation. They kept this hope alive, but another reform became more important: they wanted to be declared eligible for citizenship. This would do more than anything else to help them settle down in this country the way they wished to. At one stroke it would destroy all of the West Coast legal disabilities that rested on ineligibility to citizenship.

They were not very confident that the United States would extend the privilege of naturalization to them. Still they hoped. They wondered if they had not suffered enough to satisfy the most anti-Japanese. Maybe too, they thought, their generally cooperative behavior under the stress of evacuation and the service of almost 26,000 Nisei soldiers would convince Americans that they too are worthy to become Americans.

Issei have followed their children. For a brief period after evacuation, some of them pulled the other way. Now the war is over, they have joined their children in America.

Appendix I

ANNOTATED BIBLIOGRAPHY OF THE COMMUNITY ANALYSIS SECTION

War Relocation Authority
Community Analysis Report No. 15
February 18, 1946

Introduction

The purpose of this bibliography is to provide a guide to Community Analysis reports for the use of government agencies, social scientists, and others who may wish to study and learn from the WRA experience in management of a mass migration. After the liquidation of the WRA, copies of the reports listed will be filed permanently in the two repositories of WRA records: the National Archives in Washington, D.C., and the University of California Library in Berkeley, California. There they will be available for future students of the evacuation and resettlement of Japanese Americans.

Part II of the Bibliography lists those reports of the Section which were mimeographed for distribution to WRA staff generally and, on request, to persons and institutions outside the agency. They constitute a very small, but carefully selected, number of the total reports produced by the Section. The purpose of the mimeographed series was to furnish information on those aspects of the Japanese American background and the reaction to evacuation and relocation most essential for an understanding of the group as a whole. Listed here are seven series of mimeographed reports; the first five of which were prepared in the Washington office.

I. *The Community Analysis Reports,* begun in October, 1942, deals with the cultural behavior and social structure of the Japanese Americans, salient features of relocation center life, and aspects of West Coast attitudes towards Japanese Americans. The final numbers of the series constitute the Bibliography of the Section.

II. *The Community Analysis Relocation Studies,* begun in April, 1944, were designed to report on problems and developments in evacuee adjustment in areas of resettlement. Only one issue, on resettlement in Washington, D.C., was mimeographed.

III. *Trends in Relocation Centers (three issues),* begun in November, 1944, constitute periodic summaries of major developments in evacuee attitudes and human relations in the relocation centers.

IV. *Weekly Summaries (30 issues),* begun in December, 1944, consist of summaries of the trend reports from all the relocation centers, reporting chiefly the reactions to the lifting of exclusion and the final center closure program.

V. *Community Analysis Letters (14 issues),* begin in April, 1943, were newsletters dealing with the activities of the personnel of the Community Analysis Section, sometimes containing brief comment or analysis of current developments in the program.

VI. *The Project Analysis Series (24 issues),* begun in February, 1943, were prepared by various Analysts in the relocation centers. They consist of analyses of particular problems and events in the relocation centers.

VII. *The Community Analysis Notes (15 issues),* begun in January, 1944, were prepared by the Project Analysts, evacuee assistant Analysts, and others. They consist of biographical sketches of evacuees, notes on Japanese American customs, and notes on the pre-evacuation communities as seen through evacuee eyes.

I. COMMUNITY ANALYSIS REPORTS

(Nos. 1, 2, 4, 5, 7, 8, and 12 bore covering letters written by D. S. Myer.)

1. "Dealing with Japanese Americans," C. A. Rept. 1, by John F. Embree, October, 1942, 8 pp.: Race and culture; the go-between; sharing responsibility; project head's position; modes of employment; anxieties; food; evacuee attitudes; summary. First mimeographed issue had 9 pp.

2. "Causes of Unrest at Relocation Centers," C. A. Rept. 2, by John F. Embree, February, 1943, 6 pp.: Factors inherent in the situation; factors related to project administration; signs of trouble. First mimeographed issue had 7 pp.

3. "Japanese Groups and Associations in the United States," C. A. Rept. 3, John F. Embree, March, 1943, 7 pp.: Discussion of the nature and function of social, economic, religious, and military-nationalistic Japanese groups and associations in the United States.

4. "Notes on Japanese Holidays," C. A. Rept. 4, by John F. Embree, April 2, 1943, 5 pp.: Chronological listing and description of the chief Japanese holidays.

5. "Evacuee Resistances to Relocation," C. A. Rept. 5, by John F. Embree, June, 1943, 10 pp.: Three reasons for the relocation program; ideal program; recent leave procedure; causes for resistance to relocation; feelings of insecurity; social reorganization; importance of Issei influence; reasons for not relocating; note on administration attitudes.

6. "Nisei Assimilation," C. A. Rept. 6, by Frank L. Sweetser, July 21, 1943, 7 pp.: Are the Nisei assimilated; evidences of assimilation; material culture and manners, language, religion, and ideals and ambitions. First mimeographed issue had 8 pp.

7. "An Analysis of the Segregation Program," C. A. Rept. 7, by Edward H. Spicer, Oct. 7, 1943, 8 pp.: Analysis of segregation procedure; staff and evacuee attitudes.

8. "Japanese Americans Educated in Japan," C. A. Rept. 8, by Edward H. Spicer, Jan. 28, 1944, 14 pp.: Definitions of Kibei; reasons for studying in Japan; reasons for returning to America; pre-evacuation social adjustment; relocation center adjustment; the Kibei at registration; the Kibei and administration.

9. "Buddhism in the United States," C. A. Rept. 9, by Anne O. Freed and Katharine Luomala, May 15, 1944, 10 pp.: Buddhism and Shintoism in Japan; Buddhism in the United States before evacuation; sectarianism and nonsectarianism after evacuation; Buddhism and Christianity in the United States.

10. "Labor Relations in Relocation Centers," C. A. Rept. 10, by Rachel R. Sady, Oct. 28, 1944, 28 pp.: Dynamic factors in labor relations; pattern of labor crises manpower shortage; recommendations.

11. "Exploratory Survey of California Attitudes Toward the Return of the Japanese," C. A. Rept. 11, by Katharine Luomala, Apr. 4, 1945, 9 pp.: Purpose of the study; California localities studied; selection of respondents.

12. "Effect of the Housing Shortage on Central Valley, California, Attitudes Toward the Return of the Evacuees," C. A. Rept. 12, by Katharine Luomala, May 14, 1945, 43 pp.: Housing the first major concern after rescission; reasons for the housing shortage; spotlight on Little Tokyo; results of urban evictions thus far; efforts at solving the problem of evacuee housing.

13. "Prejudice in Hood River Valley—A Case Study in Race Relations," C. A. Rept. 13, by Rachel R. Sady, June 6, 1945, 17 pp.: Campaign against the Japanese in the 1920's; the Japanese community before evacuation; the recent campaign against the evacuees.

14. "Annotated Bibliography of the Community Analysis Section. Part I: Community Analysis Trend Reports from the Relocation Centers," C. A. Rept. 14, by Joan Ishiyama, Katharine Luomala, Rachel R. Sady, Edward H. Spicer, Nov. 19, 1945, 36 pp.:Weekly trend reports, in typed manuscript form, submitted to the Washington office by the Community Analyst in each of the following centers: Central Utah, Colorado River, Gila River, Granada, Heart Mountain, Minidoka, Rohwer, and Tule Lake. Introduction on the nature and purpose of the trend reports. Tule Lake trend reports which have been submitted since Report No. 14 was prepared will be listed and annotated in the later part of the bibliography which lists the regular Community Analysis reports from that center.

15. "Annotated Bibliography of the Community Analysis Section. Part II. Community Analysis Mimeographed Series," C. A. Rept. 15, prepared by same people as No. 14, Feb. 28, 1946.

16. "Annotated Bibliography of the Community Analysis Section. Part III. Community Analysis Reports from Jerome, Rohwer, Central Utah, Heart Mountain, and Gila River Relocation Centers," C. A. Rept. 16, prepared by the same people as No. 14.

17. "Annotated Bibliography of the Community Analysis Section. Part IV. Community Analysis Reports from Granada, Minidoka, and Manzanar Relocation Centers," C. A. Rept. 17, prepared by the same people as No. 14.

18. "Annotated Bibliography of the Community Analysis Section. Part V. Community Analysis Reports from Colorado River and Tule Lake Centers," C. A. Rept. 18, prepared by same people as No. 14.

19. "Annotated Bibliography of the Community Analysis Section. Part VI. Community Analysis Reports from the Washington Section," C. A. Rept. 19, prepared by same people as No. 14, and will include miscellaneous reports from former center Analysts received too late for inclusion in earlier parts of the bibliography.

II. COMMUNITY ANALYSIS RELOCATION STUDIES

1. "Relocation to Washington," by Anne O. Freed, C. A. Relocation Studies No. 1, April, 1944, 32 pp.: Evacuees in Washington, D. C., area; reasons for relocating; housing and employment adjustment; positions held by resettlers in Washington, Dec., 1943; social adjustment of the Nisei; individual problems and adjustment; attitudes toward Caucasians, WRA, and toward discrimination and prejudice; the organization, philosophy, and techniques of the Washington Relocation Office; comparison of Washington with Denver; negative and positive factors in adjustment; relocation needs in the Washington area. Report derived from original manuscript in files of articles prepared by the Washington Community Analysis Section.

III. TRENDS IN THE RELOCATION CENTERS

(By Edward H. Spicer)

1. "Trends in the Relocation Centers: I, Nov. 15, 1944," 4 pp.: Relocation slump; manpower shortage; juvenile delinquents; apathy in center life.

2. "Trends in Relocation Centers: II, Mar. 1, 1945," 6 pp.: Reactions to center closing; levels of belief; spread of acceptance. Attached is covering letter from Washington Chief of Community Management Division to Project Directors, dated Mar. 15, 1945.

3. "Trends in the Relocation Centers: III, Sept. 26, 1945," 7 pp.: The idea of the residue; relocation west; disintegration of the centers.

IV. WEEKLY SUMMARIES

1. "Reactions in the Relocation Centers Following Announcement of West Coast Opening and Ultimate Center Closing, Dec. 17–23, 1944," by Margaret L. Lantis, W. S. No. 1, 6 pp.: Acceptance of center closing; reaction against center closing; objections to return to West Coast; relocation plans and center organization; center differences; the future.

2. "Reactions to Lifting of Exclusion and Closing of Centers, Dec. 24–30, 1944," by Edward H. Spicer, W. S. No. 2, 6 pp.: Community organization; relocation; evacuee thinking; the Army Team; the information program; Tule Lake; the future.

3. "Reactions to Lifting of Exclusion and Closing of Centers, Jan. 1–7, 1945," by Edward H. Spicer, W. S. No. 3, 6 pp.: Relocation; community organization; evacuee thinking; outside contacts; rumor; the future.

4. "Reactions to Lifting of Exclusion and Closing of Centers, Jan. 8–14, 1945," by Edward H. Spicer, W. S. No. 4, 6 pp.: Relocation community organization; evacuee thinking; results of scouting; other outside contacts; rumor; the future.

(Nos. 5–30 by Rachel Reese Sady)

5. "Reactions to Lifting of Exclusion and Closing of Centers, Jan. 15–21, 1945," W. S. No. 5, 5 pp.: Plans for relocation; the conditional relocation position; the opposition; reaction to exclusion notices.

6. "Reactions to Lifting of Exclusion and Closing of Centers, Jan. 22–28, 1945," W. S. No. 6, 4 pp.: The All-Center Conference; other community organization; interest in relocation; rumor; outside contacts.

7. "Reactions to Lifting of Exclusion and Closing of Centers, Jan.

29–Feb. 3, 1945," W. S. No. 7, 3 pp.: The All-Center Conference Mr. Myer goes to Rohwer; pressure on property owners.

8. "Reactions to Lifting of Exclusion and Closing of Centers, Feb. 4–10," W. S. No. 8, 2 pp.: Interest in relocation; eve of Conference; Spanish Consul visits Poston Center.

9. "Reactions to Lifting of Exclusion and Closing of Centers, Feb. 11–17, 1945," W. S. No. 9, 4 pp.: Thinking about relocation; news from "outside"; the importance of being housed; closing the mess halls.

10. "Reactions to Lifting of Exclusion and Closing of Centers, Feb. 18–24, 1945," W. S. No. 10, 2 pp.: Belief in center closure; relocation problems; about the Conference.

11. "Reactions to Lifting of Exclusion and Closing of Centers, Feb. 25–Mar. 3, 1945," W. S. No. 11, 4 pp.: Actual relocation; public opinion and private planning; Nisei conference; scouts to San Mateo report back.

12. "Reactions to Lifting of Exclusion and Closing of Centers, Mar. 4–10, 1945," W. S. No. 12, 4 pp.: Worrying and thinking and planning; community solidarity weakens; locality group meetings; information.

13. "Reactions to Lifting of Exclusion and Closing of Centers, Mar. 11–17, 1945," W. S. No. 13, Mar. 29, 1945, 4 pp.: Interest in relocation; opposition to relocation; when the schools close; information; resettlement assistance; a point of view.

14. "Reactions to Lifting of Exclusion and Closing of Centers, Mar. 18–24, 1945," W. S. No. 14, Apr. 5, 1945, 4 pp.: Public opinion; kinds of locality group action; information; a new problem; the Wilson Plantation offer.

15. "Reactions to Lifting of Exclusion and Closing of Centers, Mar. 25–31, 1945," W. S. No. 15, Apr. 11, 1945, 3 pp.: Thinking about relocation; evacuee reporting; the Nisei protest; removal of opposition group leader.

16. "Reactions to Lifting of Exclusion and Closing of Centers, Apr. 1–7, 1945," W. S. No. 16, Apr. 19, 1945, 3 pp.: Evacuee organization; Rohwer relocation estimates; voice of the Nisei; box-making.

17. "Reactions to Lifting of Exclusion and Closing of Centers, Apr. 8–14, 1945," W. S. No. 17, Apr. 26, 1945, 4 pp.: Attitudes toward West Coast; influence of the opposition; forced relocation; community organization; two plans for every family.

18. "Reactions to Lifting of Exclusion and Closing of Centers, Apr. 15–21, 1945," W. S. No. 18, 3 pp.: The general picture; information; family conflicts; visitors; Councilman opinion.

19. "Reactions to Lifting of Exclusion and Closing of Centers, Apr. 22–28, 1945," W. S. No. 19, May 10, 1945, 4 pp.: Relocation opinion; community organization; the Buddhist Church and relocation; problems of parolees; White River Valley.

20. "Reactions to Lifting of Exclusion and Closing of Centers, Apr. 29–May 5, 1945," W. S. No. 20, May 19, 1945, 5 pp.: Evacuees look at the West Coast; Doi case; signs of liquidation.

21. "Reactions to the Lifting of Exclusion and Closing of Centers, May 6–12, 1945," W. S. No. 21, May 23, 1945, 3 pp.: Relocation; closings within closings; the merger.

22. Reactions to Lifting of Exclusion and Closing of Centers, May 13–19, 1945," W. S. No. 22, May 30, 1945, 4 pp.: Summer relocation estimates; informing and advising; West Coast incidents; loss of interest in center affairs; shrinking blocks.

23. "Reactions to Lifting of Exclusion and Closing of Centers, May 20–26, 1945," W. S. No. 23, June 6, 1945, 3 pp.: Attitudes toward relocation; block composition and block relocation; mess hall and block closings.

24. "Reactions to Lifting of Exclusion and Closing of Centers, May 27–June 2, 1945," W. S. No. 24, June 14, 1945, 3 pp.: Relocation geography; the "left-behind" feeling; mess hall and block closings; community interest; relocation at Tule Lake.

25. "Reactions to Lifting of Exclusion and Closing of Centers, June 3–9, 1945," W. S. No. 25, June 21, 1945, 2 pp.: The "bitter-enders"; evacuation in reverse.

26. "Reactions to Lifting of Exclusion and Closing of Centers, June 10–16, 1945," W. S. No. 26, June 27, 1945, 3 pp.: Evacuee acceptance of center closing; the problems; cooperative plans.

27. "Reactions to Lifting of Exclusion and Closing of Centers, June 17–23, 1945," W. S. No. 27, July 6, 1945, 3 pp.: Early closure dates; old problems and old recommendations.

28. "Reactions to Lifting of Exclusion and Closing of Centers, June 24–30, 1945," W. S. No. 28, July 17, 1945, 3 pp.: What will WRA do; attitudes toward relocation; schools.

29. "Reactions to Lifting of Exclusion and Closing of Centers, July 1–7, 1945," W. S. No. 29, July 21, 1945, 1 p.: Slump in relocation.

30. "Reactions to Lifting of Exclusion and Closing of Centers, July 8–14, 1945," W. S. No. 30, July 27, 1945, 3 pp.: Announcement of closing dates and reception of news.

V. COMMUNITY ANALYST LETTERS

1. "Community Analyst Letter No. 1," by John F. Embree, Apr. 17, 1943, 1 p., with attachments of 2-page mimeographed Report Roundtable No. 4, Mar. 17, 1943, by Chief, Reports Division, on reassignment of functions from Documents to Community Analysis Section, and Administrative Instruction No. 56, Supp. 1, "Transfer of Functions from Reports Division to Community Services Division," Mar. 26, 1943, 1 p.

2. "Second Community Analyst Letter," by John F. Embree, May 8, 1943, 1 p.

3. "Third Community Analyst Letter," by John F. Embree, June 5, 1943, 3 pp.

4. "Community Analyst Letter No. 4," by John F. Embree, July 3, 1943, 4 pp.

5. "Community Analyst Letter No. 5," by John F. Embree, Aug. 16, 1943, 3 pp.

6. "Community Analyst Letter No. 6," by Edward H. Spicer, Sept. 28, 1943, 5 pp.

7. "Community Analyst Letter No. 7," by Edward H. Spicer, Jan. 14, 1944, 4 pp.

8. "Community Analyst Letter No. 8, by Edward H. Spicer, Feb. 23, 1944, 4 pp.

9. "Community Analyst Letter No. 9," by Anne O. Freed, Mar. 20, 1944, 2 pp.

10. "Community Analyst Letter No. 10," by Edward H. Spicer, Apr. 18, 1944, 4 pp.

11. "Community Analyst Letter No. 11," by Edward H. Spicer, May 18, 1944, 2 pp.

12. "Community Analyst Letter No. 12," by Katharine Luomala, Nov. 3, 1944, 3 pp.

13. "Community Analyst Letter No. 13," by Rachel R. Sady, Feb. 13, 1945, 2 pp.

14. "Community Analyst Letter No. 14," by Edward H. Spicer, May 15, 1945, 5 pp.

VI. PROJECT ANALYSIS SERIES

1. "Registration at Central Utah: 14–17, February, 1943," by John F. Embree, February, 1943, 12 pp.: Staff and residents; meeting on registration and civil rights; some young people of Topaz; Issei worries; Monday night meeting; meeting with Young Democrats; family meeting; final Wednesday meeting; redemption of a Kibei; application vs. questionnaire; the Great White Father; recommendations on communication, staff education, and avoidance of discriminatory documents. Apprendices: resolution to Secretary of War Stimson, dated Feb. 15, 1943; statement of other residents of Topaz, dated Feb. 16, 1943; summary of the Wednesday meeting; statement of facts in explanation of the attitudes and actions of the residents, especially in regards to registration. Report was derived from original typed manuscript in the files of articles prepared by the Washington staff of the Community Analysis Section. First mimeographed issue had 14 pp.

2. "Army Registration at Granada," by Frank L. Sweetser, Mar. 19, 1943, 11 pp.: First phase, registration, Feb. 6–13; second phase, interim, Feb. 13–18; third phase, reconsideration, Feb. 19–Mar. 6; current situation. First mimeographed issue under title, "Army Registration at One Relocation Center," Mar. 6, 1943, 11 pp., with covering letter to Project Directors from D. S. Myer, dated Mar. 19, 1943.

3. "Registration at Manzanar," by Morris E. Opler, Apr. 3, 1943, 7 pp.: Analysis and interpretation of loyalty questions and some factors motivating negative responses. First mimeographed issue under title, "Second Special Report on Registration," Apr. 3, 1943, 11 pp. Article derived from original manuscript, Manzanar Rept. No. 3.

4. "The Fence at Minidoka," by John de Young, April, 1943, 6 pp.: Description and history of fence and watchtowers, and attitudes of residents toward them; previous history of relations between project staff and residents and military police. Article derived from original

manuscript, Minidoka Rept. No. 9, under title, "The Fence and the Watchtowers," April 28, 1943.

5. "Preliminary Evaluation of the Resettlement Program at Jerome Relocation Center," by Edgar C. McVoy, May, 1943, 4 pp.: Nine reasons for the slow peace of the leave program with an evaluation of each. Article derived from original manuscript, Jerome Rept. No. 8, May 3, 1943. First mimeographed issue, May, 1943, 5 pp.

6. "Report on an Unorganized Relocation Center," by Edward H. Spicer, June, 1943, 15 pp.: Elements of social disorganization; Minidoka social structure; present trends and attitudes; the new Charter. Article derived from original manuscript, Minidoka Rept. No. 113.

7. "Notes on Some Religious Cults at Topaz," by Weston LaBarre, June 15, 1943, 2 pp.: Main religious groups; splinter cults; administrative relevance. Article derived from original manuscript, Central Utah Rept. No. 7. First mimeographed issue, June 15, 1943, 3 pp.

8. "Factors Influencing Low Enrollment in Certain Adult Education Courses," by Marvin K. Opler, July, 1943, 9 pp. Article derived from original manuscript, Tule Lake Rept. No. 21, June 16, 1943. First mimeographed issued had 11 pp.

9. "Preliminary Survey of Resistances to Resettlement at the Tule Lake Relocation Center," by Marvin K. Opler, June 23, 1943, 15 pp.: Older Issei resistances bearing upon resettlement; general resistances to resettlement related to the relocation and project situation. Article derived from original manuscript, Tule Lake Rept. No. 3.

10. "English Words in Current Use at Minidoka Center That Have Been Given a 'Japanized-English' Pronunciation or Have Been Translated Into a Japanese Equivalent," by John de Young, July, 1943, 7 pp. Article derived from original manuscript, Minidoka Report No. 94, June 15, 1943. First mimeographed issue had 8 pp.

11. "Notes on Evacuee Family Patterns," by G. Gordon Brown, Nov. 24, 1943, 3 pp.: Husband-wife relationships; parent-child relationships; family solidarity and kinship responsibility. Article derived from original manuscript, Gila River Rept. No. 21, under title, "Community Analysis Report," Nov. 24, 1943.

12. "Studies of Segregants at Manzanar," by Morris E. Opler, Feb. 3, 1944, 13pp.: General picture; age distribution of male and female segregants; age distribution and foreign residence of Kibei males and females; age distribution and residence in Japan of segregant women

married to those "previously interviewed"; age distribution and foreign residence of female segregants married to aliens; age distribution of U.S. citizens with no foreign residence; male and female dual citizens with no foreign travel; male and female segregants who were in Japan a year or less. Appended is a summary of information concerning segregants at Manzanar. Article derived from original manuscript, Manzanar Rept. No. 69, Oct. 19, 1943.

13. "A Preliminary Survey of the Boilermen's Dispute at Minidoka," by John de Young, Mar. 3, 1944, 12 pp.: Events leading up to the walkout of Jan. 4, 1944; negotiations with the project director; present status of the janitorial situation; activities of the resident committees involved; attitude of the residents; role of threats and force in the situation; 'inu' warnings; analysis of administration role in the situation. Article derived from original manuscript, Minidoka Rept. No. 285, Jan. 17, 1944.

14. "The Tule Lake Incident," by Edward H. Spicer, Mar. 27, 1944, 18 pp.: The crisis of Nov. 1–4, 1943; background of the demonstration; evacuee vs. administration; causes of the incident. Report derived from original typed manuscript in the files of articles prepared by the Washington staff of the Community Analysis Section.

15. "The Reaction of Heart Mountain to the Opening of Selective Service to Nisei," by Asael T. Hansen, Apr. 1, 1944, 13 pp.: Early reactions; growth of opposition; community feeling; the Council takes the moderate position; Fair Play Committee gathers strength. Article derived from original manuscript, Heart Mountain Rept. No. 77. First mimeographed issue had 14 pp.

16. "The Significant Factors in Requests for Repatriation and Expatriation," by Morris E. Opler, Apr. 19, 1944, 8 pp.: Rumors of the closing of Manzanar; length of the war; the Kibei myth; delay in leave clearance; the Tule Lake magnet; effects of center life; parent-child relationship; the delicate balance that exists; the draft. Article derived from original manuscript, Manzanar Rept. No. 224, Mar. 30, 1944.

17. "Relocation at Rohwer Center, Part I: The Relocated Population," by Charles Wisdom and Katharine Luomala, July 24, 1944, 19 pp.: Description of the population; description of those who relocated; months preferred for relocation; states to which evacuees relocated; returns from indefinite leave. Entirely rewritten by Katharine Luomala from original manuscript, Rohwer Rept. No. 11, under title, "Statistical Report on Relocation at Rohwer Relocation Center," by Charles Wisdom, May 12, 1944.

18. "Relocation at Rohwer Center, Part II: Issei Relocation Problems," by Charles Wisdom and Katharine Luomala, Sept. 2, 1944, 30 pp.: The relocated Issei; Issei relocation problems; Issei suggestions for solving their relocation problems; temporary and permanent adjustment to center life. Entirely rewritten by Katharine Luomala from original manuscript, Rohwer Rept. No. 12, under title, "Issei Relocation Problems at Rohwer Relocation Center," by Charles Wisdom, June, 1944.

19. "Community Government in the Relocation Centers, Part I: One Year of Community Government at the Gila River Relocation Center," by G. Gordon Brown, Nov. 6, 1944, 20 pp.: The Constitution; the first term; the second term; the present Councils. Summary by Edward H. Spicer. Article derived from original manuscript, Gila River Report No. 51a, July 14, 1944.

20. "Relocation at Rohwer Center, Part III: Background for the Resettlement of Rohwer Farmers," by Margaret L. Lantis, Feb. 7, 1945, 27 pp.: California origin of Rohwer rural population; general characteristics of Japanese farming in California; specific characteristics of Japanese farming in Los Angeles County and San Joaquin County; recent trends and changes in the Japanese agricultural situation.

21. "Relocation at Rohwer Center, Part IV: Prospects for the Resettlement of Rohwer Farmers," by Margaret L. Lantis, Feb. 22, 1945, 42 pp.: Review of pre-evacuation experience; evacuation: leaving the farm; assembly center experience; new community: Rohwer Center; resettlement of Rohwer farmers; trends in rural resettlement from Rohwer.

22. "A Typical Block at Tule Lake Center," by an unnamed evacuee assistant Analyst, Apr. 17, 1945, 8 pp.: Segregation and old Tule Lake; block government; block statistics; block socials; block religion; block sports; block mess-hall organization; three groups of block opinion. Article derived from original manuscript, Tule Lake Rept. No. 143, under title, "An Average Block in Tule Lake," Mar. 6, 1945.

23. "Final Report on the Gila River Relocation Center as of May 20, 1945," by G. Gordon Brown, Sept. 24, 1945, 81 pp.: I. The Aims of This Report. II. Community Analysis—historical sketch; staff; method; techniques; practical procedures; Community Analysis and administration. III. The Social Organization of a Relocation Center —brief social history; the people; the administration; basic aspects of center organization; the organization; the organization of its people;

communication; the regulation of conflict; clubs and societies; associations; employment and labor problems; cooperation and conflicts; relocation; some comments on administration. IV. Appendix—population by month from July 23, 1942 to July 23, 1945; admissions to Gila River Center. Original manuscript is Gila River Report No. 67.

24. "Stresses and Strains of Center Life, Project Analysis Series, No. 24," by J. Ralph McFarling, Community Analyst at Granada Relocation Center, Feb. 20, 1946, 13 pp.: Personal narrative report on role of the Analyst; segregation; relocation; employment; problems connected with authority from the top; center population characteristics, age, sex, and citizenship distribution; community government.

VII. COMMUNITY ANALYSIS NOTES

1. "From a Nisei Who Said 'No'," by Morris E. Opler, Jan. 15, 1944, 9 pp.: Life experience and viewpoints which lie behind a young Nisei's negative answer to Question 28 of the Army registration form. Article derived from original manuscript, Manzanar Report No. 53, Aug. 31, 1943, First mimeographed issue had 8 pp.

2. "Engagement and Marriage Customs in a Relocation Center," by John de Young, Feb. 29, 1944, 3 pp.: Before evacuation and within the relocation centers. Article derived from original manuscript, Minidoka Rept. No. 188, Sept. 6, 1943, prepared by the Community Analysis research staff.

3. "Traditional Japanese Therapeutics Practiced at Minidoka," by Dick Kanaya and John de Young, Apr. 7, 1944, 2 pp.: Hari, mogusa, and anma treatments. Article derived from original manuscript, Minidoka Rept. No. 169, under title, "Report on Therapeutics Practised by Other Than Licensed M.D.'s in Minidoka Center."

4. "Social and Political Organization of the Block at Manzanar," Mar. 17, 1944, 4 pp.: Taken from a report by a Japanese American who lived in a Japanese village for several years. Article derived from original manuscript, Manzanar Rept. No. 125, Jan. 7, 1944.

5. "A Nisei Requests Expatriation," by Morris E. Opler, Nov. 10, 1944, 4 pp.: Why one young man asked to be expatriated. Article derived from original manuscript, Manzanar Rept. No. 245, under title, "Statement of a Recent Expatriate," Aug. 26, 1944.

6. "Biography of a Nisei Celery Farmer from Venice, California, by Morris E. Opler, Dec. 11, 1944, 15 pp.: Life before evacuation; war

and evacuation; reasons for going to Tule Lake; relocation plans. Article derived from original manuscript, Manzanar Rept. No. 243, under title, "Mr. O., A Farmer from Venice, California," Aug. 24, 1944, and prepared by an evacuee member of the Community Analysis staff.

7. "Nisei Report on Their Adjustment to Tule Lake," by evacuee assistant Analysts, Dec. 20, 1944, 5 pp.: Part I. Report of the Older Nisei; Part II. Interview With a Young Nisei. Article derived from original manuscript, Tule Lake Rept. No. 104, under title, "Nisei Adjustment at Tule Lake," Aug. 30, 1944.

8. "West Coast Localities: Sacramento County and City," by Margaret L. Lantis, Mar. 1, 1945, 7 pp.: Sacramento County—history, agriculture, marketing, social organization in the Florin-Elk Grove area, and evacuation; Sacramento City—population, business, other employment, community relations, social organization, since evacuation, and post-exclusion. Based primarily on retrospective accounts of pre-evacuation communities by evacuee members of the project Community Analysis staffs.

9. "West Coast Localities: Placer County" by Margaret L. Lantis, Mar. 9, 1945, 4 pp.: Japanese population; agriculture; marketing; social organization; Caucasian-Japanese relations; and after evacuation. Based primarily on retrospective accounts of pre-evacuation communities by evacuee members of the project Community Analysis staffs.

10. "Boys' Day," by an evacuee member of the Community Analysis staff, Mar. 13, 1945, 2 pp.: Symbolism, and how it is celebrated in the relocation centers and in the United States. Article derived from original manuscript, Manzanar Rept. No. 249, Nov. 1, 1944.

11. "West Coast Localities: Fresno County," by Margaret L. Lantis, Apr. 2, 1945, 8 pp.: Population; property ownership; occupations; agriculture; Japanese town, schools, and social life in the City of Fresno; other Japanese communities in Fresno County; evacuation; post-exclusion events and attitudes. Taken from locality reports prepared by the Community Analysis Section in the relocation centers.

12. "West Coast Localities: Imperial Valley," by Margaret L. Lantis, Apr. 9, 1945, 11 pp.: Population; agriculture; Japanese life in the Valley; and evacuation. Based on locality studies made at either Colorado River or Tule Lake Centers by members of the Community Analysis Section.

13. "West Coast Localities: San Francisco Bay Area," by Margaret L. Lantis, Apr. 9, 1945, 17 pp.: I. Description and statistical comparison of five urban counties in the City of San Francisco. II. San Francisco City and County—economic base of population; retail dry cleaning and dyeing business; wholesale and retail art goods business; hotel and apartment house business; domestic workers; fishermen; flower market; other occupations. III. San Mateo County. IV. Alameda County. V. East Bay Floral Industry. VI. Problems and Possibilities of Return to the Bay Area. Taken from locality studies prepared at the Central Utah Center by the Community Analysis Section.

14. "West Coast Localities: San Joaquin County," by Margaret L. Lantis, Apr. 16, 1945, 5 pp.: Population, occupations, and industries of Japanese in general; population, businesses, and social life of Japanese in Stockton; agriculture in San Joaquin Delta; French Camp; Linden; Lodi; evacuation. Based primarily on retrospective accounts of pre-evacuation communities by evacuee members of the project Community Analysis staffs.

15. "A Lexicon of Center Terms," by Marvin K. Opler, July 18, 1945, 10 pp.: Terms used by Issei and Kibei; terms used by Issei; expressions used by high school Nisei; Nisei terms for grooming and hair cuts; older Nisei general center terms; terms applied to social and political life of center; words and phrases coined by Nisei; Issei terms peculiar to the center; Hawaiian slang used in the center. Article derived from original manuscript, Tule Lake Rept. No. 161, June 25, 1945.

Appendix II

A BIBLIOGRAPHY OF LIFE IN THE WAR RELOCATION CENTERS

by

Edward H. Spicer and Janet R. Moone

(Exclusive of publications dealing with evacuation and resettlement. For these phases see the extensive listings by, for example, the War Relocation Authority, Reports Division, in the National Archives, the University of California at Berkeley, and Special Collections, at the University of Arizona.)

Adams, Ansel, 1944, "Born Free and Equal: The Story of Loyal Japanese-Americans." (Text and photographs) *U.S. Camera,* New York.

Adams, Lucy W., 1942 "Education in the Relocation Centers." *California Journal of Secondary Education,* 17:477–79.

Ade, Lester K., 1942 "War Relocation Centers: Educational Program for Evacuees of Japanese Ancestry." *Education for Victory* 9:7–9 and 9:17–18. (U.S. Office of Education, Federal Security Agency.)

Alexander, Maurice, 1943 "The Nisei—A Casualty of World War II." *Cornell Law Review Quarterly.* (June) pp. 385–413.

Armstrong, Hubert C., 1943 "Americans—To Be or not To Be." *Progressive Education* 20:12–15.

Arrington, Leonard J., 1962 "The Price of Prejudice: The Japanese-American Relocation Center in Utah During World War II." *25th Faculty Honor Lecture, The Faculty Association.* Utah State University, Logan.

Anonymous

1942 "Are Evacuees To Become Peons?" (An editorial.) *Christian Century* 59:973.

1942 "Business in Evacuation Centers." *Business Week* (July 18) pp. 19–20.

1942 "Child Welfare Problems and Japanese Evacuation." (Notes and comments by the editor.) *Social Service Review* 16:673–76.

1942 "Coast Japs Are Interned in Mountain Camp; Manzanar, California." *Life* (April 6) 12:15–19.

1942 "Life in a California Concentration Camp; Excerpts From Letters." *Nation* (June 6) 154:666.

1942 "Reaction to Internment; Letter From a Japanese Girl." *Nation* (Oct. 24) 155:427–28.

1942 "Relocation Centers in Operation." *International Juridical Association Monthly Bulletin* 11:64–65.

1942 "War Relocation Centers: Organizing the Schools." *Education for Victory* 1:17–18. (U.S. Office of Education, Federal Security Agency.)

1943 "A Visit to Jerome." *Arkansas Churchman* (Jan.) 15 p.

1943 "Along the Scouting Trail." *Boy's Life* (April) 33 p.

1943 "Art Reflects Life in Relocation Camps." (Drawings.) *Asia and the Americas* 43:584–85.

1943 "Conditions at Camp Harmony; Reply to T. Nakashima." *New Republic* (Jan. 18) 108:72.

1943 "Cooperative Community Program at Manzanar." *Education for Victory* 2:30–31. (U.S. Office of Education, Federal Security Agency.)

1943 "Life in the Relocation Camps." (A letter.) *International Quarterly* 7:13.

1943 "Life in a Relocation Center." (Photographs.) *The Commission* 2.

1943 "The Japanese Americans." (An editorial.) *New Republic* (Jan. 11) 108:40.

1943 "Newspapers Inflame Race Feeling." (An editorial.) *Christian Century* 60:1324.

1943 "Problem of Student Nurses of Japanese Ancestry." *American Journal of Nursing* 43:895–96.

1943 "Relocation Camps Destroy Families." (A news item.) *Christian Century* 60:1511.

1943 "Trouble at Tule Lake." *Newsweek* (Nov. 15.) 22:54.

1943 "War Relocation Centers; Educational Pioneering at Rohwer: the people's School." *Education for Victory* 1:27–29. (U.S. Office of Education, Federal Security Agency.)

1943 "War Relocation Projects." *American Journal of Nursing* 43: 1–3.

1943 "What Happened at Manzanar—A Report." *Common Ground* 3:83–86.

1944 *Commonweal* (Japanese-American edition.) 39:509–20.

1944 "Employment of Residents of Relocation Centers." *Monthly Labor Review* 58:993–94.

1944 "Issei, Nisei, Kibei: The U.S. Put 110,000 People of Japanese Blood in 'Protective Custody'." *Fortune* 29:8.

1944 "Manzanar," (by Japanese-American students in Manzanar High School) *Scholastic* 44:23.

1944 "Preparing Evacuees for Relocation: WRA Educational Program." *Education for Victory* 2:24–32. (U.S. Office of Education, Federal Security Agency.)

1944 "The True Story of a Victory Garden." *Evangelical Missionary World,* July:8–29.

1944 "Tule Lake Segregation Center." *Life* (March 20) 16:25–26.

1945 "Readjustment of Nisei Into American School Systems: Educating 27,000 for Relocation." *Education for Victory* 3:9–10. (U.S. Office of Education, Federal Security Agency.)

1947 "Relocation City, Arizona: Review of *City in the Sun"* by (**Karon Kehoe** [Dodd, Mead]). *Saturday Review of Literature* (March 8). 30:30.

(n.d.) "Americans too: Japanese Americans." Cooperative Council of Missionary Education, Saint Louis, Missouri, Board of National Missions.

Baker, John C., 1943 "The Relocation Center Home." *National Magazine of Home Economics Student Clubs* (Sept.) p. 10.

Ballif, Ariel S., "Reactions to Laborers From Relocation Centers." *Sociology and Social Research* 29:40–45.

Bartlett, Agnes, 1944 "Poston—Relocation Center in Arizona." *Mount Holyoke Alumni Quarterly,* (Nov.) p. 99.

Bass, H. E., and **Carlysle Thompson,** 1944 "Relocation Center." *National Teachers Association Bulletin:* 77.

Beatty, Willard W., 1942 "Democracy at the Crossroads." *American Teacher* 26:8–10.

1943 "What Makes an American." *National Education Association Journal* 32:55–56.

Bloom, Leonard, 1943a "Familial Adjustments of Japanese-Americans to Relocation: First Phase." *American Sociological Review* 8:551–80.

1943b "Familial Problems and Japanese Removal." *Research Studies of the State College of Washington* 11:21–26.

1943c "Prisonization and the WRA Camps." *Proceedings of the Pacific Sociological Society:* 29–34.

1947 "Transitional Adjustments of Japanese American Families to Relocation." *American Sociological Review* 12:201–09.

Bogardus, Emory S., 1943 "Culture Conflicts in Relocation Centers." *Sociology and Social Research* 27:381–90.

1944 "Relocation Centers as Planned Communities." *Sociology and Social Research* 28:218–34.

Bondy, Curt, 1943 "Problems of Internment Camps." *Journal of Abnormal and Social Psychology* 38:453–75.

Bosworth, Allan R., 1967 *America's Concentration Camps.* New York, W. W. Norton and Co., Inc.

Breed, Clara E., 1943 "Americans With the Wrong Ancestors." *Horn Book* (July–Aug.) pp. 253–61.

Briesemeister, Esther, 1944 "Japanese Americans—Our Responsibility." *Pi Lambda Theta Journal* 22:88–90.

Britannica Book of the Year (Events of 1943) 1944 "Aliens: Japanese Relocation." Chicago, *Encyclopaedia Britannica,* Inc., pp. 46–47.

Britannica Book of the Year (Events of 1942) 1943 "Aliens: Japanese Relocation." Chicago, *Encyclopaedia Britannica,* Inc., pp. 48–49.

Broom, Leonard, and **J. I. Kitsuse,** 1955 "The Validation of Acculturation: A Condition to Ethnic Assimilation." *American Anthropologist* 57:44–48.

1956 "The Managed Casualty: The Japanese-American Family in World War II." *University of California Publications in Culture and Society* 6:1–226. University of California Press, Berkeley.

Brown, G. Gordon, 1945 "WRA, Gila River Project, Rivers Arizona; Community Analysis Section, May 12 to July 7, 1945— Final Report." *Applied Anthropology* 4:1–49.

Brown, Robert L., 1942 "Manzanar—Relocation Center." *Common Ground* 3:27–32.

The Bureau of Sociological Research (War Relocation Authority) 1943a "The Japanese Family in America." *Annals of the American Academy of Political and Social Science* 229:150–56.

1943b "The Psychiatric Approach in Problems of Community Management: From a Study of a Japanese Relocation Center." *American Journal of Psychiatry* 100:328–33.

Cutkowsky, O. F., 1945 "Shop at the Minidoka Project." *Industrial Arts and Vocational Education* 34:96–97.

Davies, L. E., 1942 Japanese at Work for the United States; Life at Manzanar, One of the Pioneer Colonies." *New York Times Magazine,* (June 21); pp. 14–15.

Davis, Maxine, 1943 "The Truth About Jap Camps." *Liberty Magazine* (Aug. 7) 20:9.

Dawber, Mark A., 1943 *America's Changing Frontiers.* New York, Friendship Press.

Dean, George D., 1942 "Jap Relocation Centers To Have Own Papers." *Editor and Publisher* 75:

DeSilva, Gertrude, 1943 "A Schoolteacher Observes the Nisei." *California Journal of Secondary Education* 18:487–91.

Derrick, E. W., 1947 "Effects of Evacuation on Japanese-American Youth." *School Review* 55:356–62.

Douglas, C. E., 1943 "Who's at Tule Lake?" (Letter to the editor.) *Christian Century* 60:1409.

Douglass, Aubrey A., 1942 "Education of Japanese at War Relocation Centers." *California Schools* 13:261–62.

Dumas, Enoch, and **M. Walther,** 1944 "Landscaping for Beauty and Health." *School Executive* 63:40–41.

Dyo, Matsuko, 1943 "Evacuee in a Diet Kitchen." *National Magazine of Home Economics Student Clubs* (Sept.) p 11.

Eastman, Elizabeth, 1943 "Japanese-American Problems." *Interpreter Releases* 20:235–53.

Eaton, Allen H., 1952 *Beauty Behind Barbed Wire: The Arts of the Japanese in Our War Relocation Camps.* New York, Harper and Brothers.

Embree, John F., 1943a "Resistance to Freedom: An Administrative Problem." *Applied Anthropology* 2:10–14.

1943b "The Relocation of Persons of Japanese Ancestry in the United States: Some Causes and effects." (Communicated by W. N.

Fenton.) *Journal of the Washington Academy of Sciences* 33:238–42.

1944 "Community Analysis—an Example of Anthropology in Government." *American Anthropologist* 46:277–91.

Ernst, Charles F., and **Toshio Mori**, 1943 "Japanese-American Cooperation in the War Effort." *Public Welfare* 1:134–140.

Evans, Michael, 1942 "Concentration camp—USA style." *Coronet* (Oct.) 12:51–43.

Felsecker, Harold J., 1943 "Relocation Camps." *Commonweal* 38:578–80.

Fisher, Galen M., 1943 "Are the Evacuees Being Coddled?" *Christian Century* 60:984–86.

Fisk, Alfred G., 1943 "Letter From a Japanese Camp." *Christian Century* 60:331–32.

Fletcher, James Gould, 1944 "East Goes West in Arkansas." *Asia and the Americas* 44:538–41.

Fonde, C., 1944 "Community Activities in the War Relocation Centers in Arkansas." *Recreation* 38:261–65.

Foote, Caleb, 1942 "Democracy in Detention." *Fellowship* 8:205–07.

1944 *Outcasts: The Story of America's Treatment of Her Japanese-American Minority.* New York, Fellowship of Reconciliation.

1944 "What is Manzanar?" *Kiwanis Magazine* (June) pp. 6–7.

Fox, Rollen C., 1944 "What is Manzanar?" *Kiwanis Magazine* (June) pp. 6–7

Frase, Robert W., 1943 "Relocating a People." *Common Ground* 3:67–72.

Freed, Anne O., 1944 "Our Racial Refugees." *Survey Midmonthly* 80:117–19.

Freeman, Harrop A., 1943 "Genesis, Exodus, Leviticus—Genealogy, Evacuation and Law; Wartime Control of Japanese Americans." *Cornell Law Review Quarterly* (June) pp. 414–58.

Friedman, Lucille, 1943 "Training Japanese-Americans for Tomorrow." *Business Education World* 23:256–57.

Fukuhara, Henry, 1944 *Portfolio of 50 Scenes of the Relocation Centers.* Plantin Press, New York.

Gefvert, R. H., (n.d.) *American Refugees: Outline of a Unit of Study About Japanese-Americans.* American Friends Service Committee, Philadelphia.

Gerken, Edna A., 1943 "Health Education in a War Relocation Project." *American Journal of Public Health* 33:357–61.

Glenn, E., 1944 "Education Behind Barbed Wire—Difficulties in Teaching Democracy to Children of Japanese Evacuees." *Survey Midmonthly* 80:347–49.

Gottfried, Leanore V., 1944 "Medical Social Work in the War Relocation Program." *Family* (Social Casework edition) 25:108–13.

Hannaford, H. D., 1943 "Situation at Tule Lake." (A letter to the editor.) *Christian Century* 60:1476.

Hansen, H., 1945 "Governing a Troubled Community." *Survey Graphic* 34:330.

Harrison, Earl G., 1944 "Civilian Internment American Way." *Survey Graphic* 33:229.

Hascall, Tad, 1943 "I Teach Music to These Japanese." *School Musician* 14:6.

Hashimoto, Dick, and **F. Oshima,** 1944 "School Life in a Relocation Center." *Student Life* (Dec.) p 23.

Havighurst, R. J., 1943 "Educating Japanese-Americans." *School Review* 51:73.

Hoffman, B. P., 1942 "Our Japanese Brethren." *Advent Review and Sabbath Herald* (Oct. 22) p. 119:

Hoffman, William E., 1943 "Fire Protection in Relocation Centers." *National Fire Protection Association Quarterly* (Oct.) pp. 93–99.

Hoke, John C., 1943 "The Intramural Softball Program at Amache." *Athletic Journal* 23:24–25.

Hosokawa, Robert, 1943 "An American With a Japanese Face." *Christian Science Monitor Magazine Section* (May 22) pp. 3–13.

Hudson, Ruth E., 1943a "Health for Japanese Evacuees." *Public Health Nursing* 35:615–20.

1943b "Public Health in a Japanese Relocation Center." *Public Health Nursing* 35:

Hunter, Allan A., 1942a "Life Hard in Evacuee Camps." *Christian Century* 59:894.

1942b "Trouble Flares Among Internees." *Christian Century* 59:1600.

Ichiba, Sam, and **K. Toyfuku,** 1943 "Thoughts Become Visible." *Window of Y.W.C.A.* (Jan.) pp. 1–2.

(An Intelligence Officer) 1942 "The Japanese in America: The Problem and the Solution." *Harper's Magazine* 185:489–97.

Itami, David A., 1942 "Letter to the Editor." *Time* (May 4) 39:6–7.

Katayama, Taro, 1943 "Beyond the Gate." *Trek* (Feb.) p. 2 (Available University of California Library.) Berkeley.

Kawahara, Hattie, 1944 "I Am an American." *Mademoiselle* (Aug.) 19:176.

Kehoe, Karon, 1946 *City in the Sun.* Dodd, Mead, and Co., New York.

Kehoe, Monica, 1944a "Education for Resettlement." *Common Ground* 4:99–101.

1944b "Japanese Become Americans: Adult Education at Gila River Relocation Project, Rivers, Arizona." *Adult Education Journal* 3:55–59.

1944c "Relocation School at Rivers." *Arizona Teacher and Parent* 33:8–9.

Kimble, G. Eleanor, 1946 "The Disloyal at Tule Lake." *Common Ground* 6:74–81.

Kinghorn, Glenn I., 1942 "Inside a Jap Relocation Center." *The Ace* 2:2.

Kleinkopf, Arthur M., 1943 "Teacher Training at Hunt." *Idaho Journal of Education* 24:

Larison, John, 1943 "'Jap Crow' Experiment." *Nation* 156:517–19.

Leahy, Margaret, 1945 "Public Assistance for Restricted Persons during the Second World War." *Social Service Review* 19: 24–47.

Leighton, Alexander H., *et al* 1943 Assessing Public Opinion in a Dislocated Community. *Public Opinion Quarterly* 7:652–67.

Leighton, Alexander H., 1945 *The Governing of Men.* Princeton University Press, Princeton, N.J.

Lewis, Grace, and **R. Dierlam,** 1943 "School for Japanese Evacuees." *Clearing House* 17:280.

Light, Jerome T., 1943 "Relocation centers—Hunt, Idaho." *Library Journal* 68:281–82.

Luomala, Katharine, 1947 "Community Analysis Outside the Centers—a War Relocation Experience." *Applied Anthropology* 6: 25–31.

1948 "Research and Records of the War Relocation Authority." *Applied Anthropology* 7:23–32.

Lyle, Betty, 1943 "At a Japanese Relocation Center." *Women's Press* 37:57.

Manning, E. M., 1944 "Libraries in a Relocation Center: Colorado River Relocation Project at Poston, Arizona." *Wilson Library Bulletin* 18:371–75.

1945 "Hakujin Librarian in a Japanese Relocation Center." *Library Journal* 70:1124–26.

Marsh, Alice B., 1943 "Home Economics for Loyal Evacuees." *Journal of Home Economics* 35:567–68.

Marshall, J., 1942 "Problem People: In a Dozen New Communities in the West, 100,000 Japanese and Japanese-Americans Wait out the War." *Collier's* (Aug. 15) 110:50–52.

Means, Florence C., 1945 *The Moved-outers.* Houghton Mifflin Co., Boston.

Merritt, Ralph P., 1943 "Letter to Aunt Luella." *Common Ground* 3:86–88.

Morimitsu, George, 1943 "These Are Our Parents." *Asia and the Americas* 43:586–89.

Myler, Dillon S., 1943a "Democracy in Relocation." *Common Ground* 3:43–48.

1943b "Relocating a Farm Population." *Extension Service Review* 14:100–01.

1943c "The Truth About Relocation." (A speech given before the Commonwealth Club, San Francisco, Aug. 6, 1943; manuscript filed with WRA.)

1944 "Facts About WRA." (A speech given at Los Angeles Town Hall, Jan. 21, 1944.)

McCormick, Anne O., 1944 "The Outlook From a Japanese Relocation Camp." *Pi Lambda Theta Journal* 22:91–92.

McEvoy, J. P., 1943 "Our 110,000 New Boarders." *Readers Digest* (March) 42:65–68.

McWilliams, Carey, 1942 "Japanese Evacuation: Policy and Perspectives." *Common Ground* 2:65–72.

1943 "Our Japanese hostages." In his *Brothers Under the Skin.* Little, Brown and Co., Boston, pp. 147–75.

1944a "The Nisei Speak." *Common Ground* 4:61–74.

1944b *Prejudice. The Japanese-Americans: A Symbol of Racial Intolerance.* Little, Brown and Co., Boston

1944c *What About Our Japanese-Americans?* New York, Public Affairs Committee, Inc.

McVoy, Edgar C., 1943 "Social Processes in the War Relocation Center." *Social Forces* 22:188–90.

Nakadate, M. M., 1944 "Dentists Behind Barbed Wire Fences." *Oral Hygiene* (Feb.) pp.

Nakaji, Chizuri, 1943 "Relocation Centers—Manzanar." *Library Journal* 68:204.

Nakashima, Ted, 1942 "Concentration Camp: U.S. Style." *New Republic* (June 15) 106:822–23.

Nash, Ray, 1942 "Manzanar From the Inside." (A speech given July 31, 1942, and mimeographed by WRA.)

Nickel, George D., 1943 "In the Relocation Centers; Gila, Arizona." *Survey Midmonthly* 79:3–7.

Noguchi, Isamu, 1943 "Trouble Among Japanese Americans." *New Republic* 108:142–43.

Okada, Dave, *et al,* 1943 *Japanese-American Relocation.* Oberlin College Publicity Bureau, Oberlin, Ohio.

Okubo, Miné, 1946 *Citizen 13660.* Columbia University Press, New York.

Opler, Marvin K., 1945 "A Sumo Tournament at Tule Lake Center." *American Anthropologist* 47:134–39.

1948 Review of *The Spoilage,* by **Dorothy Swaine Thomas** and **Richard Nishimoto,** in *American Anthropologist,* Vol. 50, No. 2, (April-June):307–10.

1950 "Two Japanese Religious Sects." *Southwestern Journal of Anthropology,* Vol. 6, No. 1:69–78.

1950 "Japanese Folk Beliefs and Practices, Tule Lake, California." *Journal of American Folklore* (Oct.-Dec.), pp. 385–97.

1958 "Cultural Dilemma of a Kibei Youth." In *Clinical Studies in Culture Conflict* (G. **Seward,** ed.). The Ronald Press Co., New York, pp. 297–316.

Opler, Morris E., 1944 "Resistance in Resettlement." In *Agriculture in Transition From War to Peace.* Papers and Proceedings of the 17th Annual Conference of the Western Farm Economics Association. Berkeley, California.

Oyama, Mary, 1942 "This Isn't Japan." *Common Ground* 3:32–34.

1943 "My Only Crime Is My Face." *Liberty Magazine* (Aug. 14) 20:9.

Page, K., 1943 "Empty the Relocation Centers." *Christian Century* 60:715–16.

Palmer, Albert W., 1943 "Arizona's City of Exiles; Gila Relocation Project for Japanese." *Christian Century* 60:76–78.

Peterson, Erma, and **Callie O. Morley,** 1951 "History of Topaz." In *Milestones of Millard: A Century of History of Millard County, 1851–1951,* by Daughters of Utah Pioneers of Millard County. Springville, Utah, Art City Publishing Co.

Pickett, Clarence E., and **Homer L. Morris,** 1943 "From Barbed Wire to Communities." *Survey Midmonthly* 79:210–13.

Powell, J. W., 1943 "America's Refugees: Exodus and Diaspora." *Proceedings of the National Conference of Social Work,* 1943: 301–18.

1942 "Education Through Relocation." *Adult Education Journal* 1:154–57.

Provinse, John H., and **Solon T. Kimball,** 1946 "Building New Communities During Wartime." *American Sociological Review* 11: 396–410.

Pusey, Harriet C., 1944 "Counseling in a Japanese Relocation Center." *Clearing House* 18:252–54.

Ramey, Arthur G., 1943 "Student Activities in a Japanese Relocation High School." *Clearing House* 18:94–96.

Redfield, Robert, 1943 "The Japanese-Americans." In *American Society in Wartime* (W. F. **Ogburn,** ed.). University of Chicago Press, Chicago.

Robertson, Wanda, 1943 "Developing World Citizens in a Japanese Relocation Center." *Childhood Education* (Oct.) 20:

Robinson, Marianne, 1943 "The War Relocation Authority, Tule Lake, California." *Wellesley Magazine* 27:147.

Rostow, Eugene V., 1945 "Our Worst Wartime Mistake." *Harper's Magazine* 191:193–201.

Sady, Rachel Reese, 1947 "The Function of Rumors in Relocation Centers." University of Chicago Ph.D. Thesis (Unpublished).

Sasaki, E., 1947 "I Was Relocated; a Nisei's Americanism Was Tempered in the Last War." *Senior Scholastic* (May 19) 50:42.

Schafer, Phillip, 1943 "A War Relocation Authority Community." *The Compass* (Nov.) pp. 16–19.

Schermerhorn, R. A., 1949 *These Our People.* D. C. Heath and Co., Boston.

Shimano, Eddie, 1943 "Blueprint for a Slum." *Common Ground* 3:78–85.

Smith, Bradford, 1948 *Americans From Japan.* Lippincott, Philadelphia.

Smith, Elmer R., 1948 "The 'Japanese' in Utah." *Utah Humanities Review* 2:129–44.

Spencer, Robert F., 1948 "Social Structure of a Contemporary Japanese-American Buddhist Church." *Social Forces* 26:281–87.

Spicer, Edward H., *et al,* 1946a *Impounded People: Japanese-Americans in Relocation Centers.* Washington, D.C., U.S. Department of the Interior, War Relocation Authority, U.S. Government Printing Office.

Spicer, Edward H., 1946b "The Use of Social Scientists by the War Relocation Authority." *Applied Anthropology* 5:16–36.

1952a "Reluctant Cotton-pickers: Incentive To Work in a Japanese Relocation Center." In *Human Problems in Technological Change* (E. H. Spicer, ed.). Russell Sage Foundation, New York.

1952b "Resistance to Freedom: Resettlement From Japanese Relocation Centers During World War II." In *Human Problems in Technological Change* (E. H. **Spicer** ed.). Russell Sage Foundation, New York.

Stowe, Fern E., 1944 "Relocation Centers." (A letter to the editor.) *Wilson Library Bulletin* 18:594–95.

Tajiri, Larry, 1943 "Democracy Corrects Its Own Mistakes." *Asia and the Americas* 43:213–16.

Tani, William, 1943 "American Japanese—Friends or Foes." *Free World* 5:552.

Taylor, George E., 1943 "The Japanese in Our Midst." *Atlantic* 171:104–10.

ten Broek, Jacobus, E. N. Barnhart, and **F. W. Matson,** 1954 *Prejudice, War, and the Constitution.* Japanese-American Evacuation and Resettlement Series. University of California Press, Berkeley.

Thomas, Dorothy S., and **R. S. Nishimoto,** 1946 *The Spoilage.* Japanese-American Evacuation and Resettlement Series. University of California Press, Berkeley.

Thomas, Dorothy S., 1952 *The Salvage.* Japanese-American Evacuation and Resettlement Series. University of California Press, Berkeley.

Tibesar, Leopold H., 1944 "Minidoka Sanctuary." *Maryknoll, The Field Afar* (April) pp. 28–29.

Tsukamoto, Mary, 1943 "Until we get home." *Christian Advocate* (May 18) pp.

United States Government

1943a U.S. Congress Special Committee on Un-American Activities, House of Representatives, Report No. 717, "Military Views on War Relocation Centers." 78th Congress, First Session, September 30, 1943. Washington, D.C., U.S. Government Printing Office.

1943b U.S. Congress Subcommittee of the Special Committee on Un-American Activities, House of Representatives, 78th Congress, First Session, on H.R. 282, "Report on the Tule Lake Riot." November 1, 1943. Washington, D.C., U.S. Government Printing Office.

1943c U.S. Congress Subcommittee of the Special Committee on Un-American Activities, House of Representatives, 78th Congress, First Session, on H.R. 282, "Committee Print on the Majority and

Minority Report of the Subcommittee Investigating W.R.A."
November 1, 1943. Washington, D.C., U.S. Government Printing
Office.

1943d U.S. Congress Hearings before the Committee on Military
Affairs, U.S. Senate, 78th Congress, First Session, on S. 444—
a bill providing for the transfer of certain functions of the War
Relocation Authority to the War Department, Part 4, November
24, 1943. "Events at Tule Lake Center, California." Washington,
D.C., U.S. Government Printing Office.

1944 U.S. Congress Subcommittee of the Special Committee on
Un-American Activities, House of Representatives, 78th Congress,
Second Session, on H.R. 282, "Committee Print on Minority
Views on Tule Lake Segregation Center." Presented by Herman
P. Eberharter. Washington, D.C., U.S. Government Printing
Office.

United States Supreme Court

1944a Brief for the Director of W.R.A.: Brief for the Appellant
. . . Mitsuye Endo, Petitioner, vs. Milton Eisenhower, Director,
War Relocation Authority and Wartime Civilian Control Ad-
ministration, for a Writ of Habeas Corpus to the United States
Court of Appeals for the Ninth Circuit, No. 10, 605, March 10,
1944. Washington, D.C., U.S. Government Printing Office.

1944b Brief for the United States: Brief for the Appellant . . .
Fred Toyosaburo Koematsu, Petitioner, vs. United States of
America—On Writ of Certiorori to the United States Circuit
Court of Appeals for the Ninth Circuit, No. 22, October Term.
Washington, D.C., U.S. Government Printing Office.

1944c Opinion: Ex parte Mitsuye Endo, 323, U.S. 283. Washington,
D.C., U.S. Government Printing Office.

1944d Opinion: Korematsu vs. United States, 323, U.S. 214. Washington, D.C., U.S. Government Printing Office.

Viles, N.E., 1945 "Federal-state Co-operation in the WRA School
Program." *School Board Journal,* Oct.: 38–40.

War Relocation Authority

1942a "Relocation Communities for Wartime Evacuees." Washington, D.C., U.S. Department of the Interior, U.S. Government
Printing Office.

1942b "The War Relocation Work Corps: A Circular of Information
for Enlistees and Their Families." Washington, D.C., U.S. Department of the Interior, U.S. Government Printing Office.

1943a "Evacuees of Tule Lake." Washington, D.C., U.S. Department of the Interior, U.S. Government Printing Office.

1943b "Segregation of Persons of Japanese Ancestry in Tule Lake Relocation Center." Washington, D.C., U.S. Department of the Interior, U.S. Government Printing Office.

1945 "Education in the War Relocation Centers." Washington, D.C., U.S. Department of the Interior, U.S. Government Printing Office.

1946 "Annual Report of the Director, War Relocation Authority, to the Secretary of the Interior." Washington, D.C., U.S. Department of the Interior, U.S. Government Printing Office.

(n.d.) "Pertinent Facts About Relocation Centers and Japanese-Americans" Washington, D.C., U.S. Department of the Interior, U.S. Government Printing Office.

War Relocation Authority (Final Reports)

1946a "Community Government in War Relocation Centers." Washington D.C., U.S. Department of the Interior, U.S. Government Printing Office.

1946b "The Evacuated People: A Quantitative Description." Washington, D.C., U.S. Department of the Interior, U.S. Government Printing Office.

1946c "Wartime Exile." Washington, D.C., U.S. Department of the Interior, U.S. Government Printing Office.

1947 "WRA—A Story of Human Conservation." Washington, D.C., U.S. Department of the Interior, U.S. Government Printing Office.

Watanabe, Kate, 1943 "From a Relocation Center." *Progressive Education* 20:232–34.

Wax, Rosalie Hanke, 1952 "Reciprocity as a Field Technique." *Human Organization,* Vol. II, No. 3, pp. 34–41.

1953 "The Destruction of a Democratic Impulse." *Human Organization,* Vol. XII, No. 1:11–21.

Webb, J. Lloyd, 1946 "The Welfare Program of the Relocation Centers." *Social Service Review* 20:71–85.

Windsor, Elsie, 1944 "At a Japanese Relocation Project." *Travel Magazine* 84:18–21.

Yatsushiro, Toshio, Iwao Ishino, and **Yoshiharu Matsumoto,** 1944 "The Japanese-American Looks at Resettlement." *Public Opinion Quarterly* 8:188–201.

Yatsushiro, Toshio, 1953 "Political and Socio-Cultural Issues at Poston and Manzanar Relocation Centers—A Themal Analysis." Cornell University Ph.D. Thesis (Unpublished).

INDEX

War Relocation Authority *(continued):*
satisfactory relations with evacuees, 75–77; early administrative framework of centers, 77–78; weaknesses in framework begin to show, 81–83; use of Caucasian and other terms for staff, 86–87; use of practices emphasizing differences with evacuees, 87; difficulty of adjustment to evacuee reevaluation of work, 90–91; regulation against Kibei going outside centers at harvest, 115; ruling that only citizens can hold elective office, 115–116; policy of leave clearance for harvest labor, 126; announcement of resettlement policy, 126–27; Poston staff during strike, 132–35; closer contact made with evacuees during Poston strike and Manzanar crisis, 134–35,138; registration policy decided upon, 142; reactions to registration by staff, 157–58; criticisms of staff competence and fairness by evacuees, 166–68; staff antagonisms crystallize, 168; staff-evacuee adjustment process, 168–69; announcement and views of segregation, 171–72; reactions to Tule Lake demonstration, 184–85; clash of attitudes toward resettlement with those of evacuees, 192–93,204; staff, in general, a segregated minority, 205–06; liquidation of centers tied to lifting of West Coast exclusion as basic policy, 252; evacuees disagree with methods of clos-

ing, 256; administration takes steps to break *Hoshidan* at Tule Lake, 274–75; thinking behind resettlement policy, 277–78

Wartime Civil Control Administration, 43,135

Western Defense Command, 28,43

Women: new independence and freedom at centers, 106–07; in elected councils, 111–12; use of new leisure, 224

Work: early work corps concept and abandonment, 88–89; confusion among evacuees over concept, 89; feeling that work not related to economic necessity, 90; eager response of many to outside jobs, 90; complete evacuee reevaluation of, 90–91; Issei attitude about, 91–93; views of Government's obligations lead to different opinions about, 93–95; evacuee standard of becomes dominant, 95,212–14; response to harvest work outside, 126; problems upon return of harvest workers in early winter, 128; labor reduction by administration, 213

World War I, 26

World War II, 25–29,28–29,54–55,202,263,265

WRA, *see* War Relocation Authority

Yamato damashii, 201

"Yellow peril," 45,49

Young Buddhist Association, 172